Circles

Circles

Further Insights into OCS (Mild-Moderate Obsessive-Compulsive Symptoms)

Ron D. Kingsley, MS, PhD, NCSP

Library of Congress Control Number: 2009907189
ISBN: Hardcover   978-1-4415-5664-6
               Softcover   978-1-4415-5663-9

The information within this book is a culmination of data and experience gathered over the last twenty-five years. It reflects the author's opinions and inferences regarding research and active work in the field as a School Psychologist in the public school system and practicing Clinical Psychologist in the private sector. As such it is not meant to be used as a replacement for competent medical, pharmaceutical, or other professional advice. Specific advice in these areas can only be given by qualified and trained physicians, psychiatrists, pharmacists, and psychologists who are competent and aware of each individual's particular developmental history and other relevant information. Always consult your doctor or another appropriate professional for specific diagnoses and treatment.

This book was printed in the United States of America.

To order additional copies of this book, contact:
Xlibris Corporation
1-888-795-4274
www.Xlibris.com
Orders@Xlibris.com
63078

CONTENTS

Part 4 Unique to OCS

Part 5 For the Professional

FOREWORD

My first book was published in 2002. It was called *Making Sense of the Senseless*. It was my hope that it would open the door to understanding, managing, and ultimately treating OCS. This was the acronym I gave obsessive and compulsive symptoms or tendencies in the mild-moderate range. Symptoms at this level are not regarded as severe enough to cause problems. That was because they were not an actual Obsessive-Compulsive Disorder. This is true as defined in the Diagnostic and Statistical Manual of Mental Disorders IV (DSM-IV).

Obsessive Compulsive Symptoms were portrayed as being on a continuum. Actual OCD would in theory be at one end, with essentially no symptoms whatsoever at the other end. Symptoms are related either directly or indirectly to Serotonin levels in the brain. As a result, nearly all human beings can show such tendencies at times.

Stress and fatigue clearly magnify the intensity and frequency of OCS and OCD in most, if not all, cases. Attention Deficit Hyperactivity Disorder (ADHD) and Tourette's Syndrome/Tic Disorders were briefly touched upon as related genetically. These conditions are often misdiagnosed, misunderstood, or missed entirely.

The title of the initial book, *Making Sense of the Senseless*, was felt to be a perfect name. This is because much of the time the thoughts, behaviors, reactions, and expressions of those with OCS just don't make any sense. That is, they don't make sense unless you consider the underlying problem that is driving them.

Emotional instability and mental distress in this group are high. Dissatisfaction in life frequently leads those with OCS/OCD to seek out ways to self-medicate. Their goal is to relieve the anger, misery, anxiety, and panic. They also seek to curb the fear and depression, as well as the emotional explosiveness they must face daily. Mostly, these people lean towards using alcohol, marijuana, and pain killers to ease their pain. All these tend to dull the misery caused by the relentless, obsessive and compulsive push in their lives. Each can relax the person to the point that the OCS/OCD issues just don't seem to matter anymore. For those who care way too much about everybody and everything, this can be a wonderful experience. To suddenly not care so much is like a dream come true to these people. This type of relief, as a result, can be psychologically addictive in very short order.

This second book has been written to make the information easier to understand for the general public. It also adds further insights into the OCS problem that affects the day-to-day life events of so very many of us. There is no *one* or universal strategy that works for most people most of the time, other than education. Knowledge frees us from the chains of uncertainty. Education is the one universal method that truly can benefit everyone.

To manage anything effectively, one must know what it is. What works this week may not work the next. Although education is the best tool, it needs to be ongoing. Coping with obsessive and compulsive issues at any level is a journey, not a destination. If we expect this to be the case we will never give up, and hope for ever better and more helpful management methods. Remember, we should never give up, but there might still be times when we just might need a little extra help.

Sincerely,
Ron D. Kingsley MS, PhD, NCSP

Lost

lost in my own home . . . so alive . . . yet so alone
I should be loved . . . but feel I'm not
I wonder what went wrong

inside I long to be . . . anyone else but me
sometimes I'm afraid I'm living in a dream
where no one else can see . . . me at all

> it's true I have few friends
> and most who say they are don't know who I am
> they don't see the scars or pain
> see the light . . . but not the rain
> don't know I sometimes wonder . . . if I'm even sane
> I'm told to wait . . . but I cannot
> though I try . . . somehow I'm caught
> in this whirlwind that's my life
> where nothing that I do is right
> and no one there to understand my plight

hope's an empty dream . . . though I strive it seems
there's nothing I can do to change . . . my inconsistency
they tell me I'm to blame . . . I'm so lazy . . . what a shame
if I'd just try harder I could learn to play their game . . .
it's a shame

—chorus—

Words and Music by Ron D. Kingsley
May 5, 1992

INTRODUCTION

Most of us have wondered at some time or the other in our lives whether or not we might just be a little bit *crazy*. Those who swear they have never thought about this are either lying or simply have not yet done so. It's only a matter of time. The fact is that we can all be a little bit strange at times. Of course, some can be more so than others. Usually this concern regarding our own sanity will trouble our minds only during times of real stress or fatigue. High stress or overwhelming tiredness can in the end bring on actual hallucinations. These normally do go away, once the stress and fatigue are no longer so extreme.

Depending on our state of mind or mood, when OCS pops up and begins to direct our thoughts and behaviors, we may really start to worry about our own pending madness. We suddenly realize that we *are* thinking and maybe even doing some very weird things. And furthermore, we cannot just laugh it off or let go. It can be a little bit scary. However, the very fact that we *are* able to consider the possibility that we might just be a little unhinged is a good sign. It is probably one of the most powerful arguments in favor of our actual sanity. People who have truly lost touch with reality—those who are crazy—tend to be completely unaware of this fact. They are apt to think that the things they believe, say, and do are perfectly normal, when everyone else knows they clearly are not. Crazy people don't usually wonder if they are crazy. They are quite certain that they are perfectly sane. No amount of arguing or persuading will convince them otherwise. They will argue that what they see, hear, and believe is real.

At times the OCS-affected person *is* very much afraid of being crazy. Because of this fear, they have to come up with a reason why some things they do or say aren't really what they appear to be at all. They work hard to make it *seem* like it's not crazy. The OCS person's defense is often driven by fear. They don't want anyone to think they're crazy. Active psychotics truly believe that all they see, say, or do is genuine reality. To them there is nothing weird or strange in it. They see no reason to fear insanity. *They are not* insane. The OCS sufferer knows deep down that something really *is* peculiar. They may not know what it is, but they do know it's not right. They are desperate to escape judgment. They don't want to be found insane. They are constantly working to make sure others know that they're normal. At the same time, they still worry that they just might be crazy. It is never far from their mind.

When OCS begins to get in our way, we feel that some of the things we are thinking, feeling, or needing to do are weird. We often cannot make sense out of why we feel the way we do. We don't always understand the purpose of our actions. The only thing that actually does make sense is that something *is* keeping us from being who we really are. It is also hard to believe that it is *something* we cannot fully control. The little control that we may have is not enough. Feeling out of control is a symptom often feared above all others. Fear and anxiety, panic and anger, withdrawal and depression, as well as physical illnesses, are linked to this. They may arise in any combination and add to the problems. And, guess what? When such strange OCS tendencies are present we are not about to tell anybody.

Sadly, in *Making Sense of the Senseless,* the language throughout most of the book was difficult and hard to understand. This new book is a revision that I was going to title *The Invisible Enemy.* It was written with the client in mind. I got to thinking about that title and decided that it felt too negative. It is true that OCS is invisible. It is also an enemy, but not all the time. I therefore set my mind to work to find a better title. I wanted one that did not have such negative connotations. One day, while meditating, the idea came into my mind to call it *Circles.* This one word describes so well what is actually going on, that I felt it was a much better title. I shared the idea of a title change with a few of my clients and others. Their reactions convinced me even more that I had found the right title. It is my purpose in writing this to help those suffering with OCS to understand that they are *not* crazy. For those of us who sometimes worry about being crazy, knowing that we are not can be just what we need to hear.

I interviewed a young man in his early teens with an OCS scale. He was positive for forty-four out of forty-six signs. Next, I asked him, "Have you ever talked about any of these things to your parents?" He snapped, "Are you kidding? No way! I'm not crazy!" People suffering from OCS do not talk about it to anyone, unless they are forced to do so. And even then, they tend to minimize the condition or lie about it.

So this is for all of us who ever caught ourselves wondering if we just *might* be crazy. Always keep in mind that thinking you might be crazy is one of the strongest indicators that more than likely you are *not*!

PART I

What Is OCS?

1

The OCS Continuum

"I've told you a thousand times!" his mother screamed. "You just don't listen!" Chances are if you've ever found yourself saying something like this to a child, you are reading the right book.

"Why don't we ever do what *I* want to do?" complains her husband. Yet, she knows that they *always* do what he wants to do. She doesn't understand how he can possibly say such a thing with a straight face.

"When are we going to get there?" repeated thirty-two times in only one hour. You still have three hours of travel left before you arrive. You aren't sure you can make it. You want to shut those children up. You knew it would be like this. You had even seriously considered getting something from your doctor to knock them out during the trip. You didn't get the drug. By the second hour you are wishing you had.

"I've got too much on my mind and I'm just too tired," she says for the third night in a row. You know that's just an excuse. If she was *so* tired then why isn't she sleeping, you ask yourself over and over.

"There's a way to do things," she complains, "and you just don't do it right!" She says this as she refolds all the towels you spent forty-five minutes folding already. You were trying to take some of the load off her so that maybe you could spend some time together. It doesn't look like it's going to happen. You wonder why you even try.

These are just a few examples of the many kinds of difficulties that can develop when obsessions and compulsions in the mild to moderate range are present. It may not look or feel like an obsessive or compulsive thing at all.

Obsessions are persistent ideas, thoughts, impulses, or images that interfere with life. On a day-to-day basis, these obsessions cause clear anxiety or distress. Compulsions are repeated behaviors carried out to avoid or ease anxiety or distress. For these to be considered a *disorder*, they have to be fairly extreme. But what if obsessive and compulsive behavior were on a continuum? On the one end, you would have people who care way too much about every little thing. These would be relentlessly driven to think and do things. This is the extreme *drama queen* or *king*. They are likely to flare up over every little thing that isn't right. At the other end of the range would be those who do not care much about anything. These would not be especially interested in, or care much about, what's going on around them. They don't really want to do anything. This would be an example of perhaps the ultimate *couch potato*. Over the years I have come to believe that a continuum of obsessive and compulsive behavior *is* exactly what we are dealing with. Evidence suggests that even animals seem to display such behaviors on a similar continuum.

The abbreviation (OCS) is used to represent only Obsessive and Compulsive Symptoms that are in the mild-moderate range. Other professionals have sometimes called this "subclinical OCD." OCS is not an indicator of those symptoms that are more severe and better known as OCD (Obsessive-Compulsive Disorder). OCS is defined as bothersome obsessions and compulsions that lack the intensity to be labeled as an Obsessive-Compulsive *Disorder* (via DSM-IV). Yet, in spite of this, they remain strong enough to interfere and cause problems in life. These problems may not have been considered obsessive or compulsive at all. This is because OCS behaviors look very much like a whole lot of other issues and difficulties.

A common belief among many professionals is that a pattern of mild-moderate obsessive and compulsive behaviors is clearly not serious enough to justify a need for treatment. If the obsessions or compulsions are not nearly "all consuming" as described in the DSM-IV for OCD (Obsessive-Compulsive Disorder) it is not considered a *real* problem. As a result, seeking out treatment is often thought of as unnecessary, and sometimes even strongly discouraged. Such a view has not been very helpful to the many who *are* suffering with OCS-related problems. The mistaken opinion that "nothing is really wrong" is all too commonly made. Depression for family members, as well as for the suffering OCS person, is also very common. So it is with frustration, severe stress, anxiety, and blame as well. These are frequent results that make the condition much worse over time.

The list of OCS characteristics given below is in no way all-inclusive. It does represent at least some in most categories that could occur. No one has every single one of these characteristics. Some behaviors may be present for a while, and then they go away. These may or may not ever return. This is the key difficulty with making the OCS diagnosis. It is not any one or two things that are the problem. It's the effect of all of them put together. A few minutes spent here, a few minutes there; by the time the day is over, it adds up to a lot of time wasted foolishly that could have been used for more important things or just to relax.

Common OCS behavior as seen by others may include the following:

- Questions may suggest a worry about the future
- May seem afraid, or simply may not ask questions even when clearly confused about something
- Gets overly upset when a mistake is made
- Has trouble with change
- Resists transitions from one thing to another
- Very concerned with fairness and all things being equal
- Shows undue guilt after doing something wrong (whether perceived or real)
- Seems unable to forgive others
- Is upset if things don't turn out perfect, or "just right" for them
- Overly blames self if things go wrong or blames everything or everyone else
- Seems to have many senseless or unusual fears
- Seems to display an *"I don't care"* attitude; does what he/she wants
- Appears tense, edgy, or nervous
- Worries too much
- May seem to avoid physical contact in play
- Becomes angry quickly
- Doesn't seem to want to act like or to do what others are doing
- Becomes angry if asked to do something
- Is defiant when disciplined
- Wears unusual clothing styles
- Seems more at ease as a loner
- Tends to do things his/her own way
- May explode when stressed
- May reject classmates in a hostile or unfriendly manner
- Has trouble following directions or taking suggestions from others

- May flare up at classmates, siblings, parents, and teachers if teased or pushed
- Style of behaving may seem deliberately different from most
- Sulks or shows signs of a chronic bad temper
- Is difficult to get to know
- May seem dependent on others to lead him/her around
- Appears unhappy
- May show little feeling when others are upset
- May seem over-obedient
- Withdraws quickly from group activities; seems to prefer to work by self
- Avoids or shuns competition or when playing may have a need to win
- Seems to want to boss others around
- May seem overly shy or too outgoing
- Seems to set themselves up to be criticized
- Can be easily frustrated and give up passively
- May tend not to show feelings
- Wants others to do things for him/her
- Feelings easily hurt and/or be very sensitive about most things
- Often may cling to adults or friends or a spouse
- Appears disinterested in classmates or in the work of others
- May appear to be depressed
- May seem to seek constant praise

The question has been asked: "Do we truly want to treat or get rid of all obsessive and compulsive types of behavior?" The answer to this question is, "*Of course not!*" These tendencies appear to be a key reason why we go beyond ourselves. It is why we invent. It's why we become outstanding in writing, art, music, sports, and so on. We don't want to eliminate or completely take away all these drives. We want to manage them so that they can work more *for us* than against us. The goal of treatment is to ease those symptoms that are excessive. Then we must temper some, and become more aware of all others that may be present.

*   *   *

"I don't know why it *has* to be exactly like that. It just does!" he complains to his wife. "It's the *right* way to do it. That's all. You don't put food on the same plate that is likely to mix with other food. It ruin's the taste! How can you enjoy the different flavors if they all run together? Why do you think foods have different flavors anyway? Now, let me show you how to do this."

*　*　*

She throws the newly purchased blouse on the bed. "I'm not wearing *that* again!" She announces loudly. "And I'm not taking it back either! So don't even say it!"

Her husband is very frustrated. "But you haven't even worn it once yet," he says.

"I just did," she replies with finality.

"You call that wearing it! Putting it on for five minutes is wearing it?" He is upset, but doesn't know what to do. She's done this before. Why does she constantly want to throw away their hard earned money on clothes like this? What a waste! He just doesn't get it.

*　*　*

"Okay honey, I'm home," he smiles broadly as he walks in the front door. "I got off early so we could get there on time."

"Oh, don't worry about making it on time, dear. We're not going," replies his wife. "Something came up and it was postponed."

"What? Not *going!*" he shouts. "What do you mean we're NOT GOING?" With each word his voice raises in pitch. "What's this? I get off of work *EARLY!* I *set* aside time. *Time* that I DON'T HAVE to go to this STUPID reception of *your* sister! And now you're telling me we aren't going? What am I supposed to do NOW?"

His wife is crying. She knew this would happen. It doesn't matter, though. It still hurts. He gets like this whenever plans change at the last minute. To him it's as if it's the end of the world.

"I'm going back to work!" he screams. He storms out of the house. The door slams behind him.

She continues to cry. "What's wrong with him?" she wonders.

*　*　*

"I need a few more Micron 01 pens to draw with," he thinks to himself. "The ones I have are getting old. I can stop by Michael's on the way home." He is content with this plan. He will stop on his way home.

He sings with Jackson Browne from a recent solo CD playing on his car stereo all the way to Michael's. He's been listening to the same CD every day for *five* months now. He'll probably listen to it for a year or so before changing it to something else. He's happy. He's going to get more Micron 01 pens, which he needs.

At Michael's he's frustrated. They are out of Micron 01 pens. They have the 03 and the 05 sizes, but not the 01. They even have 005. Now what's he going to do? He *needs* those pens. There's another Michael's out near the mall. It's probably seven or eight miles away. Oh well, he sighs. He needs the pens.

The Michael's near the mall is in even worse shape. They have Prismacolor, but are completely out of Micron. He hates Prismacolor. He still has to have the pens. There's another Michael's clear on the other side of town. He figures he'll have to go there. He needs those pens. A desperate feeling is building up inside.

By the time he gets home, he has a hard time explaining to his wife why he is an hour and a half late from work. He's also just used up a quarter of a tank of gas at $3:14 a gallon. Good thing his car gets 30 miles per gallon. He got his three pens, though, at $2:69 each. He did manage to do that.

*   *   *

Education is still the most important and best tool for the effective treatment of OCS/OCD and just about anything else. When you *know* what it is you are dealing with, you can manage it better. When you begin to see how something either directly or indirectly influences all that you do, positive changes can be made. Such changes will then be much more likely to last.

When a person has OCS it is not unusual to be unaware that these symptoms are present. Those with OCS often come in seeking help for other troubles such as marital issues, anger management, depression, anxiety, panic, and the like. There are many possible underlying causes for such problems. Because of this, some kind of short generalized assessment is usually a good idea. If the brief assessment suggests the possibility of OCS, additional evaluative measures will bring this to light.

The idea that something like OCS might be at the heart of the problem is hard for some to take. Others are thrilled to find out that there might be an explanation for what has been gong on. Once the assessment is completed, many become instant believers in OCS, if determined present.

This is because the very questions tend to educate at the same time that they evaluate.

An illustration at this point can be helpful. They might think of OCS as if it was a *bus* (the symptoms) that's been driving them for their entire lives. They, however, didn't know this. Most of us do not like the idea that something or someone is controlling us. Some people will outright reject such an explanation because of this. They can't accept the idea that they have not been in control of their own lives. Such a thing as OCS couldn't be right as a possible cause for their troubles or difficulties. Many, however, are able to use this image of a bus driving them to begin to understand and start to resist the OCS influence.

After all, no one likes to think they are not in control of their own lives. If the bus is driving them, it means that they have to go wherever it takes them. It also means that they can only get off when the bus decides to let them off. The thought that effective treatment will work to teach them to take back control and drive their own bus is very appealing. It also makes sense in a strong emotional and heartfelt way.

I was working with a young man, trying to help him learn to drive his own bus, when a rather unique response occurred. He was about ten years old. I asked him if he would like to drive his own bus. I was a bit surprised when he said, "I don't think so."

My surprise quickly dissolved though as he went on to say, "I think I'd rather drive a car."

He was unable to imagine driving something as huge as a bus. Of course, after that comment it made perfect sense to me what the problem was. I told him "Okay then, we'll make yours a car," and we did.

So whether it's a bus, car, bicycle, or even a skateboard, it doesn't really matter. Once we begin to believe and understand that OCS may be in our lives, we can ask ourselves the following question:

"Am I driving the bus right now or is the *bus* driving me?" Many other creative possibilities have been similarly effective. Things such as: "Am I playing the violin or is the violin playing me?" "Am I playing the video game or is it playing me?" and so on.

This question can also be helpful when used by others. Children often need someone to help them see when OCS is getting in the way. A parent can do this. Spouses and friends can also become helpers as long as the one with the OCS agrees with the plan. Once OCS is noticed, this other could say, "Hey, is that bus driving you right now, or what?" Such a statement can remind the person to stop and think about what they are doing. They can then try to take hold of the steering wheel and start to drive their own bus. It can also be used as an awareness exercise. Sometimes the one with OCS might only be able to say something like, "Well, yeah, it's driving me right now. I'm going to be able to get to the steering wheel very soon, though. Can you just hang in there with me until I do?"

Such a comment provides useful information. It explains that the affected one *is* currently aware that they are being driven by symptoms. It also infers that at the moment the urge is too strong for the person to do anything about it. This knowledge can help others to react with understanding and kindness, rather than irritability, anger or frustration.

When using the *bus* allegory, others within earshot are not as likely to know what exactly is being talked about. Comments about driving or being driven by a bus can act as a code to keep embarrassment and anxiety at a minimum. It is important to note, though, that sometimes even the mention of a bus *can* be viewed as strange and as quite embarrassing. Some don't want such phrases to be used in public, or at all. Although for many it can be a very effective tool, for some the *code* does not work. When this is the case it simply should not be used.

The Masque

as I wake up each morning . . . It's already in its place
covering my emotions keeping others from reading my face
it fits much too well to notice not another soul has a clue it's there
and by the time the day is over . . . not much truth has been seen or shared

there's no hint of pain or sorrow . . . no reason or need for blame
it'll be much the same tomorrow . . . don't expect it to ever change
'cause it's been like this forever . . . at least it seems that way to me
how dare I hope for something better . . . how dare I take a chance on my own dreams

no one knows who I really am . . . though some have a need to believe they do
'cause everyone feels so much better when . . . they know if you're the threat or just a tool
they plug you in where they think you'll fit . . . and cause the least concern or strife
dodging storms and uncertain paths . . . in hope to smoothly glide right on through life

but each time I lay me down at night and try to set this masque aside
it gets harder and harder to find myself . . . am I who I think I am . . . or is it all a lie
is it me who loves the sunshine or is it me that so loves the rain
am I the one dancing merrily through life or the one who only smiles when hiding pain
is it me when I get so angry or me when I'm so calm and cool
am I the wise and patient one or am I the vengeful and stubborn fool
I'm no longer quite sure of anything . . . I've spent much too much time in disguise
trying so hard to get others to see . . . and believe that I was alright
I'm no longer sure of anything . . . I've spent way too much time in disguise
trying so hard to get others to see . . . and confirm that I was alright

—repeat—

trying so hard to get others to see . . . and believe that I'm alive
trying hard to get someone to see . . . and believe that I'm alive

Words and Music by Ron D. Kingsley
February 21, 2007
For Cam

The OCS Diagnosis: Important Points to Consider

OCS Definition

OCS is defined as mild-moderate obsessive and compulsive symptoms. These are insufficient to be diagnosed as true OCD. Nevertheless they do interfere in a person's life. They keep the person from being who he really wants to be. When symptoms are present but not getting in the way or causing distress, treatment is not warranted.

Symptoms

These are usually not seen at all, minimized, excused, or simply denied. This is often because of fear. Sometimes it is plain ignorance.

Psychopharmacological Intervention (medication)

When used to treat mild-moderate OCS, the possible benefits of medication cannot always be predicted. The full range of problems varies for each person. The severity of symptoms must also be taken into account. Often, the degree to which OCS interferes in a person's life can be withheld on purpose. It is not unusual for symptoms to be hidden in layers of explanations. These may sound a lot like excuses. This comes from distortions and misunderstandings that are so common. From childhood on, they have had to come up with explanations to and reasons for the things they do. This is not always easy. It also gets old. This is because they have to do it so frequently.

Discovery Problems

Obsessions and compulsions are only problems when they get in the way of how you want to live your life. At first you don't even know that it is OCS that *is* getting in your way. Over the years it can become so mixed up in other behaviors that it doesn't feel like a symptom. It often doesn't look like one either. It's just the way things are. It's just who you are. Problems that begin with OCS may end up looking like something else. One thing leads to another and then another, and then another. The problem you are currently struggling with may be layers above the main OCS symptom that sustains it. The issue concerning you most *now* is indirectly related. This makes it hard to believe that OCS might really be at the heart of the issue. Even the helping professional may not recognize that OCS is a major underlying cause of what is going on. When OCS is there, but not discovered, treatment is often inadequate. This is true, even though some progress may have actually occurred.

Misdiagnoses

Obsessive thoughts may be reported by a young child as something other than thoughts. As a result of this, a misdiagnosis can easily occur. The OCS child may describe the symptom as a voice, or voices, that are heard. These voices are telling him or her what to do. Actual psychosis or schizophrenia may then be suspected. It may even get treated as such by professionals unaware of this common way that children describe such thoughts. These children don't have the life experience or the words to explain what is happening. The developmental level of a person can also add to the account of "voices telling him/her to do things" and the like. It is important to figure it out. We need to determine whether or not the child truly believes a voice is actually heard. Was it a voice or was it merely a strong repetitive thought? Is the child *unable*, or *unwilling*, to acknowledge this thought as his or her own?

Another common error in the diagnosis of OCS/OCD is viewing it as Bipolar. The old name for Bipolar is Manic Depressive. When a person doesn't know about OCS and describes the behavior of someone with OCS, it does sound a lot like Bipolar Disorder. If the right kinds of questions are not asked with OCS in mind, it can be easily mistaken for many other issues. Yet another common misdiagnosis is ADHD (Attention Deficit Hyperactivity Disorder). The OCS and the ADHD affected have problems paying attention at times. Both have a hard time concentrating, but for different reasons. OCS/OCD can also make it look like a person is hyperactive. Someone who is obsessed and feels a strong need to do things will not stop until they are done. It may take hours, days or even weeks. The person may sleep very little. They may disregard other tasks as well as other people. This can and does look like hyperactive or manic behavior. It is no wonder that OCS/OCD gets labeled so often as Bipolar or ADHD.

Purposeful Concealment

Obsessions and compulsions at any level of severity tend to be kept secret. People often have no idea why they think or feel the way they do.

Most have never heard of OCS, although they may have heard of OCD. They don't know what is happening to them, but they *do* often suspect or *know* that whatever it is, it's weird. They fear others might think they are crazy if they say anything about their thoughts. They may act like or insist that they actually *want* to do the strange things they feel compelled to do. No one would believe it if they told them they just *had* to do these things. They can hardly believe it themselves. Since even *they* don't understand this *need*, they are sure no one else will either. If they don't hide their thoughts and the real reasons for their actions, others will surely think they're "crazy" or insane. There may be a passionate wish that they could hide it from themselves. Sometimes a very heated denial when confronted about OCS is an effort to do just that. "Thou protesteth too much," as Shakespeare so aptly wrote. If they don't admit to it, maybe they can't be considered crazy. Once a person truly learns about OCS, the fear of real insanity is no longer a problem.

Genetic Connection

OCS and OCD appear to have clear family ties. There is a growing research base that suggests Tourette's Syndrome and Attention Deficit Hyperactivity Disorder (ADHD) are somehow related to OCS/OCD, too. When one or the other of these is present, a check for the other two should to be made, as well. Checking for signs in family members can also be a good idea. It appears that any one of the three, or any combination thereof, found in a relative can lead to any mixture or single condition in a descendant. Treatments for one can sometimes make the others worse. Interestingly, such treatments targeting one can also make the others better.

Compulsion or Motor tic?

It can be very difficult to tell the difference between what is called a *Complex Motor Tic* and a *Compulsion*. Experience suggests that much of the time what is thought of as a Complex Motor Tic may actually be a compulsion. It can also be a combination of the two. Research is providing at least some evidence that the two may be derivations or extensions of the same thing. The basic difference may be they show up in different body systems—one in the mind and the other in the muscles. A trial on an SSRI is often a good idea. If the target concern *is* due mainly to a compulsion, the use of an SSRI can often treat the problem. Clinical practice does confirm that indirect easing of motor tics can also occur. This appears to be from the lowered stress that occurs when other OCS symptoms are relieved.

Control Issues

Those with OCS are often believed to have *control* issues. They want, seem to need, or *must have* control over others in the family. This may also occur socially, or on the job. Children with this issue are said to want to *boss* others. When OCS-driven, such an argument is generally wrong. It is a common error that is caused by a lack of knowledge about OCS. It is true, though, that the actions of those with OCS do seem to show signs of a desire to control others. The real reason is that OCS drives them to feel that things must be done in certain very specific ways. It is this inner craving that forms the false impression that the OCS-driven need to control others. If they could let go of these urges, there would be no *control* issues. The problem is not truly one of *"control,"* it is one of passionate need for exactness.

The shift—from seeing the OCS-driven as controlling, to seeing them as caught in the midst of compulsive needs—is crucial to treatment progress. If you accuse the OCS-driven of needing to work on control issues, it won't make sense to them. They are not trying to control anybody, no matter what it looks or feels like to others. Most people don't like the idea that another is trying to control them. It can trigger off strong emotions. These emotions often make things worse. As others begin to understand what's really going on with OCS, they can let go of these false notions. The idea, that the person is doing what they do for the sole purpose of manipulating or controlling another, can be put aside. This alone can bring about positive change. It can ease stress, worry, frustration, and anger linked with the thought that this person wants to control them.

Symptom Resistance: The Battle and the War

Specific battles may be won, but the war will go on. Fighting a compulsion is not easy. Paying no attention to an obsessive thought is also hard. A good rule of thumb to remember is that when trying to change something, it nearly always gets worse before it gets better. You know you are truly making progress when the anxiety, tension, and fear get worse. If you do something and it brings instant relief from tension or anxieties, don't think you've found the cure. Abrupt relief is most likely a sign of symptom substitution or ritualization. Real relief comes with repeated effort over time. True freedom from OCS takes place slowly and with much hard work on the part of the affected person. Things getting worse are a mark of positive progress in treatment. The exception to this general "rule of thumb" is when medication is used. When the right medication is used, often there can be quick improvement. This is especially true for OCS but not usually for OCD. There have been some suprisingly quick improvements, though, in the research literature, even with OCD.

Movies, Television, Books, and Experiences

It can be hard for those with OCS to let go of thoughts, needs, or experiences. It is a good idea to pay attention to and monitor all movies, television, and books. For some individuals, certain types of movies may be better off avoided. Affected children may need to be restricted from access at times. This includes TV news shows. The real life horror and drama shown on the news can trigger (trigger event) new symptoms in a flash. Sometimes, going over what happens before watching a show or reading something is helpful. Of course, this can't be done for most news shows. Sometimes, going over what happened afterwards can also be helpful. All that is looked at, heard, felt, read and experienced can instantly become a new problem. In a sort of a delayed reaction, these can also become the focus of an obsession or compulsion at a later date.

Generally, some things seem to cause problems for the OCS-affected, more than others. These include horror, true stories, TV news reports of disasters, and real life events. The effect can be especially strong when catastrophic or tragic. The OCS person tends to be quite gullible. Depending on where their mind is, they can come to believe anything told to them. This can make them a target for those who get a kick out of teasing. When something like what has been talked about above causes a new concern or symptom, I have called it a trigger event. There are often many such trigger events in the lives of OCS/OCD driven people throughout the course of their lives.

New Experiences and "Change"

Any kind of change can make all symptoms worse. This is especially true if the change is sudden. The most common outcome of this is resistance.

The strength of the resistance can vary. It could be simple comments and/or defiant, nonverbal body language. It could lead to verbal abuse, extreme tantrums and panic attacks. It depends on how important the thing being changed is to the person. It also depends on how severe the OCS drive is at that moment. New experiences and change often create great distress in the OCS/OCD affected for many reasons. When faced with a change or a new upcoming event, there are ways to lower the distress these people feel. One must talk about (process) the future change over and over before it happens. Doing this prepares the person in advance for what is going to occur. In this way they can become more "comfortable" with the situation. They are made more ready for the novel experience or change. It can also create a backlash of complaining and obsessive thinking. Still, this tends to be better than tantrums or panic. These responses are highly individual and can differ, depending on the person.

Choose Your Battles

From the observer's point of view, this plan can look as if the parent is being ruled by the child. Too many OCS children are viewed by others as spoiled brats. OCS children can tantrum and not give in to a parent who won't buy them a bubblegum. The same thing may occur if told they are not allowed to play in a busy street. On the one hand, the child's life is in danger. On the other hand, it's whether or not a piece of gum is purchased. Is the long-lasting, screaming tantrum worth the price of a nickel bubblegum ball? Choose your battles. If it is important to say no, then by all means say no, and do the battle. If the concern is simply one of alleged control, or might be considered fairly meaningless, then don't fight. Why battle even if the child seems to have manipulated and won, when the matter being fought over is harmless? So what if they take their shoes off in public? Is it worth a thirty-minute tantrum, each time you have to try to get them back on? Think about it. Save your energy for the next really important issue for which a battle is truly called for. Maybe she had seven cavities the last time she visited a dentist. If so, that extra bubblegum may be worth battling over.

Remember, the OCS-driven battle does not go by the same rules as the battles of the will for those who don't have interfering OCS. When the response is OCS-driven, such a battle rarely teaches the child (or the adult) not to tantrum. In such a setting, consequences tend to be meaningless. Since the person is overreacting from within, the consequence is not a focus of attention at all. Of course the strength and total length of time the reaction may last varies with the environment and the OCS severity. Still, when OCS is a factor, choose your battles with wisdom and restraint. As a result, they will occur less frequently. It will also have less of an overall harmful effect on family relationships. Finally, it will have less of a damaging effect as well on the self-esteem of the OCS-driven one.

Stop and Smell the . . . What? Where? I Didn't Even See Any Roses

Those with OCS appear busy all the time. They always seem to be doing or thinking about something. Even when depressed or feeling hopeless or worthless, the mind is busy. As a result, most of the time, they go through life in a series of time-pressured units or events. They may constantly feel overwhelmed by the moment. This is particularly true when stress is high. In later years, a person can develop into a workaholic. Many who have this trait see themselves as too busy for interruptions. If interrupted for any reason, they may get very angry. This anger comes from the loss of time caused by the unwanted or unexpected break, no matter how brief it may have been.

The OCS person tends to respond in one of several ways to such intrusions. They may pay no attention at all to the interruption. It's as if the disruption had never occurred. There may be a brief verbal warning, followed by a return to earlier activities. There could also be an explosive angry outburst. Such an outburst is usually not justified. It is out of order and well beyond what would be expected. The interruption may or may not have in fact interfered with their activities. Their feelings about time tend to be very tightly wound. As a result they think they cannot tolerate even the briefest of intrusions. A dozen freshly cut roses could be placed in the person's lap. The OCS-driven might not pause long enough to even notice the fragrance. They may also wonder a bit later on how their pant legs could have gotten wet. They may have no idea what could have caused the cut on the back of their hand (a wayward thorn). The pain, at that juncture, would have worsened to the point that ignoring it was no longer possible.

The OCS-driven, beset by an endless stream of things to do and think about, can ignore friends and family. Finally the OCS-driven, like Albert Einstein sometimes was accused of doing, may pay no attention to the basic needs of their own body. There were times when Mr. Einstein wouldn't eat, unless someone reminded him. It wasn't really important to him. As a result, he once ended up in a hospital and had to be nursed back to health.

It is important to point out that keeping busy also serves to relieve many of the OCS/OCD-driven symptoms that might otherwise cause even greater problems.

Justifying the Neglect

The reaction of the OCS workaholic, when faced with proof of neglect, is often one of intense bewilderment and frank disbelief. They cannot comprehend how someone could possibly think they are neglectful. They are often unable to see its effects on their own or in their loved ones' lives. It is not uncommon for them to stubbornly cling to their work record as proof of how much they care. The time spent working is cited as the best evidence of how well they provide for a spouse and children.

"Why do you think I go to work?" they may claim. "Of course I care!"

The OCS mind frequently believes that the time and effort put in at work has been solely for and on behalf of the family. As such, this stands out as absolute proof of their self sacrifice. It shows quite plainly how absurd the notion is, of so-called negligence. Any success achieved is seen as the result of the time and effort they have already put forth. They feel that altering their already proven effort or time schedule might damage the level of success. Doing so could end up creating an actual failure to provide.

A common belief is that the time needed to be successful should somehow make up for any personal moments that may have been missed along the way. This belief can be very powerful. Alternative notions or beliefs have no way of getting in or having enough influence to change it. This belief stays intact long into treatment. It needs to be recognized, processed, and worked with. In time, as long as treatment continues regularly, it can change.

There may also be a fear (usually unconscious) of what they would do with *extra* time. This may be a camouflage to cover up for symptoms they may not even be aware they have. Not being busy, however, may cause a very uncomfortable awareness. This may be underneath the anxiety and fear that they my not willingly admit to at any time. This may be why it can look so much like a personality disorder.

Distractions

It has long been an argument of mine that ADD or ADHD without hyperactivity (now called ADHD predominately inattentive type) is really

OCS. Both those with ADHD and those with OCS are prone to distraction. The pure ADHD person cannot seem to focus on anything at all for very long. The OCS mind *can* focus like nobody can. When intensely focused on one thing, though, they may have trouble focusing on something else. So if the OCS child or adult is focused on something other than what is being said or taught to them, it can be a problem. The same holds true during conversations. If the OCS mind gets stuck on an idea, it is no longer attending. If there is already a thought in the OCS mind, it can be very hard for them to attend to a new idea or to something different. When obsessively focused on one thing while asked to do something else, the something else often doesn't get done. This is because the person does not adequately process the request. Even if they answer and tell you that they *will* do it, they quite regularly may not. This is not done on purpose. All too often, it may seem like it *is* purposeful to others. Others take it personally. When something else is taking up the OCS mind, new information doesn't stick. This *looks* like distraction. It *sounds* like distraction. Well, it *is* distraction. It *is* a different form than the kind that occurs from ADHD, though. It *can* therefore easily get misdiagnosed as ADHD.

All-or-Nothing/Black or White

This could be a main principle for OCS. It is such a common factor. If the OCS person doesn't think she is going to win, she doesn't want to play. If *he* can't do something well, he'd rather not do it at all. If in the midst of a game and she or her team starts to lose, she may get upset. She may come down on teammates or call them names. She may try and cheat. She may fake or magnify an injury. The blame for a loss may get transferred to an umpire or referee. It may get blamed on injury or team members. It may get blamed on not trying.

"I wasn't trying," he may say, "or you would have really been in trouble."

If he can't finish something in time, he may not want to start. Losing is *not* an option. Everything seems to be all-or-nothing. There is no in-between. Things are right or wrong, black or white. There is no gray. This can be very difficult to live with for the OCS-affected, as well as others.

The Critic Within

Nobody is harder on themselves than those with OCS. Nothing is ever good enough, not really. "If I would have *just* done *this* instead," they sob. "I *should* have done this," they sigh. If only, if only . . . is said so many times, it becomes redundant. "*Nobody* likes me," is a very common report. "Everybody *hates* me," is another that is common. "I hate myself," is something that gets said far too often. "I'm ugly," "I'm too tall, too short, too fat, or too skinny." "My feet are too big." "My hair is the wrong color." "I've got freckles." You name it, and the OCS person has most likely blamed themselves, if it is negative. The OCS-driven is gloomy, glum, pessimistic, distrustful, and unhappy. They either *love* it or *hate* it. There is no in-between.

There is also a polar opposite, though. This is the person who can't find it within themselves to be responsible for anything. They are to blame for nothing! Everything and everyone else is to blame for everything that happens. As stated elsewhere, I call this Paradoxical Inclination.

Driven to Read or Disability in Reading Comprehension?

In that same style of *all-or-nothing*, those with OCS can be either compulsive readers or typically *hate* to read. Those that are driven to read may read everything they can get their hands on. They may also read only one kind of book and nothing else. It may be only science fiction, mysteries, or horror. They may only read books about the supernatural or about romance. Whatever they choose, they may be driven to read or to study the subject.

On the other side of the coin is the "*I hate reading*" group. This person may actually read very well. When OCS is present it's not the ability to read that is the problem. The real problem is obsessive thoughts. While reading, the OCS mind gets caught up in another thought. It may come from a sound overheard that starts them thinking. It may stem from a thought that is already in their mind. It may begin with a word that is read from the book that reminds them of something else.

This is like a small trigger event. It often goes something like this: You start to read. The trigger occurs and your mind begins to think about something else while still reading. You don't realize you are thinking about other things until you get to the bottom of the paragraph or the page. All of a sudden, it hits you. You don't have a clue about what you just read. You may go back to the start and try again. A few lines into the first paragraph it happens once more. Again you go back to the beginning. After the third or fourth time this happens, you throw the book down. You say to yourself or mutter under your breath, *"who wants to read anyway?"* You do this enough times and eventually you stop trying to read. You don't like it anymore even if you once did. It's not that you can't read. It just takes so much effort and energy to read, that you don't want to any longer.

Depression

This is maybe the most common problem related to OCS. People with OCS are depressed off and on throughout their entire lives. Nothing they do is good enough. Nothing is as good as was expected or hoped for. After a while that alone can be quite depressing. Then, if you add up all the other problems that occur with OCS, you can begin to understand why depression might be so common. People often describe it as feeling as if they're on an endless roller-coaster. They can go from happy to sad in an instant. They can be singing in the rain one day and cursing it the next. This is another feature that can lead to a misdiagnosis of Bipolar. Usually the longer OCS goes on undiscovered, the worse the depression can become.

Sometimes there may be cycles of energy and despair. If the compulsion or obsession is strong enough, it will drive the person to act. Because of this they may look very energetic or driven. They may even seem to be hyperactive or in a manic state. Their mood can be high and positive. They can do anything. A person may be awake for days or sleep very little when compulsively driven. The roller-coaster is at its peak. Eventually they may wear themselves out physically. Their bodies just can't take anymore and they crash into exhaustion. This is similar to what happens to those who have Bipolar, but tends to cycle way more often and much quicker than with true Bipolar.

They can also wear themselves out mentally. Despair may surface because something did not go right. It may arise from a negative comment made by another. Suddenly the obsessive drive to do gets pushed out of the way. It is replaced by excessive *doubt* and *fear*. Did I do it *right*? Could I have done it *better*? I *should* have done it differently! These are a few common examples of the questions that create doubt. Doubts such as these run over and over in the OCS mind. This leads to thoughts such as "I never do anything right," or "I'm just not good enough."

The *fear* part of this equation can often come from being worried that others are judging them. "What do they think of me?" "They must think I'm stupid." "Surely they think I'm crazy." Self-directed questions such as these bring about anxiety and fear. Being anxious and fearful can also cause despair or depression. The roller-coaster is heading down into the ravine of desolation. You can also become afraid of fear itself. The thoughts can transform. "I probably *am* stupid." "I'm the *dumbest* animal on the planet." "I *don't* even like myself." "I'm *bad* at everything." "I *never* do anything right." "I *should* just give up."

Suicidal thoughts may begin and even flourish. After all, it is the perfect situation for feeling self-destructive. "Maybe it would be better if I just *wasn't here* anymore." "I wish I'd *never* been born." "I *wish* I was dead." "I *should* just kill myself." Such thoughts are frightening for all those who have them. For many, it never quite gets that far. Sometimes, though, it does.

Literal Thinking

This tendency can sometimes be deliberate, though for most of those with OCS, it is not. It's almost as if there is a brain freeze. The moment something is put into words, the OCS mind takes what has been said literally. They cannot seem to shift to any other conclusion.

A mother scolds her son: "Why did you hit your sister when you were playing with the football?" He responds instantly, "*I* didn't hit her, the football did."

Similarly, a father watches as an older son appears to reach out and smack his little brother. He rushes out back as the younger boy comes screaming into the house. The father tries to play it cool. He doesn't want to *lose it* with the older boy, but he's *really* mad.

"What just happened?" he asks.

"Nothing," the older boy replies. He's also playing it cool.

"Why is your younger brother crying?" Good old dad wants his eldest to come clean. He's giving him this chance.

"I don't know," says the older boy.

"Did you hit him?" This is his *last* chance to come clean.

"No, dad."

Without going any further in the story, let's take it further along in a discussion. The older boy would not confess to having hit his younger brother. The father got so angry veins were bulging from his neck. He was turning purple in the face. He shouted and screamed at his oldest son. He cursed and called him a blankety-blank liar. He threatened him with a whipping. Still the boy would not admit to having *hit* his little brother. All this occurred because the boy felt he hadn't actually *hit* his brother. As far as he was concerned, he'd only *pushed* him.

It doesn't really matter how the father got the idea that the younger boy had been hit. It could have really *looked* that way. It could have been that the little brother told the father he'd been hit. It could have been someone else told the father and used the word *hit*. It could have been the father's general word he used for anything that happened. It could have been that the older boy did hit the younger, but convinced himself it was just a push. It doesn't matter. Until the father said it right, that older boy was not going to confess to anything. To the boy, such a confession would have been like lying. His father hated anything to do with lying. The dilemma here seems obvious. For a great many people in the throes of this type of a situation, however, it is not so obvious.

Polar Opposites

I believe this is one of the main reasons why obsessive and compulsive symptoms are so often confused with Bipolar Disorder. Of course both conditions *can* be present sometimes as well. This causes great concern for medical professionals because the medications that treat OCS and OCD often make things much worse for someone with Bipolar. An obsessed or compulsive person can appear to be in a manic (overexcited, agitated, or hyper) state. They can also appear to be very depressed. The OCS-driven frenzied behavior, with little or no sleep, can last for days, depending on the strength of the compulsion or obsession. Generally it lasts until the obsession or compulsion has run its course or is satisfied.

The main difference between the OCS behavior and Bipolar appears to be one of time and frequency. OCS can go from being manic-like to a hopeless state of depression in an instant, and certainly many times during a day. Bipolar generally stays on one side or the other (manic/depressed) for a much longer period, or cycle. When the OCS person is in the manic-like phase, if one little thing goes wrong immediate despair can result. If then something else happens to make things suddenly go right, complete cheerfulness may return. It's a true Dr. Jekyll and Mr. Hyde type of response. The triggering event that brings on this change can be so trivial that it is hard for others to believe it could have caused the switch. It is also common to miss the trigger entirely. This is usually due to its apparent lack of importance. As a result, the triggers are not reported. When this happens it becomes much easier to believe that the condition is Bipolar rather than OCS.

The constant flip-flopping from one emotional side to the other of the OCS person drives people crazy. Parents talk of loving their children and not being able to stand being around them in the same breath. They often feel horrible about this, but don't know what to do. They feel they never know what their child is going to do or say. Will they freak out or be okay? It is very distressing.

Afraid to try

The OCS reasoning goes something like this: "I can't fail if I don't try." "Nobody can say I'm not smart if the reason I don't do well is because I'm not trying." "I'm not really a *loser* if I'm not trying to win." Plus, if the OCS person does do their best and doesn't get a 100 percent or do really well, the emotional outcome can be unbearable.

Excuses for Everything

"We only lost because we weren't trying." Maybe that was the reason or perhaps, "several of our players were playing hurt." It could have been that "the other team cheated," or, "my teammates all suck" or "the refs were all against us" and so on. Those with OCS are driven by a real need to have a logical explanation for every single thing they do. If they can't find one that makes sense, they'll invent one. If not able to come up with something that sounds reasonable, they tend to go back to the old standby, "I don't know why but there's got to be a reason." If there is a reason for something happening then it's not *their* fault. They're off the hook. They don't have to be so upset about losing or having made a mistake. No one can point the finger of blame in their direction. They don't have to feel so bad. They often still do feel bad, but they try and believe they don't.

The Truth and Nothing but the Truth

Quite a few OCS-driven people have a very strong need to be honest. Not long ago the mother of a nine-year-old was worried over what a liar her daughter was turning out to be. She shared an example of the kinds of things that were happening.

"I had a bag of candy left over from Halloween. I'd put it in one of the less used cupboards of the kitchen. The next day I decided I should probably keep it on the highest shelf in my bedroom closet. I didn't want either of my two girls to get into it. They would surely polish the whole bag off in one day. If *I* kept the candy in *my* control we could all enjoy it as a special treat for quite a while. I went to get it from the cupboard but when I opened it was surprised. The candy was no longer there. Did someone take it? For a moment I thought that maybe I'd opened the wrong one. A quick search of the cupboards on both sides led me to the conclusion that my hunch about it being taken was probably right. I went to my oldest daughter. She was in the living room watching TV.

'Do you have that extra bag of candy left over from the other night?' I asked.

'No, mom,' she replied. Her big brown eyes gazed directly into mine. There wasn't a second's hesitation. There were no guilty gestures or movements of any kind. She didn't act as if she'd been caught in a lie. She didn't *seem* to be lying. She wasn't nervous. I believed her.

My youngest had the same kind of response. I believed her too. I was ready to start pulling my hair out. Was I getting Alzheimer's? Did I only think I had put the bag in the cupboard because that was what I'd planned but never got around to actually doing it? Did I even have a bag of candy left over that night?

Three days later, I was doing a little cleaning in my eldest's bedroom and came upon a scrunched up, discarded bag. It was *the* bag of candy that I hadn't been able to find. She *had* taken it. I was furious. How *could* she look me straight in the eye and lie like that? She never used to tell lies at all. In fact, she was so truthful that it sometimes hurt. Was she a pathological liar? Is she becoming one? Doc, what am I going to do? Now I'll never know whether she's telling me the truth or not. She's turning out to be such a liar. My daughter is a bold faced liar."

This mother was very concerned about her child and what she perceived was a bold-faced lie. There were other similar examples that further supported her concern. The problem with this example, though, resides in what might be best described as *intent*. From the perspective of the nine year old girl, the answer she had given was not a lie. It was the truth. This is why there was no anxiety or nervousness in the way she responded. Her mother had described this girl in the past as easy to read. That is, she could always tell if she was about to tell a lie. The girl would pause and sometimes stammer. Her eyes would seem to roll back and she would have difficulty making eye contact. Her voice would falter and she would simply *appear* to be very nervous. Let's go back to the mother's own words.

"That afternoon she came back from a friend's house where she had been playing. I took her into my bedroom alone and confronted her.

'Why did you lie to me?' I asked her.

'About what?' She seemed confused. 'About this,' I shouted. I pulled the empty bag out of my back pocket and shook it in her face.

'What *are* you talking about, mother?' she said, using that *tone* of a typical teenager (she's only nine, remember). 'I never lied to you about anything!'

I suddenly glared intensely at her.

'Well, uh, at least not recently,' she added.

'Yes, you did,' I shouted. 'You *did* just the other day! And *now* you're even lying about not lying.' I held the bag up in front of her nose. 'I found *this* in your closet.'

'Uh-huh,' she looked at me expectantly.

'What was it doing there?'

'Oh, I'm sorry, mom. You're right. I should have thrown it in the garbage. Sometimes I just tell myself I'll take care of that later, and then I forget. I forgot again. I am sorry.'

Now I was a bit confused. 'This is *not* about the garbage,' I reminded her firmly.

'It's not?' she said. She looked genuinely surprised. 'Then what *is* it about?'

'*You lying,*' I hissed through gritted teeth.

'But I *already* told you, mom. I *haven't* lied.' 'I can't *believe* you're denying this,' I told her. '*I* have the evidence right *here* in my hand.'

'What's it evidence of?' she asked in a very convincing, sweet and innocent voice.

I counted quickly to ten. 'Three days ago I asked you if you had this candy.' Again I held the crumpled empty bag up for her to see. 'You looked me *right in the eye* and told me that you didn't have it.'

'I didn't,' she reaffirmed again, while staring directly into my eyes.

I took a deep breath. I so wanted to just scream *LIAR* into her face but I remembered what we've been working on in here (counseling sessions). Instead I said, 'Honey, I found this in your room today,' indicating again of course the empty bag.

'I know.'

'So you admit *now* that it *was* there?' I questioned.

'Yeah.'

What was wrong with her? 'So you *did* have it.' She was cool as ice.

'It was in my *room*, mom.'

'But when I asked you directly the other day if you had this candy, you told me no.'

'Well, mom,' she looked at me as if to say *Duh*! 'I *didn't* have it at the time. Like I told you, it *was* in my room.'

This mother had been mistakenly concluding that her daughter was becoming a pathological liar. She, however, was actually a pathological truth-sayer. She was so very conscious about telling the truth, and nothing but the truth, that she took it to the limit. Her mother had asked if she had the candy. At the moment the question was raised she did not have it. It truly *was* in her room. Therefore she felt compelled to simply say, no. Now, if her mother had thought to ask her if she knew where the candy was she would have informed her that it was in her room. The *intent* here was not to lie or even to stretch the truth. The truth *was* that at the time of the query the girl did not have the candy.

Sometimes the OCS person accused of lying, as in the case above, is perfectly innocent of wrongdoing. Other times, though, the person may be praying every second of the way that the parent or teacher doesn't ask the *right* question. The right question will force an admission of guilt. When this is the case, it's usually because the one with OCS is terrified of getting in trouble. Often this fear is greatly exaggerated. The trouble or consequence for their wrongdoing is often nowhere near as bad as the OCS person imagines. They usually fear the worst. So it is a good idea to keep in mind that this tendency to answer only what is literally asked can actually be *innocent*. It is also important to remember that it can also be done on purpose to mislead. In either situation, though, the answer that is given (it can be argued) remains true.

Lazy Is Better than Crazy!

For those with OCS, there is often a perceived *need* to do things (tasks, actions, or chores) in a *certain* way. When the way that things *need* to be done is the same as how most others would do them, it's *no big deal*. When their way is not *too* strange or different, the person can usually come up with good reasons for the difference, if asked. Again, it's no big deal. The reason given though *can* sometimes stretch the truth a little or a lot.

The rationale may be taken from a common cultural or community held belief. When the manner of doing something is *very* different or *bizarre* the stress felt by the person with the need can be huge. In such a case the *strangeness of* one's actions may be noticed by any who happen to see it. When this happens the person may simply refuse to perform the task.

These people usually *don't* want to be noticed. They may simply refuse to talk about it. There is no reasonable explanation for why they acted like they did. So, rather than be caught in weirdness, they may not respond at all. They may do nothing. When asked *why* they aren't doing anything, they may reply that they don't know how. Put more simply, they may say that they *can't* do the task.

There may be pressure to keep trying from the one asking. This is because they are *certain* that the OCS person really *can* do what is being asked. If this happens, the one being pressured may actually say they don't *want* to do the thing. If pointed out that they *should* want to accomplish the task, they may declare that they *don't care what* they should or shouldn't want. They *don't* care! They don't and *no one* can make them care either.

Quite often the OCS-distressed person, as described above, is viewed by others as *"lazy." Lazy* is a term common to many cultures and communities for those who continually do not finish tasks. This can be especially hard for those OCS-influenced people who feel guilty. The term *lazy* is also used for those who will not even try.

Many OCS-driven folks work very hard to simplify everything. They might choose not to eat at all, rather than have to go through the steps needed to make a sandwich. This may sound a bit crazy, but it's not. It is very easy to identify such behavior as *"lazy,"* though. For this type of OCS-influenced person, it is not unusual that they might consider *themselves* as lazy.

"I'm just lazy," said George, almost immediately after sitting down at the start of his first session with me.

"What do you mean?" I asked.

"Well, I guess I'm not very good at picking things up or putting them away," he replied, "and I don't really like to *do* things."

"You don't like to do things? Like what kinds of things?"

"Oh, pretty much anything I don't want to do," he said soberly.

"And there are a lot of things you don't want to do?"

"You got it."

"Such as . . . ?"

"Oh, you know . . ." he paused and grinned, "dishes for one."

"And . . . ?"

"Well, there's school and work and chores and getting up to change the TV channel . . ." George paused and looked at me keenly.

I regarded him blandly. He seemed to be waiting for me to say something.

He was still looking at me expectantly. "Well?" He said.

"Well, what?" I responded evenly.

"Aren't you going to tell me how *lazy* I really am after all?"

"Not just yet." I smiled, "Now, you were saying . . ."

"I was saying that I'm just *lazy*. There's no two ways about it. What else could there be to explain why I don't seem to want to *do* anything?"

I queried, "Have you always been this way?"

"People have been telling me as long as I can remember how lazy I am. I guess that probably means I have always been that way."

"*What if*," I began, "every time you were asked to do something you were told after you'd finished that it wasn't good enough? *What if* no matter how hard you tried it was *never* quite good enough? *What* if you were always told to do it over again? *What if* no matter what you accomplished it never seemed quite right or good enough to you? *What if* you weren't satisfied with *anything* you ever tried to do? *What if* after every task you completed you felt like a failure?"

George obviously thought long and hard about this stream of questioning. Suddenly a thin smile grew on his face. He sat forward.

"Well," he began, "I suppose I might . . . well, I just might . . ." he paused, "stop wanting to do things, I guess. I'd just sort of give up."

"So we have here at least one way that you *can* see how a person might get labeled as lazy, even though it might not be true, right?" I reasoned.

"Yeah," George said, a little tentatively. He was still sitting forward and now looking eagerly in my direction.

"*What if*," I started off again, "no matter what you were doing it seemed very important to you? *What if* there were already fifteen things you wanted to do that you felt *should* have been done already or absolutely *had* to be done next? *What if* somebody told or asked you to do something different than you had planned? *What if* this not only interrupted you, but added yet another thing to your already huge and growing list of things to do? *What if* you began to realize that there was *no way* you were going to be able to get all those things done? *What if* everything you had a need to do felt like it was just as important as everything else? *What if* you just couldn't figure out which thing to do first?"

Again George paused and seemed deep in thought. "I might not do anything," he announced. "I mean, there are already *too many* things to do. If each thing is just as important as all the rest, I might not be able to decide. If I can't decide which one should be done first, I might just procrastinate and not get to any of them."

"*Voila*," I said (which is French for 'you see'), "here is yet another way a person might be considered *lazy*, even though they may not be lazy at all."

"But that still doesn't explain why I don't even want to get up and change the TV station when the remote is broken or lost," complained George. "How is *that* not being *lazy*?"

"Well," I told him, "I can actually think of quite a few ways that that might not be regarded as *lazy*, believe it or not. However, in your case perhaps, this is actually an example of your being just that; a bit *lazy*."

George seemed surprised by that comment. He regarded me for a moment and then burst into laughter. "Yeah," he laughingly admitted, "that probably really is me being lazy."

I laughed with him and then added, "You know, the person who invented the TV remote control would probably be thought of as *lazy* by a lot of people.

"What," they might argue, "you can't even get off your lazy bum to change a TV station? What is this world coming to?"

We laughed a little more. "The real reason, though, for inventing something like that it would seem to me," I told George, "has to do with how long it would take to change channels or to check out other channels. The inconvenience of having to get up and then sit down over and over again would add to the length of time taken. You could also argue that the remote control enhanced the ease with which channels could be changed."

"It's also a lot easier," George cut in, "on the wear and tear of the equipment." George was a real technology buff, which is why his thoughts went in that direction. "And," he added, "It also cut down on the size of the parts needed to adjust the set and change the channels." He was on a roll. "And it changed the shape and look of the front of the TV, too. No more ugly knobs sticking out and eventually looking old and worn."

"So was it a *lazy* person's invention or was it *progress*?" I wondered aloud. "I guess it depends on your point of view, doesn't it?"

George nodded his head heartily in the affirmative. He remained sitting forward in his chair. After a fairly long moment of silence George spoke.

"Do you really think, Doc," he asked candidly, "that I might not *be* just lazy? Do you think it really could be something else?"

I sensed a glimmer of hope in his vocal tones. George's eyes seemed to have just a bit more light shining in them than had been present when the session started.

"Yes, indeed I do," I told him truthfully. "Let's see if we can figure out what it really is and work to change that and make it better."

George *did* have OCS characteristics that were at the heart of his so called *laziness*. We figured it out, treated the symptoms and also practiced methods to keep him from falling back into old patterns. Before the OCS was identified, George did have a kind of a sense that *lazy* just might not be all that he was. He had no idea what was wrong, but he felt that there was something that wasn't right. He was aware that thinking this way seemed a little weird or maybe even crazy. Being thought of as *lazy*, though, he realized was a whole lot better than being considered *crazy*. So he embraced the notion that he must be lazy. Who wouldn't, given these circumstances?

Too Trusting for Words . . . or Not

Like many other OCS symptoms, the tendency to be overly trusting has a flip side that could also be of equal concern. Usually the issue of trust will lean towards one side or the other. The person will be either too trusting, or too skeptical. In some situations, though, a person can sort of waver between both sides.

The too trusting OCS person is subject to being taken advantage of by dishonest or scheming others. Those on the overly trusting side of the coin tend to be gullible, naive, childlike, easy to fool, and too suggestible. They tend to shy away from confrontations and, more often than not, believe at face value what others tell them.

It seems to me that these people might be over represented in the group of placebo responders. No research that I know of thus far, however, has studied this or shown this to be the case. It makes sense, though. The overly gullible person would, by nature, be more likely to truly believe they were going to get better. They might be more certain than anyone that the medication—or whatever method is used—*is* going to work for them. Perhaps the physical body of those who believe the deepest (in other words a bit obsessively) responds in kind to this obsessive type of thinking. The hyper-trusting OCS person also really believes that others are going to do exactly what they say they will. These are genuinely surprised when someone does not do whatever it is they may have promised to do.

On the other hand, the OCS skeptic doesn't seem believe a word that anyone says. These people tend to trust no one but themselves. These are undoubtedly the ones that helped the idea of "reverse psychology" gain its popularity. The lack of trust can be so strong that the OCS skeptic will tend to lean towards doing the opposite of what another suggests. This skeptic can feel very lonely at times. Relationships are hard to build and maintain when the seeds of doubt are constantly sprouting. This person can't be sure of anything that anyone says. These are the cynics that find it hard to believe that anyone could possibly be helpful simply out of the goodness of their heart. Cynicism, suspicion, sarcasm, and pessimism are this skeptic's calling cards. Hyper-negativity runs wild in the OCS skeptic.

Perfect in Public

Have you ever been in a community or church setting where you couldn't help but admire a certain family? This family seemed to be on top of it all. The husband and wife appeared to have the ideal relationship. You only wished yours could be as good. The children were all well mannered, adjusted, and perfect examples of how *all* children ought to be. If only your children behaved half as good as theirs, you might have whispered to yourself on any given Sunday. This is the family everybody wants theirs to be like. They are everyone's role model.

The family portrayed above doesn't really exist. That's not to suggest that you don't *think* you know such a family. Probably you do. It's just that when out in public people usually work very hard to look as if they have it all together, even when they don't. The OCS-driven persons who have an intense worry about what others may think will work even harder than most to appear "normal." We all tend to want others to see us as capable, good-looking, good parents, good husbands or wives, good people, and so on. When in the public eye, most of us try to put our best foot forward. Some of us are very good at doing this. Some of us, though, really *need* to do it, and are clearly *driven* to do it.

"At home my kids are animals," one parent reported in a group setting. Other parents in the group nodded their heads knowingly. She sighed heavily then added "they're like little angels everywhere else. I *don't* get it. It's like they have two personalities. How can they behave so well at school or at their friend's houses and so *horribly* at home? You know, one of my daughter's friend's mothers told me just the other day that she wished her daughter behaved more like mine, and I almost fainted."

There were a few chuckles from others in the group. Obviously other parents could relate.

The original parent continued. "After surviving my knees almost buckling I took a deep breath and grilled her, maybe a little too fiercely. I came on like someone's nightmare. You're talking about *my* Jennifer here right? I asked her seriously. My daughter is Jennifer, you know. She told me she knew who she was, but I was having a hard time believing her. She must have thought I was nuts. She reassured me that she was indeed talking about Jennifer. Then she told me that she just loved having her over. She went on and on about how thrilled she was that her daughter had met mine and they were becoming friends. She said my Jennifer was such a *joy* to have around. This was the second or third time Jennifer had been over to this new friend's house, as they had moved into the area only recently. I almost asked her if her daughter had more than one friend named Jennifer. I kept thinking: 'How could this be?' It had to be a clear case of Dr. Jekyll and Mr. Hyde. Maybe it was multiple personality."

I had asked this mother to share her story with the group because it was so typical of the OCS-driven concern over what other people might think. According to her mother, Jennifer's teachers actually felt pretty much the same way about her as did her new friend's mother. At school she was a model student. She was always polite and did whatever her teacher asked with no hesitation whatsoever. Jennifer also always did her homework and always turned it in on time.

At home, however, her mother got a very different child. If things didn't go Jennifer's way she went ballistic. She would leave her stuff lying all over the house. She *"never"* put anything away after using it. Her room was a *"disaster area"* and she would *"freak out"* and scream and yell over "stupid little things that hardly mattered at all." Jennifer walked around in their home with a permanent scowl on her face. She was *"always"* mad.

Her mother once confided in me that she wanted some of that *"angel dust"* they must throw on her when she arrived at school each morning. This was because by the time she got home it had clearly worn off. Jennifer's mother was more than frustrated. She was hurt. She was taking her daughter's behavior quite personally. She once asked, "Am I that bad a mother?" while tears fled from the corners of her eyes.

Jennifer was much like the members of that *"perfect"* family characterized earlier. She had a very strong need for others to view her in a positive light.

It was very important to her that no one outside of her family thought of her as a *bad* kid. She worked very hard whenever she wasn't at home to present herself in the best possible light, *always*. This required a huge investment of effort and mental energy.

By the time Jennifer got done with school she'd be both physically and emotionally drained. Once home, she could no longer hold it together. If the most minuscule thing went wrong, she would *lose* it. When with her family Jennifer seemed to "let her hair down." At home it didn't matter if she wasn't *perfect*. Her family already knew she wasn't. Family members *had* to accept her. Besides, nobody could be perfect all the time. What did they expect? It wasn't as if what *they* thought mattered to her all that much anyway.

Special Note

Most often it does matter to the OCS person what members of their family may think. However, symptoms cannot be held in check forever. They tend to come out eventually. This is yet another example of what I named Paradoxical Inclination. If OCS persons admit that they do care about how they act around family, they will beat themselves up over it mercilessly. This is one of the reasons so many affected ones have suicidal thoughts, and sometimes, attempts.

The only way out of this dilemma is for the person to focus on the opposite of caring. They must convince themselves that it doesn't matter what the family thinks at home. They must deny that they care at all. Compassion often gets locked away along with concern for the family and what they truly believe.

At home all Jennifer's repressed irritations and emotions of the day could no longer be held in check. They would burst forth at the slightest provocation. Jennifer would be riding an emotional roller-coaster. Her mother once described her as an *"emotional basket case."*

Jennifer's mother had asked why her daughter couldn't act at home like she did everywhere else. "How can she be this perfect angel that I always hear about and this crazy *demon* child at home?" The answer was complicated, but the heart of the matter was in that OCS-driven *need* to look good to others. It was simply impossible for her to look and act good all the time, and so her family got the shaft.

I honestly believe that if Jennifer had been capable of controlling her symptoms in other places as well as at home, she *would* have. So many

OCS people face this dilemma all too often. There is often quite a lot of arguing and denial about how this person treats others in the home. The overreacting OCS person argues that their response is the fault of something or someone else. They'll also argue that the reaction they had was justified. It wasn't excessive at all.

Frequently the OCS person is truly unaware that their reaction was a little *over the top*. Remember, by the time this person gets home from school or work after holding it together for six to eight hours, already they are *stressed*. They are like a balloon already blown up to full capacity. All it will take is one more breath and, *POP!*

This person is in a frazzled state. They are feeling intense emotions inside. These emotions have been bottled up all day. Responses tend to happen at the same level a person is feeling, unless managed or controlled. Control is no longer an option at these times. When they react, it doesn't seem like an overreaction to them. The tension built up throughout the course of the day is magnified by the act of keeping it in check. It is well-known that over-control is linked to over-responsiveness. Eventually it comes out.

On Being Self-centered and Self-focused

The divorce was bitter. He didn't want it. As far as he was concerned, everything was just fine. She had to get away from him. She had to get her eighteen-month-old son away from him too. As long as she did everything he wanted, everything he expected of her, all was well. The moment she did not, he got angry. If she relented quickly, the anger would subside. If she failed to yield, the anger would intensify. Sometimes it got so bad that her husband would literally seem possessed. That scared her greatly.

When she first met him she had thought of this intensity as just confidence. He seemed so sure of himself. He knew exactly what he wanted and would let nothing get in the way of his obtaining it. She admired him for that in the beginning. It was something that she felt she lacked.

It wasn't until a few years into the marriage that she realized her husband's self-confidence was actually very poor. If criticized in even a very minor way, he would fly into a rage in defense of his assaulted self-image. She had been walking around on *eggshells* (in her own words) for years, afraid to say or do anything that might upset him.

She was going to have to take a job in another state where she would be near family who could help. Her family was willing to babysit for free and for both their sakes the move was necessary. After the divorce she could not afford to live on her own, and she didn't have a job. He was a musician with no steady income.

Still, because she wanted to leave the state, the lawyers had to meet with her ex-husband. Apparently he had to say it was okay for her to move and take their son to another state. The statement he made at the mediation hearing said it all.

"What do I get," the lawyer reported him asking, "out of her moving out of state?"

Self-interest, self-focus, selfishness, self-centered, and narcissistic are commonly used to describe OCS-driven people. If you stop and think, it makes sense that this might be so. The OCS-driven person is constantly worried or anxious about all that is happening around them. They don't have time to focus on others. They are too busy trying to survive their symptoms. This makes them look very self-centered. They usually don't see it this way, though. To them everything they do can feel like it is done for someone else. When accused of being selfish, they either don't have a clue as to how the accuser came to such a conclusion or they passionately deny it.

The paradoxical inclination to this self-centered behavior is that of being overly focused on everyone but themselves. Those who take this opposite extreme may take very poor care of themselves. As long as they are able to succeed in constantly helping or focusing on others, they may be just fine. Problems arise over time as they take on too much without taking care of their own needs.

The Chameleon

Some with OCS can change how they behave to whatever may be desired or needed at the moment. For example, the character Eddie on the old TV show *Leave it to Beaver* was quite good at this. Whenever he was around other kids, he did cruel things. He teased them unmercifully. He also tried to con them into doing things that he knew were wrong. Anytime that Eddie was near an adult, though, he at once became the *perfect* model of politeness and good manners. The adults in the show could sense this change. He was just *too* polite. But they could never quite catch him at it red-handed. They never were quite able to confront him and accuse him directly.

When talking with others the OCS person may take on similar vocal tones or patterns. They may begin to make the same kinds of gestures or body language. Also, they may have a sudden attitude change to match that of the one with whom they are talking. Observing a change like this can be confusing to those who are familiar with the person in other settings. It can also be unsettling to the person acting in this way, when such a change is pointed out or questioned by another.

The one with OCS may not be aware that such a change had occurred. It's kind of like a chameleon changes color naturally for protection. They don't have to think about it. Those with OCS become less noticeable and blend in by adjusting to others in this way. This is often driven by a strong need to be liked and accepted by everyone. They don't want to be singled out. So they do what others do and try to sound like they sound. They may dress like they dress, if possible. They may defend the issues they defend and say they like the movies they like, and so on.

Sometimes this tendency to be like a chameleon can keep a person from feeling like they know who they truly are. When you don't know who you are, you may have trouble relating to others on a heartfelt personal level. This is because you're never quite sure if what you might be thinking or feeling is really coming from you.

What if the thoughts and feelings you sense as your own aren't really yours? What if it's just *you* reacting to the other person's ways? The worry caused by this can be very hard to deal with. It can drive an OCS person into a state of chronic despair. The OCS can end up feeling that *no one* likes them. They may think that others only seem to like them because of what they are pretending to be. Often the person doesn't dare take a chance on actually sharing what they truly think. What if they do that and are rejected? This is a devastating prospect. They just don't have the self-esteem or ego strength necessary to survive such a rejection. So they just go right on, trying to be everything they think others want them or imagine them to be.

"Does he like me for who he thinks I am," Jill wonders aloud, "or for who I *truly* am?"

Brenda, her best friend, shoots back with: "And just *who* are you, *truly?*" She ends with a little laugh to let her friend know that it's just a joke.

But Jill bursts into tears. "That's just it," she sobs, "*I* don't *know who I am. I don't know!*"

There is a wonderful example of this same situation found in the movie *Runaway Bride.* Julia Robert's character is a woman who has accepted three offers of marriage in the past, but never married. On each wedding day, she runs from the altar just before the actual ceremony can start. In the opening scenes of the movie we see that she is engaged and preparing for her fourth attempt. As the plot develops, scenes show her choosing all the very same kinds of things that her fiancé—a high school football coach—likes. He wants to climb *Annapurna* (a very tall snow capped mountain) for their honeymoon; she says she does too. He orders his eggs for breakfast specially prepared as "egg whites only." She does the same, and so on.

This woman has been trying hard to be everything that others want her to be. She changes colors depending on outside needs much like a chameleon. Each time she approaches the altar at the start of her wedding, she gets uneasy. Unconsciously she knows that something isn't right. The guy she's about to marry doesn't have a clue who she really is. He thinks she is exactly what he always wanted. This is because she has been so good at making him feel that way. She suddenly realizes that it's a recipe for disaster and runs away. She can't go through with it because she *knows* she is not what she has portrayed herself to be. It's her fault, but in the movie she doesn't know that yet.

Along comes the character played by Richard Gere. He is a columnist who loses his job because he wildly exaggerates a story about this "runaway bride." He alleges that her escapades make her a man-eating shrew. He falsifies some of the things about her real life, so people will be more interested in the story.

Julia's character's written complaint to the editor of the paper he works for gets him fired. To vindicate himself and perhaps get his job back, he goes to the little town where she lives. He plans to do a story on her and get the facts right. He believes that she will once again run from her fourth fiancé when it comes right down to the wire. He is bent on proving this to the world and to himself. He believes that most of the exaggerations of his first story were essentially correct. He wants to prove it.

While doing the story, Richard's character gets closer to figuring out who she really is than anyone ever has. They fall in love and her fourth fiancé gets dumped a week before the wedding. He commiserates later that it was better than being dumped at the altar. The church was still reserved for the fourth wedding and announcements were already sent out. The new lovebirds think to take advantage of this. They decide to get married on the same day that she was supposed to marry groom number four.

It's made pretty clear that this fifth fiancé really does know her. She is also very aware of that truth. Once again, though, when put on the spot she runs. She does this just prior to reaching the altar. Although Richard's character did know her much better than all the others, she realizes that something still isn't right.

Later we learn what the problem was. Although her fifth fiancé *did* know who she was and knew therefore what he was getting into, *she* was completely full of doubts. She didn't know who she was. She still needed to find out for herself who she really was.

Being chameleon-like can keep us from ever being sure about what we think and how we feel about things. Like a leaf in the wind, we're blown to and fro in whatever direction the next breeze may go. Self image is fractured into many pieces rather than being one strong whole.

In the movie Julia's character finally understands. She figures out what has been keeping her from being able to commit to a relationship. Then she sets out to do something about it. She sits at a counter with eggs prepared in many different ways and tries each of them. She then determines which eggs she likes best. She is no longer going to rely on someone else's tastes. She also decides to pursue her lifelong dream. She invents and sculpts intricate lamps out of pipes and parts from her father's hardware store. In the movie we see that these end up being sold in New York City.

She spends enough time, energy, and effort to figure herself out. Finally we see her in the New York City apartment of her last *victim*. He had been devastated when she ran out on him. She literally *gives* him her running shoes. Now that she's found out who she *really* is, and what she *really* wants in life, she is ready to go forward. Julia's character asks *him* to marry her. There's a stipulation that they have a small wedding ceremony with only a few of their friends. It turns out that she never wanted a *BIG* church wedding like those planned for in her first attempts to marry. It's a happy ending after all, but only because she became aware. She learned about her inclination for chameleon-like conduct and worked hard to get rid of that behavior.

Sometimes playing the part of a chameleon can work to the OCS person's advantage. The sales person, who picks up on another's language, vocabulary, and manner of speaking, is ahead in the game. The one able to blend in with others has an advantage over those who do not. Then there are actors who can be so convincing in the characters they play that others tend to believe that's who they really are. Their ability to be chameleon-like makes their true selves invisible. During a performance we don't think about who the person really is. If they weren't able to completely immerse themselves in a part, though, they would not be very good actors. Nobody would pay money to see them act.

The truly major distressing part for the OCS chameleon is the not being sure if they are who they think they are. They may wonder, "Is it me, or just a reflection of someone else? If even *I* don't know who I am, how can I possibly know anybody else? Also, if I don't know who I am, how can another ever know me? How can anyone ever *trust* me? I can't even trust myself to be who I think I am."

Most of us spend all our lives trying to figure out who we are. The OCS chameleon is truly handicapped in this area. It tends to be much harder for those with OCS to figure out who they are and it usually takes a lot more time and effort as well. It's worth working on, though.

The Chameleon

I am the chameleon and no one knows my name
by day I am another at night more of the same
sometimes I have to wonder if I even know myself
I am the chameleon and changing is my hell

a little boy of six am I . . . an innocent beleagued
such that really I am forty and tossed by weathered seas
the wind has swept away my youth . . . the water drowned my soul
I am the chameleon and in no way am I whole

chorus

I stretch the truth to fit my needs or at least what I believe
I lose myself amid the lies . . . only parts can I retrieve
and just when you think you know me . . . the me part slips away
this may go on forever so don't get caught up in all that I say

chorus

it hurts so much inside sometimes I try to run from all the pain
to take on the guise of someone else fills me up with guilt and shame
but I am so scared . . . so afraid . . . of what you may think of the truth
I am the chameleon acting out this role since early youth

chorus

Words and Music by Ron D. Kingsley
March 15, 1988

PART II

Symptoms of OCS

2

Crazy or Not?

Have you ever wondered if you might be *crazy*? I know I have, and there have been many times when I actually worried about it as well. What if I *am* crazy? Someone's bound to find out. When they *do*, I'll be toast. Maybe, I can just go with the flow and just *fake* it. I've done it before. I don't think anyone noticed. But, what if they did? What if they do?

"So Doc," she asked with concern in her voice, "do you think, I mean uh . . . am I . . . you know, *crazy?*" She covered her face with her hands.

Without hesitation I told her, "No, you're not crazy."

The sigh of relief she uttered was easy to hear. "Are you sure?" She whispered timidly.

It was clear that she had been thinking about this for a long time. This fear alone had kept her from looking for help for her chronic depressive states, anxieties, and problems. She'd had trouble getting along with others throughout the course of her lifetime, thus far. She had never sought out help before. It is a common tale, a very common tale.

"Uh, yes," he responded uneasily.

It was the twentieth question of the inventory he'd answered "yes" to out of the twenty-three that had been asked thus far. There were twenty-two answers left that he had yet to give.

A little later, he was more tentative. "Well, yeah . . . sometimes," he faltered. Then, wringing his hands in obvious distress, he added, "I think."

He had just answered question number forty. It gave him a total of thirty-six *yes* responses and only four *no*s. It seemed he was now very worried.

"Are you worried about all the *yes* answers you've given?" I probed gently.

"Well, now that you mention it," he replied, "*YES!*"

Again, in a very gentle voice I told him, "Try not to. It just means that we're probably going in the right direction. It's actually a good sign. Hang in there. I'll explain it all to you as soon as we get finished. There're only five questions left."

He was wondering if he might be crazy.

"Okay, Doc, whatever you think."

*   *   *

There have been occasions when I have actually joked with a client. Of course, this depends on the relationship, or rapport, developed before such an inventory is started. It also depends on the apparent personality of the client. Some people you do not want joke with. Laughter, though, is a very good thing emotionally and mentally, when appropriate. Thus, sometimes when I see that a client is beginning to realize that he or she has answered *yes* to nearly every question that has been asked on the inventory, I have tried to become witty to relieve their anxiety.

I have in fact commented, "Hey, do you ever say *no* to a question?"

Usually this gets a little chuckle, especially after it becomes clear that they now have to answer *yes* once again to this very question.

Thinking that you might be *crazy* is no laughing matter. It is one of the major reasons, if not *the* major reason, why a great many people do not try and get help. If you are an adult, all you had to do was see the film *One flew Over the Cuckoo's Nest* (1975) one time, and you won't want to have anything to do with psychiatrists or psychologists ever again.

The image of Jack Nicholson being stuffed into a straight jacket and taken away to a mental institution will be forever stamped in your mind. What happens to him therein is even worse. Actually, there are many more movies that can be cited, both bad and good, whose accuracy is too often very much in doubt. Nevertheless it leaves a vivid image in your mind of exactly what you now think might happen if you *are* considered *crazy*. Can you blame anyone for not being willing to go see a psychologist and find out?

There was a young man who absolutely refused to eat a banana in public. He never told anyone about this, even though he had been haunted by this issue since Junior High. You might wonder what the big deal was. You might wonder, that is, until you hear the *rest* of the story.

After having been in counseling a while, he finally brought up the banana issue. It went something like this:

"You know I haven't been able to eat a banana in front of someone since *forever.*"

"Uh-huh," the counselor replied. What else does one say to a statement like this?

The young man went on, "It really made me feel like I was crazy."

"Not being able to eat a banana in public."

"Yeah, but it wasn't just in public. I couldn't do it in front of *anyone.*"

"Was it the banana or the people watching that bothered you?"

"Oh," he blurted out, "both." He then hesitated for quite a long time before going on, "you see, uh, bananas sort of resemble . . . uh . . . well, you know what a banana looks like, right?"

The counselor nodded, thinking, 'yeah, they look like bananas'.

The man became even more nervous. "Well," he said, "have you ever seen one of those movies where the nurse comes in to talk to the high school kids about birth control and safe sex?" He was barely whispering now. "*You know and they pass out bananas for the girls to put the . . . uh . . . the rubber over?*"

"You mean condom?"

"Yeah, *well!*"

"Well what?"

"Well, I saw one of those movies when I was thirteen. I can't get the thought out of my head that every time I put my mouth over a banana, other people watching might think it's like I'm putting my mouth over . . ." there was a pause before the young man finally finished that sentence.

For many years this young man had been afraid that this thought (among others) that kept reoccurring whenever in the presence of a banana might just mean that he was crazy. That or something he feared perhaps even more; that it might mean he was gay. These thoughts had been tormenting him for years.

That was an obsessive thought that had been bothering this young man for a very long time. It wasn't frequent enough or interfering enough in his life to be considered a mental *disorder.* Nevertheless it caused him significant distress off and on throughout those many years. He wondered why he would think such a thought. How *could* he possibly think it if there wasn't some sort of truth in it? Isn't that what that guy Sigmund Freud had said? Isn't that what psychologists believe? Isn't there supposed to be a piece of truth in everything anyone thinks or says?

If only it had been that one single thought, it might not have been as big a deal as it eventually became. That specific irrational thought, however, was merely one of many. Even though certain thoughts such as this might not occur for days or weeks at a time, there were a great many floating around in his mind at all times. He was never quite sure that some of them weren't going to pop up suddenly, without warning, at any time day or night.

Luckily, there is a truism that can, when finally understood, relieve people of much of their concern about being regarded as *crazy*. Simply said it is as follows:

"People who think they're crazy are not."

Ponder this simple idea with me for a moment. The term *crazy* most likely has as many meanings as does another popular and rather vague term *love*. Both can be interpreted in many ways; consequently, they can also be *misinterpreted*.

If we think of the word *crazy* as meaning *out-of-touch-with-reality* (or *psychotic*), then this may be a little easier to understand. A person who is really *crazy* or *out-of-touch-with-reality* thinks that what he or she may be doing or thinking or seeing is real, when no one else in the world does. The truly *crazy person* is liable to argue wildly with anyone who tries to tell them that what they are doing, thinking, or seeing is not real.

A person beset by obsessive thoughts like the banana example or who has the urge to do or say strange or repetitive things, knows very well how strange or seemingly crazy this appears. They are terrified by the prospect of others finding out. They typically are very reluctant to say anything about this to anybody. This is not *crazy*, nor is it *out-of-touch-with-reality*. These people are afraid because others *would* view the things that they have been thinking and doing as weird or strange. That is, they would view it this way, if they knew about it.

Welcome to the world of the OCS-driven. They have just enough thoughts and compulsions to make them think that they might be crazy. On the other hand, it's not enough to be identified as having a *disorder*. What do they do? They get depressed. They get anxious. They panic and have panic attacks. They are constantly afraid. They worry. They do a lot of unnecessary little things that take time out of their day, and by the end of the day exhaust them. It's only a little bit here and a little bit there, but it all adds up. They explode over trivial issues like someone bumping their rearview mirror out of alignment. After all, it takes a long time to get it just right, you know. They cry. They scream. They shout and yell. They don't understand what is going on in their lives. They think they might be crazy.

Satisfied? Never!

oh . . . oh . . . oh . . . oh . . . oh . . . oh . . . oh . . .

it's said life is hard . . . though sometimes not

and we should be thankful . . . for all that we've got

thankful . . . yeah . . . on that I agree

but satisfied? . . . never! . . . no one can force that on me

oh . . . oh . . .

I want to be rich . . . I want to have fun

I want to do some things . . . nobody has done

go all the way . . . around the world

find the right one . . . and marry that girl

there's still so much I want to be

and I . . . oh, I . . . just got to be free

sometimes things are so hard to see

'cause we're blinded by what we already believe

oh . . . oh . . .

Words and Music by
Ron D. Kingsley
March 3, 1987

3

Dissatisfaction Guaranteed!

Most of those who have OCS getting in their way will have spells of negativity throughout the course of their lives. This is one of the most common and enduring features of the condition. If we think about this, it makes near perfect sense.

Although there may be moments and some longer episodes of *happiness*, many with OCS are not very happy. Most are said to be "chronically unhappy." Think about it. For those with OCS, nothing is ever good enough, right enough, or exactly the way they wanted. It makes sense that overall true happiness would be like an elusive butterfly. It would often be just within reach, but terribly difficult to catch and hang onto.

There is a tendency to obsess over every little mistake that occurs during the course of a day. This leads to dour and irritable moods that can unravel upon arriving home after school or work. Success itself is too often perceived by the OCS-affected as failure. Usually this is because it wasn't the "right kind" of success or it wasn't successful enough. I believe this is what drives the workaholic, never-say-die, businessman or woman. The OCS factor drives them to continue reaching for more. It will drive them to go far beyond whatever level of success they may have already achieved. As far as they are concerned, they are not really successful. It doesn't matter how much wealth or societal acclaim they get or have obtained. In their deepest thoughts these people have not yet arrived at the zenith of true "success." These are the "successfully unsuccessful." The OCS-affected never quite feel that they've made it, and so are driven on and on and on. Many of them are anyway.

There are some within the OCS population who are also driven to succeed, but other things get in the way. These people may not have the talent, the genius, the luck, or the same favorable environment as those mentioned above. Perhaps their OCS is just a bit worse off or more severe than the successfully unsuccessful. In this group the emotional reactions to failure are stronger. They linger longer and are much more painful. Rather than continue to reach for the unattainable satisfaction and success that they desire, they just give up. Why even try when you already know failure awaits you at the end? These people begin to wallow in negativity and self-defeating thoughts. This can bring on difficult, depressive episodes. The old adage, "You can lead a horse to water, but you can't make him drink," comes to mind.

You *can* point out the personal accomplishments of an individual in this group. There are sure to be some and maybe even many. You can't, however, make them think or believe that this means he/she is successful. Nor can you make them believe that the things mentioned are really accomplishments at all. The OCS-affected can always find something wrong with the logic used. They will always find some reason why an identified success or level of skill is really not what it seems to be.

For example, a high school diploma may mean nothing to a young OCS-driven man. When asked, he will tell you that the only reason he got it was because his counselors felt sorry for him. According to his story, they somehow arranged for him to be able to graduate. He didn't really earn it. HEY! Isn't that what all high school counselors do?

Also, it means very little to the young woman who will quickly inform you that she didn't graduate, her parents did. If they hadn't kept pushing, nagging, and in other ways forcing her to do her homework, she wouldn't have finished high school. She'll tell you flat out, "It's their diploma, not mine!" In this way, the usually valued act of getting a high school diploma can be viewed as a negative event. Its attainment can actually work against, rather than for, the receiver.

There was a man, who upon receiving his fourth college degree, had fearful and anxiety-provoking thoughts. He thought, "What if they find out I don't really deserve this?" and "So, *big deal*, you've got a PhD . . . . now, what?" It must have been an OCS person who came up with that mocking description of what the acronym PhD really stands for. Somebody came up with the idea that it really means "Piled higher and deeper."

It is yet unclear what causes some of those with OCS to end up as one of the successfully unsuccessful? How is it they become successes in society's eyes and yet not in their own? What is it that triggers others to become chronically depressed? Why do some feel like worthless underachievers when they are not? How *can* they feel this way? A few ideas have already been explored up to this point. Surely there are others. More study and research needs to be done in this area. Nevertheless, an attempt will be made at this point to explore other possible reasons.

First and foremost, when OCS is evident it means that there is probably a brain chemical involved. Low levels of serotonin tend to be related to behavior that is obsessive and compulsive. Treatment with a medication known as an SSRI is effective. It often reduces the negative mind-set of those with OCS. It can also rapidly diminish thoughts of chronic failure. In fact, this change can be quite dramatic.

Parents, siblings, and others often describe the transformation that occurs as "amazing." In the beginning, the treated person may not even be aware of the so-called "change." This is because it is chemically driven. It's just the way the world looks to them now. They have not made a conscious choice to change; it has just happened. They didn't see their comments and behaviors before the change as having been "negative." Nor were their actions and words from before thought of as unreasonable. It's just the way it was.

Sometimes, after the start of a medication, a person will sense that others are reacting to them in a different way. These others are not treating them the same as before, but they don't really understand why. In their hearts they still feel like the same old "Joe" or "Jill" that they always were.

Since the early changes come from the inside and don't have much to do with thoughtfully planned actions, they may go unnoticed. There was no map drawn up to achieve behavioral change. The opening reaction is more like a state of being or a new state of consciousness than a real "change." It is simply, as already suggested, the way it is. This might explain why in the early stages of treatment with a medication, the person treated often reports that it is not working.

Medication must be taken for a while, sometimes, before the treated one can see results. There has to be an obvious change in another's attitudes or behavior over time. Without clear evidence of the change in them reflected by others, it is unlikely they will notice. Otherwise, it is difficult for the one treated to see and believe in the transformation.

You cannot see or feel the internal healing process after suffering a broken leg. You can only trust in the actions of the physician who sets it right. Then you must follow the instructions given, so that the leg will heal. You cannot know it is truly healed, until when running and jumping you no longer feel weakness and pain. The OCS-treated often only begins to truly experience an awareness of their healing by means of others. It is revealed in the actions and reactions of others towards them.

There is another chemical issue that can be a part of not being satisfied with success. The same issue can also impact the inclination to just give up in defeat. This is the commonly co-occurring condition known today as ADHD or Attention Deficit Hyperactive Disorder. The aim of this discourse is to reflect on the ADHD-primarily hyperactive type.

It makes sense that the energy behind the never-say-die, "successfully unsuccessful," might be the hyper form of ADHD. They are always on the go. They seem to never need much sleep. They always need to be doing something. There is an edgy liveliness in ADHD. This, in combination with OCS, may be at the heart of those who are never satisfied but unwilling to give up. They do not slip into depression easily even though they feel like failures. Instead, they go on and on and on in spite of their perceived lack of success.

Perhaps an inference from the hyper group may in part explain those that seem unable to go on. It may clarify why these others do quit trying. Perhaps those who tend to quit don't have the energy needed to continue forward in the face of all odds. Perhaps this group does more easily get depressed when they feel they've failed. Maybe they give up because it's too hard to press forward when you can never be happy with how things turn out.

Then there is, of course, the severity or strength of the symptoms. This may be linked to the amount of the serotonin deficit. It makes sense that such might be the case. When OCD or Obsessive-Compulsive Disorder is treated with medication, the dose range is fairly high. For Prozac, it usually spans 40 to 80 mg daily for an adult. When OCS is mild to moderate though, the effective dose usually ranges from 20 to 60 mg daily.

Next, there are the conditioned or learned behaviors. These can develop from the main chemically-driven thoughts and actions. Sometimes, they might also arise due to the environment. They come from modeling the actions of parents and/or others as well. These behaviors also tend to endure. They may keep fruitless behavior patterns going over time. Even when primary symptoms have improved, these second and third layer behaviors can continue. This also makes sense. An example of a situation such as this might be as follows. At the heart of it all, let's say there is a hypersensitive emotional response. This response is set off each time a mistake is made, or something doesn't go right in the eyes of the person involved. The reaction every time this occurs is to get very emotional. In fact, the person is so upset that others begin to take notice and react.

Some are irritated or angry and warn the person to "Shut up!" and "Quit whining!" Others resort to name calling, "Oh . . . you big baby!" and "What a spoiled little brat!" Still others may try to console the individual and reassure them. They might say: "Don't feel bad, everybody makes mistakes," or, "Just try to shake it off, it's no big deal," and so on.

The response made by others gives rise to later responses, which then bring on yet other responses. The person may begin to feel picked on or singled out needlessly. He or she may start to verbalize this fact angrily, in return. This can lead to the individual being labeled as a trouble maker or as a "bad seed." Eventually a person can begin to think of himself or herself as just plain "bad." This assumed "badness" can begin to seep into everything they do and say.

The mind-set that begins to show forth, as well as the view of being bad, can set the stage for other unwelcome behavior. The unwanted behavior might never have occurred, had it not been for those that did occur thereafter. Each action or behavior would bring on the next, which would then bring on yet another new reaction. Yet, most of these behaviors are indirectly connected to those that came first. As a result, it takes a lot longer for them to soften and change or be let go of.

After treatment begins many behaviors tend to remain in place for some time. This is true, even though the key underlying problem is noticeably improved. The issues directly related to the serotonin deficit clear up first. Then the issues related secondarily to those that were first can clear up. Then those that were third, fourth, fifth and so on improve for as many layers as may exist. Once the direct chemical-driven response is no longer there, the next one in line may then fade, and so on.

The behaviors that are not directly caused by the earliest response should not be expected to change right away. This is because these interrelated responses have been born of other factors. These later behaviors have no direct ties to the initial chemically triggered reaction. So medication may take months and even years to show the full positive effects that are possible.

As the main chemically driven base gives way sooner or later, the entire behavior response structure will fall. New behaviors can then take the place of the old dysfunctional behavior. The key words in this are "sooner or later." Many of the interrelated behaviors of OCS can be extremely complex.

Sometimes, it is impossible to see the links leading back to the chemically driven beginning. This may be so, whether considered by the professional or those with OCS. In such cases the connections only become clear with extended treatment and study after the fact. As the related issues finally fall away, the earlier unseen crumbling support system is easily connected to the fall.

Fortunately, the complex behavior network formed and built often many years in the past does not stand alone. It is usually surrounded by behaviors more or less closely connected so that the assessment of OCS can still be made. It is not unusual though for the strong-willed to find alternate explanations. This explanation is often just as realistic, and at times can even seem more so. They find logical and believable reasons for the presence of these very same behaviors.

Often, this hunting for a reason has been considered a form of "denial." Sometimes it actually is. When it is, it may be conscious or unconscious. This means the person may or may not be aware of their use of denial. The reason for denial is to protect themselves from finding out or having to face bad news. In the OCS population, it seems that such an interpretation is often not true. As a result, it tends to be counterproductive to view it in such a way.

Those with OCS often come to believe in whatever reasons or causes that sound good or right to them. They have no better explanation. If they did, they would take it. There is often a strong need, though, to find a cause for their inexplicable behaviors. Frequently these reasons naturally flow out of the common beliefs and insights of their culture. Thus, "I just have a bad temper like my dad" becomes the accepted reason for angry outbursts.

It doesn't matter that these explosive episodes are really due to a chemically driven reaction. You believe it's because you got it from your dad. In fact, you are sure you probably *learned* how to do it from him. It also stands to reason that if you learned it you can also unlearn it. The fact that you don't unlearn it is puzzling. You don't want to do it. It's also very frustrating, especially to others. They blame you. You begin to blame yourself. What else can you do? It's your fault. You must not want to stop. You must be doing it for attention. Yeah, that's it.

Even negative attention is better than no attention at all. At least that's what everybody seems to believe. So it must be true. Often, however, such an explanation is about as far from the truth as you can get. Once a culture accepts a belief, however, it is nearly impossible to change. To do so would require a paradigm shift. Such a shift takes years, and even then remnants of the old beliefs can linger on.

This is not an attempt to suggest that all angry outbursts are biochemically driven. They are not; of course, that is the problem. Many people were never told or taught that sometimes an angry outburst can be caused by a chemical imbalance. These same people, though, may have witnessed such outbursts in family members. They may have heard stories of similar outbursts in extended family members for their entire lives.

They have also been told: "You've got a bad temper, child. You must've got it from me and I got it from my Dad, I'm sure." Such a belief system can make it very difficult to be open to other explanations. When this occurs, it is not denial; it is pure and simple ignorance.

As already pointed out, the OCS-successful, who does not feel a success, is usually unhappy. They aren't satisfied with life or anything about it. They constantly focus on the negative. They don't look for the silver lining on the cloud. They are sure that it doesn't exist without having to look. They usually don't see themselves as focused on the negative, although most others do. Rather, they tend to see themselves as being "realistic" or "honest."

They desire realistic appraisals of life's experiences at all costs. They cannot tolerate the pretender. They often suppress laughter and do not think jokes have a place in this world. They strongly prefer that one not profess success or positive outcome where none exist. They are serious and sober observers of life. They don't want or need to exaggerate the positives, in order to feel a measure of success. As far as they are concerned, too many people concentrate on the positive so they can run from or ignore the negative. They tend to view those who do so as either naive or liars.

Success, to this person, is a "journey . . . not a destination." And since success *is* a journey, it follows as night does into day, that there is no such destination as success. If there is no such destination, then it makes sense that no one will ever get to such a place. So it is contrary to reason to make a declaration that you are a success.

A deep-seated discontent and negative outlook has been subtly entrenched into their being. Because of the extreme intertwining of causes and counter-causes, even the capable adult is hard put to figure things out. There may be years of intricate and long standing webs of deceit. It's been like that far too long and the connections are much too powerful.

If discovered in time, though, most versions caught up in this pattern can be successfully treated. They can then steer clear of much of this negative, chronic, personal dissatisfaction. They can develop a new and different world view than those adults who are too entrenched in their longstanding complex patterns and unable to let go of the negative focus.

As with other OCS symptoms, the chronic-dissatisfied group also has a polar opposite. These hardly ever seem to show up for treatment. This may be due to the fact that relatively few of those with OCS seem to experience this side of the coin. It's more likely a direct result of the impact it has on others in the world. Ultimately, most others wouldn't think of this behavior as a symptom at all. They might find it hard to believe that it could be considered something for which one might seek out or need treatment.

If you have not already guessed it, this is the extreme Pollyanna type of outlook. It is the great optimist. Such are the constantly elated, and at all times happy people. They are the self-satisfied, always triumphant, positive thinkers. These individuals gloss over and cannot accept or see the bad in any way, shape, or form at all. They cannot allow themselves to feel or accept even the tiniest of resentments. There are no laments, disappointments, or negative attitudes. They will not admit to dissatisfaction with anyone or anything. Of course, it's those like the extreme case just described, if any, that are most likely to end up in treatment.

Most of those in this group, though, are on a continuum and not nearly so extreme. A positive attitude and outlook is highly valued in most cultures. Such attributes are not considered a problem. These people are rarely, if ever, singled out as having symptoms. Some who are severe enough in their optimism can irritate and grind on the nerves of others. It can be especially hard on those who must deal with them on a daily basis. These tend to have an unquestionable positive point of view, no matter what happens. When extreme, it can be too much emotionally for most others to have to deal with. Strong optimism can seem far-fetched, questionable, and even fake when present at this level.

The OCS-affected can cycle from leaning more towards one side of a symptom pole and then suddenly shift to the opposite side. Further study is needed to try and resolve why some with OCS go back and forth from positive to negative poles. It may have something to do with the all-or-nothing feature common to them. Generally, most do seem to display their symptoms in just one main direction.

The strong positively or negatively driven person may very well have OCS. It may be the principal reason why someone might focus strongly in one direction or the other. So an intense negative or positive focus might just be an indicator of possible OCS influence. It should at least be considered. If OCS is present, there will also be evidence of other signs. No real OCS characteristic stands alone. When supporting indicators are not present, an OCS diagnosis should not be made. Other possible sources or causes should be considered instead.

4

Driven to Please

People with OCS can often have a strong need to be liked. This pattern can lead to undue efforts to make sure that others don't think bad thoughts about them as well. A related need also likely to be part of this is to *never* let anyone down. Similarly to never do anything that might cause another pain.

This specific need can seem quite contradictory at times. In order to change such a behavior pattern, the seeming contradiction must be understood. After it is figured out, then true progress can be made. This is written to examine and share common examples of this OCS pattern. Also to explain in sufficient detail what it mens to have this *need to please*. The hope is that by doing so, behaviors linked to this need may be identified. Once identified, symptoms can be treated suitably. These symptoms need to be understood for what they are, rather than for what they so often appear to be.

At the heart of this *drive* or *need to please,* there is often a constant longing for acceptance. The self-esteem or self-worth is frequently low. Self-image also may tend to rely on the appraisal of others. As others approve of them, self-esteem soars. All too often this is only temporary. The moment the tiniest hint of disapproval is felt, self-esteem drops. The person can straight away appear very distressed. They may also become quite negative and gloomy. The thought of others being dissatisfied with them may cause an extreme reaction. To those with this obsessive *need to please*, it can seem as if their whole world has just collapsed around them. Feelings of complete worthlessness often follow. Although such a reaction is clearly over the top, it doesn't' seem that way to the person. At least, it doesn't seem so over the top at the time.

There is a tendency to feel a need to fulfill every whim of others. This can be a big problem. It can't be done. This need results in an inability to say *no*. When asked to perform favors or tasks by another person, they feel they must do whatever was requested. The person often agrees to take on everything asked of them. Then they spend much of their time completely overwhelmed. Some are actually able to complete the many things that they've taken on. However, doing so takes its toll. Many end up feeling like total failures. This can occur even though *no one* in their *right mind* would have expected success under such conditions. Knowing this should enable them to be less self-critical about the unfinished tasks. This is too often just not possible for those who are driven to please.

The inability to say *no* virtually insures that there will be times when there is too much to do. At least some of the time we should assume that things won't get done. Most people would quickly realize this. They would see that they had overstepped their capacity. It would be clear they had agreed to do more than they had the time or energy to finish. Most would then shrug it off and maybe use it as a learning experience. Probably they would make a mental note to remember not to take on as much in the future. This would help to keep things more manageable the next time, so that there would be a better chance of success.

The OCS pleasers often simply cannot do this. They don't seem to realize they had set themselves up to fail. Many obsess over the failure itself. They beat themselves up mentally. Sometimes the more deeply distressed can even do so physically. They blame themselves. As far as they're concerned, they *should* have succeeded. This is one of the common distortions of the mind that the OCS pleasers simply cannot shake off. They are convinced that the failure was entirely their fault. Some even feel the need to be punished. They feel a need to pay for this *terribly awful* error or mistake. Guilt abounds.

There are other subtle, yet related, problems linked to the characteristic of *needing to please*. Over time, the constant lack of success creates other issues. These include conditions such as depression and anxiety. Anger control issues and feelings of inadequacy are also at the top of the list. The development of co-dependency is common. Distorted versions of life events are frequent. Self-loathing may be chronic. This loathing of the self is often misunderstood and thought to be something else. Negative expectations can be embraced as a way of life. Optimism is usually shunned. Hope is sometimes viewed as unrealistic. Positive, hopeful people are disdained and labeled as not living in the *real* world.

In time, pleasers can also develop physical problems and illnesses. Chronic fatigue is one such physical reaction that is fairly common. Headaches (including migraines) and stomachaches (including acid reflux disease) evidence suggests can result from this as well. Sometimes physical problems may be used as an excuse for failure.

Much of the time, these physical responses are automatic. It is the body's reaction to stress. If a person won't willingly rest, eventually the body will make sure that rest occurs. It will shut down. Physical illness is often the only excuse accepted for any type of failure. If you don't do what you promised you had better really be sick. In this way, the pleaser may not have to feel the great distress of continual unexcused failure. When acceptably ill, there exists a genuine reason for the failure. No one who is truly ill is condemned for task incompletion or a lack of attendance at work or school.

So the excessive pleaser's brain sometimes takes care of things by shutting down physically, which is the only way it can rest. It is constantly working to balance all bodily functions. It attempts to relieve stress caused by the guilt of the driven pleaser's failures. This it does by directing a breakdown of some bodily functions. With a good excuse, relief may finally occur. The emotional relief that comes when this happens can be huge.

The act of taking care of other's needs first, often leaves the pleaser feeling empty and alone. Personal needs are ignored or set aside in favor of doing for another. Usually, though, these pleasers secretly yearn to have their own needs met too. These people dream of someone taking care of *them* in much the same way that they take care of others. This can be difficult. The pleaser usually has a stronger drive to deny rather than make known personal needs. They also feel very uncomfortable if another does try to take care of them. Getting their own needs met is not something they know how to do. Allowing it to happen would bring about strong feelings of guilt. More guilt is not something they want or need. So they push others away.

For instance: An OCS pleaser is working on a project. You ask him if he could give you a hand after he finishes what he is doing. He immediately puts down his work and comes to your aid.

After he spends more time helping you than you really needed or wanted, you politely ask, "Is there anything I can do for you?"

"Oh, no," he replies smiling warmly. "I'm *just* fine."

You are not quite convinced and so continue: "Are you sure? I've got a little extra time right now and it looks like you still have a lot left to do . . . ."

The pleaser's smile gets bigger. He repeats, "No, no, I'm fine. Really I am." To emphasize his point he starts shooing you on your way with big sweeps of his arms. "Go on. I don't need anything. Yes, that's right. I'm good."

The case outlined above is an example of a common OCS pleaser's response. Why would you try to help another when told point blank and more than once that no help was needed? As unbelievable as it may seem, the pleaser in the situation above can often become upset after you leave. He'll start back to work on his project, all the while grumbling under his breath about how much work he still has to do. Chances are he would also complain about the fact that no one *ever* helps *him* with anything.

Without even realizing it, such pleasers often dig their own deep holes. Then they throw out the shovel. A very important point to remember is that these people may not understand what is happening. Even if they are aware, they just may not be able to stop the pattern from repeating again, and again, and again.

The OCS pleaser privately longs to be pleased. They aren't very good at allowing it to happen, though. They don't want to impose on someone else's time.

Jim smiled, "C'mon, honey, you sit right here on the couch. *I'm* fixing dinner tonight."

"What!" Jill cried. "Let me help." She stood and took a step towards the kitchen.

Jim placed his hand on the small of her back and gently guided her back to the couch. "You stay here," he said. "I'm going to bring you something." Jim picked up the TV remote and placed it in her lap. He patted the back of her ring hand with his own. "Stay," he told her. Then he quickly left to go to the kitchen.

Jill sat with one leg over the other. Her fingers tapped out a random code on her knee.

Jim returned with a glass of cold lemonade. He placed it on a coaster on the small table just left of the couch. He then caught Jill rounding the other side of the couch. He took her by the hand and led her back to the place he'd chosen for her to relax. Jim then picked up the glass with the freshly made lemonade. "For you," he said. "I hope it tastes good."

"You shouldn't have," she said trying to push the offering away.

"Why not," Jim asked? "You deserve it."

She tried to tell him that she didn't. "No, I . . . ."

Jim smiled. "Just take a sip."

"Okay, okay," Jill finally agreed. She pressed the rim of the chilly glass to her lips.

"Now, stay," said Jim. He returned to the kitchen.

During the course of the next fifteen minutes Jim had to shoo his wife out of the kitchen five times. The lemonade remained on the end table untouched after that one sip. She kept coming back. Jill just couldn't seem to let her husband make dinner for her. He finally quit trying and ended up sitting on the couch himself. He was angry. He felt that Jill didn't trust him to do it right. He drank her lemonade.

Intense guilt invades the mind of the pleaser. Often there is enormous guilt at the very thought of taking even the smallest amount of time and energy for personal needs. It is not unusual for pleasers who try to take time to meet their own needs to feel miserable when they do. This, then, can actually increase the pleaser's stress levels, rather than decrease them. Why continue to try and get your own needs met, if it only makes you feel worse anyway?

The dynamics of the OCS drive to please represents another form of an OCS paradox that frustrates and depresses. They desperately strive to please others and desire the same. Yet they cannot accept it when offered or enjoy it when it occurs. How could this be anything other than frustrating and depressing? In psychology they call this a *double bind*. In popular terms it's called *catch twenty-two*. It means that no matter which choice is made, there are negative consequences to deal with, at least at the start. One choice may be less painful than the other or they may be equally painful. One choice may lead to a more desirable outcome eventually. It doesn't make the choice any easier at the moment, though.

A chronic need to please or make others happy is destined to be a failing enterprise. No one can know another's wants and needs well enough to truly satisfy him or her. Failure is almost certain over time. Attempting to do so will result in a false sense of security. The belief that you are succeeding when you are not, leads to good feelings that can be lost in an instant. This puts the pleaser on an emotional roller-coaster. Their moods vary from great joy to incredible misery. This emotional roller-coaster ride tends to keep the pleaser full of worry and doubt. They don't trust their own plans or abilities.

Over time, this doubt can grow to the point that they may for a short time suffer an emotional or behavioral type of paralysis. During such an event the pleaser isn't sure if he or she is coming or going. Uncertainty may set in, as well as strong feelings of inadequacy. These can become a constant symbol of personal worthlessness. At such times others can persuade, coax, and influence the pleaser in just about any direction they wish. When extreme self-doubt is present, the decision making process becomes dysfunctional. When this happens, others can often quite easily take advantage of the situation. They can make the pleaser believe just about anything.

Variations of this drive to please can and do occur. The pleaser may have a strong personality. That, or they may become very frustrated or irritated. When these factors are involved, anger can be the result. Sometimes this anger can build up until finally there is an outburst. This can be quite intense and downright frightening. The strong-willed pleaser may come right out and demand that others *be* pleased by what they do. They had darn well *better* be pleased *or else*!

*   *   *

A father shouts down the hall in his home. "You kids, get up! I made pancakes for you and you're going to eat them and like it!"

The kids enter the kitchen, rolling their eyes.

"Don't you *dare* say it," he whispers under his breath. "If you do I'll *never ever* do something like this again, *ever*! And you know I mean it!"

*   *   *

A mother complains with bitterness in her voice. "I gave you children the best years of my life without asking for a thing in return. I could have continued my career as a dancer and gone on with my friends who went to Hollywood. I could have made movies. Who knows, I might have even become a star. But *no* . . . I chose to give it all up, for you. I gained fifty pounds for you. I gave up my glamorous wardrobe. I never could fit into any of them after that first child was born. I once had a figure to die for. No, no, no . . . don't look at me with that sad expression on your face. I gave it all up willingly. I did it for you. I left behind all the glamour of the bright lights for the dirty diapers and the dingy apartments and you *children*."

She pauses to take a breath and lets out one very long sigh before continuing: "If only even one of you seemed to be grateful for the sacrifices I made. The ones I still make *every* single day for *you*. It's not like I could *ever* regain my once greatly admired and shapely figure. I'll *never* recapture my form and fitness on the dance floor. It's gone . . . all gone . . . So what's the big deal if I want to talk or spend a little time with my children now that they're grown up? How can you think about going to your friends when your very own mother needs you? It's not like I haven't done *everything* for you . . ." The mother drones on.

*   *   *

In the first scene outlined above, a parent who insists that others must be pleased is described. He orders them to eat and like it, "or else!" This type of pleaser often has the same fears and anxieties about needing to please, as do the other kinds. They use their strong personality to get needs met. Size and intimidating physical strength may be used in the same way. These traits put them in a position to force others to at least act as if they are pleased. When others appear to be displeased, problems ensue. The strong-willed pleaser can respond with anger or explosive reactions of rage and disbelief. Such reactions can create a conditioned response. Soon others learn to hide it when not pleased by this pleaser. The strong-willed pleaser can be viewed as a kind of a bully or even a control freak.

In the second example, the mother shows her anger in an indirect way. This is known as being passive-aggressive. Her words are full of weak retractions and heavy doses of inferred guilt. This is often the path taken by the strong-willed pleaser who does not have the physical strength to intimidate others into action. These pleasers have a will and mind just as strong and powerful as their counterparts that use brute strength to intimidate. They need to find another way to vent their anger and frustration. This person's complaining, relentless, guilt-ridden words can work to irritate and wear down others. In time, a conditioned response can also develop. Whenever this type of pleaser feels others are ungrateful for what they've done, they can't stand it. This type of pleaser can be very annoying.

"Okay, mom, enough already. I love the dress, *really* I do. It's wonderful! I'll be wearing it every chance I get. Just please stop . . . ." So says the daughter, in order to avoid her mother's reaction. These would be the aversive half-hidden knives and daggers that she has learned to expect. They show up whenever she is unhappy with her mother's actions or gifts on her behalf. The embarrassment of the ugly out-of-date dress is less painful than her mother's bitter verbal barrage. Anyway, she'll just leave one of her other dresses at her friend's house down the street. That way she can change each time she wears it before actually going anywhere. She can always change back before coming home. Yeah, she decides silently, that's what she'll do.

The examples portrayed of these strong willed pleasers act in different ways. Although differing, they *are* working for the same ultimate goal. Usually the goal itself and how to get there is not consciously sought after. These people are not aware of why they respond and act towards others in the ways that they do. Their actions are not usually intended to be hurtful. Others, though, may feel that they *are* trying to hurt them. Both types of responses aim to fulfill that inner drive to please others.

This pleaser may know intellectually that no one can really be expected to please others all the time. The need, however, causes them to work hard to make sure that others at least act pleased. Such acting allows the pleaser to feel much better, even though it may have been done under a false pretense. Actual displeasure or rejection would be worse. Faking pleasure at least lets the pleasers pretend. They've got to feel this stubborn, deep-felt inner-need-to-please has been fulfilled. /they must be sure that no one else who might be observing can tell.

Eventually, those strong-willed pleasers who try to force others into satisfaction are going to reap their rewards. They are going to have to work through the inner conflict created by the lie that they are constantly living. This conflict refers to the awareness that those being forced to state their satisfaction may not be pleased or satisfied at all. Often, in fact, they may feel just the opposite.

The internal need for the strong-willed pleaser to deny the knowledge of this can be very strong. Often, accepting the truth can damage their self-esteem. They would have to admit that their self-image had been built up around false pretenses. To accept it would mean they have completely failed and fooled themselves in life's personal goals. They have been liars to themselves and to the rest of the world.

This is typically a distorted view. It tends to be overly simplistic. Such a belief is not even close to describing the whole of what has been going on. Still, the idea permeates the mind and frightens this person into denial. Denial is a much safer pathway to follow. This path is rarely chosen on purpose or based on actual consciousness. Instead, it is simply a reaction. To deny reality often seems easier than to face it. To confront a painful truth is sometimes much more difficult. For some, this actually proves to be impossible. To do so would completely destroy the blueprint that made them who they are. They wrongly fear they'll have to rewrite the entire plan. This is simply not true. It is an irrational thought. In order to heal and change, however, they *will* have to rewrite certain parts. This *is* true.

The emotional overreaction of the OCS-affected is what drives this irrational fear. Insight into this tendency to go over the top is important. Knowing that it truly *is* a driven symptom can help the person to get past it and not feel so overwhelmed. The prospect of redefining or redesigning parts of themselves can be quite daunting. This process leads them towards the goal of finally figuring out *who* they *really* are.

The absolute most important thing an OCS pleaser can do is to become educated about their OCS. Accurate knowledge is power. The fact that being driven to please is such a common symptom of OCS makes it important to learn about. Education truly is a powerful tool for change. It is just as vital to learn about the many other OCS patterns too. Each pattern influences and impacts one another in a variety of ways. This knowledge can then work to allow the person to deal with symptoms much more effectively. It can help them predict responses to future events. In this way, they can better prepare ahead of time for possible difficult situations. When prepared for beforehand, they are less likely to simply react to these events. Various symptoms are less likely to be set off. They will be better able to act than react. Acting, not reacting, is the ultimate goal. When we can do this, we are truly free from all symptoms. Once free, we can drive our own bus, any direction we choose.

5

Negativity Squared

"I *never* win, so why should I even try?"

"My teacher always picks James to read the story. She *never* picks me!"

"Are there olives in this salad? I *hate* olives. You *always* put olives in everything."

Do any of these statements sound familiar? Most of those affected with OCS will experience bouts of negativity off and on throughout their lives. This is one of the most common traits related to the condition. In part, this may happen because organizations and the media all over the world tend to do exactly the same thing. In schools, the focus is on how many questions you get wrong on a given test. In the media, the focus is on the tragedies and bad things that occur everywhere. The spotlight is mostly on what's wrong or bad, rather than on what's right or good. People are constantly bombarded by potential negative "triggers." These triggers can set that obsessive compulsive gun into action. It starts firing down the road towards negativity. It makes sense that negativity would result from having been fed negativity on a daily basis for years.

There really can be moments and periods of apparent "happiness." This, however, is not the norm for the typical OCS negatively affected person. These might be better described as "chronically unhappy." Think about it. Nothing is ever perceived as good enough, right enough, or exactly what they want. So it makes sense that as mentioned true happiness is like an elusive butterfly, often just within reach, but terribly difficult to catch and hang onto.

It's Gotta Be Done Right

There is one very interesting thing about this tendency to be so negative. Often the person caught up in the pessimistic behavior may not be aware of their own negativity. They will frequently describe themselves as "realistic" or "honest." They may say something like, "I'm not being negative. I'm just being realistic," and so on. There is a tendency to highlight the negative, though at the expense of ignoring the positive.

Let me share an example of a ten-year-old boy I once worked with for a time. We'll call him Billy Green. Billy's father showed many signs of OCS, himself. He was totally unaware of this as a driving force in his own behavior though. Mr. Green had brought his son to see a psychologist and the boy was the identified problem. The real problem in this case was the father. He said that Billy *never* followed through on chores or anything else. According to this man "that kid doesn't do anything right, even though he knows exactly the way things should be done."

Actually, Mr. Green had expectations that were way too high. You could say that he was obsessive about these expectations as well. They were so stringent and specific that it was simply impossible for Billy (or any other ten-year-old) to meet them. One example of Billy's "problem" was said to be the way he went about mowing the lawn. Mr. Green kept coming back to the fact that over time, he had shown Billy again and again exactly how the lawn should be taken care of. He would check the job immediately after Billy said he was done. This boy, remember, was only ten. Billy would cut the yard like a child, not like an adult. He was ten years old. His dad was forty-seven.

As Mr. Green inspected the yard, he would fire his negative comments, telling Billy what was still wrong. He would do this check on the average three or four times before he'd finally agree that Billy was done. Even then Mr. Green would not be truly satisfied. This was because of his anger. He would be furious that he'd had to keep telling his son what to do. Thus, even after Billy finally got it right, his father still had many negative things to say.

Mr. Green would complain to me that he knew Billy could do it the way it was supposed to be done. He was just lazy. He didn't *want* to do it right. There were even times when Mr. Green thought that his son was doing it wrong, just to get him mad. Mr. Green painstakingly explained that each time that he showed or told Billy what to do, he did it. His angry conclusion was that Billy was perfectly able to complete his chores the way they were supposed to be done. The fact that he repeatedly did not do so was evidence that he was choosing not to. Furthermore, he felt his son was clearly not doing the jobs right just to get back at him for making the boy do them.

Mr. Green's inability to say positive things to his son was the real problem. The man found only fault at every turn. Unfortunately, they did not stay long in therapy. It was pointed out to the Mr. Green that his son had never really mowed the lawn at all. Billy was simply an instrument in his father's hands. If his father expected the lawn to be mowed like an adult would, Billy was going to need continual supervision and direction. Mr. Green did not bring him back. This, however, is an excellent example of how obsessive negativity and hyper-critical behavior can develop to be a big problem.

The Barrage of Complaints

Another common problem when someone is overly focused on negative outcomes is the inclination to complain. They grumble and whine about everything. My foot hurts. Nobody likes me. Do we have to eat *that* for dinner? You gave me too much. You didn't give me enough. Jimmy got more than me. There's *nothing* to eat in this house! I hate my teachers. I hate homework! School sucks! There's nothing good on TV. School lunch smells disgusting! It looks disgusting too! Some of the complaints may actually be justified. However, like the boy who cried "wolf," these comments are eventually no longer heard, and less likely to be believed. The complaints never seem to stop. Who wants to be with someone who is always complaining? Such people are just not much fun to be around.

The Workaholic

The trend to obsess over every tiny little thing takes its toll. This can be commonly done throughout the school or work day. It can lead to dour and irritable moods. The mood often shows up upon arriving home for the day. Negativity abounds in such an environment. Even success itself is too often seen in a negative light as failure. Usually, it's because it wasn't the "right kind" of success. Either that, or it wasn't successful at the level desired or anticipated.

This is frequently the hidden dynamic that drives the workaholic. He or she is the never-say-die OCS-driven person. They continue looking and reaching far beyond the successes already achieved. They constantly doubt their success. It doesn't matter how much wealth or societal acclaim they receive. In their deepest thoughts, they never quite arrive at the pinnacle of "true" success. These people are driven on and on and on. They are successful, and yet feel unsuccessful in life.

Giving up before Starting

There is yet another group within the OCS negatively driven population. These are similarly driven. They however do not have the talent, the genius, the luck, or the favorable environment. Perhaps they have stronger symptoms and are a bit worse off than the "successfully unsuccessful" described above. For this group, the emotional reaction to failure is stronger. It seems to linger longer, and may be much more painful. Instead of continually striving to reach the unreachable, the individuals in this group tend to start giving up. Why try when you're already sure that failure awaits you at the end? These individuals begin to wallow in negativity. They have persistent self-defeating thoughts. They also experience heavy-duty depressive episodes. The old adage, "You can lead a horse to water, but you can't make him drink," comes to mind. You can point out to this person her successes and accomplishments, but you can't make her believe that this means she is successful. She may not be able to see these things as successes at all. The OCS-affected can always find something wrong. They can always come up with some reason as to why an accomplishment is not really what it appears to be.

Downplaying Success

A high school diploma means nothing to a young man. He will tell you that the only reason he got the diploma in the first place was that his counselors felt sorry for him. As a result the counselor somehow arranged for him to graduate even though he didn't deserve it. HEY, isn't that what all high school counselors do? It also means very little to the young woman who tell you that she wouldn't have graduated if her parents hadn't been continually pushing, nagging, and forcing her to do her homework. She'll tell you flat-out, "It's their diploma, not mine!" There was an individual who received his fourth college with trepidation. He had fearful and anxiety provoking thoughts such as, "What if they find out? What if I really don't deserve this?" He also thought, "So, *big deal*, you've got a PhD, now what?" It may have been an individual with OCS who came up with that humorous definition for the oft heard acronym relative to the degree of PhD, "Piled higher and deeper."

Who, Me?

When pointed out that their negative focus is beyond the norm, the OCS-driven often react with total disbelief. Since they don't view themselves as being negative, they may start to wonder if the accuser has some kind of ulterior motive. Denial is common and can itself become an obsessive symptom. "I'm not being negative," they may respond, "I'm just being realistic!" It's almost as if they think you can't be positive and realistic too. It doesn't make any sense, but it happens.

Remember, over-responding emotionally to things that happen is nearly a sure bet for someone who has significant OCS. When accused of being negative, sometimes the affected one can get very angry. He or she may respond, "So you think that's negative, do you? Well, I'll just show you what negative is then!" What may follow is an incredible amount of negative action, thoughts, and behavior. Often these people are reacting to ward off any further attacks on their emotional well being. Although they still haven't acknowledged that they are negative, they are trying to show that things could be much worse. So leave it alone. This tactic of over responsiveness is more of a gut reaction than a thought-out planned answer. Usually the overreactions are so distressing to others that they simply quit saying things like that. They may even try to retract their earlier comments. "Well, I guess you're not really *negative*. I must have had it wrong." Life goes on. The negativity continues.

A Way of Life

Side effects of constant negativity tend to be difficult to live with, as far as others are concerned. A focus on the negative sets one up to consistently expect to fail, or expect others to fail. The negative attitude can seem quite stern, sour, and even downright mean. Their focus is on what's wrong, rather than what is right. As a result, it can be very difficult for such a person to smile or be happy about much of anything.

Constructive criticism is another term these individuals will frequently use to justify their negativity. Dr. John Lund has said, "There is no such thing as *constructive* criticism. It's always destructive." Think about it. If someone is chronically critical of themselves and others, can they ever truly acknowledge an accomplishment? Will Billy be able to hear: "Good job, son. You did well," if it is followed with "but . . . you could have," or "you should have," or "if you just did this or that . . ."? A critical comment such as this, whether it comes before or after a supposed positive remark, takes away or cancels whatever praise may be intended. The inability to compliment another without also adding "constructive criticism" can encourage others to stay away. The intent of a critical remark doesn't make it any less critical. This intent, however, does interfere with the ability of those that have OCS to label their actions or behaviors as "negative." They are more likely to consider their negative comments as "helpful" or "needed."

Hope

The earlier the negative core is discovered in the OCS-affected and work begins to manage it, the better the outcome for everyone. As people get older and more set in their ways, the negative focus becomes rooted ever deeper into the heart of their being. It can get to be such a way of life that others begin to see it as "personality" rather than a symptom. Negativity can become tangled up in every part of a person's life. It can be such a part of them, that to eliminate it completely could result in an emotional breakdown.

One of the first steps in managing negativity is to figure out exactly what "being negative" really means. If the affected one is aware and actively trying to change, it will be much easier. In order to help, it can be pointed it out to them verbally. Also, others could use a cue to help the OCS person notice when they are being that way. Cues could be such things as an already agreed upon word, a touch, or a visual hand movement and the like. Most of the time it is the inability to accept being negative that gets in the way of change. If someone cannot be convinced that what they are doing or saying is negative, then why in the world would they want to change it? Therefore, an argument or fight ensues.

As the negatively inclined grow from child to adult, certain patterns emerge. They tend to justify negativity to escape blame for the consequences of their behavior. This can look like a personality disorder or flaw. "That's just the way I am," is a common declaration. "I can't help how I look at the world," is yet another. Again, these individuals also imply that they are simply being open and honest. This "so called problem" is actually a virtue that they have been cultivating over the course of their entire lives. What else could such an affected one think? They may have learned this through modeling or teaching by similarly affected parents. Also, as we all know the media can be very influential in our lives as well. It can set us up to develop a primarily negative focus on the world and in our personal views of life.

Sometimes, the negative focus is so ingrained that there is a great fear of what might happen if they were to lose this perspective. There can be an underlying terror that to change such a point of view would be to lose themselves or who-they-are. Since they have never really been able to look at the world differently, it is not surprising that a strong fear of losing the self might exist.

For family members, friends, and those in the workplace, being made aware is helpful. Others need to know of this person's unconscious negative outlook. Knowing what's going on allows you to better predict and manage another's actions and reactions. When they react to environments, stressors, and situations, you can deal with it better and help them do the same. Knowledge makes it much easier to be involved with these negatively-focused OCS individuals. There are things that can be done to effectively deal with another's negativity, once you know that it's a problem. Education is the most essential tool to use as all other interventions depend on it.

For those of you who might be getting a glimpse of yourselves in this chapter, there is hope. Change can occur. When OCS is the driving force behind a person's negative point of view, treatment is available. Appropriate treatment does bring about positive change. Wonderful news, don't you think?

The Need

you ask me why . . . but I don't know . . .
you say I lie . . . but it's not so . . . it's just not so . . .

it's like inside a voice just keeps right on telling me . . .
there's one and only one way things can be . . .
and I can't let go of this need . . .
even though I've tried I can't get free . . . of the need . . .
some things can't be ignored . . . even if you try . . .
and sometimes when there's a door . . . you still can't get inside . . .

—chorus—

it's like my own mind just won't stop reminding me . . .
there's one and only one way things must be . . .
and I can't let go of this need . . . even though I try I can't pull free . . .
and I don't really want to know what this might mean . . .
that so often I just can't let go . . . of the need . . .
some things can't be ignored . . . no matter how hard you may try . . .
like the very fact that you and I were born . . . and one day . . .
will just as surely die . . .
you ask me why . . . but I don't know . . .
you say I lie . . . but it's not so . . . I tell you it's not so . . .

some things can't be ignored . . . even though we may try . . .
and sometimes though there's a door . . . we just can't get inside
you ask me why . . . but I don't know . . .

Words and Music by Ron D. Kingsley November 17, 1998

6

The Empty Bucket

Here we have a very common symptom. This one is closely related to another that has been called Dissatisfaction Guaranteed. In fact, this particular tendency may only be different in the way that it is expressed. It most assuredly stems from the same main idea of never quite being satisfied with anything. The focus this time, though, has shifted just a bit. Instead of continually being dissatisfied with their own actions, the focus changes to that of not being satisfied with what others do. This includes developmental needs. These are things such as the need for security, love, attention, nourishment, friendship, and the like.

No matter how much water you pour into a sink, unless the drain is plugged up it will *never* be filled. You *could* say such a sink might remain *forever* thirsty. Efforts to fill the sink with water would result in complete failure. The image of someone desperately trying to fill an unplugged sink is similar to that of someone trying to meet the needs of the OCS-driven. The needs of such a person almost certainly will not and cannot be met. Their drains *never* seem to be plugged. They cannot be filled, though they may really desire to become full. They are like an empty bucket with a hole in the bottom.

"Dad, will you do something with me?" A young boy asks.

The father, who has just spent two hours playing football with the boy, sighs and says, "Not right now, son, I need to rest a bit."

The youngster, hardly daunted, repeats his request, not three minutes later.

"Not right now," his father echoes.

A few minutes later the plea is once again repeated.

"What did I just tell you?"

"But . . . Dad . . ."

"I said NOT AT THIS TIME! Now, will you *please* just leave me *alone?*" The boy walks away angrily muttering, "You *never* do *anything* with me!"

There are several things going on in the scene above that are worth noting. The boy is displaying the empty bucket situation. He is also showing the all-or-nothing tendency so typical of those with OCS. The boy states, "You *never* do anything with me!" If you won't do it this time and at this moment then you *never* do.

For this boy, the intensity of his desire at the time was so strong that it *was* how he truly felt. He wants what he wants *right now*. The two hours of playing football just before are no longer a conscious thought in his mind. At any given moment there is only one thought to which an OCS individual is responding. The pleasure he had only moments earlier while playing football with his dad is gone. It's as if it had never happened. This is because it is no longer a conscious experience. All the boy can think about is the present. Nothing else really matters. He is *locked in* on a specific target. For the moment he is unable to consider any other options. Remember, this is not an excuse, it is an explanation.

When the person wants something that desire may be very strong, due to the influence of OCS. If, then, they are prevented from getting that thing they *so* want, their reaction tends to be very strong as well. Remember, the strength of OCS symptoms changes frequently. This intensity can vary dramatically during the course of just a single day. The inconsistent ups and downs can make it quite difficult for others to relate to them. When the OCS influence is not too strong, the person's response to symptom interference also tends to be less strong. Of course, knowing this doesn't necessarily make it easy to deal with during the heat of the battle. Over time, this knowledge about OCS, along with having a few practical strategies, can and does make a real difference. Eventually, living with a chronically dissatisfied person can get easier.

So what *can* be done to make life with these *empty buckets* a little easier? Well, what if you were actually attempting to fill a bucket with water and it wasn't filling up? Chances are you would soon give up and walk away. You'd either do that or try to find out what the problem was. You might then take action to correct the problem. If you were unable to figure out what the problem was, taking action might not help at all. Without knowing what's wrong, the specific actions that you take may not even come close to solving the problem. Much effort and time might be wasted. When effort and time gets wasted, people tend to be less than happy about it. When a lot of effort and time, as well as materials and resources are put into use, progress is expected. If progress is not forthcoming people may get frustrated. They may even become *very* angry. This anger may be directed at the bucket (the OCS-affected child or adult).

Sometimes buckets become damaged as a result of misdirected anger. When this happens, the initial *problem* may then develop into *problems*. When *problems* are present things often become very complex. Then as things get more complicated, you get—you've probably guessed it—even *more* problems. When the bucket remains empty although you've been trying to fill it daily, it can be a big problem.

A way to make things better is to try and learn as much about the problem as you can. Then, with that knowledge, you can begin to better manage the situation. It becomes easier to enhance the positives and diminish the negatives. Believe it or not, sometimes this requires a shifting of perceptions and beliefs in order to make it work. For example, there will undoubtedly be times when you've simply got to quit trying to fill that bucket. Instead, you will need to accept that at least for the time being it's *going* to remain empty.

The difference is huge—between walking away from an actual bucket that can't be filled and an OCS-affected person. The bucket isn't alive. It can't get up and follow you around. Furthermore, a bucket cannot ask and eventually demand again and again to be filled. Buckets don't whine. They don't cry nor do they get angry. They don't throw tantrums, scream, and lash out physically. They don't break stuff.

What you are dealing with in the OCS person, of course, makes things a lot more complex and difficult to manage. The word manage is a good word to describe what you do in any situation involving those who are OCS-affected. Symptoms are *managed*, not cured. The ability to successfully cope with OCS varies with time. It is also managed at some times better than at others.

Parents, teachers, and others need to become informed and begin to truly understand OCS symptoms. Such knowledge greatly enhances their ability to respond to and deal with it effectively. Patience tends to improve the same as does tolerance. Also, the often-experienced negative thoughts about those with OCS tend to diminish. Sometimes, relationships can get better simply because of this knowledge. Occasionally, there is no need for any other actual treatment. To realize that someone is *not* totally in control of their actions, thoughts, and behaviors is important for progress. This helps those who *are* in control to respond differently than they might have if they hadn't known. They can then openly consider other ways that might actually help the OCS-affected. Helping instead of criticizing them for their lack or weakness does wonders for the relationship.

A synonym for awareness is education. Education means learning about something. The more we know about a something the easier it is to be around it. As we understand and learn about things we are likely to be able to deal with them more effectively.

If a professional tells us to do something that we don't understand or want to do, it's probably not going to work. It is important that you feel comfortable with what you are attempting to do. If you don't understand how to do something, are you really going to be able to do it?

One important thing to practice when dealing with the "Empty Buckets" of this world involves patience and tolerance. This is especially true for children. You must try to develop the ability to withstand verbal onslaughts. Get used to tantrums. Sometimes there may even be suicide or death threats. When the OCS-affected child is denied access to wants or "needs" while in the empty bucket mode, they tend to react in very dramatic ways. When the parent or other person is able to tolerate the reaction long enough, the involved one often will come around. They will accept at least momentarily that access has been denied. The ensuing sulking behavior may last from just a few minutes to hours and even days.

The older the person is, the more likely it is that the bad mood will continue for longer periods of time. Usually, once the process is complete, the person will act as if there never had been a problem at all. This tendency to seem to totally forget what happened baffles and angers parents and others. Others still have to sort through their own battered and bruised feelings. There is often real emotional distress from enduring such behavior. It is helpful to remember during the empty bucket outburst that this reaction is a symptom. It is due to a biochemically induced underlying cause. It is only partially controllable. This, of course, is *much* easier said than done.

Dr. Russell Barkley gives excellent advice in his book *Taking Charge of ADHD*. He reminds parents and others to work hard at trying not to take things personally. This reminder also fits those with OCS. Try not to take what is said and done personally. Don't allow the child's responses to dictate how you feel about them or the incident in question. Situations such as these are not a competition to be won. You don't have to win out over your child. You don't have to force her to demonstrate her respect in order to appease your inner needs. A lot of the time it can be so difficult to back away emotionally, that many just can't do it. Keep trying. Never give up. This is one of the reasons that medication to treat the underlying cause is often so important. When a person responds to the medical treatment, these problems tend to get better. They either stop or at least become *much* less intense or fewer in number. In this way, symptoms no longer create anywhere near the turmoil and distress that they used to.

When dealing with an older child, especially in the teenage years, or with an adult, it can be much more intense and long-lasting. Part of the problem is that the older ones often have no idea that something is actually wrong with them. If they are in distress and truly want to change, educating them can be quite rewarding and not all that difficult. When not in distress it is nearly impossible to get them to see their behavior for what it is.

If there *is* a reason or need for change that is more powerful than the symptoms, progress can still be made. For instance, one spouse says to the other, "Get treatment or I'm leaving." If the affected spouse doesn't want the other to leave, it can get them into treatment. It might also keep them there long enough to achieve positive results. The picture can at times dramatically turn around. If a teenager is faced with losing the privilege of driving the car, he may choose to attend treatment sessions instead. It is then up to the professional. Quick results must be attained, that will then be likely to *sell* the the person on treatment. Nothing works like rapid positive results. This can keep someone in treatment long enough to make a real difference.

Without the right treatment and education the holes in the empty buckets are not found. They continue to drain everyone they come into contact with. The strain this can put on relationships can be monumental. It can get so overwhelming that parents may experience terrible pangs of guilt. Most often the guilt relates to their dislike of being around their own child. They love the child but they can't stand him either. A spouse may shut down emotionally and withdraw. They can also become so embittered that anger is a constant companion.

The affected ones may sense these emotional changes in those around them. They too often do not understand any more than their partner does why it is happening. They may start to feel rejected, unwanted and unloved. This of course can fuel the emptiness already felt. It may also drive them to work even harder to get their buckets filled. The result is a circular, downward spiral. Recognition and treatment begin to finally provide the answers. Answers are the only thing that they really wanted.

7

Hey, Don't Look at Me . . . It's Not My Fault

The title of this chapter could have just as easily been one of the following: "Lies, Lies, Lies . . . and More Lies" or "Don't Blame Me . . . I Didn't Do It" or "A Million and One Excuses . . . for *Everything*" or "Storytellers Anonymous" or "The Rationalization and Justification of a Life" or "The Irresponsibility Syndrome." Perhaps these titles provide enough of a picture to get the point across. I believe, though, that I could have easily gone on.

The *bottom line* is that there is a common tendency for the OCS-affected to avoid blame at all costs. During intense moments they often redirect it. This can be towards any*one* or any *thing* nearby. The OCS-driven intensity makes this person quite convincing. Their arguments and stories tend to be very difficult for others to resist or refute. They can be bullies at times, but they don't see it that way.

Jill, an OCS-driven teenager, recalled a time when a new family moved into her neighborhood. Theirs was a newly built, very large house. Jill had been about ten years old at the time. There was a girl, Sara, in the new family that was close to her age.

The very first time Sara came over to her house, Jill remembers feeling ridiculed. She also felt embarrassed about the size of her own house.

Sara was given a tour of the home and its surroundings. Afterwards she'd made insulting comments about the "*small size*" of the house. Jill began to experience a strong need to justify and rescue her home from this mean-hearted attack.

Suddenly, Jill found herself telling Sara a story about the house. She told Sara that the previous owners had actually had it built especially for them. They were a family of "little people" or midgets. With her details and emotional investment in the telling of the tale she made a believer out of Sara. This gave Jill immediate relief from the sense of shame she'd felt. It was no longer a disgrace to live in her house. The new girl had implied theirs was such a *small* house that it somehow didn't "measure up." Now it did.

Sara's focus then shifted. It went from apparent contempt (perhaps out of a need to feel "*special*" or superior herself) to one of awe and admiration. Jill promptly became the "*special*" one.

The need to defend the self against personal attacks can be very strong in those with OCS. It can be relentless. Defenses immediately come into play with no thought of the possible consequences. The internally felt "*need*" becomes the sole focus of attention. Thus the absurd and illogical can, and sometimes does, occur. It can actually be fun and amusing to listen to these people try and explain their behavior at times. They may go to great lengths to try and make sense out of some ridiculous explanation. They can work very hard at making the illogical sound logical. It can be fun and amusing, that is, if you know what is going on. When you know that this is a *need* that is *driven* and not totally in their control, it is easier to forgive them. Releasing your bad feelings towards those with OCS is important. It is a big step in making positive progress within relationships.

Jill said the incident with Sara was the main example her parents would use of their early concern about her. It was then that they began to fear that their daughter was becoming a liar. Sara had been taken in by Jill's sincerity. She had gone right away to tell the story of the midget house to her mother. Jill might never have been caught, had Sara's mother not mentioned it soon after. She was at a social event and Jill's mother was there as well.

"So you're the family whose house was built by midgets, right?" She asked innocently.

The defense of the self is often automatic like a gunshot. When the trigger of a gun is pulled, the bullet is immediately launched out of the barrel. Once struck, a bullet cannot be called back. It's not like you could say, "Hey, wait a minute. I don't want you going in that direction. In fact, why don't you come on back and we'll just forget that I ever fired you at all." Of course, that isn't going to happen. Bullets can't be talked into coming back or into changing direction in mid-flight. They just can't. The power behind the discharge makes it impossible for this to happen. The OCS-driven reaction to an assumed attack on the self is a lot like a gunshot. Once triggered, the path that the bullet takes is immediate and the direction sure.

The reactions, embellishments, stories, and lies of the OCS-driven can be creative and quite different. A bullet is affected by gravity to some degree. It is also influenced by friction and anything else in its path. In a similar vein, the OCS reaction may depend on the environment. It can also involve previous experience and overall strength of the drive or the perceived need.

Another example may help clarify the nature of this problem. In the earlier case, a child was the center of focus. Let's look at an adult's response to the need to defer or escape from blame.

Sherry told of the occasion when she had just come into the family living room to work on the computer. She was carrying a glass of water in one hand. Upon entering, she found the furniture had been rearranged by her husband. He had temporarily moved some things around. He needed additional space for a project he was working on. The structure would not be there for very long. On the coffee table was their fifteen-year-old son's new 1000 piece puzzle. It was about 90 percent completed. The table had been shoved up next to a stool. It was the stool they usually sat on to work at the computer.

Sherry set her full glass of water down on the edge of the coffee table, closest to where she was sitting. She had to bend over and lean way back towards the rear of the computer to reach the switch to turn it on. Sherry became frustrated when she seemed unable to find it. She kept stretching her arm and reaching out to the side of the computer and the cabinet wall wherein it sat. Finally she barely touched what she thought was the switch panel. It was right there at her fingertips.

If she could just lean in a little bit farther, she was sure she could reach it. It was a very awkward position to try and stretch. Suddenly her shoulder bumped the water glass. It fell spilling its contents all over the nearly completed puzzle. Screaming, she jumped up and ran for something to soak up the spill. She was sure that the puzzle had been ruined. She mopped up the water as best she could. She kept praying and hoping that it might dry out and be okay.

Later that day she confronted her husband. He was shocked by the degree of anger she leveled at him. Sherry informed him that it was all *his* fault. It would have never happened if he hadn't rearranged everything. Why did he have to place that side table behind the computer cabinet? He'd put it right on top of the cords. The position of that table had pulled the switch box to the very back of the cabinet. That had made it impossible for her to reach in and turn on the computer. If he hadn't done that then she wouldn't have knocked over the water glass. Then their son's prize puzzle would not have been ruined.

The logic of this woman's argument almost seems sensible. There are, however, a few holes in it. If she wasn't symptomatic for OCS, it might have been different. She might have been better able to accept the responsibility for what happened. She may have realized that *she* was the one who had set the glass down on the same table as the puzzle. She didn't have to do that. Then it was *she* that had knocked it over as well. *She* knocked it over. She might have slowed down long enough to assess the situation. In so doing she might have realized the danger. Then she may have removed the glass to another place. She might have concluded that this would be a good idea to avoid knocking it over. This too would have saved her son's puzzle from getting drenched.

The OCS-driven sometimes cannot bear the thought that something might have been their fault. Often it's because to accept the blame would mean acknowledging flaws. They can't stand the idea that they might make stupid little mistakes. These are mistakes that in their heart they feel *no one* should *ever* make. Making such mistakes would mean that they are defective in some way. Being seen as inferior is something that they cannot bear the thought of. It may also mean that when others see that they are flawed, they might then think things about them, and so on.

Those affected by OCS often have trouble dealing with failure of any kind. It doesn't seem to matter whether it's a perceived failure or real. Typically fears of failure swirl within the minds and hearts of these people. To simply shrug it off and continue on can be impossible. To keep on trying in the face of failure is not something they can easily do. The feeling that they might deserve to be punished for being "so stupid" can be very real to them. Like the fired bullet, they cannot be talked out of the path or direction they suddenly find themselves moving. They must go on, until released from the path. Deliverance may occur as the drive weakens over time. There may also be a release when something else interferes with its course.

A reported incident in the life of Thomas Edison (whom I clearly believe had ADHD as well as OCS) seems like a good case in point. A reporter was said to have asked Mr. Edison a question relative to inventing the light bulb. He asked him how it felt to fail 2,000 times. Mr. Edison's quick reply seems to demonstrate the common OCS inability to admit to failure. His alleged response was:

"Fail? What do you mean fail? I never failed. It was a two-thousand step process!"

The making of mistakes or not doing something right feel like "the end of the world" for the OCS-driven. A thing as simple as not understanding a concept is so awful that it cannot be tolerated. It too must be defended against, if noticed by another. To have problems of any kind is "a bad thing."

The first defense is usually denial. The next best thing is coming up with a reason or an explanation to divert the blame. Another common word used to describe this very same thing is "excuse." OCS-driven people are the grand masters of "the excuse" or as others might regard it, "the lie." The fact that others interpret a given OCS response as a lie is a problem. Getting caught in a lie can create great difficulty for some of the OCS-affected. It is often true that they would not tell a lie on purpose. When a lie *is* told and they are confronted with it, they are in a real bind. They must now defend their own defense. Getting caught in a lie is a huge mistake. This they can't stand. So they now have to somehow get others to believe that their lie was actually the truth.

At this point, one can begin to sense how incredibly complicated the OCS-driven life can be. It is often overwhelming. Most of the time, after the fact of being caught in the lie, even the OCS person is frustrated and disheartened. They can be just as distressed as everyone else is about their behavior and reactions. They may not let others know this. They may be terrified to do so. They may be too embarrassed as well. Some of the false tales are over such trivial things that even *they* have no clue as to why they felt the need to lie. It literally makes no sense. This very fact can actually help us to make sense of these actions and begin to understand. It is one of the important indicators that suggest possible OCS as the driving force. Don't forget that the title of my first book about OCS is *Making Sense of the Senseless*.

We all search for the reason why behavior occurs. It's interesting. We want to know. Those with OCS can be desperate to know. This can become an unconscious tool used to keep blame at bay. As already stated, these people have a need to be free from blame. They don't like making mistakes. To be considered at fault for anything is anathema. They cannot bear it emotionally.

This, of course, makes no sense because making mistakes is a human certainty. It is by recognizing our mistakes and working hard to learn from them that we become more proficient in all things. Those with OCS often cannot stand the thought of personal culpability. At least, this seems to be true initially.

Perhaps the following dilemma of the OCS is lurking at the back of your mind. "*If*," you might wonder, "the OCS-affected can't handle being wrong or deal with it when they make a mistake, how do they ever make it though life?" *This* is a very good question.

Usually, those with OCS get very good at justifying and rationalizing their actions and behaviors. As mentioned earlier they can barely, if ever, admit to wrongdoings and mistakes of their own. They instead place the blame, fault, or reason for their actions on something or someone else. They cannot be blamed when the reason for what they did is not under their immediate control. When they *can* come up with a rationale for their actions that does not include them, they are able to admit that a mistake was made. But since it was not their fault, the mistake they admit to is seen as not truly their own. This then protects them from that OCS-magnified inner turmoil and emotional distress. Often the OCS person knows that everyone makes mistakes. They can tell you that right off. What they feel, though, is more like "Sure, everyone makes mistakes, but not me if I can help it."

Obsessive thoughts are common when the OCS-affected are unable to shift the blame. It can trigger long-lasting hyperemotional responses. These can include anxiety, anger, explosiveness, and depression. To avoid this, they may act out or shut down completely. The emotional pain linked to such a response each time it occurs becomes traumatic. It can turn into something to be avoided at all costs. In situations like this, a fabrication can be seen as the lesser of the two evils.

One major problem related to this dynamic is a stubborn resistance to change. Many who cannot accept responsibility for their actions do not see the need for personal change. After all, if it's not my fault why should I be the one to change? This may be boldly stated, but is usually observed rather than shared. Over time, this pattern quite often becomes automatic. The idea that it might result from a biochemical cause seems absurd. Pointing a finger at this person would only result in an abrupt turn of the head to see who was at fault behind them. To attempt and pin the blame on the OCS is to risk immediate retaliation. Often such retaliation will be in the form of an explosive and heated denial.

The OCS-affected do not see their responses as making excuses for their actions. To them it is not an excuse. It is the very rationale that truly explains what happened. To argue is to invite an intense and unrelenting beating from their often unforgiving mind.

Overreaction to the insignificant suggests a possible OCS presence. This means that the reaction tends to be equally strong no matter how trivial an incident may actually be. The misspelled word may be regarded as an error of equal severity to actions such as breaking the law. The error may not really bother the OCS person, until pointed out as such by someone else. This is a common trigger associated with the OCS defensive mode.

Significant others, parents, spouses, teachers, and friends simply cannot understand. They wonder why anyone would feel they have to deny some of the silly and incredibly trivial mistakes that occur. It often seems ridiculous to think that any one could become so defensive over such a stupid thing. When someone constantly excuses their actions, no matter how insignificant they may seem, it should be considered a strong indicator for possible OCS.

At the moment of confrontation the defense mechanism will erupt without so much as a second thought. The harder others push the OCS person to accept responsibility, the more stubborn they become. They will obstinately deny their part or stand by their explanation of the event in question. Ever on the defense, they frustrate and exhaust nearly all those who must deal with them on a consistent long-term basis. They literally wear their opponents down.

It is important not to forget that this response tends to be black-and-white and all-or-nothing too. Also remember, as most other OCS behaviors it can sometimes be manifested in the form of its polar opposite. That is to say that some OCS individuals will accept responsibility, blame, or fault for the things that they've done. But they also tend to accept blame for things they haven't done, as well. Such a person cannot let go of the idea or thought that something they might have said or done may have somehow tipped the scales or caused the problem. They may come to believe that they are at fault for every mishap, misunderstanding, and misconception that might occur. It doesn't seem to matter how remotely involved their participation or influence might have been. It makes sense that the OCS dynamic is not nearly as common as its opposite. Taking the blame for everything is quite depressing. It tends to lead to more serious and frequent bouts of depression, hopelessness, and suicidal ideation in general.

OCS may be present when a person is unable to accept responsibility. They are not to blame for anything. It also may drive those who seem to blame themselves first in all things. These are people who act as if they are responsible for the woes of the world and everything in it. There are also some who seem to vacillate between these two extremes—blaming the self at times and then everyone else at other times. This too suggests underlying OCS. Recognition and awareness is a big part of the successful treatment battle. Without awareness no war can be mounted against the symptoms. Change is not sought after; nor does it occur where it is not recognized as being needed.

8

Time and OCS
"I'm late . . . I'm late . . .
For a very important date . . ."

People with OCS commonly have troubles with time. Again, as is true for most symptoms, there tends to be an all-or-nothing type of reaction to time issues. In other words, the OCS person can be very organized with a timetable and schedule. They may map out virtually every second of their day. These *live* to be early or on time. They are *never* late. They can get very upset at others who are late. That or they may be severely disorganized in their management of time.

For these, the word overwhelmed becomes their constant companion. There is always one more thing that needs to be done before they go anywhere. Their sense of how long it takes to do something is very poor. They are perpetually late. Regardless of which "pole" one may lean towards, it can be a problem.

The bottom line is that *time* is an issue that influences everything in their lives. It can affect relationships, whether personal, social, familial, or at the work place.

"I feel rushed all the time," is frequently heard from those with OCS.

"There is *never* enough time to do everything that needs to be done."

There is an all-too-common feeling of being cheated by time. This results in some very problematic and misunderstood situations. These need to be identified and explored. This identification is not meant to excuse the OCS from the consequences of their actions. It is offered as an explanation.

This new awareness allows OCS-driven actions to be seen in a fresh light. As a result, everyone involved can better understand why the OCS and those without OCS feel the way they do. With this awareness they now have a better chance to choose to react differently.

For example, parents learn that Jimmy's horrible *"attitude"* is not just something of his choice. When asked to do something, his blowups are not because he doesn't want to do his part for the family. Knowing this makes it is easier to manage the resistive behavior when it occurs. And it *will* occur, many times. In fact this knowledge allows for a plan to be made ahead of time. Having a plan in place can help you deal more effectively with the reaction. This can make things better all around.

Often, when someone asks the person with OCS to do an unexpected task, the first reaction is one of resistance. Sometimes this resistance can be in the extreme. These reactions occur most often in and around the home setting. At any given moment persons with OCS see themselves as busy. They are engaged in whatever it is that they may be doing. This tends to be true even when it looks to others like they are doing *nothing*. The OCS person often feels upset the moment another tries to get them to do anything other than what they are already doing.

"I always have to do *everything* around here" is a common complaint.

Some examples are explainable, although such instances rarely tend to *be* explained. This may not seem to make sense. Therefore, allow me to offer a case in point of the kind of situation the OCS-driven often find themselves facing.

*   *   *

Billy is minding his own business. He is sitting on the panel-brown living room couch and staring at the ceiling tiles overhead. He is busily counting the holes in each one to see if they are all the same. He has no idea why he's doing this, but he is.

His mother calls from the kitchen. "Billy!" she says. "Will you please come in here and take the garbage out? I've been canning peaches all afternoon. It's so full I can't get another thing in there."

Billy is caught up in what he is doing. He goes right on counting.

"Billy?" she calls again. "Come and take the garbage out, will you?"

"Two hundred and eighty-nine, two hundred and ninety, two hundred and . . ." Billy goes right on counting. He is keeping a silent track inside his head.

"*BILLY?*" His mother is beginning to sound frustrated.

"*BILLY!*" Now she *is angry.*

Finally her voice gets through to him and Billy replies, "Just a minute, Mom." Three hundred . . . three hundred and one, three hundred and two . . . .

The minutes tick on by.

Suddenly there is a jerk on Billy's arm.

"Ow," complains Billy. "What'd ya do that for? Now I got to start all over again."

"You're not starting anything over again *YOUNG MAN* until that *garbage* is taken out." She pulls him roughly from his sitting position on the couch.

"I was gonna do it," he whines as her nails dig in and she drags him by the arm out to the kitchen.

In her current angry state if Billy's mother happens to say what's on her mind, the problem could get much worse very quickly.

An argument might begin if she were to say: "No son, you *weren't* going to do it. If I hadn't come in here to get you, you would have let *me* take that garbage out. In fact," she might add, "that's probably what you were hoping for anyway!"

In a situation where OCS *is* driving the bus, this interpretation may *seem* accurate, *but it is not.* In his mind Billy *was* in fact planning to take that garbage out. Just as soon as he got done with counting that one more square, he was going to do it. He would have done it, that is, if he remembered. Not remembering is the most common reason for not following through in this kind of a situation.

If his mother *had* accused him of not wanting to take it out, he probably would have argued that point with her. Then, if she had also told him that he *was* purposefully trying to get out of doing the task, an angry outburst could occur. If she'd accused him of putting it off until someone else did it for him, he would probably deny that such a thing was true. He might deny it heatedly. He might dig his feet in and stubbornly hold on to that opinion until his last dying breath.

Such a dispute could get even nastier. His mom might start listing out aloud the many times in the past that Billy had said he was going to do something and then did not. At this point he would probably get defensive.

He might then try to justify and make excuses for each and every situation his mom came up with. Billy might not be able to remember many of the specific facts. Nevertheless, he would probably start to defend himself as if he did.

In the example given above, Billy could have flown into a rage. It could have happened when his mother grabbed his arm and forcibly pulled him away. When an extreme overreaction to being interrupted occurs, it is quite often OCS related. Stop and consider what might be driving such a reaction. In those affected by OCS, it may be the time they've lost for other things. It could be the need to finish a task. The OCS often can't stand being told what to do. They also don't like being having to start something over again because it was interrupted. Being asked to do something out of the blue is to them a *huge* request.

Barbara describes it thus:

"When someone asks me to do a task for them I immediately get this empty feeling in the pit of my stomach. Even though it may only take five minutes of my time to complete the task, I have this sense of loss that is *incredible*. It's as if I can think of nothing else but the fact that 'there go five minutes of my life.' Five minutes that would have otherwise been mine are going to be *lost* forever. I know this sounds silly, but it's true. It's not that I don't want to do things for other people, because I do. It's just that it's a lot easier if I have it planned and have set aside the time for it. Does this sound selfish? I think it does. So then I feel guilty. I'm such a self-centered and selfish person. It's no wonder I'm miserable most of the time. Actually, I'm miserable all the time."

Barbara really was miserable. She saw herself as a loving and caring mother, wife, and person. She freely gave as much as twenty hours or more of service each week to her church and neighborhood community. The thought that she might resent unplanned intrusions on her time went against everything she believed in.

She would actually think of herself as *evil* at times. This was because she simply could not accept the idea that a good and kind person could feel this way. The fact that she had reacted again and again in this manner caused her great distress. It represents a form of what psychologists have called *cognitive dissonance*. Her thoughts went against what she thought of as her true nature. In time, with counseling, she was able to identify this common OCS pattern in herself. She eventually agreed to attempt medication. She did so even though she remained somewhat anxious about it.

Within two weeks after starting medication she was feeling better. Barbara recognized improvement in many of her specific symptoms from an Obsessional Inventory. She stopped thinking of herself as "*evil.*" She began to see that she was indeed the loving and giving mother that she had always thought she was, and wanted to be. She began to focus more on what she *was* able to get done, rather than on what she did not get done. She was no longer miserable. In fact, she came into a session after about a-month-and-a-half with a smile on her face. She announced that for the first time in a very long time that she was actually *happy*.

*   *   *

Don, on the other hand, experienced the difficulties of time loss a bit differently. For him it was a matter of never having enough time. He expressed it as follows:

"It doesn't matter where I am. It doesn't matter what I'm doing. I feel rushed! I *am* rushed. If I'm heading to an appointment . . . I can't get there fast enough. No dilly-dallying for me. No stopping to smell the roses. Heck, I don't even notice if there are roses. Every moment in another moment is gone . . . forever. It's gone *forever*. Think about it. We're talking about *forever* here. That's a long time. No moment can be wasted. Before I'm finished what I'm doing I'm already kicking myself for being late on the next project. It's either that or the next *place* that I need to be. Time is my enemy. It keeps me from getting things done. What I really need is more time. If I could just have a little more time, I could manage. I'm sure that I could. So you can imagine how I take it when someone wants me to do something extra or outside of my schedule. There is *NO WAY!*"

For Don, being interrupted was like disrupting his progress in life. Progress keeps moving forward and lets nothing stand in its way. If someone did get his attention through his projects and appointments, Don's reaction was explosive. It was as if he was saying, "*HOW DARE YOU INTRUDE ON MY TIME AND SPACE!*" Then, just as quickly he would be off once again. He would be off and running on his chronic time chase. The wake he left behind was often an emotional roller-coaster ride for anyone who had to be around him for long. It was especially so for those in his immediate family. He seemed angry all the time. His wife said that she couldn't talk to him at all. Whenever she attempted to have even a brief conversation, she felt that Don resented the time it took. His body language would suggest that he was annoyed. His responses to her words would be short. They would be mostly one-word utterances. The tone of his voice would seem to imply boredom or a rising irritation. For his wife, this was very demoralizing. She was concerned about the stability of their marriage.

She or any of the children could not interrupt him for any reason. If they did so Don would explode angrily and with great intensity. Sometimes his wife actually feared that he might physically harm them. This was in spite of the fact that he had never hit any of them before. Don's wife also felt unable to ask him to do anything around the house. She couldn't ask him to do something for the children either. Whenever she had done so in the past, it would result in an angry outburst. For her it got to the point where it was simply not worth asking anymore. The possibility of a divorce finally motivated Don to try and get help.

*   *   *

Daniel was experiencing difficulties while driving. Others traveling with him were often frightened by his behavior. They would find excuses not to be in the same car that he was driving. This luxury, however, was not always available to his wife and children. They were often terrified when going places with him in the car. His wife described it as follows:

"I don't know what gets into him. When someone cuts in front of him or tries to pass him in another lane it makes him mad, *really* mad. He yells and curses and makes obscene gestures. He swerves in and out of traffic. Once he chased another car for five or six blocks out of our way after it had cut in front of us. Me and all the kids feared for our lives. It's a good thing the guy in the other car didn't have a gun. It's almost like Dan just can't stand it if someone else gets ahead of him. My sister once had a horse like that. Her horse simply would not allow another one to get in the lead. Whenever another horse would try to get past her, my sister's horse would race ahead. It didn't matter what the current rider wanted that horse to do. I even fell off because of that once."

Daniel's response might have been a bit more complex than simply a time issue. However, *time* was a major part of why he'd suddenly become so upset. He often reasoned that he was in a hurry (also a part of his OCS symptoms). He'd also catch himself thinking: "How *dare* that driver squeeze in front of me. He may be in a hurry, but so am I. I was ahead of him. *I* was there first. He should have consideration for someone else."

Other counselors had worked with him extensively. They taught him relaxation exercises and worked on cognitive methods. These were meant to enable him to learn how to control these thoughts and rages. The fact is that he knew he was overreacting. But once the reaction got started, he felt helpless. He was in the grip of something that now simply had to *happen*. He didn't plan it. He honestly did not want to react in that way. It just happened. Daniel was unable to talk himself out of it. No one else could calm him down either, while he was in the midst of such a rage. He was aware that many of his thoughts during these reactions were irrational. He knew they were not worth risking his life or anyone else's over. It didn't seem to matter. At the time of each incident, rational thoughts could not be held in his mind. No thoughts to counter the problem could be kept in his mind long enough and consistently enough to make a difference.

To be calm or relaxed was practically impossible for him anyway. When driving a car it was completely unworkable. The only reason he came to counseling was that it had been court-ordered. He was cited for reckless driving. Dan had been given the choice of paying a hefty fine or attending counseling sessions. He was diagnosed with OCS. Work was then begun to help him understand his behavior in relation to this. As a result, Dan agreed to try a medication. He was started on an SSRI. Thereafter, things changed rather dramatically for Dan. He describes his experience in his own words:

"I was driving to work several days after starting the medication and I was late. Normally I would have been tearing down the road. I'd be weaving in and out of traffic and muttering under my breath or even out loud. Suddenly I realized I was just cruising along and thinking, 'I'm late . . . oh, well. There's nothing I can do about it now.' This was formerly inconceivable to me. I wasn't cursing. I wasn't driving recklessly. I wasn't angry. I couldn't believe it. I kept thinking, 'this is really different.' It was *GREAT!* I wasn't overreacting. This was something very new to me and I liked it. There was nothing I could do about being late that day. It wasn't my fault. Still in the past I would have been in a frenzy and nearly *crazy* about it. This time I was not upset. I was calm. *I was* calm. It was really weird. I kept thinking, 'I'm late', and it was no big deal. No big deal at all! This was the beginning of a *HUGE* change in my life for the better."

Daniel's wife agreed wholeheartedly with her husband's review of the situation. He still tended to strongly desire to be early or on time. He no longer went "nuts" about it, though. If he wasn't on time because of something that couldn't be helped, it was not that big a deal. She felt he was now *concerned*, whereas before he had been *obsessed*. Now he was *conscientious* as compared to *crazy*. Dan she related was easier to live with. He was also a *much* safer driver.

When time is an issue for the OCS, there is no stopping to *smell* the roses. Every moment in another moment is gone *forever*. They cannot slow down. They can see no good reason to do so. Often to get their attention, they must be on the verge of losing something that is very important. This might need to be something like their freedom, job, spouse, or children. The extreme is often the only kind of motivator that works. It's this that might enable them to seek out assistance.

There is an old popular song that includes the lyrics "time . . . is on your side." For the OCS driven nothing could be farther from the truth. Time is their enemy. Much like it seems for the white rabbit of the popular story *Alice in Wonderland*. Those with OCS are prone to running about uttering something along the lines of that now infamous phrase, "I'm late, I'm late, for a very important date." We sense, however, that there really is no *very important date*, don't we?

9

Literal Thinking
I'm Not Blind, Stupid, or Deaf . . .
Just Extremely Literal

"*DON'T YOU LIE TO ME, BOY!*"

His mind whirled. A confused look appeared on his face, "But . . . I'm not . . . ."

"A lie on top of a *lie!*" his father shrieked.

"No!" the boy stammered, "I'm not . . . You don't understand."

"Oh, I don't, huh?" The older man crossed his arms and stood up straighter just a bit.

The boy barely allowed his head to move from side to side.

"Let's just look at the facts, shall we?" announced his father. He took a notepad and pen out of the stained left breast pocket of his faded blue work shirt.

The boy said nothing.

"Were you or were you not at the scene of the crime on the night in question?" his father began.

"No," Ryan replied without hesitation.

"NO!" Mr. Green shouted. The tip of his pen ripped right through the top sheet of the tiny spiral pad. He quickly tore the rest of it from the pad. He crumpled the tiny paper in one hand and threw it towards the blue-gray carpet. "No?" he queried again. "Now you're trying to tell me you weren't even at the party?"

Ryan's brow began to furrow ever so slightly. "I didn't say that."

"Yes! You *did!*"

"No, *Dad*, I didn't."

"You did! You lying little . . ." He paused and took a deep breath before continuing. "I just asked if you were at the party and you said no . . ."

Ryan cut him off. "No you didn't," he said with drop-dead intensity. "You asked me if I had been at the *'scene'* of the *crime*."

"Same thing," his dad declared.

"No, Dad," Ryan crossed his arms. "It's not the same at all. There *was* no crime!"

"Guess that depends . . ."

"Depends!" Ryan cried in desperation. "Depends on what?"

"On whether or not you were the victim, of course," Mr. Green smirked.

"Dad, there was *no* victim . . ." Ryan scurried to his left and bent his knees just enough to retrieve a battered old dictionary from the bookshelf. He madly flipped through the pages until he reached the V's. When he finally got to the right page, he was all over the page scanning with his eyes several times before being able to mentally remind himself that the words were in alphabetical order. He silently cursed over this lifelong pattern he faced whenever searching for information. It was always the same. The moment his eyes took in the immense amount of information crammed into the one little page it seemed as if they rebelled. It was like they got instantly overwhelmed and started saying, "Whoa . . . look at all that stuff we've got to look through!" It would take a while for the initial shock to settle. Then his eyes would begin to scan through the myriad words and phrases with no rhyme-or-reason whatsoever. He *always* found what he was looking for, eventually. That wasn't the problem. It just took him a lot longer than everyone else (or so it seemed to him) to finally get there. It made tasks tedious. It was a pain in the butt!

His eyes settled in on the page "Vic." As he began moving from word to word down the page he sang that stupid kindergarten song in his head, "A, B, C, D . . . E, F, G . . ." This was another annoying routine he'd catch himself in, over and over again. If he didn't sing that alphabet song as he searched each letter on his way to "Victim," he'd get lost on the page. Then he'd have to retrace his steps and start all over again. At least he didn't have to sing the song clear to the end for each letter he was searching for. That would have been *really* annoying. Sure enough, he ended up having to turn the page. Luckily, by this time he wasn't as likely to get as overwhelmed by the amount of information on the next page. Ryan continued searching word after word until he finally arrived at "Victim."

"And for the fourth time! Ryan!" his father's arms were bent. His hands were clenched into fists. They rested on his hips. This was *never* a good sign. "What *are* you doing?" he demanded.

"What am I doing?" Was his dad joking? Ryan looked up from the dictionary. "I'm showing you," he answered. He returned his gaze to the book.

Mr. Green threw up his hands. "You haven't heard a word I've been saying."

"Dad," Ryan insisted. "Listen . . ." he began to read from the dictionary. "Victim: a person or animal killed as a sacrifice to a god in a religious rite." He skipped over the number two definition and continued with the third. "A person who suffers some loss, especially by being swindled." Ryan kept reading and included some of what was under the word "Victimize" for good measure. He read, "To kill, destroy, and to dupe or cheat . . ."

"Ryan . . . ," Mr. Green breathed. He was clenching and unclenching each fist now. Again, not a good sign.

"There was *no victim*, Dad," Ryan repeated. "Do you want me to look up the word *crime* for you too?"

"No!" his father cried. He couldn't contain himself any longer. "I don't want you looking up *CRIME*. I don't care what the definition of *VICTIM* is either! We're discussing that party you went to and what *you* did there, son. I don't care if what you've done is a little white lie or a felony."

Ryan dropped the dictionary. The big toe of his right foot broke the book's fall. He bit his bottom lip and held his breath. He was afraid to respond to the pain. It was intense. Beads of sweat began to form on his forehead and at his temples.

"Now!" his father continued.

Ryan had bent his head just a bit. He stood there staring at a tiny circular stain. It was on the carpet, a little to his right. He waited.

His father began speaking slowly and deliberately. "Did you or did you not" he said, "purposefully set out to embarrass and humiliate a classmate of yours by the name of Jill last Friday night? It was at the school's eighth-grade Halloween Festival or party or whatever it was called."

"No," Ryan half whispered.

"What do you mean . . . NO?"

Ryan demurely added, "No . . . sir?"

His father was grinding his teeth by this time. He suddenly began sucking in great gulps of air. It reminded Ryan of a snorting bull getting ready to charge. He'd seen one do that on a Spanish channel not long ago. Just before heading full-tilt towards the cape-swirling matador, the bull had done something like that. It had snorted and sniffed and blown gusts of air into the dirt. There was enough force behind it to cause a miniature dust storm around its front legs. Then it began bobbing and darting its head from side to side. The likeness between his huffing and puffing father and that bull Ryan had seen on TV was uncanny. Thinking about that caused a very slight upward turn of Ryan's lips.

"You think this is funny?" Ryan's dad shouted. His cheeks and the tip of his nose turned a fiery crimson. They were well on the way to mottled purple.

Ryan took a step back.

"I don't know what's wrong with you, son. First you deliberately hurt someone. Then you lie about your part in it. And to top it off you have the nerve to laugh about it?"

"I wasn't laughing about *that!*" Ryan tried to explain. "I . . . I . . ." he stammered.

His dad's red-hot face blustered only inches away. A few degrees more and his heated breath would surely burst into flames. Ryan thought better of what he'd been about to say. He tried to move back a little further. An unyielding catamaran halted his retreat. His knees were shaking badly. So were his father's.

"There . . . were . . ." his father stated evenly. He took a new breath after each word, "witnesses."

Ryan stood his ground. He knew he had not intended to hurt Jill. He hadn't meant to even embarrass her. Not really. It was just a joke. It was a harmless prank. He could never admit to what his father was accusing him of having done. It would be a lie.

"Son," his father said. He seemed to be trying so hard. "The psychologist said you can't change your behavior unless you first admit to it."

"But I didn't do what you said I did."

"Yes, you did," his father's voice was flat and void of emotion. "Maybe we ought to quit that psychologist. Six months we've been seeing him and nothing's changed."

That was okay with Ryan. He didn't like the guy anyway. His dad began talking softly, to no one in particular.

"Why would a teacher call me and tell me that he did something, if he didn't do it?" He glanced at Ryan. "That boy can be so convincing," he thought.

Mr. Green wanted to believe Ryan. He used to believe every single thing the boy said. That was, until the principal got involved a while back. The principal had forced Ryan's father to rethink his position about his son. If Ryan had lied about that then maybe, just maybe, he'd lied before, as well. It unnerved Mr. Green a bit. There were all those times in the past that he'd come to his son's defense. He had confronted other adults and parents and even yelled: "My boy wouldn't lie!" That's what he had once thought. Reality can bring you to your knees in an instant.

Ryan watched his father. He walked away still mumbling. As the man shuffled into the kitchen Ryan heard him say something clearly. His father had probably wanted him to hear this.

"I wouldn't really plan anything for awhile if I were you," he said. "I don't think you'll be going anywhere soon. I won't tolerate lying, son, not from you. Not from anyone."

But Ryan hadn't lied. Why wouldn't his dad believe him?

And, in fact, Ryan truly had not lied. Not if you look at it literally. This scene is not an example of a lying child. It is not hard to see, though, how it might seem to be just that. What it actually demonstrates is a subtle and very common tendency of those with OCS. This problem often wreaks havoc within the family group. It also can do the same in most other relationships as well.

This can be simplified down to perhaps several representative words or phrases. A few might be as follows: Rigid Thinking; One Track Mind; Tunnel Vision; All-or-Nothing Responses; Exactitis; and there are many more.

We already know that many of those with OCS have an obsessive need to be right. This can also be expressed as a need not to be *wrong*. To be wrong is often an emotionally devastating event for them. It is particularly so when it is pointed out publicly. Making mistakes is another way to be wrong. It could be literally any kind of a mistake. It doesn't matter how tiny or insignificant it may seem to others.

The need to avoid making a mistake can be relentlessly held on to. The affected person can sometimes become immobilized when one occurs. They may feel compelled to start a task over if a mistake is made. It may not matter how close to completion they were before the mistake. It's not as if they walk around constantly thinking, "I can't make a mistake." It's not conscious. When they make an error they simply overreact, in varying degrees of intensity. It depends on the strength of their symptom levels (mild-moderate, and so on).

The OCS-driven will often hold others up to a rigid standard. This is one of the single most important factors that interfere with communication. It commonly leads to communication breakdowns. It is also at the heart of many misunderstandings and distortions. The scene between Ryan and his frustrated father is a classic example of this miscommunication problem. Let me share another example before attempting to make better sense out of Ryan's situation. This one is not quite as complicated as Ryan's scene.

In this scene the OCS affected family has just finished dinner. One child starts to leave the table without clearing his dishes used for the meal.

"Wait a minute, Joey," his father's voice boomed out.

Joey stopped and looked back.

"Don't forget to take your dishes to the sink," his father reminded him. "You know the rule."

"Yeah, okay, dad," Joey's reluctance seeped into his vocal tones, but he moved to comply. Seeing Joey begin to do the requested task, his father left the table.

Joey finished and once again headed away from the kitchen towards the hall. His father rose up just a bit from his position on the couch. He took a quick glance at the table, just to be sure.

"Joey," Mr. Davis shouted, "*You get back in here,* NOW!"

"What?" Joey returned from the hall, looking irritated. He poked his head back into the living room area.

"What is it, dad?"

"I thought I told you to take your dishes to the sink?"

"Yeah, well . . . I did."

Immediately Mr. Davis jumped up. He stood a full six foot five inches in height. Mr. Davis towered over the mere ten-year-old Joey. He pointed towards his son's place at the table. "What do you call *that*?" he demanded in accusing tones.

Joey glanced back at the table. "Call what?" he asked. He was honestly surprised.

"You can't see that fork! What about the spoon, and the knife you left behind? I specifically told you to take them to the sink?" His father's voice grew louder as he spoke.

Joey shot back at his father, "You told me to take the *dishes* to the sink. You didn't say anything about the silverware. I thought somebody else was going to pick *them* up."

"Don't get sassy with me . . ." Mr. Davis returned, "You get your smart little . . ."

"NO!" Mrs. Davis interrupted suddenly. "George, don't you dare say what I think you're about to say." The authority in her voice stopped him cold.

Joey glanced at his father. He was sure if were possible that steam would have been shooting out of the man's ears. It would look just like the spout of a teapot on the stove.

"Get your butt . . . your behind," his father stammered. He quickly rolled his eyes towards his wife: "Get over there and finish picking up your place." Then he spoke with an exaggerated emphasis and a very slow tempo, "Take your fork . . . and your spoon . . . and oh, do I need to *spell* them out for you too?" he added sarcastically.

Joey shook his head.

"And don't forget the knife!" With that he plopped his two hundred-and-sixty-pound frame back onto the couch.

Joey quietly removed the offending pieces of silverware. He carried them to the sink. He could hear his father muttering to his mother. Maybe he was grumbling to himself.

"I can't believe that little . . ." He was saying. "What is he, stupid? Does he think we're stupid? Of course not! He's just trying to get my goat. He doesn't want to do a damn thing around here. That's what it is. That lazy little . . ."

Joey almost made it to the hall.

"He knows he's supposed to take his dishes to the sink. We only do it every meal! He thinks he's funny, I suppose. Oh yeah, he's hilarious." His father quickly glanced towards the table once more. He suddenly got very silent.

There it was. Still sitting on the table at Joey's place for the entire world to see was his milk glass.

It's not hard to imagine the kind of response Joey's father probably had the moment he saw that glass. This situation may sound ridiculous. It is not. There is a difficulty in believing this situation is related to anything other than the first thing that comes to mind. It is that it really seems like the person involved is being passive-aggressive. In other words, it looks like Joey is purposefully attempting to irritate his father. The passive-aggressive response pattern has been completely rooted into the belief system of most of the world cultures. As a result, when such actions are present it tends to be the very first cause considered.

Another theory (although in my mind a weak one) is that Joey might have had a desire or need to be in *control*. This point of view suggests that Joey's actions relate to the satisfaction he gets by causing his father to become under his *control*. This is like an employee/boss relationship. The employee is unable to confront the mighty authority figure. He might lose his job. As a result, the only way to express anger is to do it in a secretive way. In this way no one knows who did it. It looks innocent, although it is not.

These behavioral patterns have been described by experts for generations. They have been written into the world community's books and literature. These ideas have also been performed in theater, as well as displayed in movies. So it is not surprising that when such patterns do exist, they are generally thought to result from passive-aggressive maneuvering.

My experience in working with OCS has led me to believe that a third option needs to be considered. These actions are sometimes biochemically driven. Sometimes, they are mistakenly thought to be either passive-aggressive or control issues. When this mistake is made, behavior problems are inevitable. Treatment strategies designed for the first two tend to be ineffective when actions are really OCS-driven. In Joey's situation where OCS is present and it is made known, his actions suddenly take on new meaning and start to make sense. Were his father to accuse Joey of being out to get him, he would deny it. Denial, in such a case, is the true and honest answer.

The OCS-driven tends to be just that, driven. Often ideas and thoughts come to the mind that cannot be easily dismissed. Those that *are* able to be let go often return again and again in a relentless pattern. All symptoms as well as times they occur can come and go. They rise and fall in strength. They change with time and experience. They are also made worse by stress, intense emotional reactions, and fatigue.

When those with OCS are focused on something, there is a tendency to be unable to think about anything else. So if OCS *is* involved in Joey's story, the following might have been true. It could have been that he was wolfing down his food. While doing that Joey also felt the pressure to hurry. He had to get on to the next thing at the forefront of his mind. Then again maybe he was only picking at his food. Perhaps he was eating slowly and lost in thought. His mind was going over and over a specific idea. In either case, after finishing dinner with his mind in such a state, he could truly rise and leave the table without taking his dishes to the sink. It might not have even entered his mind. He was caught up in other thoughts. This could have happened, even though it had been an established family rule throughout his entire life. The need to think about other things sometimes overrules all else.

Obsessive thoughts and compulsions, whether in the mild-to-moderate or severe ranges, can interfere with life. They can do so at different levels of intensity with any and all activities. Joey couldn't wait to get on with his driving thought. His focus is interrupted when he reaches the hall of his home. Knowing about the OCS, perhaps, one can comprehend the reason for the frustrated reply he gives his father: "What?" The reaction depends on the symptom's strength and urgency. Such an interruption can bring on mild irritation or excessive emotional resistance. Without the OCS explanation of chronic hypersensitive reactions, it simply does not make sense. Let's return to the story of Joey and view it from inside of his mind.

Responding to his father's annoyed request, Joey headed back towards the table. The obsession or compulsion kept on pounding in his head like a silent drum. His father had told him to put his dishes in the sink. He had said the word *dishes* and that's the word Joey clung to. *Pound . . . pound . . . pound*. Dishes, *pound*. Joey took them to the sink. "Finally," he thinks. Now he can return to his quest, *pound*.

Upon being interrupted a second time, Joey is annoyed and confused . . . *pound, pound, pound*.

"What now?" His thoughts scream out in protest, *pound*. "There's more?"

Joey honestly can't think of anything else he's supposed to do. He did what his father had asked, *pound*. Why didn't his father just say, "Take the dishes *and* the silverware to the sink?"

The silverware never even entered his mind. *Pound . . . pound . . . pound*. All he saw was the dishes that were getting in the way of what he really wanted to be doing just then. *Pound . . . pound . . . pound*. Precious time was being lost. *Pound . . . pound . . . pound*. Joey was getting angrier by the minute. His father was now yelling at him. He was putting the entire blame for the matter right in *Joey's* lap. But it clearly wasn't Joey's fault. It wasn't fair.

Pointing this out to his father, though, did not seem to be helping to settle the matter. His dad just kept on yelling about his insolence. It was not going to be tolerated. Joey had better just stop sassing and get his a—rhymes with sass) in gear and blah, blah, blah.

"Okay! Okay!" Joey had to yell to be heard over his shouting father. "I'm doing it." He headed back towards the kitchen. Joey's father finally left the room. Joey could still hear his voice, though.

He was talking loudly to Joey's mother. Joey wondered if his father even knew how to speak softly. His voice usually carried all through the house, no matter what room he might actually be in. Joey glanced up at the air-conditioner and heating vents. He decided it probably had something to do with the air ducts.

"Your son," Joey's father was saying, "is doing this on purpose. He knows *very well* what will make me angry. He's a little . . ." The last part seemed muffled. Joey could imagine his mother placing her hand over his father's mouth. He wished he could get away with something like that.

"Now James," Joey heard his mother's voice say, "You don't *know* that. You can't be sure he's doing it just to make you mad . . . ."

"Caroline, PAH-LEEEZE," The please was distended and had that familiar sarcastic twist. His father often said it like that to strike the point home. "Please, honey. C'mon, *you* heard him. *You* didn't tell me to take the *silverware*. As if he didn't know. Is he really that *STUPID?*"

She must have shaken her head.

"I don't think so either. So," he continued, "we both agree it's not stupidity. We see this kind of thing every day right here in our home in front of our own eyes and ears?"

There was a short pause.

"I . . ." Joey's mother began, "I don't know. I'm not sure. He does have an awful lot on his mind, you know."

"And *I* don't!" was his father's curt retort. Then there was nothing.

They seemed to be taking a breather. Joey carefully picked up his fork, spoon, and the knife. He also picked up the napkin, even though his father had neglected to tell him to get rid of that. When the task was completed, Joey rinsed his hands. He dried them on the dishtowel hanging from the handle of the refrigerator. Once again he started towards the hallway and his bedroom.

As he passed his parents closed bedroom door, he heard his father whispering. "So he does know how to speak softly!" Joey thought.

"Caroline," his father confessed, "I'm actually afraid to go back out there. What if he's taken the silverware, but left his napkin?"

Joey gave himself a mental high five. A smile spread across his face. He'd remembered the napkin.

"Or," his father continued, "He's left the milk glass? I will go nuts! I'm afraid I'll hurt him or something. After all, how long has this been a rule in our house anyway? We didn't just now make it up. We've all been doing it for years. What is wrong with that boy?"

Joey had just been patting himself on the back. Then he heard his father mention the milk glass. He quickly retraced a couple of steps to get a clear view of the kitchen table. The moment he did, he slapped himself hard on the side of the head.

"Stupid idiot," Joey scolded himself. "If I'm not the dumbest jerk . . ." he raced to get back to the table. At about the same time Joey got past the hallway, his father also stepped out of the bedroom for a recheck.

This type of situation is extremely common for those with OCS. It can take place from one to many times on a daily basis. This means there are usually lots of instances throughout the course of a single day in which children like Joey are getting into trouble. The parent/child relationship is weakened just a bit each time. It also means that the children in these situations are likely being self-critical many times daily. They are telling themselves things such as, "I'm so stupid! What a jerk, of all the good-for-nothing," and so on.

Although common, the OCS don't always react quite as literally as Joey did in the example. Normally, Joey wouldn't have a problem remembering to put things away after eating.

This fact further complicates the matter. It *is* unfortunate. Adults often feel that if children have behaved correctly in one situation, they should be able to do so again. Those who do not are thought to be making a conscious choice to act inappropriately. This is not necessarily true. On the surface, thinking this way does seem to make sense. Perhaps the following example will serve to dispel this sensible, but sometimes faulty, notion.

Jimmy is an excellent first baseman. He rarely misses a throw from a teammate. He has also not yet missed a ball in the field for the entire season. Similarly, he is well-rounded in the batting area too. He has not struck out even once this season. He has the most RBIs on his team and the entire league. Furthermore, Jimmy has hit thirteen home runs in his last fifteen at bats.

At the start of this particular game, his coach has him bat in the cleanup position. Coach Redd has high expectations. This is an important game for them. Jimmy strikes out for the first time ever. After taking the field, Jimmy single-handedly allows six runs to be scored by the opposing team. These runs score due to his errors at first base.

Fans are booing. The coach is astonished by these actions. As a result, his frustration has been quite slow in coming.

What happened? What's going on? He finally pulls Jimmy from the game. In the dugout he demands an explanation.

It turns out that Jimmy had lost one of his contacts earlier in the day. He then had somehow misplaced the other. He didn't tell anyone because it was the third pair he'd lost in a month. He didn't want his parents to find out. If they did, he'd be in *big* trouble. Jimmy naively thought that he could get by without them. He'd just fake it. Surely he could make it at least until he was able to search his room just one more time. This time he'd search a little more thoroughly.

Jimmy's actions and behaviors when he could see well were very different from when he could not. He needed those corrective lenses. His eyesight was pretty bad without them. Without the help of his contact lenses, reactions that were as easy as breathing for Jimmy suddenly became next to impossible. The problems Jimmy had make perfect sense once you have all the important information.

Admittedly, the example given above is clear and simple, as well as easy to accept as truth. Of course, in many real life situations such causative factors are nowhere near as direct. Neither are they easy to understand. Sometimes they may even be difficult to imagine.

When those with OCS respond so rigidly to the "letter of the law" as did Joey at the dinner table, there may be several elements involved. Significant fatigue and stress can add strength to symptoms. Emotional hyper-sensitivity is also known to make symptoms worse. This sensitivity can also be either positive or negative. This worsening of symptoms can make focusing difficult. It can also result in a hyper or obsessive focus. Such a focus often comes at the expense of being unable to focus on anything else.

Another factor likely to interfere involves competing thoughts. If the OCS mind is caught up in other thoughts, it can be difficult to stay in the here and now. A single-track mind or what might be called "tunnel vision" can get in the way, as well. During such episodes, the OCS brain is already engaged in an idea or thought relating to something else. This thought cannot be let go. It is a very common OCS happening.

When an OCS-driven persistent thought is keeping the mind busy, it can be very difficult to attend to any other ideas or thoughts. At the dinner table Joey may have been thinking of a video game. Perhaps he'd been in the middle of playing it when called to dinner. He may have had a constant and increasingly strong "need" to return to his room to "the game." Throughout the entire dinner he may have scarcely been able to think of anything else.

As a result of this obsessive concern he ate fast. He was then ready to go before anyone else in the family had finished. Maybe they reprimanded him for this. He could have been told that he must sit for five more minutes at the table after the last family member had finished, as a consequence. This only stressed him more. Irritation grew while the intense and incessant thought and need he felt also was stronger. As soon as his little brother Billy finally left the table, Joey started watching the clock. His mother set a kitchen timer for five minutes, as well. The moment the chime rang out his freedom, Joey jumped up. He dashed towards the hall leading to his bedroom.

It was in the midst of such inner turmoil that his father yelled out for him to stop. Then he told Joey that he needed to go back and put his dishes in the sink.

Another thought occupied most of his consciousness. While in this state of mind Joey could only think: "Dishes . . . dishes." He grabbed them and actually dumped them, plate and all (little did his father it know at the time), in the garbage can under the sink. He then surrendered to the unrelenting desire of his tormented mind.

The end result of an ordeal such as Joey's tends to be due to very literal and concrete thinking. There is no extra mind-space for processing information. There is just a hearing of the request and responding, just as Joey had. Often, the information simply doesn't make it into the conscious mind. There can then be no response. In such a case new data is unable to be considered, even briefly.

The symptoms of OCS are familiar, although not well understood. On any given day Joey may be perfectly capable of acting in a proper manner. The situation wouldn't really matter. Then the very next day, he may be practically non-responsive. He may appear to be lost in his own world for half of the day or more. The child caught up in his or her own world is often given the label by teachers "space cadet." This is common when trying to describe the behavior observed.

The OCS features portrayed in this chapter and called "rigid" or "literal" thinking are fairly common. As with other common symptoms, if OCS does exist, there will also be many other signs. These too can be observed if one seriously looks for them.

Without supportive evidence for OCS, other ideas should be considered. Almost always these individuals are far from being blind, stupid, or deaf. At any given moment, though, they may be accused of any one of these, or even all three.

10

Confronting Laziness

Charlie's Dilemma

He wanted to do it. He really did. Each time his parents or another adult got mad and told him to *stop,* he tried. He meant to do what they asked. He truly did. The trouble *was,* no one believed it.

"If you *really* wanted to, Charlie," they'd say, shaking their heads, "you'd *do* it."

"You're just not trying," his mother would tell him again and again. "You could do it if you'd just *try.*"

His father would shout, "If I have to tell you ONE MORE TIME I'll . . . ." But his father never seemed to finish that speech. So Charlie didn't know just what to expect if his dad told him that *one more time.* As a result, his imagination would take over.

And Charlie had a very vivid imagination. He was *more* than just a little bit worried about it.

Charlie's teachers wrote bad remarks on his report card. It wasn't fair! He knew other kids in his classes that had *never* had even a single bad comment written on their report cards. Yet, he knew that *they* had done some of the very same things that he had.

"He's lazy!" Charlie had heard his father say to his mother late at night time after time.

"I don't think he's *lazy,* Jim."

At least Charlie's mother tried to defend him more often than not.

"I just think . . . well . . . ."

Charlie would hardly breathe. Sometimes just the sound of his breathing was louder than everything else. It made it hard to hear through the walls of their bedrooms.

His mother would go on. "I'm not sure what I think."

And there it was. He yearned for his mother to say what he knew was in his own heart. It was time to set things straight with his dad; to tell him the truth . . . .

"Charlie's a good boy!" his thoughts supplied. "He truly wants to mind. He *wants* to do what his teachers expect of him. He listens to us. He hears what we say. He tries. He really *does* try. He feels bad when he doesn't do what we ask him to."

Charlie's thoughts would then sort of bog down. He wasn't sure what else he might want her to say. There was surely more, though.

"Lazy." His father would repeat. "Face it, Marge, he's just *lazy*."

"Oh, Jim!" she'd exclaim.

It was at about this time in their ongoing debate that Charlie would hear his mother begin to get all-emotional. It was usually pretty hard then to tell exactly what she was saying. Charlie's need to breathe would overrule his need to hear.

"Isn't that," his father's voice would get softer and kinder, "what his teachers at school have been saying all along?" Often there would be a definite pause. Then it would seem to Charlie that his dad was actually quoting from his report card. Line-for-line he could hear the comments from his latest one.

"Charlie could do better, I'm sure;" he heard. "If the level of his effort matched the enthusiasm he has for certain other pointless activities throughout the day."

Did his mother cry harder then? He thought so.

His father's words would become gentler then, "Isn't that what it sounds like to you, honey?"

Things would then start to get mushy. Charlie would begin to breathe normally and his own vivid thoughts would take over.

"Am I lazy?" He'd wonder. He didn't feel lazy. There were so many things that he wanted to do. It seemed to him that there was never enough time to do any of them. Wasn't being lazy when someone didn't do anything? When they didn't want to do anything? Charlie wanted to do EVERYTHING.

Sometimes he would lie awake at night for hours just thinking. When this happened he couldn't get to sleep even though he wanted to.

It *was* true Charlie figured that there were *some* things he was supposed to do that he didn't do. But that wasn't because he was lazy. There were just too many other things that needed to be done instead. Too many things were on his mind.

Still . . . even when he'd try so very hard to do his chores and the other stuff he was supposed to, he would forget. He didn't want to forget. He didn't try to. It seemed to him that it just happened. There were even times when he forgot about things that *he* really wanted to do. Like the time he was going to go to the state fair with his friend Winchell.

Winchell's family had decided to go to the state fair practically at the last minute. After school on a Friday they out of the blue had announced they were going Saturday morning. Charlie had been invited too.

"Can I go, Mom, please?" Charlie was practically jumping up and down. He was so excited.

"Settle down," she said. "Now what's this all about? Go where?"

"Winchell!" Charlie nearly shouted. "He just asked me to go to the state fair with him tomorrow morning . . . Can I? Can I, Mom? Can I, huh? Please?" He knew by the look on his mom's face that there was a problem of some kind. "Please, Mom?" He barely breathed.

"Well," she began "I'll have to talk it over with your father . . . ."

"Can you talk to him now?"

"He's at work now, Charlie-honey."

"Yeah, but Dad doesn't get home until 5:30 or 6:00. Winchell said his parents need to know by five." They had actually said no such thing. Charlie couldn't resist the little white lie. *He* needed to know *NOW!* "C'mon Mom, please?" He gave her his sad little "I'm-going-to-die" look. The rolling of her eyes told him she was weakening.

"Pretty, please?" Now, had his father been involved, he never would have gotten this far. That was why he so desperately wanted her to call him. Now!

"Well . . ." Her voice wavered, "I suppose I could, just this once."

"YES!" Charlie shouted triumphantly. He leaped up and shook his fists in the air. Unfortunately, he'd forgotten he still had the telephone receiver in his hand. It was the old kind. It was the kind that had a long accordion-like cord. The cord went from the receiver to the main body part that made up the phone. It was hanging on the wall.

The tightly wound phone cord whipped around from his sudden upward motion. Small brown bottles with white capped lids were swept off the counter in one stroke. There was a moment of complete silence that seemed to last forever. Charlie shouted in his mind, "That stupid cord! It was that stupid cord's fault! If we had a cordless phone this never would have happened!" Luckily for him he hadn't said a word out loud.

Suddenly his mother burst into gales of laughter.

"What the . . ." he thought. Then he felt relieved by her reaction. He'd been afraid she would yell at him. He started laughing as well.

Charlie didn't really know what they were laughing at exactly. But he did know that laughing was a lot better than yelling. His mother had a tendency to be weird like that. She could go from laughter to tears without a moment's notice. And most of the time there seemed to be no reason for her sudden change. Just then it was in his favor so rather than question it he simply went with it.

Charlie could see tears forming in her eyes. His mother was laughing so hard. He put the phone receiver back on the wall hook.

"I'll get them," he said. He edged around her to where the bulk of the plastic bottles lay on the floor. Charlie's mother took a step backward and away from the counter. She'd been leaning on it heavily for support during her fit of laughter. As she stepped back a loud crack marked the place where her foot came down.

Charlie jumped. Loud unexpected noises always freaked him out. His jumpiness actually made his father angry. Whenever Charlie reacted that way his dad would usually yell, "*WILL YOU STOP THAT*, you overreact to everything!" Charlie wasn't sure if he was actually overreacting at those times. It's just what always happened. It didn't feel like much of an overreaction to him.

At the sound of the smashed pill bottle his mother started to laugh again.

"Charlie?" she managed to get out. "Why don't you clean this up while I call your father?"

"Okay, mom."

Charlie picked up all the little bottles and placed them once again on the counter. By the time he'd finished his mother was just hanging up the phone.

"What'd he say?" Charlie cried, "What'd he say?"

"Calm down, Charlie," she took his hands in hers and held them over the counter. "Calm down." His mother's eyes drifted downward.

"Your father asked me a question," She told him. "He asked me what your room looked like."

Charlie groaned and tried to pull his hands away. But she wouldn't let go.

"I got him to agree to let you go," she said, "if your room was clean enough to pass his inspection."

Charlie groaned again. "*HIS* inspection," he thought. His mother must have seen the effect this declaration had on him.

She patted him on the shoulder.

"C'mon, Charlie," she soothed, "you can do it."

He looked at her with a doubtful frown.

"You *do want* to go to the fair, don't you?"

"The fair," he had totally forgotten all about that! Yeah. He wanted to go to the fair. He could do it. He *would* do it. Charlie started towards his room.

"Wait honey," his mother called after him. "That's not all."

Charlie stopped and slowly turned to look at her. He should have known.

"Your dad wants it done before he gets home tonight."

"Oh, great!" thought Charlie, "So much for going to the fair."

"It's not so bad, Charlie-boy," she cut into his thoughts before they could get much more negative. "He said he's going to be late tonight. He won't be home until around 8:00."

Charlie regarded his mother just standing there. She was acting like this was supposed to make him feel better. Clean his room good enough to pass his father's inspection? He might as well grow wings and fly.

"C'mon, Charlie-boy" she encouraged, "go on in there and show your dad what you can do!" She was smiling.

He really did want to go to the fair. But his *room*! Why did it have to be his room? He glanced at the wall clock above the kitchen table. It was four-thirty. That gave him maybe three-and-a-half-hours if he was lucky. Could it be done?

The phone rang.

"I'll get it," his mother waved her hand to get him moving, "you go and get started on that room."

Charlie nodded. He turned and moved quickly down the hall. At the doorway of his room he heard his mother's voice.

"Charlie!" she called. "The phone's for you."

He made his way back to the kitchen.

His mother smiled. "Don't talk too long, hon. Remember the room."

It was Winchell, of course. "So Charlie can you go?" he asked. Charlie told his friend about the situation.

"Why don't I come over and help you clean it?" Winchell offered.

Charlie was surprised. "Sure," he said. "That sounds great." Then he felt guilty. He wondered if he'd be offering to help Winchell clean *his* room if the roles were reversed. "Uh . . . I better tell my mom, though. Hang on." Something nagged at the back of his mind. It was telling him that his mom should probably be advised about the situation.

"I'm sorry Charlie-boy," his mother patted him on the shoulder again. She did that a lot. "That was part of the deal. Your father was very clear about that. *No* help. He made me promise. Of course he *was* talking about me . . . ." She let her sentence sort of trail off into the air.

"Yeah, okay, mom, I get the picture." He took his hand from the muffled receiver. Charlie told his friend it was a no-go. Winchell made him promise to call as soon as his dad came home and saw the room and said it was okay for Charlie to go. Then he said goodbye.

Charlie hung up the phone.

"Don't look so glum, Charlie," his mother commented. "You can do it. I know you can."

Once again he took off towards his room. He opened the door and walked inside. He then quickly closed the door before actually looking at anything.

Then he looked.

The situation was even worse than he'd imagined. There were clothes on the bed. They covered the dresser. They were draped over his desk and chair. They were also in little piles all over the floor. Papers covered the rest of his desk and the nearby floor space. His collection of rocks had been tipped over. The whole assortment was scattered between the bed and his closet. Nintendo-64 games were scattered everywhere. Here and there mounds of assorted junk were visible that were hardly recognizable. The bottom of his closet was hidden by at least two feet of *stuff*. What a mess.

Charlie had seen enough.

He slumped onto the bed and then instantly jumped back up. He reached towards his bottom. Then he grabbed the jumbled up quilt that he'd sat on and lifted it. A fork was dislodged from the thick folds. It fell to the carpet. He rubbed his left backside and counted himself lucky. It's a good thing he hadn't sat down any harder than he did.

His room was a disaster area!

He slid his hand over the spot on the bed now uncovered. He felt around carefully with his hands, just in case, and then laid the quilt back on top of itself. His roving fingers had found a peach pit. He tossed it towards the corner of the room. The wastebasket was over-full. He'd put up a tiny basketball hoop over the cylinder, using parts from a Nerf basketball set. The pit hit the rim and bounced away. "Darn," he thought. "It probably wouldn't have gone in anyway." The basket was just too full already.

Again he sat down on the bed. What should he do first? He didn't know. He leaned over and picked up the fork. What had he been eating with this? He couldn't remember. He wasn't supposed to eat in his room. Lucky thing it was *he* who found it there, and not his mom. It was especially lucky that it wasn't his dad. He could imagine if his father had found it.

"I've *told* you a thousand times," he'd shout. "No eating in your room. When are you going to start *listening*?"

Since no food had been found with the fork, Charlie could also easily picture his own impulsive response.

"I wasn't eating with it, dad," He'd say. "I was doing an experiment . . . uh . . . for school."

Charlie knew that his father valued his education above all else. That was because he'd never had the chance to finish school himself.

His grandfather had died at a fairly young age from *the croup* (whatever that was). Charlie's dad had then been forced to go to work to help support his mother and three little sisters. He regularly lectured Charlie about this whenever he got grades below a B in school. Charlie had gotten that lecture a lot. He'd heard the story at least once every quarter since he'd been in first grade. He practically knew it by heart.

He might have gotten the lecture in kindergarten too if they'd actually given letter grades back then. During the lecture if his dad thought Charlie wasn't listening he'd get mad. He regularly yelled at him. Charlie hated it when his dad yelled. He hated it so much that he'd almost rather do anything than get yelled at. He'd *even* lie. He hadn't been using the fork to eat with. Yeah, right.

Charlie took the utensil into the kitchen. His mother was standing over the counter cutting potatoes into tiny squares. He grimaced. That meant potato soup for sure. It wasn't all that bad, but it certainly wasn't his favorite.

"So . . . how's it going Charlie boy? Are you getting a lot done?"

Charlie glanced at the fork in his hand. "Yeah, Mom," he said, "tons."
"Dinner should be ready in about 45 minutes," she announced. "Your
father can eat later."

"Yeah, Okay, Mom." Charlie wanted to tell her that he wasn't all that
hungry. He returned to his room instead. He began picking up clothes. He
had a hard time trying to figure out if they were dirty or clean. Should they
go into his drawer? Should they be hung up in the closet? Or should they
be put into his dirty clothes basket? What a pain!

Maybe he ought to just put all the clothes in the dirty clothes basket.
But wouldn't that upset his mother? Besides the basket wasn't nearly big
enough for the mounds that still lay here and there all around his room.
There was no *way* he'd *ever* get the entire mess into that tiny little basket.
Maybe he should do clothes last.

Charlie knew he had to do something with them to get them out of the
way. He needed to be able to see what else there was that had to be cleaned
up. He decided the bed was a good central location. He threw the T-shirt
already in his hand onto the bed. He did the same thing with the rest of
his scattered wardrobe.

After about half the clothes in the room had been shifted from the floor
to the bed, Charlie came upon an unusually large pile. Beneath a pair of his
old pajamas there was a shirt that even he had no trouble seeing belonged
in the dirty clothes basket. Under these were several pairs of pants. Beneath
the jeans he found something he hadn't seen or even thought about for a
long-long time.

It was a partially built model replica of the *Titanic*.

A while back his mother and father had seen the movie with Leonardo
DiCaprio as the star. Not long afterwards his father had been walking
down an aisle in a Target store. He happened to see a model kit of the ship
on sale. It was a *huge* model. Charlie thought it surely had about a billion
pieces that all had to be glued one-by-one in place. Right on the top of the
box it said in big dark letters "WARNING! NOT FOR BEGINNERS."
Charlie's dad bought it for him anyway. He'd said it would be fun as well
as *educational*.

Fun? Not really. Educational? Well, Charlie supposed it was that.

He hoped his father had learned a lesson. You really ought to pay
attention to label warnings. Also, Charlie hoped he understood now that
his only son didn't really like model building.

There it lay on the carpet unfinished.

He wondered if the real *Titanic* had as many pieces as the model. Then he laughed. It probably had a *lot* more. He thought about the time it must have taken to actually build the real boat. All that work just to see it end up at the bottom of the ocean. What a waste! He was sure that the inhabitants of the ocean didn't think the *Titanic* was such a big deal. Maybe educational, though.

Then all the weeks he'd spent trying to follow the pages and pages of diagrams and directions. He grimaced. Just to have the model end up uncompleted on the carpet underneath some dirty clothes.

What a waste! He supposed it was fitting in some strange way that he couldn't really explain in words.

Charlie glanced once more around his room. He had no idea what to do with the unfinished ship. It wouldn't be completed. He was pretty sure about that. Perhaps he should just throw it away. But then again he couldn't really do that either. After all, his father had bought it for *him*. He'd have to figure out *some* place where it could go.

The box with the remaining pieces was sticking out noticeably from under his bed. He pulled it the rest of the way out and dusted off the top.

He immediately sneezed twice. Charlie always sneezed in twos.

He lifted the top off the box and peered inside. A three-quarters-used tube of Testor's model glue and an old Exacto knife lay side by side on top of the instructions. The directions were opened to page thirty-three.

That had been as far as he got. Charlie knew he'd really disappointed his father on this one.

Maybe he should just sit down right here and now and complete it. No wonder his dad didn't trust him to finish things. He hadn't finished this. Some things were hard to finish.

He pushed aside some socks that might have been worn several times without ever having seen the inside of a washer. He also shoved away a few of his scattered rocks. Charlie cleaned out a flat space on which he could work. He lifted the instruction booklet. He placed it and the glue as well as the Exacto knife directly in front of him on the carpet.

He began to read aloud from page thirty-four.

As Charlie labored, he wondered what his dad would think. How would he react when he came home and saw that he'd finished the ship? Would his dad even remember giving it to him? Surely he would. For sure he'd also be surprised. Finally Charlie had actually followed through with something and completed it. Would he be proud? Of course he would. Why the educational value of the task alone . . . .

His father would undoubtedly be speechless at first. He would then grandly congratulate Charlie on a job well done. He would no longer doubt that his son could start a project and finish it. The proof would be there. No one could deny it. They wouldn't dare.

His father would then stop calling him lazy. He would know by the completed ship that Charlie wasn't lazy.

Charlie became intensely focused on what he was doing. He never consciously heard his mother call him for dinner. Nor was he aware that she had come to his bedroom door and had a brief conversation with him.

"Charlie-boy," she'd called ever so softly, "don't you want to come out and eat? Dinner's ready."

Charlie was so intent on the task at hand that his answer was automatic. "Not now, Mom! I got to finish this." He'd said it, but his single-mindedness on building the *Titanic* was intense. It kept him from recording in his mind that anything had been said. At some level it *must* have registered in his brain. After being reminded about it later, he remembered that it had happened.

"Okay honey," his mother had replied through the closed bedroom door. "I understand. You go right ahead. I know how much this means to you. You can eat later too."

Charlie was putting the final piece in place. It was a banner that said "*Titanic* the Unsinkable." There was a knock at his door. It made him jump. He dropped the banner and the tube of glue to the carpet. "Just a minute," he called towards the door. "I'm almost finished."

He snatched up the banner and the glue. He completely ignored the glob of cement that had spilled onto his well-used carpet. Charlie dabbed the needed portions on the proper places. He put the tube down. Then he quickly placed the banner over what must have been the . . . what was it called? Maybe it was the Bridge. Or was that just on *Star Trek*? Oh, well . . . anyway it was the place where the captain stood over the steering wheel. Who really cared about its name?

He heard another firm and insistent knock at the door.

"Coming," he said. He let go of the banner. It stayed in place.

Done! Charlie jumped up and flew towards the door. He fumbled to unlock it and threw it open. He stepped back. Ta Dah! He felt like one of those magicians on TV. They raise their hands into the air after a trick. It sort of invites everyone watching to take a good long look at what they've done.

"Charlie's been working in here all afternoon," his mother was saying. "He didn't even want to come to din— . . . ." her voice trailed off without finishing as she looked past Charlie into the room.

His father's eyes had been turned away. As he brought them back around to face Charlie and the room, he froze.

Charlie gestured towards the completed *Titanic*. "So what do you think?" he asked. He didn't get the reaction he'd expected. Something was wrong. He promptly glanced back at his father.

His father stood clenching and unclenching his hands at his sides. As Charlie watched he saw the muscles in his father's neck begin to tighten. The color of his face started to turn a sort of bluish-red.

Suddenly, with a quickness and force that was frightening, the man turned and pushed past Charlie's mother. He strode away muttering. "Stupid, lazy, good-for-nothing . . . ."

"What have you been doing, Charlie?" his mother asked.

"Working on the *Titanic*, mom, what do you think? I actually finished it. The *whole* thing!" Charlie lowered his head sadly, "and dad didn't even look at it!"

"Well . . . ." she began.

"Well, what!" Charlie insisted.

His mother just stared for a moment saying nothing.

Then it dawned on him. The fair. His room.

Suddenly he knew that his father wouldn't care a whit about the *Titanic*. He'd probably long ago given up on Charlie ever completing that.

It was the *room* he'd been interested in. That was what he'd come in to see. Charlie didn't know what had happened. He'd honestly started out fully intending to clean his room.

Later that night he could hear his dad talking to his mother, "Charlie doesn't care about going to the stupid fair. If he *did* care . . . if he'd really wanted to go . . . he would have cleaned up his room!"

Could that really be true? Was it possible that he actually didn't want to go to the fair? He didn't think so.

He'd almost cried over the phone that night. His dad had forced him to call Winchell. He'd had to tell his friend that he couldn't go.

It was only with the greatest effort that Charlie had kept from bursting into tears. He didn't want to give his father the satisfaction.

So he went right on acting. He pretended that what his dad thought actually *was* true. He worked very hard on it from that moment on. He tried to convince himself and everyone else that he could've *cared less* about the stupid state fair.

It almost worked too. He almost convinced himself. Almost.

"Why didn't you call me earlier?" Winchell was clearly upset.

"My dad didn't get home until around 8:30," Charlie told his friend.

"What happened? Didn't you get your room done?"

"Not the way he wanted me to." Charlie was unable to tell his friend what had really happened. Winchell would probably conclude just like his father had, that Charlie didn't want to go to the fair in the first place. Heck, it was even starting to seem that way to him. At least that reason sort of made some kind of sense. He was confused.

Something was wrong. There had to be something wrong. But what was it? What could it be? Charlie *just* didn't know. He wondered if he ever would.

THE END
(Or perhaps it is actually the beginning.)

There *was* something wrong with Charlie. Charlie and his parents were interviewed. He seemed to have a number of characteristics consistent with a mild-moderate obsessive-compulsive symptom picture. As we visited, the decision to administer an expanded version of the Leyton Obsessional Inventory for Children was made.

Charlie responded positively to thirty-nine out of the forty-five questions asked. This meant that he felt he had thirty-nine of the symptoms. Interestingly, when shared with his parents, they questioned the results. Many of the traits he'd said were there they had not seen evidence for. They had a hard time believing it was true. This is not that unusual. Think about it. They had never seen it. He had never spoken of such things before. The OCS persons frequently tell no one about much of what they experience. They do not talk about the feelings they have that they "must" do certain things. They will avoid it at practically any cost. It tends to embarrass them. There is also an enduring fear that others simply will not believe them. They fear others will get angry or make fun of them as a result. Alas when those with OCS do tell the truth about their symptoms they are often not believed. Also, peers *do* make fun of them. They also look down on them and treat them as if they might be crazy. And finally, parents, along with well-meaning teachers, often do get angry.

The extended family history was explored. Parental eyes began to widen. They recognized various characteristics of OCS in their siblings. There was also evidence in both sets of Charlie's grandparents as well.

Charlie's symptoms were not limited only to those mentioned in his "story." His symptoms also included such things as a short temper. He had poorer school performance than he was capable of. Peer relationship difficulties abounded. He had problems getting to sleep at night. There was a tendency to be irritable and slow getting ready for school in the morning. There were frequent arguments, especially with his father.

A recommendation was made to Charlie's physician. It was suggested that he consider starting him on a medication about one hour before bedtime. Given available evaluation data, the physician agreed. Charlie's mother brought him in for the first session after he had started this medication.

She was obviously pleased with his response, but was also slightly confused. Charlie's doctor had told her that it would be three to six weeks before she would likely see any benefit. Her confusion came from the fact that something had happened the very next morning after he had taken just one dose. Charlie had, for the first time in as long as she could remember, gotten up with his alarm. He then got dressed and ready for school. He was in the kitchen eating his breakfast before she got there to start up the coffee maker. She indicated that she had been "amazed." Furthermore, this same thing had continued every day since.

Charlie's teacher had also sent home a note spontaneously. She congratulated him on his newly found efforts with a personal note. That note said, "You see, I told you you could do it if you tried!" She had not been informed as yet that a medication had been started.

In an interview with Charlie it was determined that he had noticed that he felt calmer and less angry. He had finished all his work at school since starting the medication. As a result he had only had one homework assignment. He completed it easily, much more quickly than before. It usually took him hours to complete even a small amount of homework. It often would not be completed at all without his parents sitting next to him, urging him on.

The Leyton was re-administered. Charlie reported that twenty-five of his initial thirty-nine positive symptoms were "better." Symptoms were less frequent and less intense when they did occur. He also recovered more quickly and let go sooner. He indicated that five of the remaining fourteen were actually "gone." Either that or they just hadn't been noticed anymore.

Of the final nine symptoms there were several that he wasn't sure of. These actually might not be noticed one way or the other due to the type involved. For example, the question relating to keeping various odds and ends that others might think he should get rid of had not changed. Nor had the one changed regarding his unwillingness to eat certain foods *"no matter what"* and so on.

After about the fifth or sixth session, Charlie's father took me aside briefly. As the others walked out of the session, he whispered, "So can adults take this medication too?" Eventually Charlie's father was also diagnosed with mild-moderate OCS. He too was treated medically. Fortunately he also responded positively. I have found that it is not unusual for one or both parents to wonder about treatment for themselves. After they see the positive results that have occurred with their child it makes sense.

"What a lazy bum."

"He never wants to do anything."

"If you give *him* something to do you can be sure it won't get done. He just doesn't care whether or not tasks are completed. He never finishes anything."

Some of the above statements may sound familiar. They probably seem realistic as well. Experience has taught me that such blatant comments are hardly, if ever, true. Such remarks almost certainly come from those who are frustrated with another's behavior or lack thereof. Individuals making such remarks often feel at the end of their rope. Often they are not only at the *end* of that rope but it is also dangling over a chasm. They're going to let it go if they have to face such slothful, neglectful, and indolent behavior one more time. This person's grip on emotional control is getting loose.

A parent berates her child. "Why don't you want to succeed?" This statement can be taken in a couple of ways. The first is that the child being questioned is not at all interested in success or succeeding as it were. Another notion is that this child *is* believed to be absolutely capable of succeeding. She, however, is simply choosing not to do so.

In my twenty-three years of clinical work I have not yet found even one person who didn't want to succeed if it was possible to do so. It doesn't matter whether it is a child or an adult. There have been those who thought that they must *not* want to succeed. It's hard not to feel this way when told this repeatedly again and again by so many others. But even these, when one reaches the true heart of the matter, realized that this was simply not the case.

I have also worked with those who would argue and insist that they in fact *do not* want to succeed. Most people, if knocked down repeatedly enough times when trying to stand, will eventually give up. The "sour grapes" fable will sometimes lead this person to believe that he or she did not truly want to stand up anyway. This distorted pattern of thinking is often used to preserve self-esteem. What else can someone do when others are seen all around getting up and standing successfully and even beginning to walk? The inability to join in is frustrating and embarrassing.

Sometimes the only way to feel "okay" when most others are succeeding while you are not is to deny that it is important. If it's not important, then it no longer matters if you are less than successful. You simply don't care. "I can't" becomes "I don't want to," which is much easier to deal with emotionally at times. The fact remains that it doesn't matter who you are. If every time you try to stand up you fall down because of some interfering force, you will soon find something better to do. As long as this "force" is present and getting in the way, the effort put forth to reach your goal will tend to diminish with each unsuccessful attempt.

Before too long this constant failure will probably develop into a noticeable lack of trying. Others will probably label such behavior as "laziness." This only makes sense. It is a circular trap. Try not to get caught up in this trap. Remember, being considered lazy is the easy way out. It is better than getting branded as incapable or being judged as an absolute failure.

"Yeah . . . I'm lazy all right. So what? Who cares about standing up anyway? It's *so* overrated. It's also a *stupid* thing to want to do. And since I'm *not* stupid I wouldn't be caught dead trying to do it. Who needs to stand anyway? Look at me. I've been crawling all my life and it hasn't hurt *me*. Standing is just not that big a deal, you know."

A parent or teacher trying to help such a child might point out that standing is an essential first step. They might say it's the first step in a process. It must be accomplished before someone will be able to walk.

"So what?" the argument may continue. "I don't want to *walk* either. As soon as you start to walk people start asking you to do things. They make you go places that you don't want to go. Nah, walking is for the birds."

After hearing something like this, a parent or teacher may be doing all they can to hold back their laughter or their disdain. "Everyone has to walk," might be the next comment made.

"Not me!" comes the angry reply. "I don't *have* to walk. You'll see." The OCS will often tend to carry this farther than their non-affected peers. This is due to the tendency to obsess over it. "When I'm ready, when I *want* to . . . I'm going to just get up and *run*. Standing and walking are overrated actions, anyhow. Who needs to stand? Who cares? Not me! I don't. Do you hear me? I don't care. I don't! I'm not going to *stand* or *walk*. One of these days I'm just going to *run*." Of course there is also an OCS group who may not be so sure. These may feel so defeated they are unable to even imagine that they'll ever be able to walk, let alone run.

The situations related above are quite simplified. This is in order to aid in understanding. These models are representative of the many other types of situations and experiences that can occur. There are many variations that may be encountered during the course of a lifetime. Patterns of so-called *laziness* such as those explored above can be developed in any area of one's life. This is especially true for the OCS-affected. This is because not only do they obsess over such things, but they often see themselves as failures anyway. Often this is due to their overly zealous self-expectations for perfection. They consider themselves to be failures in areas where an unaffected peer might be dancing in the street for joy. The unaffected is excited, though having only performed at the same level of proficiency.

Thus if the OCS-affected expects that he or she *should* be standing RIGHT NOW and they are not, it's a problem. This might be in spite of their being developmentally too young for such a task. To them it doesn't matter. As a result there may be a conscious or unconscious decision to give up or actively quit trying. This course of action can appear to observers as purposeful idleness. With no other motive available, the label of *lazy* may be adopted.

Parents and relatives may repeat that age-old line, "If you would just try, you could do it." Or, "If you'd just try a little harder, I'm sure you'd find that you can."

If we could get inside the mind of those with OCS bombarded by such unhelpful comments, it might help. Their thoughts might go something like this, "Try? If I'd just try? Where have you been? I've been *trying* and *trying* and still failing. I don't like failing. I can't fail. If I do fail it will mean I'm *nothing*. Trying harder to stand will only make my bottom take on more shades of color than I want to think about. That's not the worst of it, though. I could stand a little bruise on my bottom. I could even take a massive one. But I can't endure the bruise that would result in my mind and heart if I were to *really* try hard and *then* fail. If I don't try it stands to reason that I also can't fail. I won't fail if I don't try. And I really don't want to fail. So I'm done with this trying business. Thank you very much."

"What a lazy bum," says the angry stepfather. "Your kid," he directs his comments at his wife, "is the laziest . . . ."

What the OCS one often hears when such a statement is made is not the literal meaning. Rather there can be a running translation in his or her mind. It goes something like the following: "At least I'm not *disabled* or incapable. I'm not too stupid or incompetent for the task or situation. I'm not handicapped. Nope, I'm none of those. What *I* am is *lazy*. Lazy isn't so bad. It's certainly better than being handicapped."

A professional facing such a situation may see strong resistance. They may also observe downright angry denial. The idea that this problem might be due to something else other than laziness can be hard for most to swallow. The so-labeled person may have ego and self-esteem issues underlying their use of denial. They may liken a lack of success, even if only in just a few areas, as proof of their ultimate worthlessness. *Worthless* or *lazy, hmm . . .* let's see . . . which one would you rather be?

Parents often have a hard time believing that something could be interfering that cannot be overcome by sheer will power. They may fear that by thinking this way they are also accepting that their child is *defective*. The reasoning goes further. If a child is *defective*, the fault must lie with the parents. Such parents must be doing something wrong. They must therefore be *bad* parents.

Unfortunately the idea that genetics and inherited traits are involved may not make these parents feel much better; at least not at first. They still may blame themselves for having passed it on to their child. There may be a very real need to avoid blame. Parents can become heavily invested in believing that the problem has to be that the child is just *lazy*. It must be. Children who are *lazy* are to blame for the problem all by themselves.

The parents then can be free from guilt. They can take on the role of concerned bystanders rather than a part of the actual cause. As you can see both sides have some rather compelling reasons to reject any other explanation. A manifested chronic lack of effort *has* to be due to simple laziness. As long as the problem is one of laziness, the status quo remains the same. Life can go on without getting everybody all uptight or upset about who is to blame and for what. No one has to think about neglect. No one has to feel inadequate. Nobody has to be thought of as damaged or deficient.

A great many of those with OCS interference, who've come to see me over the years, have felt that their problem was one of being lazy. This was often brought up within the first or second session. It is common for the OCS-driven to feel this way. When it is brought up in an initial interview, a note is made to screen for possible OCS.

Laziness or not caring are often accepted as explanations for actions that appear to otherwise make no sense. "What else could it be?" This question is thrown in the face of anyone suggesting that there might be a different explanation. A professional may not want to suggest this too soon. Clients may reject such explanations right away. It's too hard to believe. They may leave the session wondering if the professional is a quack.

In order to radically change a way of looking at something takes time. Sufficient knowledge and education must often be acquired first. This may have to happen before such ideas can be considered and explored.

It is not unusual for the OCS-affected to have no idea why they don't finish things. When projects need to be done, they may put them off or delay them as long as possible. Either that or they don't complete them at all. In interviews they can make a strong case to support the idea that their problem really is one of laziness. They will provide much evidence "I just can't seem to get started," is a fairly common statement. "I can't seem to get myself to do it. I just don't want to." They may also add: "And I don't even have a good excuse for not wanting to. I just don't get it done."

The elements at the heart of this guise of laziness are many. They are insidiously interwoven into the OCS mind. As one might guess, untangling them is a difficult process. The following was suggested in my earlier writings.

"When lies are easier to believe than the truth, the truth is not welcome."

A person's lack of performance resulting from being *lazy is* easy to believe and accept as true. It is a lot easier to believe than the complicated truth about those with OCS.

What those with OCS experience might better be termed *Pseudo-Laziness*. In my mind this is somewhat like the concept of *Learned Helplessness* as envisioned by Martin Seligman. The difference between the two appears mainly that of intensity, duration, and frequency. Time of recovery and choice of treatment are also differences that need to be taken into account.

Ask yourself this question. How would *you* react? What would you do if every time before starting a task you found yourself thinking or worrying excessively? You might worry about a host of bothersome issues such as the following:

— Should I be doing this right now? Is there something else I should do first?

— Should I be doing this at all? What if it's the wrong thing to do?
— What if I don't do it right? What if I fail? What if others don't think its right or a good job?
— What if I don't finish?
— What if I can't do it? What if I'm not good enough?
— What if it takes too long? What if I don't have time for all the other things I still need to do?
— Why do I even try? It won't be good enough anyway. It never is. Oh, why try at all?
— I wish I didn't have to do this. Hey, maybe I'll get sick. That's a good reason not to finish.
— As long as I don't try too hard when I fail, it won't bother me as much as it would if I had been trying.
— This is going to take so long. I wish it was tomorrow. I wish it was already done.
— What if no matter what I do it's not good enough? Wouldn't that mean that I'm not good enough?
— Maybe I can get someone else to do it for me or with me. Then the outcome won't be my fault.
— There's got to be some way out of this. It's not fair to have to do all this work.
— I have to do everything around here.
— What if I copied down the wrong assignment? Was this what my teacher wanted me to do?
— Maybe I should wait until I find out for sure if this is what I'm supposed to be doing.
— What if I do the stuff I think I'm supposed to do and it turns out that it isn't what I'm supposed to do. *That* would be stupid. That would mean I'm stupid too.
— I don't think I'm stupid. Am I? Maybe I am. I can't be sure.
— I'll never get done with this. It's going to take forever. Why does it have to be me? Always me.

The list above is not all-inclusive. There are many pathways to Pseudo-Laziness as experienced by the OCS population. Often it is a combination of these factors and not just a single pathway that causes the problems. Together these work to reduce the person to the level of being considered *lazy*. Some of the more common and obvious paths need to be explored.

Those with OCS often feel emotionally overwhelmed. The intensity of this feeling regularly rises and falls whenever stress or fatigue is present. The reasons behind this tendency to be overcome with emotions are varied. Sometimes the person has simply *taken on too much*. This one is not unusual. The tasks they expect to complete can be difficult. They may be time-consuming. They can be more numerous than any normal person would ever be able to complete. As such they simply cannot get them done. Those with OCS often feel a strong *need to finish* all tasks they start. When they find themselves in a position of not being able to do so, it can create great emotional distress. This distress cannot be easily soothed. It can't be ignored either, and may cause a partial or even total shutdown.

Another tendency that can lead to a shutdown is the *desire to complete all tasks perfectly*. That is, perfect in the sense that it is exactly the way the person thinks or feels the task *should* be accomplished. Sometimes, *the element of time* can also be an important issue. To make sure things are *just right* usually takes time. It often takes a lot more time than is typically required by the non-affected person. If a time limit has been set, the OCS-affected often can get anxious and worried. They fear they might not have enough time to adequately complete the task. They may therefore refuse to comply. They also may be unable to get started. The *not being able to get started* can look like dawdling or fooling around. It can also sometimes look like purposeful resistance.

If for any reason *the OCS believes he or she will not be able to perform at the best of his or her ability*, this may cause a shut down as well. They may make comments such as "I can't do it" or "it's too hard." Such comments can be confusing to others who have observed the person do just fine with similar tasks before. Others may be hard-pressed to understand. Why would someone insist that they can't do something when they clearly can?

Paradoxical Inclination can play a role in this as well. This occurs because of a perceived inability to perform at personally acceptable levels. They do the task slothfully or without really trying. This response may be conscious or unconscious. This person has decided that there is a need to at least do *something*. These people can't just sit there and do nothing. They may respond quickly and halfheartedly without much focus or effort. As a result, they may be labeled as *lazy*. It is obvious to others that they are not trying. They are known to be capable of much more. They don't put in the time or effort necessary to do a good job.

People commonly comment "She doesn't care if she does a good job or not." When OCS is truly present and getting in the way, such a statement is absolutely false. The comment hits the OCS-affected like a slap in the face. Often the affected one has no idea why they can't seem to put forth effort at times. Their saving grace is that they are aware that their effort has been poor. They are therefore able to forgive themselves for their poor performance. Had they been trying hard and still performed poorly, the self-esteem would have taken a beating. This would have triggered all kinds of negative emotionally-driven thoughts and feelings. Sometimes it's too much to bear. It should be noted that there are also those who cannot seem to forgive a poor performance as well.

Negative beliefs or thoughts can become intense or extreme. These can reach a level such that the mental energy required to get past them is monumental. When those with OCS do make an attempt to get past such thoughts, by the time they are through, they are exhausted. Upon reaching such a point there may be no energy left to give to the actual task. Then if there is enough energy left whatever time constraints may be connected to the task are likely now to interfere.

Time issues can actually interfere to a huge degree in other ways as well. Sometimes the OCS ability to keep things clean, organized, and neat is a problem. They may have trouble cleaning up after themselves. It may be a struggle to keep a bedroom, a garage, or a counter top in the kitchen orderly and clean. These are all fairly common problems for many OCS-driven persons. Again, as a result of this, the label of *lazy* could easily surface and be applied.

Usually the OCS mind is intensely focused on whatever it is doing at a particular moment. It may also be focused on the very next thing planned or the next idea that enters the mind. The *next* thing scheduled is often impatiently waiting in the wings of the mind. It can't wait for the chance to get in and get going. There is no time in-between these thoughts, plans, or needs for anything that goes beyond the activity of the moment. As soon as the sandwich being made is finished, the next thought rushes madly in. The OCS-driven is then off to the races. Left behind may be the opened bread loaf. An open jar of peanut butter with the knife still leaning on the lid can be there too. Maybe a lidless jar of grape jelly waits to be put away. Also bread crumbs may be spread across the counter top. There may be no consideration whatsoever given to the matter of clean up.

The next thought pushes its way in at the very moment the current task is completed. In this case the making of a sandwich was the current task. This next need immediately takes over the mind completely. The idea of cleaning up and putting away the supplies and sandwich mess is left hanging. You have to make the sandwich before it can be eaten. But you don't have to clean up the leftover mess in order to eat it. Once the sandwich has been made the very next goal in the mind would be to eat it.

Often, while a specific task is being worked on, the OCS mind is hyper-focused on completing the task. The focus when done is in getting right to the next urge, need, or locked in thought. If another person happens to interfere by asking a question or making a request, the OCS reaction can be extreme. The response may be one of instant resistance. It could result in frustration or anger. Sometimes the reaction can be explosive. The other's request has placed a cog in the otherwise smoothly running gears of the OCS mind-set. The formerly quiet gears are now grinding and squealing in an intense effort to dislodge that unwanted cog. A perfectly running and comfortable mind-set has been interrupted. It's a loss. That same mind-set is now gone. It can never be recovered. It will never be the same. Emotional grief must be given. But there's no time available even for that.

The other major *Time* element has to do with how long a task is expected to take. The OCS-affected typically desire to do things very well. If it seems the task is one that will take a huge amount of the person's time, attempts may be made to resist. The person may try and put off starting the chore for as long as possible. Examples might be the tasks of cleaning a bedroom, the kitchen, bathroom, or garage.

When the OCS-driven finally accepts that a time-consuming task must be done, they will start. Once it is decided a chore is to be done the obsessive-compulsive part may kick in. When it does take over, it's like the bus begins to drive that person rather than the other way around. It takes control until the entire chore is complete. It will need to be done *just* so. This may take hours and hours and at times even days.

The person with OCS knows this is the way they are. It may not always be a conscious knowledge, though. They may procrastinate and complain. They may gripe and whine in an attempt to delay beginning the task. They may try and get away with a half hearted *quickie* while mouthing the words silently: "It doesn't matter because I'm not really trying . . . ."

Others without the interfering OCS influence just can't understand. When these others see the methodical and overly perfectionistic performance, they don't get it. They may belittle the one with OCS without realizing it. They may make statements like, "Well, you didn't have to do all *that* . . ." or "you could have just done what I said."

The non-affected do not believe the OCS-driven explanation that it had to be done a certain way. They will argue the point. To those with OCS it's as if the other is saying, "It's your fault it took so long, stupid. You could have just done what was asked and been finished in thirty minutes. But no, Mr. Perfectionist . . . you had to scrub the tile three times on your hands and knees. Then you had to take a toothbrush to the grout along with all that other picky little stuff you did. It only serves you right that it took so long. Next time, *dummy*, do it the *easy* way."

Those with OCS cannot usually help others to understand without the assistance of a professional. Too often they don't understand it either. This causes an even further gap in communication within families and relationships. This of course only adds to the OCS-driven one's despair.

Distractibility and obsessive over-focus can also lead to the OCS being labeled as *lazy*. An excellent example of this can be found in the story at the beginning of this chapter called Charlie's Dilemma. It is actually a case history. The names were changed to protect confidentiality.

As you remember, Charlie has an opportunity to go to the state fair with his friend's family. All he has to do is clean his bedroom. It is an absolute disaster area. He eventually enters the room fully intending to clean it up before his dad returns from work. It has to be done that evening so that he will be allowed to go with his friend the next day.

In the process of picking clothes up, he uncovers a half-completed model. He hadn't seen or touched it for nearly a year. He starts thinking about the strong negative emotions linked to the unfinished model. All on a sudden he decides to complete the model. In his mind he believes that if he does this, his father will be proud. It might just make up for the fact that he had been so extremely disappointed when Charlie seemed to lose interest before. Completing that task, Charlie reckons, will show his father that he *can* get things done. It will prove to him once and for all that he can follow through to the end and finish things.

Charlie spends the next five or six hours working on that model behind a locked bedroom door. He skips dinner with his mother in order to get it done. He finally finishes just as his father gets home from work and knocks on his bedroom door.

As he unlocks the door, his parents enter the bedroom. Charlie's father immediately gets very angry but tries not to show it. He leaves the room mumbling that Charlie hadn't really wanted to go to the fair with his friend. If he had truly wanted to go he would have cleaned up his room. It wasn't until that moment that Charlie even remembered the fair. He'd forgotten that he *had* actually gone in there to clean up his room.

Charlie had become totally and completely sidetracked. He was focused on what he was doing in the moment. It was so intense that during the five hours of model building he didn't even think about the fair or cleaning his room. He couldn't help but wonder if what his father suggested might be true. Maybe he hadn't really wanted to go to the fair after all. He sure thought that he wanted to go.

Those OCS-affected who do not finish tasks because of this over-focus are often confused. They don't see what's happening, until it gets pointed out to them. This tendency to become overly absorbed in something else is not directed or intentional. They sometimes have no idea why they don't seem to be able to finish what they start. As a result, they may even reach a point where they don't even want to begin tasks. This is because they have a sense of impending doom hanging over them. It seems to be warning them that it's useless to try. It's a waste of time because they'll never finish anyway. That's why statements like, "that lazy bum never wants to do anything," and "even when he does start on something he *never* finishes," and "He's just a lazy good for nothing bum," ring so true. After all, what other reason could there possibly be for not finishing tasks than laziness? I must be lazy.

Self-doubt about their ability to do the task right can keep the OCS-affected from finishing. It may also keep them from starting. There is always the possibility that others will see the OCS performance as inadequate. Taking such a chance, however unlikely, can be extremely difficult. The welfare of their self-worth and esteem is at stake. If such a thing were to happen, it would be devastating. It would be like the end of the world. Sometimes it is considered better to *never* find out than to take a chance that it could happen.

It's often easier to avoid such a situation altogether. If one does not perform at all one cannot be found inadequate. Ignorance is bliss (though not really) seems to be the right cliché to apply. Ignorance may preserve the self-image of those with OCS, but it doesn't feel very good. Fearing that you might be a failure can be infinitely better than actually finding out that you *are* a failure. To find out is to know, and to know is to be certain.

Certainty versus uncertainty, which would you choose? Perhaps it's best to simply doubt or fear. Doubt and fear can be easier to deal with than certainty or reality. "*I don't care*" or "*I don't want to,*" along with "*I'm not interested in that*" are common defensive declarations. Such postures are used to keep others from figuring it out. They must never know the horrible, awful, much feared, and likely truth. After all, the dreadful truth just might be that the person *is* actually defective or inadequate. Or maybe the person's just lazy.

Depression can contribute at times to the OCS appearing to be unwilling to work. It can also make them seem indifferent or idle. It is common knowledge that people who are depressed often don't want to do anything. Depression is a very common consequence brought on by OCS. It is a reaction to the chronic obsessive and compulsive symptom presence. It makes sense that it too can often play a part in the observed apathy displayed by those with OCS.

Sometimes, a *fear of success* can be one of the underlying OCS-driven symptoms. The fear of success can give others the impression of laziness in an OCS-affected person. This person may excessively fear that if too successful they might be promoted. A promotion might mean they would be given even more to do. These individuals are often chronically uncertain. This can be especially true when facing the unknown. They don't need more to do. They don't want more to do. If they succeed, others will expect things from them. What if they can't deliver? Better to stay put. Better to just keep the status quo.

"Sure, they think I'm good," the affected one might think, "but I *know* better. I actually suck. I'm not really succeeding at all. They just think that I am. What if they find out?" The fear that someone might find out how incompetent they truly are, can keep them from advancing. It can cause them to appear a bit *lazy*. This is because others believe the person could do better if they only chose to do so.

This discussion of *laziness* and the OCS has explored many different and related pathways to the problem. There are many routes that lead to indolence, apathy, or lazy-like behavior. The root of the problem needs to be determined and treated properly. When this is done, the alleged idleness usually improves dramatically.

Exploring the underlying influence of obsessive and compulsive tendencies can be important. Determining how OCS affects behavior can be vital for everyone involved. It can be especially important for those with OCS, who have come to actually believe that they are indeed *lazy*. In the case of an OCS-driven person this is often a false assumption. The assumption arose over time because of a lack of awareness or knowledge about OCS symptoms. It makes sense that such a conclusion can occur due to the unenlightened state of the person. These people must be educated about the reasons for their behaviors. Then they must be provided with strategies for change. Unless correctly applied, true change does not occur. Either that or it is fleeting when it does.

11

Issues of Control or Not!

Is it Control . . . or Something Else?

The notion of control is another major issue for many of those who truly have OCS. The charge that the affected person is a "control freak" is an extremely poor substitute for what is really going on. As the familiar adage goes *"appearances can be deceiving."* It is important to understand exactly what *is* going on when issues of control seem to be a problem. To deal with this issue effectively, it must be recognized for what it really is. This is essential not just for those with OCS, but also for others who must live or work with them.

Let me try and shed some light on this situation. Normally, anxiety is a constant companion for the OCS population. There is also a sense of certain or impending doom that always seems to be lurking nearby. An entire host of *"needs"* can be experienced that simply *"must be* adhered to *or else."* When another interferes with a need or ignores the "rules" the OCS-driven will try to enforce these rules.

The person with OCS feels a need to make sure things are done right. The efforts to do so quite naturally *appear* to be controlling. The OCS-driven has a need to make sure everything turns out like it should. This is not an attempt to *control* the situation or the others involved. It is an attempt to insure things are done right. If someone else isn't doing it right, the OCS person will try to help them do it right. Things *have* to be done right. If everything isn't exactly the way they need it to be, something horrible will happen. It will be an inconceivable disaster.

There is no argument that in trying to achieve this goal, the OCS do indeed appear to be controlling, but they are not. This is why those with OCS stubbornly deny such a claim when confronted. For them the issue is not one of control at all. For the OCS-affected it is one of doing and getting things *right*. Are these individuals manipulative? You bet. The reason, though, is not what others often perceive it to be. It is easy to believe the OCS are controlling. It is much harder to believe the truth.

When things don't go exactly as planned, no real disaster occurs. Although this is usually true, it doesn't matter. In the mind of the OCS, getting it right feels like a life-or-death situation. This can create a frenzy of activity. It can also result in intense emotional outbursts. Anyone on or near the path of the OCS person is likely to get *blasted.*

A great deal of the anger displayed by the OCS can be misdirected. This is brought on by the mounting frustration, anxiety, and fear felt over the course of the day, month, or year. Emotions build up day after day from minor things that didn't turn out the way they were supposed to. This is not due to the desire to have *control*. There is an internal standard that is felt must be met sometimes at all costs. The problem is that this standard is hardly, if ever, met.

When discussing human behavior it is often the intent that is most important. Those who are OCS-driven are locked into their intentions, which have nothing to do with controlling anyone. The pattern is like that of a circle. Around and around they go. They cling to these intentions doggedly. They can no more let them go than they can stop breathing. At least that's how it feels to them until they learn how to manage.

Because there is no real intention to control others they simply cannot see their actions in the same way that others do. They don't know that they are exhibiting controlling-like behavior. When it is pointed out they can't believe it. Denial is inevitable. Remember, these people are obsessive. How can they admit to being controlling when they honestly do not think that they are? That's just it—they can't and won't.

Consider the following conversation. This illustrates how easy it can be to view someone as controlling, when in fact they are not. The underlying driving force in this case is none other than OCS in disguise.

*   *   *

"How can you say that?" Jeff whirled on his heel and confronted his wife.

Brenda was leaning back against the counter. Her arms were crossed: "Because it's true."

"TRUE?" Jeff shouted. "True? Nothing could be farther from the truth."

Brenda stood firm. "Face it, Jeff. You *are* a control freak. You have to control everyone and everything around you."

"I DO NOT!" The muscles in his neck grew tight. His face began to redden. Finally he threw his arms into the air. "When?" Jeff shouted, "When? Give me one example of when I've tried to control everyone and everything."

"How about this morning?"

"What about this morning?"

"You made me redo your eggs. They went fifteen seconds past the timer. *You* had to cook two new ones. You wouldn't even try the eggs that were already cooked."

"They were overcooked!" He threw up his hands again. "You don't expect me to eat something that's overcooked, *do* you?"

"Fifteen seconds," she repeated.

"Fifteen seconds is fifteen seconds," his come back was fast.

"You see," Brenda affirmed, "it *is* control."

"That's not control," Jeff was nearly shouting now. "It's basic common sense. Three-and-a-half minute eggs aren't three-and-a-half minute eggs if they're cooked for three minutes and forty-five seconds, now, are they?"

"I'll bet," she said, "if you hadn't heard the timer you couldn't tell the difference between a three minutes and thirty seconds egg and a three minutes forty-five seconds egg."

"I'd know!"

"Yeah, right!"

"Could it be," Jeff began sarcastically, "that you're just mad that you made a mistake? Are you sure you're not just trying to blame it on me and make it a *control* issue? Maybe, it's really a simple mistake that *you* just can't own up to."

Brenda was nearly in tears. "Call it what you will but I know *control* when I see it." She took a deep breath. "I'm surprised you didn't say something about your fork being on the wrong side of the plate. What about your napkin being folded incorrectly?"

Jeff twisted his head around. He wanted to look her in the eyes. "I was going there next," he informed her matter-of-factly.

"Ohhh . . ." Brenda brought her hands up to her face and ran from the kitchen.

"Hey, where ya goin'?" Jeff called after her. "The eggs aren't done yet."

*   *   *

Was it really control? There certainly was no doubt in Brenda's mind that it was. She felt like she couldn't do *anything* without having to revise or correct it. It had to be the way that Jeff wanted it done. As far as she was concerned, *he* was trying to control her every move. She even confided once that she was sure her husband would try to control her breathing if it were possible. The little laugh she released after saying this was a bit forced and rather sad. It wasn't really funny. It was just too real for her.

Other counselors had told Jeff that he would have to let go of his control issues. If his marriage was going to survive, he needed to quit trying to be so controlling. They might as well have been speaking to him in an alien tongue. He had no clue what they were talking about. To him they all seemed to take sides with his wife. They believed her every word she said about him.

No counselor had *ever* listened to him. Not even one believed him when he said he wasn't trying to control anyone or anything. The consensus of his former counselors and his wife was that Jeff was in denial. And it was *big time* denial. For that reason, progress could not be made therapeutically in their marriage. According yo them until he recognized the denial and began to let go of and work through his issues of *control*, nothing could be done for the marriage. This, however, was something he simply could not do, because there *were* no issues of control. Consider the following allegory.

Human beings in general are able to choose many of their actions. Because of this there is a natural tendency to believe that all actions are chosen. This, however, is simply not true.

A blind man stands before a table. On the table there are two sandwiches. Each rests on a paper plate. They are side by side. Written boldly on one paper plate for all eyes to see is the word *"poisoned."* On the other plate are the words *"safe to eat."* The blind man is then told to make his choice. He is supposed to choose and eat one of the available sandwiches. He is informed ahead of time about the message written on each plate. If then the blind man picks the poisoned sandwich, can it be argued that he chose to die? Would he have been responsible for his own death?

This example may sound far-fetched or ridiculous. However, it is really not so very far from what actually happens to many people every day. At least, it happens symbolically. There are a lot of people every day who, for one reason or other, make choices that are harmful. These may be hurtful to themselves or to someone else. The reasons for such choices are also not readily obvious to observers.

Furthermore, these people are then held responsible for their actions. This is done even though there was no awareness of the possibility of either harm or real intent involved. Often they are treated as if the intention was present. But also as if they knew exactly what they were doing as well.

A lot of times those who place such blame have a very real need to see the actions of others as purposeful. Doing so enables them to justify their own responses that are meant to teach these perpetrators a lesson. Those with such a mind-set tend to feel that if certain behaviors are not paid for, justice is thwarted. And when justice is blocked, a change in behavior will not, and cannot, occur. This is also not necessarily true.

Let's do a re-enactment once again of the blind man choosing a sandwich. Just one small change may provide further insight and understanding regarding the point being made. This time there will be an observer present. This onlooker is in an adjacent room behind a two-way mirror. The observer can clearly see the sandwiches. She is informed about the messages clearly inscribed on the paper plates.

There are no outward visible signs of the subject's inability to see. The eyewitness is not told that the man choosing is blind. The man's behavior in making his choice does not in any way suggest blindness. This fact, therefore, remains unknown to the uninformed participant.

The observer can clearly see the man appearing to gaze intently at the available choices. The subject's fingertips are already touching each of the plates. Because of this, the choice he makes is smooth and sure. The consequence is witnessed. The observer is questioned afterwards. She is a bit hesitant in assigning responsibility. She is allowed, however, to ask questions.

First, the observer asks if the man making the choice was mentally ill or intellectually impaired.

He was not.

Second, she asks whether or not the man could read.

The answer to this question is a resounding *yes*, although no mention is made that he was only able to read Braille.

Was he learning disabled?

No.

The observer fails to ask whether or not the man is blind.

This is because it seemed to her that the man could see. She was not informed otherwise. Since it had looked like the man *could* see, she never thought to question this assumption. The observer felt compelled to conclude that the man *was* responsible for his own death.

What if the individual facing such a choice *is* sighted? What if he has perfect 20/20 visual acuity but is severely depressed? Depression is not always obvious. At times it can remain hidden during brief or even extended observation periods. Such a person may see the poisoned sandwich as a way out of his or her misery. The only way out. Depressed people frequently do not think very clearly.

This is widely known.

*   *   *

Let's go back to Jeff and Brenda and the three-minute egg. In his own words, Jeff put it like this:

I never wanted to control anybody. Not ever! I honestly don't understand why people are always accusing me of this. In that famous *egg* example Brenda is always bringing up, I wasn't trying to *control her*. All I wanted was for my egg to be cooked for three-and-a-half minutes, no more, no less. Hey, I don't even mind cooking it myself. Not really. But Brenda is always trying to be the *best* wife. She tells me over and over again that she wants to cook for me. If she doesn't cook she feels like she's not being a good wife or something. It's like she feels she's not holding up her part of the marriage.

I'm not trying to control her into making my egg a certain way. Eggs *need* to be a certain way or they aren't *right*! Just like oatmeal needs just the right amount of water. Just like cutting the grass. It needs to be one and one-half inches tall and mowed evenly. *Evenly.* Then there's the trimming. I just don't get it! Nobody in our family does things the right way but me. So I have to do everything. Everything! Nothing ever gets done right, so I have to do it all. It's wearing me out. I can't do it any more. I just can't.

There was something that other counselors in Jeff's past appear to have missed. It was the fact that he wasn't in denial at all. In his mind the problem was not one of him trying to control others. To him the problem was that he ended up always trying desperately to make everything *right*. If things weren't done the way he *knew* they were supposed to be done, then the world was not right. Jeff couldn't stand it when the world wasn't right. And since it was hardly ever right, he was frantic and miserable most of the time. His *control* issues were born of his inner need to get things right or correct. He was not interested in actually controlling anyone or anything.

The discovery of what was truly at the heart of Jeff's issues was extremely important in his therapy. Real lasting progress had not been made over the course of several years and several different therapists. As soon as the focus was on the OCS symptom of needing things to be *right,* progress took a huge leap forward.

Awareness and knowledge combined with couple's therapy relating to the common OCS dynamics was begun. Appropriate medication also helped Jeff to see that a problem did exist. This marked the beginning of Jeff and Brenda's real journey on the road to psychological and emotional health. It was not a problem control. Jeff, for one, was very relieved to know that.

When OCS is present and the person is believed to have issues of control, it is nearly always related to their need for rightness in the world. Although it may look, smell, feel, and sound like a control issue, for these people it is not. Progress will be hard to come by unless this is discovered and worked through.

No one in his or her right mind could argue that it doesn't seem like control is the issue. It does indeed feel like a control problem. A shift in thinking must be made. The focus needs to be the often hidden issue of the obsessive-compulsive *need* to make things right in the world. When this happens true growth and change can, and often does, occur.

12

Manipulation, or Not?

As surely as we all breathe, every one of us has manipulated or at least tried to manipulate others. Usually the reason is to avoid punishment, distress, or to simply get something that we want or think we need. This is when our behavior is directed solely at getting personal needs met. There is no awareness or concern for how what we are doing might affect others. We tend to call those who do this a lot, *manipulators*. It is generally seen as a negative label. To be so branded can have quite a negative impact on a person's life over time. The negative influence can be subtle and pervasive. People tend to dislike those who are known manipulators. Some even steadfastly declare that they *hate* those who manipulate others for their own personal gain. The word manipulate has taken on an offensive meaning. It's now a *bad* thing. In the original English use of the word, this negative interpretation was only one of many. Just say the word in this day and age and instant emotional responses from others are likely to occur. If you take a poll you will see that most, if not all, of these responses will be negative.

Webster first defined the word manipulate as *to handle or use, especially with skill*. Another definition was added as time went by. It was *to manage or control artfully or by shrewd use of influence, often in an unfair or fraudulent way*. Yet another meaning developed which is *to change or falsify for one's own purposes or profit*.

The word *manipulation* is defined as *skillful handling or operation*. It is also regarded as *artful management or control*. Later on this came to be used to describe relationships and people. Most of us do not like the idea of being controlled by another. To be *artfully* managed or controlled, however, is even worse.

When one person manipulates another, the manipulated person is often thought of as a victim. Once it is made clear that you were manipulated, you may become upset. You may even get *very* angry. To be the kind of person that others can manipulate has serious implications. It must mean that you are not very bright. Others might even think you're *stupid*.

The manipulator is viewed as the *bad guy (or girl)*. It is they who are taking advantage of you. It's probably because you are less fortunate in some obvious way. Just the idea of the one being manipulated as somehow being *less fortunate* has a negative connotation. The manipulator is seen as trying to *control* everybody and everything for purely selfish reasons. This is also something most of us do not like to happen. The idea of *control* is discussed in detail in another article titled "Control or not?" This essay can be found in my book *Making Sense of the Senseless*, 2002.

You may be wondering what all this talk about manipulation has to do with those who have OCS. The connection is actually quite strong. It also tends to be rather indirect. The real problem with manipulation in its negative sense seems to be related to intent. Why is the person being manipulative? As stated before, when we think that someone is being a selfish manipulator with no concern for others, our emotions can intensify. We may have bad feelings, anger, frustration, and depression. The manipulator is condemned the moment his or her actions are discovered. So also is the person who was manipulated. The one is censured for having acted to control another. The other is scorned for allowing themselves to be acted upon or controlled. As if anybody *ever* actually starts out by letting another manipulate them.

People with OCS or other lifelong conditions often turn out to be the masters of manipulation. They *have* to. A large part of the reason for this is because these people are constantly driven by a host of believed needs. As a result, they *must* manipulate others to even come close to getting those needs met.

Sometimes a need can be so odd or strange that others can hardly believe it. It's impossible for them to believe that anyone would manipulate another to meet such a need. They can't imagine it. It's too ridiculous. At other times, the need may be such a common one that no one even thinks twice about the reason because of what they already believe. They just assume it's the same. This easy-to-believe reason, though, can be totally off target.

There will be those who will insist they are absolutely sure why a manipulative behavior has occurred. Often they are so certain of their conviction that they simply cannot imagine any other cause. Most are blinded by what they already believe they know. This is where the real trouble starts for those with chronic conditions, like the OCS-affected.

Within cultures, a common belief system about regularly observed behaviors does develop over time. It is often quite rigid and unyielding. Once an entire culture believes something, it is very hard to get any of them to so much as consider other options. They tend to believe what they believe and there are no other possible explanations or reasons they are willing to accept.

Sometimes a *need* is very strong and the driven person does not have the means or a way to get the specific need met. In that case they may fight that inner drive or desire as long and as hard as they possibly can. Eventually though, they can reach a point where they simply cannot withstand the anguish and inner turmoil that such a delay causes. They *must* satisfy that urge or need. To do so they may stoop to lying, cheating, stealing, and any other means they can think of to *manipulate* others to get the need met. They must find a way to quell the growing anxiety, fear, and sometimes panic that threatens to overwhelm them. If that *need* does not somehow get taken care of, they become more and more frantic.

If still unable to ease the constant urge, behavioral breakdown is usually the next thing that happens. These behaviors like tantrums, screaming, crying, withdrawal, stubbornness, fear, anxiety, and panic, to name just a few, are often misread. Others declare them to be proof of yet further manipulation. For the truly OCS-affected this tends not to be true. They are reacting to a symptom. When behavior reaches this level of intensity it is a reaction, not a manipulation. These people are only reacting to the internal distress, worry, anxiety, and panic they feel at the moment. The reaction is caused by their not having obtained their goal or need. It is extreme because of the great sensitivity brought on biochemically from within.

Every one of us at one time or another has used manipulation as a tool to try and get what we want. That, or in an effort to get someone else to do something we believe may be good for him or her. We have often put it to use as well to avoid a feared or deserved punishment. Once it is pointed out that what we are doing is manipulative, we were able to back off and let it go.

The OCS-driven is frequently unable to do this. This can be true for those with other disabilities as well. They just can't seem to let it go. If one manipulative tactic fails, another is attempted in its place. The more manipulations tried and failed, the more intense things generally become. Sometimes when the OCS drive is strong, a manipulation can seem pathetically weak or silly. Emotional deterioration causes this as needs are not met.

Intensity levels play a large part in how others interpret the actions of the OCS-affected. The OCS person's reactions are clearly beyond what is generally regarded as the norm. As a result, others are much more likely to view the behaviors as manipulative and in a negative light. Also, these behaviors tend to go right on with no regard to another's response. As might be expected, others become more and more tense and irritable as the behavior continues. The OCS-driven seems to ignore the emotional impact their pushiness has. So those getting pushed tend to feel that this recurring behavior is a ploy or a manipulation.

There is an interesting difference between the related words "perseverance" and "perseverative." Obviously the root is the same. *Perseverance* is usually thought of as a positive trait worth having. It's the stick-to-it, never give up, never surrender attitude that we have come to admire. It is someone who is determined to do something. They persist even though odds may be against them.

The word *perseverative* is used to describe what is considered a very negative behavior. This is the person who is beyond determination. This person seems unable to stop. They are viewed as out of control. Often, their behavior is seen as annoying.

On the one hand, history is filled with those who because of their persistence or perseverance were able to do many great things. They are said to have persevered and succeeded as a result. Almost assuredly these were OCS-driven people. Their own generation surely thought their behavior was annoying at the time. It was also probably perseverative. That's the main reason they contributed wondrous things to society and the world. They were obsessive and compulsive about things. They felt driven to do the things they did.

People who are so driven are annoying to others. It's almost a given. They will let nothing get in their way, including other people. These persons such as Thomas Edison, Albert Einstein, and the like are viewed sometimes as great optimists. They had a never-say-die kind of attitude. Eventually this allowed them to achieve success. This was true even though others observing them at younger ages often felt they would not succeed.

I believe these types of individuals were OCS-driven. As a result they displayed many of these negative and manipulative problem behaviors.

They were beset by them throughout the course of their lives. Once they made it big by discovering, writing, or inventing something that others valued, things changed. Those *problem* behaviors were suddenly seen in more of a positive light and direction. *Perseveration* became *perseverance. Enduring to the end* took the place of *perseverative,* and so on.

Einstein had a tendency to forget anything and everything that wasn't important to his own interests. This included dates, times, and facts. It was one of the main reasons he ended up being referred to as the bumbling genius or the *absent-minded professor.* He was, however, a very difficult child, at least in the schools. He was a difficult young adult as well, described in *Einstein the Life and Times* by Ronald W. Clark.

There was a time when Einstein was expelled from what roughly equates to high school in the United States. He was cast out on the grounds that his presence in class was disruptive and negatively affected the other students. He was further described as a precocious, half cock sure and insolent youth, which lasted into early adulthood. Einstein was also said by one of his teachers (Minkowski) to be a "lazy dog who never bothered about mathematics at all." This was said of the man who gave us E=MC² and the Theory of Relativity.

I can actually imagine Mr. Einstein when he might have been better known perhaps as *little Albert.* That or maybe when he became an older youth as *the big Al.* Just as likely though, I can also imagine him pictured by others as a self-centered, impudent brat. Perhaps he would have been called the *space cadet* who thinks he knows everything. I can see it now.

"Hey, Al!" calls out one of his co-workers at the Suisse patent office. "Why don't you hop a light wave into the future? Maybe they'll like you better when you get there. Oh, and you'd better make sure you go far enough. You know, because when you get there, if we're alive and old while you're still young, nothing will have changed."

It seems likely to me that as Mr. Einstein got older he may have become better able to ignore comments and jibes from others. He did what he had to do to get his ideas across to the rest of the world. He did this because he was absolutely convinced he was right. If that meant behaving in ways that might be misperceived by others, then he behaved in those ways. All things centered on him, or so others thought. This in itself may have been his most misunderstood manipulation. Others report that if something didn't relate to what he was thinking about or trying to do, it didn't matter to him at all.

This perception may not have been entirely true. Had someone taken the time to actually ask Mr. Einstein if something was important at a moment when he was not actively engaged in another task, he might have actually agreed. When busy in thought or the pursuit of his ideas, however, Einstein's behavior would have made him look like a liar. Perhaps some of those accusing Mr. Einstein of neglect in some areas did ask him if those things neglected should be considered important. Maybe he told them, "Yes, of course, such things are important."

Perhaps because of the OCS driving him, he was unable most of the time to show by his actions what he believed to be true. Actions are supposed to speak louder than words; so it is said. If such a thing did indeed happen, surely, most wouldn't have believed him. They would have reasoned that he had been lying outright. They also might have thought he was trying to somehow justify his neglectful behavior.

Many would be unable to see how Mr. Einstein could agree or say that a thing was important, and then act as if it was not. Those who have interfering OCS usually can and do understand. As an obsessive thought or compulsive need plays itself out in the mind, nothing else at all matters. Attention becomes riveted on that thought or need. From the time that a symptom begins *driving the bus* (if you will), until something else of more intensity interferes or the strength of the symptom naturally starts to ease up and go away, the bus drives on. There tends to be no ability to accept that any other idea or thing could possibly be as important. The focused OCS-driven mind is unable to attend to or care about anything else at a particular driven moment. This can explain the apparent dishonest nature those with OCS seem to show when they say one thing and then do another.

Is it true that those with OCS are more manipulative than others without such a driven interference? The answer to this question must be an unequivocal *yes*! These people have so many worries and concerns, how could it not be so? They also have so many things that they want or *need* to accomplish, create, make, or fix that are constantly interfered with. This interference comes from both the environment and the wishes and wants of others.

Another important interfering feature can be the lack of time to complete these needs and/or goals. So the manipulation of others can become a way of life. If my legs don't work or I feel pain every time I move, it is easier for me to simply ask another to bring me a glass of water than it is to go and get it for myself. If the OCS-driven is forced to interrupt something they're doing because of thirst, they may act like the person in pain. To get it themselves or even to respond to another's request is an issue of momentous effort. The OCS-driven cannot change tasks easily. Remember, all humans manipulate to some degree during the course of their lifetimes. This is to be expected and, unless taken to extremes, is a normal part of living.

The intent of manipulations when OCS symptoms are behind them tends to be an unknown. Often the attempted manipulation when OCS is the driving force may not make any sense at all. One such seemingly senseless manipulative act is paradoxical. The paradox is that it's not hard for those with OCS to let others think whatever they want about the reasons for a behavior. Often what they believe may not be true, but at least it's not usually too weird. The real cause behind a behavior may be too difficult to explain. It also may be so unbelievable that it's better to let the easy believe cause stand. A lot of energy and time can be wasted in useless attempts to explain, argue, or defend the true reason.

Some things are too hard to accept as true when they appear senseless or beyond belief. The only trouble with this is that when you try to change behavior based on methods designed for a different cause, it doesn't work. When something doesn't work, professionals assume that the method must not have been applied correctly. When OCS exists, the failure to change a behavior can also be due to something else entirely. Chemically-driven behavior responds to very few, if any, externally derived techniques. Methods must be derived to treat the OCS, for true progress to occur.

Is it manipulation or is it choice, *that* is the question. Sometimes, managing behavior is best done by not managing it. Let me explain. This method is called choosing one's battlegrounds. It is almost a sure thing that those affected by OCS will become more manipulative than those who do not. It is very important for others working with or around them to pay attention to this. If I have a constant feeling that there is so much to do that I will never find the time to do it all, I am going to tend to want others to do things for me. I might also feel this way if I had very strong doubts about being able to do anything good enough. If someone else does it for me, I don't have to feel bad about how poorly I did it. Since such a feeling is not something others can see, they would believe my actions were all choices consciously made. They would be angry and feel that I was taking advantage of them. They also might think I was just being lazy. A child in such a situation may appear to observers as whiney and manipulative.

Knowing when and where to draw-the-line in such circumstances is not an easy thing to determine. Consider the following:

A three-and-a-half-year-old was brought into my office by her parents. She was screaming and thrashing wildly. It was the first session. She had been happily playing with blocks in the lobby. When it was time to come in, she did not want to stop that activity. This started her going just a bit. She was clearly unhappy and became a little defiant. Her parents also began to insist that she put on her discarded socks and shoes. This put her over the top and she went ballistic. They never did get those shoes back on her feet. The tantrum she threw was so disruptive that they simply scooped her up and carried her into my office barefooted.

"She takes them off whenever she can," the little girl's mother informed me. "She hates them."

It took the little girl twenty minutes to recover from that outburst and calm down. As you might imagine, those first twenty minutes were rather difficult. It was hard to hear what anyone was saying as she carried on. The parents shared that such behavior occurred "all the time." Most of the time it was over silly things like putting on her shoes or picking up a toy she'd been playing with. Wasn't this manipulation on her part, they wanted to know. There are a great many that would jump on the bandwagon and shout out "YES." Not only that, but many would also point out how well-trained those parents were. Surely that child had them both wrapped around her little finger.

It turned out that this behavior was not manipulation in the purest sense of the word. It was true the child's actions seemed to focus on getting her own way. When OCS is driving the bus, though, there are other interpretations. Rather than just a manipulation, the little girl's behavior was more like a reaction. The response *was* way more intense than might be expected. I mean, what's the big deal about putting on your shoes anyway? What's more, it did not stop after she got her way either. It lasted another eighteen minutes more than was necessary. She was carried into my office without those dreaded shoes on her feet. This was not just a calculated goal-oriented action. Too often though, actions are interpreted as having been exactly that.

At the conclusion of the session the little girl was playing intently with some toys on the carpet. The moment she realized she was going to have to pick up and leave, she started to react. A subtle re-direction helped her to start picking up without incident. As soon as the toys were put away, her mother mentioned the need to put on her shoes. There was an instantaneous change in her demeanor. I quickly waved both parents off and got her attending to something else. Their daughter calmed right away.

"How important is getting those shoes on her feet right now, really?" I asked.

Her parents regarded me blandly. I added, "Does it matter? Will you even remember next week whether or not on this particular day she wore shoes?"

Both mother and father sort of shook their heads. They seemed to be saying that they might not remember. A quick glance at each other suggested that maybe it didn't really matter.

"Why trigger such a reaction?" I gently counseled them. "Why start a war when you already know what it will cost in time, energy, and frustration?"

These parents stared at me as if I were suggesting something utterly shameful. It seemed like they were surely thinking such things as: "Can you do that?" "If we do that doesn't it mean we're *giving in?*" "We can't allow her to get away with not obeying us on the little things." "Won't that teach her to disregard us on the bigger things later on?" and so on. Such nagging concerns and questions haunt our every move as parents. These doubts can undermine the natural parenting skills in us all. It can lead to anxiety that weakens our ability to take direction and apply it. The ideas and plans suggested by professionals and the like can be rendered useless.

When walking across the Arizona desert it is probably more than just a good idea to wear both socks and shoes. It is similar if going for a walk in the winter after a snowstorm. In the snow one might find it quite useful to be wearing adequate socks and shoes or boots. Going from a reception area to the office itself or from that office to a car is not nearly as critical. Also, going from a car to a house pales incredibly in contrast to a walk in the hot desert or a snow-filled landscape. Having socks and shoes matters greatly in the freezing snow or the cacti-filled desert. One can easily imagine what might happen to someone who is barefoot under such conditions.

The emotional distress brought on in some situations is worth whatever it may take to stand firm. To confront and withstand the disturbing onslaught is the right thing to do, when to have done otherwise could cause serious consequences. When there are no serious costs to giving in to an OCS demand, the emotional distress that comes from not giving in may not be worth going through.

It is not manipulation if the supposed manipulated one freely chooses their response. Even those who consciously manipulate others are not getting away with anything if the one responding to them does so by choice. If I am aware that you are trying to manipulate me, but I choose to go with it of my own free will, no manipulation is taking place.

Remember the example of the little girl who went nuts every time her parents tried to put socks and shoes on her feet? If I choose to allow her to go barefoot, I am not being manipulated. It doesn't matter that the reason is to avoid a fifteen to twenty minute hysterical reaction. I am making an intelligent decision for myself and often for the rest of the family. The little girl's reaction is not intentional. Something is interfering with her ability to respond normally to such an event. Managing this may mean letting her go barefoot. Sometimes it is okay, although in some specific circumstances even this would not be allowed. Shoes and socks were not the only things to which this little girl reacted hysterically. Hopefully, that isn't a surprise.

Chronic illness or a factor such as OCS can interfere with development of skills at all ages. Let's consider another example.

Years ago, as a school psychologist, I worked with a young boy who was in the third grade. He actually should have been in the second grade, but he was intellectually gifted. He was also rather big for his age. To best meet his educational needs, he had been promoted to third. This was so he could attend the gifted program of the school district. Normally it was not offered until a child had reached the third grade. The boy also had cerebral palsy which was not readily obvious. Still it did interfere with coordination, both at the fine and gross motor levels. He was, in addition, a very sensitive child.

As a result of these things and a strong need to do well in school, the boy began to have some academic/emotional problems. In the third grade penmanship is taught using cursive writing. When spelling tests were taken the teacher would require all students to write each word in cursive as they were dictated. The boy's writing was so painfully slow that he simply could not write the words quickly enough to keep up. He would fall behind on the first word and begin to get frustrated often to the point of tears. The times during which he was expected to write in cursive were causing him great distress emotionally. He began doubting himself and hating the third grade. He felt like a failure, even though he was an otherwise brilliant and capable boy.

I met with this young man's mother to try and figure out what to do. I soon found that at home the boy did all his writing on the computer.

He had been successfully keyboarding for years. Moving his fingers on the keyboard was not as difficult as holding a pen or pencil. The pressure needed, as well as the sequencing of fine motor skills and muscles in cursive writing, made it a slow and arduous task. I thought we should have a meeting to suggest that this boy use a laptop computer. He already had one he could bring to school whenever writing tasks were assigned. His mother also thought this was a good idea, and a meeting was scheduled.

At this meeting was the school psychologist (me), the school counselor, his third grade teacher, his teacher for the gifted, the boy's mother, and the principal. I presented the case and the solution that the boy's mother and I thought would perhaps solve the problem. There is a general feeling among grade school teachers that *every* child *must* learn and be able to do some basic things. Such is the feeling about cursive writing. This was the general feeling of the educators at the meeting too. This is true in spite of what happens once you begin searching for employment. Every job application will have printed at the top of the first page in big bold letters *PLEASE PRINT OR TYPE ALL RESPONSES.* Applications written in cursive are returned or just thrown away.

The principal addressed us by agreeing that the problem was worthy of solving. He was unsure, though, of the approach recommended. His concern was that eventually everyone has to learn to write. He thought that the suggestion on the table might further handicap the boy. How would he manage in a world where everyone else could write? He also added that, "After all, he can't take a laptop everywhere he goes."

My hand shot up and the principal called on me, "Why not?" I questioned. "I know some people who take a wheel chair everywhere they go."

That statement was followed by a few moments of rather intense and reflective silence. The principal was open-minded and a good man. He took a deep breath and said, "Okay, write it up as a 504 plan and let's do it."

The boy blossomed under the plan and the tears and frustration were seen no more. There was only one problem he had after the plan started. Every once in a while a kid might come by and bump something on his laptop and erase all his unsaved data. This, however, he could handle, since it was actually a rare occurrence. I am also pleased to report that this simple solution was continued on through junior high and high school. The young man flourished.

If we had not made accommodations and modifications for the boy, I can share from experience what might have happened. First the boy might have started to complain about school. He might say teachers were "mean" and not understanding. Classmates might be accused of making fun of him for crying. They actually might do this as well. Then he might start to develop stomachaches. These would be worse just before the scheduled spelling test. He would start asking to go see the nurse.

It probably wouldn't take long for educators to start to believe that the boy was manipulating them. He was claiming to be ill in order to get out of taking a spelling test. This might lead to his becoming ill at home rather than at school. This would cause him to miss the entire day of a test rather than just the class. Is this manipulative behavior? You bet it is. It is also emotional survival to the boy. And from here it would only get worse.

There was a very bright young lady who had, as one of her major OCS symptoms, the need to get very good grades in school. She also had some very strong social needs and ADHD symptoms that could interfere with her performance in school. She would start a semester in high school doing very well and then midway become overwhelmed by all the demands. She would then get behind, start doing poorly, and eventually withdraw from school. She did this four times in high school at four different schools.

Finally she decided to just take the GED, which she passed easily, and go on to college. Unfortunately she continued to have similar problems at the college level. Eventually this bright young lady dropped out. She was so intent on getting good grades that each time she realized it wasn't going to happen, she ran. Rather than buckle down and face the music she manipulated the system by withdrawing. She cut her losses and received no grades whatsoever. It was better to do that she would reason than to have even one grade below an A. She then enrolled at another school only to end up doing the same thing. She would have done anything rather than get a less-than-perfect grade. The manipulations that the OCS-affected employ are often not in their own best interests.

We all manipulate others and environments at times in the attempt to meet ours or another's needs. It's only when the use of manipulative tactics is frequent that it becomes worthy of attention. Those of us who are chronically ill or have an interfering condition tend to be more manipulative than those who don't. Here are a few general principals worth thinking about when faced with someone who is overly manipulative.

1. Find out the real reason for their manipulative behavior. Knowing this can help you to perhaps meet their needs before they resort to manipulation. Understanding leads to less frustration and less

anger relative to the behavior. Many weeds have long deep roots. If the entire root is not pulled completely out of the ground it will result in a return of the weed. Getting to the heart of the matter can be an important key. Solving the problem there can reduce future frustration and anguish. Manipulations often become less frequent as a result.

2. In the case of demands made, decide if the goal could be harmful to the person or someone else. Try and determine if the demand is to be allowed. If serious consequences are likely to occur, stand firm. Do not bend to the manipulative behavior. If the goal is inconsequential, let it be achieved. Doing this will defuse the manipulative intent. It will then become a legitimate choice rather than a reaction to manipulation.

3. When a person is being manipulative in an effort to avoid doing a requested task or chore consider the following.

A. Is the person capable of performing the task?

B. How important is it that the task be completed? In a week or a month will it really matter whether or not the task was completed? Will it be remembered?

C. Could the task be completed at a different time or day equally well?

D. Is my need to be obeyed or in control interfering with my judgment of the task's importance?

E. Is my impression of the task's importance distorted in any other way?

F. What will it really mean in the life of the individual or in my own if the task is not completed?

G. What will be the impact of standing firm in the request? What will happen if I take steps to insure that the task is completed as wanted? Is it worth it?

H. Would modifying the request result in a more positive final outcome? Would paying attention to the person's strengths and weaknesses help?

I. Would withdrawing the request for the moment be wise? Such an action could help both involved to save face and avoid an emotional battle that no one can ever win.

PART III

Treatment of OCS

13

The Nearsighted Archer

"I don't want a pill controlling my life," the young lady said to me. I was trying to explain the potential benefits of a medication for her OCS symptoms.

"If God had wanted me to be different . . ." she started in that well-worn argument that never really explains anything. It occurred to me that although her point didn't really explain much, it certainly did show the depth of this young lady's convictions, or fear.

This got me to thinking. Just what does it mean to need what are known as psychotropic medications? The term psychotropic is defined as "mind and mood altering." It is also defined as "affecting behavior" and as "having an effect on the mental state of the user."

Webster defines the term psycho itself as: "*A victim of a severe mental or emotional disorder.*" Is it any wonder that when medications carry the prefix "psycho" most of us are not that thrilled to take it? The general public tends to shy away from medicines that have a primary effect on the mind.

Several years ago, I had a casual conversation with a trusted friend and long time colleague. We were chatting about the difficulties people had in not wanting to take antidepressants. He shared an example that he regularly used to try and get around this. In cases of ADHD or depression, this physician would compare the need for medication to insulin-dependent diabetes. Somehow this analogy did not ring true in my heart. During our conversation, his explanation kept bouncing around in my mind. I kept searching for that all-important connection. It did not happen. For some reason, this comparison seemed weaker than logic dictated it ought to have been.

As I gave voice to these thoughts it occurred to me why his response didn't seem to work. The reason his analogy wasn't that helpful was due to a major difference between them. It was in the nature and treatment of those other disorders versus that of diabetes.

All may be treated with medication. When left untreated, all significantly influence behavior. The insulin-dependent individual, however, if left untreated will soon die. The death would be as a direct result of the insulin-related problem. The OCS or depressed person is not going to die if the disorder is not treated with medication. It is true that their behaviors can sometimes lead to possible injury. They might even lead to death. However, these dreaded consequences are not directly caused by the biochemical lack. Individuals don't die from a lack of impulse control. Still, the moving car that their impulsive behavior influenced them to run out in front of *can* injure them. It could also be the cause for their early demise.

The OCS-affected will not die if they do not take medication. If they do take it, though, their quality of life may drastically improve. My colleague's use of this inexact analogy led me to search for a new parallel that might make more sense. Here is the analogy that I came up with for similar situations.

The Nearsighted Archer

A nearsighted archer makes use of corrective lenses to sidestep the problem of a defect in her sight. Now that she can see clearly, she can compete on equal grounds with those whose vision is not flawed.

If we follow the logic shared by the young lady at the beginning of the chapter, there's a problem. One might easily conclude that providing corrective lenses to this nearsighted archer is the same as "cheating."

I can imagine the argument even now.

"If God had wanted that archer to see clearly . . . he would have . . ."

It sounds quite silly in this setting, does it not? And yet the use of contacts to correct her sight is not that different from taking medication for something such as ADHD or depression or OCS. The "pill" in this case represents the corrective lens. The biochemical lack represents the flaw in eyesight.

"Wait a minute!" I can picture the young lady's next argument. "Glasses don't change the personality. They don't make her into somebody she's not! They don't make her into somebody different!"

"Ah, but they do indeed," would be my reply.

Of course, just how much of a change occurs depends on how severe the flaw actually is. Contact lenses allow those whose eyesight is poor to appear as if they do not have such a defect. Others are no longer able to clearly see their flaw as they can when glasses are worn. There is great psychological power in being able to hide imperfections. For those who see themselves as "less than whole" or defective, this can be a boost to their self-esteem.

The nearsighted archer with contact lenses in place can achieve a much higher score in the archery tournament. She will also be able to read signs more easily as well as recognize friends and acquaintances from a distance. She may begin to smile more often and more readily. A spring may return to her step. Or, in the case of someone who never did see well in the first place, a spring may arise for perhaps the first time. Stepping with a spring is a reflection of an inner confidence. It says, "I can see clearly now . . . the pain is gone." This person then becomes surer of herself and of her actions as well as reactions.

Other's opinions of this nearsighted archer are also likely to change. She will no longer be seen as an incompetent bumbling fool of an archer. Now she can be a competent and maybe even prize-winning expert in the field. Perhaps now she'll be admired. Others will stop seeing her as an apparent aloof and self-focused loner who ignores friends and acquaintances. Now she can see and wave to them on the street or across a crowded room. She'll know who they are. Now she can be the warm, observant, and conscientious friend who always notices others and greets them kindly.

Does wearing contact lenses change one's behavior? Of course it does.

Can these lenses also affect the mood? Yes, they can. Could it be that contacts actually alter one's mind? Oh, yes, it could! Can others see these changes? Will others respond to the change by altering their earlier views? You bet they will! It may take a little time. Is there anything that doesn't?

Can new bias develop as a result of the corrective lens intervention? Sure, it can. After all, life is no bed of roses. The thorns may need your attention as well.

"I don't want a pill controlling my life!" she said.

"So," I responded to this declaration. "Would you rather be controlled by a chemical deficit which you barely understand? Do you want something directing your life that you have no idea how to manage? What influence has this already had on the way you think? What effect has there been on your life choices up to this point? How much of what you do has been dictated by this unseen ruler? Do you really want to be controlled by something other than yourself?"

"Yes," is the answer many have given when asked these questions. They mostly don't come right out and say the word "yes." But their actions, or lack thereof, say basically the same thing. They don't want their behavior influenced by a pill. They simply do not realize that a deficient chemical or brain glitch has already been doing just that. In effect, this physical deviation is and has been influencing their behavior all along. Without the brain irregularity their choices and behavior might have been quite different.

A weakness of the eyes may require corrective lenses to enjoy good and accurate vision. Behavior also changes in time as a result. Medication may be required to correct chemical levels in the brain, which then will have an effect on behavior. Corrective lenses do not "control" the eyes or the person using them. They correct the physical defect in the ability to see as long as they are in.

The lenses simply clear up the eyesight so that a person can see as well as everyone else can. This clarity gives a poorly sighted person the chance to act differently.

The person is now freer than ever before in all responses that depend on good eyesight. The lens itself is not a chain lock binding someone down for life. Rather, it is a liberator. Without some kind of intervention the poor-sighted are already chained and restricted. The individual is not to blame for the poor eyesight. It is often a genetic weakness completely out of their control. It is true that corrective lenses will probably have to be used for life if they want to see clearly. So what? Changes in lenses will need to be made from time to time as the vision worsens due to damage, age, progressive disease and so on. These days an operation can modify the eyes and fix the sight for some. Even these will someday need glasses in order to read and see things that are close up.

Those using a medication to adjust brain chemical levels are also freer in their ability to respond. They will have choices available to them that they did not have before. Similar to contact lens changes, medication may also need to be adjusted as time goes on.

Interventions within the realm of the biochemical are still in their infancy. Corrective lenses have been in use and constantly refined for over seven hundred years. It has not been nearly so long for the biochemical.

Let's go back to the nearsighted archer. This archer had the opportunity to choose to study and practice the sport of archery. She was not free to perform at her highest potential. It didn't matter how much she practiced; nor did it matter how persistent she was in so doing. Her free will may be to choose to work hard and long to become a master archer. Her weak vision, however, is interfering with the goal of that free will. Thus her free will alone is not sufficient to enable her to reach her potential as an archer. It doesn't matter how strong her will may be.

Free will is difficult to conceive of because it is not visible. It cannot be touched, measured, heard, smelled, tasted, or depended upon. Brain chemical deficits also cannot be observed.

Brain chemical fluctuations that influence behavior and interfere with free will are also intangible. These fluctuations too cannot be seen, felt, heard, smelled, or tasted. Relying on them is probably not a good idea either. The mechanism of this interference is invisible.

Many believe that taking a medication will change who they are. They fear their basic personality structure is in danger. They only recognize themselves as who they currently are and always have been. The lifelong influence from internal biological defect is subtle. This makes it nearly impossible for them to imagine *who-they-might-have-been* if the chemical or other defects had not been there.

Those with biochemical interference can have a hard time accepting that this could be true. The idea that the person they really are might be different from one they think they are, is tough to swallow. The biological weakness has always been there. If this interference is lessened or removed, how can they see this as anything but an actual loss of the person they think they are? How can they be expected to view it as a successful attack on the actual problem? The answer to this question is through education. They must be informed ahead of time so that none of this comes as a surprise. They need to be told what to expect. Then they need to see these expectations come to fruition.

In my experience, most of those involved view the end result of taking medication for OCS in a positive light. Distraught parents sometimes see the changes in their child as a welcome return to the way they used to be. Over the last twenty-three years I have worked a great deal with children and adults in the diagnosis and treatment of OCS/OCD, ADHD, and Tourette's syndrome. There have been many occasions in which mothers of treated children have thanked me for "returning their child" to them.

So many times in early sessions, parents feel "caught between a rock and a hard place." They are attempting to explain the problems that caused them to bring their child in to see a clinical psychologist. Usually by this time the child's behavior has reached a point of intolerability. Almost without exception as parents unfold the story about their child they are a bit shocked by what they are saying. There is discrepancy between the descriptions that they are painting and how they feel about their child. Often they exclaim in anguish, " . . . but she really is a wonderful child . . ." and " . . . he truly is good in his heart, you know . . ." and so on. It often seems as if these parents suddenly feel like they are traitors. What are they saying about their child?

Many seem to be seeking reassurance that what they truly believe about their child is right. They want sometimes desperately to hear this psychologist tell them, "Yes! You're absolutely correct. He does have a good heart." "Yes! She is wonderful." They want to hear this, in spite of the apparent evidence that seems to indicate the opposite.

Fortunately, I can honestly report that in all my years of private practice and in-depth work in the public school setting, the parent has been right. Every time in the case of their declaration of goodness relative to a child, they have been absolutely correct. There have been times when the child didn't think so, however. There have even been times when a child has declared adamantly that he or she was anything but good. What else can some of them think? When you can get past the barriers and defenses to the heart even these weary children are able to see that goodness is there.

The child is good. The real problem is that something else is interfering with the child's ability to demonstrate their true inner goodness in a consistent enough way that others are able to see it and respond to this goodness, rather than to the interference. I do not believe I have ever worked with an "evil" child, although I readily admit to having worked with many who, for all intents and purposes, certainly appeared to be that way, at least initially.

With the right kind of treatment OCS adults who want help for themselves are often relieved of long-standing burdens of guilt. They are also relieved of chronic frustration, and anger. This remorse, irritation, and wrath often come from how badly they feel about their own past misbehaviors. Reframing childhood memories can free them from these burdens. This should be done after being educated about OCS, ADHD, or whatever. They can then look back and revisit events and traumatic incidents with the knowledge of what having such a disorder means. It can help them see how things may have been distorted by them, as well as others. It can heal old emotional wounds because *now* they know why.

It can give them insight into why others acted in the ways that they did towards them.

The sometimes enormous emotional stockpiles of guilt, self-hate, and self-directed fury can be put to rest. Also, if there has been misappropriated anger leveled at parents and others, this too can be eased. This experience alone can significantly boost a person's energy levels. As already stated, it can make it possible for important old emotional wounds to finally heal. And it can bolster the desire and motivation to persist in this difficult journey. It is a long journey of discovery, liberation, and healing. The treatment process is ongoing. It will require continuing education and appropriate interventions. It will also call for an acceptance that these particular biochemical disorders aren't likely to go away anytime soon. Typically, they are *managed* (more or less successfully over time) and not *cured*.

14

Treatment is a Journey, not a Destination

Clinical experience and research over the years have revealed what I believe are the three most effective methods in the treatment of mild-moderate OCS. They are education, medication, and CBT (Cognitive Behavior Therapy). Please keep in mind that this chapter is not meant to be an instruction manual for treatment. Rather, it is an attempt to foster a higher level of awareness. This alone is your greatest tool.

Education

The first and most important method in the treatment of OCS is awareness and education. Once the symptoms begin to be understood, social and family dynamics often improve. In fact the goal of this book is to do just that. The hope is to inform and educate the reader. OCS is widely prevalent. Yet, it is still a largely unidentified and misdiagnosed condition. It is a biological, behavioral, social, cognitive, and emotional problem.

Parental reactions as well as teachers, siblings, and even friends, tend to change when true understanding is achieved. It is not uncommon for others to view the OCS-driven behavior as a personal attack. Others can also feel that it is an assault purposefully directed at them. The camouflage tends to be quite thick around the true origin of the symptom source. Even those with OCS tend to wonder if their actions might really have been purposeful. Once the problems are identified as coming from the biologically driven OCS, change occurs. A new perspective often dawns.

A seventeen-year-old said it in his own words:

"It's like," he shared, "I'm seeing everything from another point of view . . . like I'm seeing things for the first time through someone else's eyes."

When understanding truly sinks in, parents are often relieved and sometimes even thrilled. They discover that there really is something exceptional and unusual about their child. They somehow knew this all along. The behaviors and responses of the OCS child that seemed so strange begin to make sense. The parents have not been exaggerating their experience. They have an odd and difficult child. They begin to realize the child's behavior problems are not primarily their fault. The troubles the child has are not due to their having been overly permissive or lacking in discipline. They are not *bad* parents, as others may have hinted at and even blatantly declared. Relationships improve in time. The journey towards healing these stormy and painful emotional bonds begins.

This journey tends to be a slow process that fluctuates greatly. For some there is an initial burst of tremendous growth and progress. This can be followed by a period where progress seems to greatly slow down. For others it may be slow going all the way. Some can experience moments of substantial insight. Improvements can be interspersed between lags or periods of seeming stagnation. Whatever the pattern of progress, therapeutic assistance can be beneficial. It is an ongoing process of discovering and learning about OCS. Its influence is felt in every area of life.

At this point in time I have not come across any body of literature specific to OCS (mild-moderate). This is the reason that I wrote these two books. There is a fairly extensive literature base for what I consider the severe form of this problem identified in DSM-IV as Obsessive-Compulsive Disorder (OCD). It can be useful for all involved to read this available literature. It can allow for a more comprehensive understanding of the entire spectrum of OCS/OCD. It also can scare them to death. The OCD level of symptoms is so much more severe than OCS, that many with OCS conclude that obsessions and compulsions must not be their problem. Generally speaking, what works in the treatment of OCD can also work for the milder version of OCS. There are several books that can be very useful as reference tools and to gain further depth and knowledge. They are as follows:

The Boy Who couldn't Stop Washing, Judith Rapaport, M.D.
Brain Lock, Jeffrey M. Schwartz, M.D.
Getting Control, Lee Baer, PhD.

Talking Back to OCD, John S. March, M.D.
Freeing Your Child from Obsessive-Compulsive Disorder, Tamar E.
    Chansky, PhD.
What to do When Your Child has Obsessive-Compulsive Disorder,
    Aureen Pinto Wagner, PhD.
The Imp of the Mind, Lee Baer, PhD.

The therapeutic strategy of education and gaining insight is ongoing. It should be thought of as a never-ending process. Another way to more eloquently put this might be, *"it's a journey, not a destination."*

It is vital during the therapeutic process to instill within the minds and hearts of all involved another very important concept. The concept is this:

OCS is an EXPLANATION; NOT AN EXCUSE!

People need to be held responsible for their behavior. It doesn't matter if their actions are pre-planned or biochemically driven. It doesn't make a difference if they are under the influence of drugs, or whether it's an accident. Otherwise, chaos would eventually reign. Disorder would disrupt the family unit and society as a whole. A worldview stated as follows can be used to put into practice the goal of the concept related above.

"Okay, you may have done that (problem, action or behavior) because you have OCS. So now what are you going to do about it?" If amends need to be made, they need to be followed through on. Plans and strategies should be developed and written down. This is done in an attempt to prevent similar incidents in the future. Either that, or at least diminish the intensity of the next response. Knowing what to do ahead of time can help the OCS-driven person to respond as planned.

Medication

Another element in the treatment of OCS involves the use of medication. Evidence suggests that the brain chemical serotonin plays a role in the emergence of OCS/OCD. Medications which inhibit the re-uptake of serotonin can diminish the strength of OCS as they do for OCD. Improvement occurs however at much lower doses than needed to treat symptoms at the OCD level. This only makes sense. The mild-moderate symptoms seem to be caused by levels of serotonin that are "less deficient" than those of OCD. Hence, if this is true, it follows that OCS would respond to lower medicinal dosages than those required for OCD. In fact, this is exactly what OCS does seem to do. Less medication is directly related to fewer side effects. Fewer side effects play a part in a greater willingness to take medication. This then relates to a greater success rate when medication is used.

There are several SSRIs that are antidepressants that effectively treat those with OCS. It is important to talk to your doctor before taking a medication. You want to know about all the possible benefits as well as potential side affects.

Once a medication is begun, it is important to track its effects on the target symptoms. Progress in general should also be monitored. As a part of the diagnostic process, I use a slightly modified version of the Leyton Obsessional Inventory. I code the Leyton with a plus (+) when a person reports a symptom's presence. A minus (-) is noted when not present. A re-administration of the Leyton is used to monitor progress. The client is usually asked only those questions with a prior positive response. If the specific symptom seems better it is coded (B), the same (S), gone (G), and worse (W). Sometimes the response will be more specific in regard to the variations mentioned above. They might say "it's a lot better" or "just a little better" and so on. When this happens, I code it in whatever way I feel will help me to remember the response.

Through the use of this instrument, progress reports are made to prescribing doctors. Impressions are shared in regard to how effective the current medication level appears to be. This helps the physician determine if raising or lowering a given dose is warranted. In clinical practice, this tool has proven to be useful as a measure of a medication's impact. It is also a useful tool for those with OCS and others in the pursuit of the OCS "knowledge" or "education" base.

Through the re-administration of the Leyton, the OCS-driven learn what responses really are symptoms. As symptoms respond, and behaviors as well as thoughts change, awareness blossoms. The OCS-affected begin to recognize how broadly their lives have been influenced by this biological problem.

The goal of medical intervention is threefold. There are three possible means by which improvement can occur as follows:

1. Symptoms may become less frequent or occur less often.
2. When they do occur, they may be less intense or less severe.
3. The person with OCS may recover sooner after symptom occurrence. In other words, they can let go of it sooner.

Also, a part of the hope is that those with OCS will become believers in the true biochemical nature of the problem. When they respond to this treatment positively they do indeed become believers.

There are no strict guidelines available for the appropriate length of time to be on a medication. A ballpark figure of three to eighteen months seems reasonable. This is based on clinical experience or an experienced based approach. It often depends on the severity of the symptoms. The successful withdrawal of a medication and management of returning symptoms may take more or less time.

Clinical practice has suggested some common response patterns relative to the use of medication. Research has yet to be completed before these ideas and practices can with some degree of certainty be endorsed. With this in mind, impressions coming from the treatment of OCS via the medicational route will be introduced. Perhaps these ideas will enable some to open their minds to other notions and possibilities.

Occasionally, after a therapeutic level has been reached and treatment has continued over an extended period of time, a problem may occur. Some who are treated appear to take on an extreme "I don't care" attitude towards things. Whereas, prior to treatment they had been overly concerned and seemed to care way too much about everything. With this outcome, the person no longer seems to react as if things mattered much at all. This makes perfect sense. Not enough serotonin seems to result in a tendency to over-respond. They care too much. If so, then it stands to reason that too much serotonin might produce a tendency not to care. This is part of what led me to infer that OCS might be on a continuum. It appears that discontinuing the medication or lowering the dose when this apathetic response occurs once again boosts motivation. This should always be done through the prescribing doctor and under his or her supervision.

The bottom line when working with medication and OCS seems to be to "start low and increase slowly." Usually the lowest dose typical for the age and/or size of the person is begun. Symptom response is monitored weekly with the Leyton. Data is shared with the prescribing physician in the form of progress notes on an ongoing basis.

Exposure and Response Prevention (Cognitive Behavior Therapy)

As treatment progresses, symptoms are consistently monitored. Awareness of OCS grows and has a positive effect on a person's day-to-day life activities. The understanding of OCS enables a person to better apply what may be the most important method. The only other method shown by research to be effective in the treatment of obsessive and compulsive symptoms is a form of CBT.

This is the behavior modification technique of "exposure and response prevention." It is beyond the scope of this work to outline in detail this well-established treatment method for OCD. The interested reader is referred to an excellent source for this information in a book by Lee Baer titled, "*Getting Control.*" In this volume, Dr. Baer presents what I consider to be one of the best available descriptions of exposure and response prevention and its use in the treatment of OCD.

In fact, I frequently recommend to my OCS clients that they purchase Dr. Baer's book to be used as a reference tool. I do so because of its excellent coverage of the exposure and response prevention technique. Included are an explanation, history, and step-by-step procedures for its use.

The exposure component of this method involves repeatedly confronting a situation that causes fear, anxiety, or distress. The component of "response prevention" comes into play with each exposure incident. It is put into practice when the exposed person consciously does not act out the response they feel they must in order to feel better. Similarly, if a person feels that they need to avoid some situation, someone, or something to feel better, they are instructed not to do so.

Persistent and frequent exposure is required for success. At the moment of exposure the need or compulsion must also be resisted successfully. With daily hard work over time (usually two to six weeks) symptom strength will weaken. So also will associated anxiety. For this method to be successful, it often requires close work with an experienced behavior therapist. It can also be important to have a knowledgeable coach and/or helper. Medication may be needed as well, along with a strong desire to be free of symptoms and a willingness to work hard.

In my opinion, a working knowledge of exposure and response prevention is important for all those dealing with obsessive and compulsive issues. It can be useful information, no matter how severe the problem. It has almost always been clearly beneficial. CBT is a benefit as an integral part of the overall treatment process and future maintenance of positive gains.

Once there is sufficient knowledge of exposure and response prevention gained, it's like riding a bike or playing the piano. After having once been learned these skills are hardly forgotten. Later they can be readily accessed when the need arises.

Dr. Baer reports more problems and less positive results in the treatment of OCD-affected children. He does suggest some encouraging outcomes, though, when several specific factors are also present.

The position taken by Dr. Baer in regard to the treatment of children does not seem notably different from my own. The most important thing that children need in order to succeed in this work is motivation or incentive. A child has to be willing to endure intense levels of anxiety. Children must tolerate serious assaults on their emotional well being for extended periods of time.

To overcome symptoms through behavior treatment methods, a child must have strong motivation. A child is not in danger of losing his job if symptom relief is not achieved. His family won't *divorce* him. He or she won't be thrown out into the street due to foreclosure. A child won't be going hungry if symptoms don't improve. The motivation for children to get better is weak to nonexistent, when compared to how strong actual serious OCD symptoms can be. This is not necessarily true for OCS. The symptoms in the mild-moderate range may surrender more easily to CBT.

The role of a child in the context of a family, as well as his or her place in the community at large, is one of dependence on others. It is such that the child is not likely to work seriously on any proposed behavioral changes that are too challenging. Neither will they work hard if it requires long-term effort to achieve the goal. CBT is of no use without ample motivation.

It is true that those with the most "control" over a child's life may be able to manipulate the environment to some degree. If careful, it may be possible to coax exposure and response prevention methods into action. In fact, the initial step (exposure) naturally occurs off-and-on throughout the course of a day. The other part (response prevention) is also something that the person gets a chance to confront on a daily basis. When forced to face situations in life that bring on OCS during the natural course of the day, it is called *in-vivo* exposure. Loosely translated, *in-vivo* means "real life."

The OCS-driven will often persist in their actions far beyond that of their non-affected counterparts. Behavior modification works a bit less cleanly when OCS is driving the actions. Even when behavior changes, those with OCS can have persistent lingering thoughts and desires. At times this can promote a form of chronic mental distress, irritation, and/or torment. They are not happy campers. They can also influence how others around them are feeling. Others may get the impression that those with OCS want them to be as miserable and unhappy as they are.

Another difference between those with and without OCS is the intensity of their actions and reactions. Those with OCS tend to react in absolutes and extremes. This is especially true when things do not seem to go the way they want or "need" them to. This tendency to "over respond" to stimuli has been discussed elsewhere in this work. It is essential, however, to keep this in mind when working with the OCS population. Their overreactions often seem unjustified and don't make much sense. They tend to be much stronger than would be expected, based on the identified trigger. A combination of education, medication, and behavioral therapy is usually best. This can bring meaning to the otherwise senseless acts, reactions, and baffling situational events. Making sense of the senseless is what this work is all about.

Please see all of me

there is so much more to me than you see . . . this I want you to know
there are thoughts that I've thought . . . there are things that I've done
there are places i still mean to go

please see all of me . . . not just the outer (obvious) parts
please see all of me . . . open up your heart
please see all of me . . . don't be worried you might get too near
please see all of me . . . or you may turn away I fear

if the package we're in is pretty we've got a better chance
if there's a wonderful song that we sing people may get up and dance
there's a difference to us all you know . . . and I'm sure thankful that it's true
when I imagine another just like myself it scares me . . . how about you?
                    —chorus—
I know no one learns how to be a friend . . . by staying away
or a song on the piano . . . by never sitting down to play
hey . . . I may not laugh when you laugh . . . you see I may not understand
but if you reach out to me with your own . . . if I can . . . I'll give you my hand
                    —chorus—
there are some people who never even seem to see . . . past their very own nose
and some would call the grand canyon a ditch . . . or say a rose is a rose
but deep inside we all know that just isn't true . . . at least that's not the way it ought to be
yet at times we still do it any old way . . . 'cause some things are just too hard to see
                    —chorus—

Words and Music by Ron D. Kingsley
March 12, 1988

PART IV

Unique to OCS

15

The Process of Grief

Emotional changes occur when someone is first told that they or a child of theirs has a possible disabling condition such as *OCS*. These changes are often a lot like those experienced by people facing the loss of a loved one. Often after it has been confirmed that OCS is present, those involved may go through a "grieving process." Typically there are five stages. These are: denial, anger, bargaining, depression, and acceptance. For ease of reading, the rest of this article will be written as if you are involved in this situation.

Each of these stages will be reviewed as they relate to those with OCS as well as the parents of a diagnosed child. As such you must come face-to-face with the reality of what it means to have this biological condition. Unfortunately, the diagnosis of OCS is commonly missed, ignored, and misdiagnosed throughout all ages and stages of life.

The first emotional change often comes with the diagnosis. The underlying factor is the idea that you who have OCS can no longer be considered "normal." You may be thrilled at the prospect of being thought of as "different." You may be devastated at that thought. You might be one who is actually relieved to know that there really is something wrong. You always suspected something, but didn't know what it was. To some it really doesn't seem to matter and still others may be very upset. This can be a time of shock that frequently leads to a complete rejection of the diagnosis. You may immediately think, "This can't be true." Parents of a child and those with OCS facing such a verdict can feel that their entire world has just collapsed. Those who are in this situation also commonly feel very much alone.

OCS can be diagnosed at virtually any age. It is somewhere around the time of diagnosis that the first stage of grief is experienced. As soon as some unexpected, shocking, or traumatic news is suggested, your mind may put up a hasty defense. This is done in an effort to protect emotional stability. The first such defense is almost always a form of denial. Often you may not even be aware that this process of denial is happening. This "mechanism of defense" is not planned. It acts as a shield to deflect unwanted information that you are not yet able to handle. Inconsistency is a hallmark symptom of OCS. It can be very easy to fool yourself into thinking that OCS-driven behaviors are deliberate. This can lead you into the trap of long term denial. It is at this point that "doctor shopping" can occur.

A second opinion is often a very good option to choose. In the case of denial, though, a second opinion is not really the goal. You may go from professional to professional. You are hoping that the diagnosis will be reversed. You hope it will be revealed that you or your child is in fact *normal*, after all.

If not found normal there is yet another hope and prayer. It is that some other perhaps better informed professional will be able to figure out what the problem really is and fix it. Of course, after the problem has been corrected, you believe that the so-called OCS diagnosis will have been exposed as incorrect. Then proof will exist that your child or you is and has always been "normal."

You may convince yourself that the tests themselves must have been in error. Either that or the diagnostic reports must have been somehow switched. In their hearts, though, all that are involved may sense there surely is something wrong. No one is yet able to accept the existing problem as it has been diagnosed.

At this time in the process of grief, denial often plays a very important role in keeping people from "going off the deep end." Not having to face the abrupt and mind-numbing truth can allow you some needed processing time. This extra time enables you to slowly adjust and reorganize your thoughts. You can stretch your mind and make room for new possibilities. Most of the time such a reaction is not really a refusal to acknowledge that there is a problem. Rather, it is an inability to even consider that this *problem* might just be a permanent fixture in your life. OCS is managed, not cured. It will be there with its subtle influence, sometimes getting in the way and sometimes not, for the rest of your life.

Tied in with this first stage is the unshakable feeling of being the only one. Along with the new diagnosis comes the fear that you are all alone singled out and somehow set apart from everyone else. This can be especially true if there is no local support from others with similar problems. These feelings of isolation can foster a withdrawal from your usual ways of life. This can then actually act to create the very isolation that is feared, at least for a time.

Another common reaction during the stage of denial is fear itself. Usually this fear is triggered by the unknown extent of the problem. What does it mean to you or your child? What will it mean to friends or to immediate and extended family members? What changes will have to be made? How will it affect personal, family, and social life? What new responsibilities will be added to your load or expected as a result? What will this mean in relation to your child's school experience? How about what it may do to current or future employment? How is it going to affect social relationships? Will the ability to stay or even become self-sufficient be a factor? Just what is going to happen? Most have no idea at the start what will happen and that's why they are scared. They may have a hard time admitting fear, though. This should be kept in mind.

Other common feelings that occur during the denial stage are guilt and shame. Parents often can view their children as extensions of themselves. In the case of the diagnosis of OCS, you as the parent may have experienced the very same kinds of problems growing up. You may have been told over and over that you were *bad*. You may have also been told just as often that if you would "just try harder" you could behave, and so on. As a child you may have been placed in special education classes. Once there you may have had a horrible experience. This would have been because educators did not understand the real problem. You may be treating your child in much the same way that your own parents treated you. Sometimes there may be actual mental or emotional abuse. Sometimes there is physical abuse. Parents do not do this on purpose. They do not set out to be abusive like their parents. They don't want to be that way.

When parents are faced with the proposition that they may have been abusing their children, guilt and shame may amplify exponentially. This can happen even if the abuse has only been on occasion. The idea that your child's actions were the result of a biological cause not completely under their control is hard to take. You may realize "I've been abusive for actions that my child couldn't always control." How is *that* for guilt? It is no wonder that such a diagnosis may be rejected. The guilt and shame you would feel and have to face if you accept the diagnosis can be overwhelming.

This can be further complicated by the feelings you may have towards your own parents. This could be true for you if, with your child's diagnosis, you begin to recognize your own similar symptoms. Questions arise: "You mean I wasn't really bad?" "I wasn't lazy?" "I'm not dumb?" "I was unknowingly biochemically influenced?" Feelings of both love and hate (known as ambivalence) toward your child, your parents, and even yourself, may surface. This can make emotional reactions much more difficult to understand and deal with, effectively.

Usually the stage of denial with its emotional issues is only temporary. As you complete this stage, you begin to experience what can be thought of as a "partial acceptance." The initial reaction of "NO! This can't be true!" is replaced by "Well, I guess it could be."

Whenever you or your child is unable to meet expectations, it results in disappointment. This shattering of parental and personal hopes and dreams can bring about anger. This is a common second stage of the grief process. The anger may be directed at your child. It may be directed at others or even yourself. You may become angry because of your "lost opportunities." Also, anger can come from the fear that you may now be unable to meet your child's needs, or your own. Doctors are suddenly blamed for the medical condition they have diagnosed. Teachers may be blamed. Attempts may be made to try and hold them responsible if there have been academic or learning problems. Parents themselves may be blamed by a newly diagnosed adult or by older children.

The spouse of a married adult or significant other may be blamed for creating all the problems. This can happen more often if the spouse or other was first to recognize the symptoms, leading to a diagnosis. Honest outrage at the ignorance of others for missing the diagnosis can occur. Time and again they misunderstood what was going on and then judged you or your child mercilessly. This kind of experience is common when OCS is the diagnosis. There may also be justifiable anger directed at doctors and professionals. They may have misdiagnosed the condition and then minimized the problem.

Well-meaning doctors may have often made statements such as: "He's a boy" or "She'll grow out of it." There may have even been a comment such as: "Have you ever thought about taking a class on parenting skills?"

The third stage in the grief process to be explored is called bargaining.

As the reality begins to sink in, you may try to postpone this thing that can no longer be avoided. You may do this with promises of good behavior. Most of the time commitments such as these are made secretly and are religious in nature. Common bargains include promised changes. The bargain may be a large religious donation to be exchanged for granted requests and prayers. Sometimes these oaths are driven by added feelings of guilt. There may be remorse for not having been faithful in attending religious services regularly. Perhaps the shame is from not having been consistent in offerings and donations.

Eventually you realize that bargaining has not and will not alter the final outcome in your situation. This is when the fourth stage in the process of grief may enter the picture. It is depression.

Hope and anger are abandoned as useless. The new focus is on the great loss that you feel for all the things that "might have been." Usually each family member and sometimes close friends share in these sorrowful feelings. It is during this stage that you may actually begin to accept that which cannot be changed. It is also at this point that newly diagnosed adults may start the process of correcting distorted memories. Past events are reframed in light of your new found knowledge. Memories begin to more accurately reflect reality. This is a very difficult and sometimes overwhelming task. You may need experienced professional help to succeed.

After the depression has run its course, there can be a period of time which may best be described as a lack of feelings. You are no longer depressed; nor are you angry, or even envious. It is at this time that you may truly begin to understand that things really could be worse. Not that this is going to make it all better, somehow.

This is the gateway to the last of the stages in the grief process. The final stage is acceptance. Acceptance has at its heart two distinct and separate levels. One is emotional in nature, and the other intellectual. In order to work through this stage you need to do a couple of things. One is to be able to talk about and understand the realities of the diagnosis at a clear intellectual level. You must also be able to have and support this knowledge at an emotional level, as well. Either level of this stage without the other does not constitute complete acceptance.

An example of true acceptance might be: "I know it takes Rebecca a lot longer than most of her peers to do her school work. Most of the time, she can only finish about half of what has been assigned. I need to let her do it by herself. This is because it is important for her to experience the benefits that come from personal accomplishments. She has the right to do her own work at her own pace and at her own level."

The acceptance stage is the beginning of the process that marks a healthy adjustment. Adjustment, though, is an on going process that covers every aspect and phase of our entire life. Each new phase of life brings new challenges and sometimes new grief. A few examples of such phases include age, physical development, and social life. There is also marriage, your vocation, and other personal time limited goals.

Perhaps, for the first time, old misunderstandings and emotional wounds can be successfully cleared up and in due course, healed. The diagnosis promotes new insight. You learn why certain events and incidents may have happened while growing up. You also get a chance to understand the real reasons things were the way they were. This insight can free you from what may have been a tremendous lifelong burden of anger and guilt. Most times, such insight has the literal effect of changing the past you may have thought you knew. Looking through this new frame of reference at life's events often results in some radically changed views. Incidents long believed to have been caused by specific people and circumstances may be seen quite differently.

When this happens, you are in the process of figuring out who you are by redefining your past. Much of what you believe about yourself—who you were and what you did—you realize may not be altogether accurate. You embark on a journey of rediscovery. You want to know what memories may have been accurate, exaggerated, distorted, or simply misunderstood. You may fear at least momentarily that your entire existence up until the present day may have been a lie. This of course is simply not true. But the actual fear itself can be *very* real.

A re-inventing of the self must be undertaken. When an unseen lifelong condition like OCS is finally diagnosed, there is much work to be done. A reframing of the past enables a true healthy adjustment to occur. This is a difficult task that requires patience, persistence and hard work. Also, to accomplish this adjustment usually takes a fairly long period of time. To ensure success, this needs to be undertaken after reaching the acceptance stage. It is best if this stage is resolved first, but this may not be possible. As in some of the other grief stages, professional help may be needed.

It is important to clearly understand that even though you may have reached the acceptance stage, it does not mean you are home free. Getting to this stage is not a guarantee that your pleas and hopes for a cure will be gone entirely. The true resolution of this stage comes as knowledge and emotions have evened out and become stable. With this stability you can now face the reality of your situation and begin to make the best of it. The hope that the doctors were wrong has now matured. It has become, instead, a new hope of making as normal a personal and family life as possible.

Concluding Remarks on Grief

You should be careful not to assume that once emotions have been accepted and explored, they will never bother you again. Even when our emotional wounds seem healed, the memory still remains. It is equally helpful to know that the stages in the grief process do not always come one right after the other. Some stages may run into each other, or may even take place at the same time.

Not everyone experience emotions at the same level. As a result, you may respond in a different way to the challenges of moving through these stages. For some, it may not take very long to complete the grieving process. For others, it may require years. Throughout the process of adjustment, certain stages can resurface and may need to be once again worked through. Usually this happens because another event with the same kind of issues has occurred. You should always keep in mind that humans are extremely complicated beings. Because of this, no one is ever entirely predictable.

When present, the grief related to the diagnosis of OCS should be taken seriously. It represents an honest struggle with what can be regarded as a "symbolic death." The child that parents had anticipated and dreamed about is not what they got. The person that you thought that you were, is not who you really are. That hope and belief, about who you were or your child was, is buried by the diagnosis. A true loss is felt and this impacts your life, not only in that moment but forever.

The ultimate role of spouses, friends, parents, and teachers is not to actually counsel those in the process of grieving. Professionals and specific support groups are better suited to accomplish that task. The healthiest role for most others is one of awareness, understanding, allowance, and support.

When a child or an adult with OCS is first diagnosed, others can be most helpful if they are sensitive about this. They can also be supportive in relation to the grief process, should it begin. Others need to be made aware that, once in the process, people must be allowed the time and space needed to experience the stages. A supportive and nonjudgmental attitude can be of great comfort. It can be a lot like a shelter in a storm.

One final thought worth repeating is in relation to what it takes for true healing to occur. Those who are grieving must be allowed to work through these emotionally laden stages. They must be allowed to redefine who they are. They need time to set new expectations for their children or themselves. They also might need some time as well to learn new skills with which to cope. Another's willingness to understand, respect, and keep communication lines open can speed up the healing process. During this traumatic period of life, this can be all that is really needed.

16

Life with OCS

Intimate Partner Relationships

How could we both have it? Don't opposites attract? The genetic link in OCS is speaking loudly, and has been for a long time now. Interesting things sometimes happen when a child is brought to my office and found to have OCS symptoms. Before too long, parents may begin to make comments such as the following:

"Doesn't *everybody* have this? I mean . . . I do."

"Hey! I used to do that when I was his age too . . ."

"Uh . . . can this be treated in adults too . . . uh . . . like me?" and so on.

The tendency for a parent and other family members to also have OCS symptoms is not surprising to me. When OCS is present in a child it is pretty much expected. What did surprise me at first, though, was how many times *both* the mother and the father would have it too. OCS could also be observed in both parents' extended families. Often each parent's symptoms would show up quite differently.

Sometimes a parent can easily recognize their own symptoms. Sometimes they can't. This may have something to do with marital power structures. When the power in a relationship is not the same, it seems that the stronger one has the more trouble seeing his or her OCS actions. They often seem to feel there could not possibly be anything wrong with them. "Just look at how I'm doing. Who do you think is making this marriage work anyway?"

Informal interviews with these OCS adults were completed. This was done in an attempt to try and find out why those with OCS seem to have a tendency to marry other people with OCS. The following premise seems to make the most sense.

Much of what people learn and the behavior that follows over a lifetime comes from the "patterns" that occur. For me the word "patterns" refers to everything that happens repeatedly. This includes all behaviors and thoughts. These then become a part of the "self." They are considered to be a part of "who that person is."

A child who grows up in a family with two alcoholic parents learns how to survive or "live" with such people. This results in a style of behaving, thinking, and reacting that becomes one of the many "patterns" of life for the child. Such a pattern is often carried on into adulthood. The person's behavior as an adult, to some degree, is shaped by the pattern.

An *only* child learns the pattern of living with adults. Such a child always has a parent's attention. The *only* child also shares the weight of having the duty to be all that her parents expect her to be.

When a child grows up with one or more OCS-affected parents a similar "pattern" is created. This specific "pattern" is often made up of two parts. First, there is the part of the "pattern" created in response to the actions, reactions, and behavior of the OCS-affected parent(s). Second, when the child also has symptoms, this too becomes a part of the "pattern" of living in the OCS world.

Such a "pattern" as described above commonly becomes a powerful core "blueprint." The child typically lives in it, around it, and with it for eighteen to twenty years. This "blueprint" then, more than likely, has at least some influence on most other "patterns."

Now we need to consider the fact that the OCS-affected are usually not aware of the problems created by their symptoms. It then becomes easy to see how this "pattern" is often experienced as a part of the "self." That's just who they think they are. It is often thought of as "personality." At least that's what most people might think. "It's just who I am," they would say.

It is not unusual for children with OCS, who have parents with OCS, to have quite stormy and even abusive relationships. This often happens throughout the years that the child is developing and growing into adulthood. Anger is often an added factor. Quite commonly, the child can also be very adamant that he or she is not going to grow up to be like dad or mom.

Without education and treatment though, they probably will become a lot like their parents. Often they seek to find a partner that is as far removed as possible in personality from either parent. And yet the OCS "pattern" often interferes with this goal. They are determined that such a relationship "pattern" as their parents had will not be repeated. In spite of this conviction, it *is* nevertheless repeated.

The young people who have grown up with the OCS "pattern" around them all their lives know almost instinctively how to survive. They are aware of how to get individual needs met when living with those who have OCS. They usually don't like what they may have to do, but they can do it. As a result, when the OCS "patterned" young person meets another such person, there is an instant attraction. There is a sort of "celebrating of the souls" to give it a creative label. They instantly feel at ease with each other. Each has had years of experience in how to respond to those with OCS. They tend to respond to each other almost instinctively. It can be a very warm and fuzzy kind of feeling feeling.

Interestingly, these relationships may become quite "rocky" prior to the wedding date. This really ought to act as a warning signal to the couple. Typically, it does not. These young people often end up deciding to marry. They go on with plans anyway in spite of some misgivings. Once a relationship has begun, the comfort and ease felt at the start becomes secondary. Love-at-first-sight gives way to the more immediate problems brought on by OCS symptoms.

These OCS issues can include an obsessive need to be with the other person. Also there can be an obsessive fear of rejection. There may be unrelenting fear that no one else would ever want to be with the OCS person. It may also be that an obsessive commitment to the partnership itself exists. There can be an obsessive need to smooth things out. Likewise, there might be an inability to admit that the partnership might be a mistake.

Don't think this is everything, though. There can be many, many other mixtures and symptoms that are likely to come into play over time. When such symptoms are activated, perceptions of reality can't help but get twisted and influenced. It occurs to me that the OCS pattern may very well be responsible for a popular notion. This notion is so entrenched in society that jokes are commonly made about it. This is the idea that children grow up and marry their parents. Generally the girl would marry someone just like her father. In the case of the boy, of course, he would marry someone just like his mother.

The Family

This is where it all begins. The OCS-afflicted child is born into a family in which one and often both parents have OCS or OCD themselves. Often, there is no awareness at all of this fact.

Interactions among OCS family members tend to be quite intense. Attempts to joke with one another tend to fail miserably. Often this is because the target of the gag takes it too seriously or literally. It's as if the meaning of the actual words interferes with their capacity to see the humor. They cannot remove from their minds the literal meaning long enough to see how it is funny. Those with OCS can miss the subtle hints and slight variations in vocal tones of others, because they hear it straight. Their responses to jokes also tend to be greatly exaggerated. This is because the OCS don't get that it's only a joke they over-respond. Efforts to lighten up a bit and laugh about difficult situations often fall short. In place of humor, what can occur are bitter arguments and family strife.

Growing up in such a family is difficult. This is often made even more difficult by the fact that no one knows why it is so hard. Family members have no idea why they react to each other and to the outside world like they do. Often there *is* an unconscious awareness that something's not right or not "normal" if you will. At the same time, there may be a *desperate* need to at least appear "normal" to others. This conflict has a profound impact on each of the family member's lives over time.

A mother of three children in an OCS family will joke that she really has four children. The three she gave birth to and her husband. She'll laugh about it to friends with whom she spends time. But in secret she will shed some very real tears.

When obsessive thoughts and compulsions are actually intruding, not much may get done. Chores and homework as well as special requests and the like take a back seat to symptoms and are left unfinished.

An eleven-year-old girl walks through the family room in front of her dad who is sitting on a couch watching TV. She is going towards the kitchen.

Her father has noticed her socks that had been lying on the carpet by the end of the couch. He says to her, "Ellen!" in a somewhat gruff and frustrated tone, "Will you PLEASE pick up your socks? And from now on, will you please try a little harder to quit leaving your clothes scattered all over the house!"

Ellen pauses and leans over to retrieve the socks before continuing on her way. From the kitchen, the sound of a refrigerator door being opened and closed is heard.

Ellen once more crosses in front of the couch where her father is sitting.

Suddenly his voice fills the room. "Ellen," he calls out. He sits up straight and glares at her. He shakes his head and lets out a big sigh. "*Where are your socks?*"

Ellen freezes in her tracks. With eyes wide she stares blankly at her father. A tear trickles out of the corner of her right eye. She hesitates and then slowly glances around the room. She seems to be looking for something. Then in a soft, but choked-up whisper she replies, "I don't know."

And she doesn't. She really had no clue. This is a true story.

"You've got to be kidding," her dad comments as he pushes away from the couch and gets to his feet.

Ellen automatically shies away from him as if afraid he might hit her. She does this in spite of the fact that she was four years old the last time her father actually spanked her.

Ellen's father heads straight for the kitchen. "Where could they be?" He asks, to no one in particular.

Later many times he laughs hysterically as he shares the story about his "brainless" daughter with others. He guffaws especially hard when he gets to the "punch line" of this very real joke of life.

"They were in the refrigerator," he'd roar.

Most of the time, others would laugh out loud right along with him.

"She left them in the fridge!" He'd sometimes say again. "If that don't beat all," Then he'd laugh again.

His daughter didn't laugh, though. There was a tear in her eye.

Ellen never did laugh at this. To her it had not been funny. She was terribly embarrassed whenever her dad told the story. It only got worse with each subsequent telling.

These are the kinds of dynamics that become entrenched within OCS families. One specific event like that described above is not usually catastrophic in and of itself. What can be catastrophic are the countless similar incidents over the years. Such occasions often just continue on and on. Because they have been a part of a person's behavior for so long, these same issues can carry on later in life. This is true, even though the family members no longer live together.

Individuals in a family learn early in life to "walk on eggshells" within the home. There may be one or two in the family who do not feel this need, though. When this is the case, the eggshell walking occurs to keep those with OCS from blowing up or freaking out.

A wife complains, "I can't tell him anything important! Every time I do he just blows up. Then after that he doesn't hear a single thing I say."

Another woman points out, "When I tell him he's done a good job he comes back angrily with all the reasons why it's *not* a good job. If I don't say anything he complains that I don't ever notice or care about the things he does. If I happen to suggest one more thing that could be done, or a different way something might be done, he goes ballistic. I can't win!"

Another explains that her husband is just *lazy.* "He never does ANYTHING around the house," she carps in a loud and bitter voice.

Later, in confidence, the husband shares, "Why *should* I do anything? No matter what I do, no matter how much or how hard I try it's never, ever, good enough. She wants me to do it again. That, or she does it again herself. Then she grumbles and whines that *she* has to do *everything* around the house. What's the use?"

Parents have said things like, "The kids are addicted to playing. They never come home when they're supposed to. They don't listen. They don't mind and they *don't* care. Grounding doesn't work. Neither does spanking. Yelling doesn't work. Nothing does. Those kids don't care about consequences of any kind. They just don't care."

Consider this scenario:

I was so afraid they might forget. I was sure we wouldn't even get there. We were supposed to go to the beach at 10:00 in the morning. I was up at 6:30 AM. I was *so* excited. I love the beach. I couldn't wait to get there. By the time it was 8:00 I could hardly stand the anticipation. I was running around the house, making sure I had everything. I got my swim fins and mask. I got my beach towel. I got everybody else's beach towel. I ran into the garage and got the ice chest.

At 8:30 I was making so much noise that my stepmother and father began to yell through their closed bedroom door for me to settle down and be quiet. They liked to sleep in on Saturdays. Besides, the toll beach didn't open until 10:00 anyway. I tried to be quiet. I tried to settle down. Really I did. By 8:45 my parents were screaming at me again. This time they were also swearing.

At 9:00 I could take it no longer. If we didn't get moving we'd be late. It was a long drive to the beach. How were we going to get there in time if we didn't get going? I had to get them up. Dare I knock on their bedroom door? No, I'd better not, I told myself. Something else inside of me said, "You're going to be late." It also cried out, "You've got to get going!" I knocked softly on my parent's bedroom door.

"WHAT NOW!" a shrill voice screamed.

It screeched my name then said, "If that's you . . ." but it didn't go on. Then all of a sudden it bellowed, "One more sound. One more knock on any door. Just *one* more and we're not going to the beach *at all!*"

It was 9:30. They still weren't up. If we got there too late the beach would fill up. They only let a certain number of people out on the beach at a time. When it's full they close the beach down. People can't get in then even if they want to.

It was 9:35. I stood outside my parent's bedroom door. I hardly dared to breathe. Then it was 9:36. We were *never* going to get there on time. I shouldn't do it again. I knew that. They had said if I did we wouldn't go at all. I really wanted to go. I love the beach. The beach was waiting for me.

I decided to just sort of bump their door. My bedroom was right across from theirs. I could pretend that I was bringing something out of my room and accidentally hit their door. What could I use to hit it with? I entered my room and began to look around. It would have to be something that was big to make it look like an accident. I started going through my closet.

It was 9:40. I was frantically moving things around. I dropped some. I shoved some other things out of the way. It was making quite a racket. I wasn't paying attention to the noise I was making. I was so intently focused. My closet was right next to their bedroom.

Suddenly I heard someone holler, "*That's it!*" a voice said. "No beach today. We're not going."

I was devastated. We weren't going. No sand in my shoes. No building sand castles. No finding sand dollars. No chasing and catching sand crabs. No running from waves. Nobody surfing or using my mask and fins to look for mermaids or sunken treasure. No playing in the waves. No lying in the hot sand after nearly freezing to death in the cold water, and then doing it all over again. No skim-boarding over the retreating water an inch above the hard, wet sand. No cold fried chicken and watermelon on the blanket covered sand. None of that was going to happen now and it was all *my* fault.

As an adult, looking back on scenes like this, the man that tells about that beach incident was able to finally begin to make sense out of what had happened. His parents had most likely already decided that they were not going to go to the beach on that Saturday. They simply neglected to tell the boy.

You might wonder why parents might choose not to tell a child about such a change in plans. It's a good question. Think about this. What if the parents didn't really want to go in the first place? An OCS-driven child can be relentless. Perhaps the boy had been begging to go all week. The more the parents put him off, the more intensely he pleaded.

"I'll wash dishes for a month," he might have promised, "if we can just go this Saturday to the beach. "I won't ask to go again for a whole year. I'll wash your car. I'll shine your shoes. I'll do everything you say without complaining. *Please*, can we go? Please, can we . . . can we?"

After listening to his incessant pleas day after day, what would you do? It's not hard to imagine a parent getting very frustrated and annoyed with it all. Telling the child they didn't want to go didn't help. Warning the child to shut up didn't work. Threatening him didn't work. How hard is it to picture a beleaguered parent finally giving in?

They might say something like, "Okay, we'll go," just to get the kid off their back. They are weary of the constant nagging. They allow him to think that they *are* going to the beach. After all, what's the harm in that? They now get a whole week of peace about the matter. They deliberately do not tell him they aren't actually going to go. All they want is for him to *shut up* about the stupid beach.

On the morning when they are supposed to get up to go, they sleep in. After the child's antics wake them several times they know they are home free. They can now place the blame for not going to the beach squarely on him. They are no longer going to the beach because of something *he* did. *He* was the one who woke them up before they had gotten enough sleep. Now they have to sleep in even longer because *he* woke them up too early. It's *his* fault that the beach trip got canceled. "If only you had waited, son, to wake us up at the time you were supposed to!" If only *you* had done things right, we would have gone. If only.

Chew on that one for a while. The child now focuses the blame intensely on himself. He will probably beat himself up pretty bad verbally. He may question his ability to ever do *anything* right. How could he be so stupid? No wonder he never gets to go anywhere. On and on and on it goes. His parents, however, can now stay home. They can sleep in peace and not have to worry about going to the stupid beach.

How often do you suppose something like this has to happen before there is lasting emotional damage? How many emotional wounds does it take to cancel or cover up any happy times that may come along? The answer is that it depends.

In my professional opinion, no book will ever completely portray all the directions in which OCS can have an effect on a family. This is because symptoms vary and are so numerous. They come and go over time. Environments in which people live are different. Symptoms are constantly misinterpreted and misdiagnosed. Individual chemistries change.

This is why it can be pivotal for families to seek out a knowledgeable professional. They need someone who understands what is really going on and can work with them in the discovery process. The goal is to disentangle the complex family dynamics of OCS. The information presented in this book should be viewed as fairly common examples. Even so the depths and types of the possible problems may never be entirely described in books. Also, the issues and concerns that are related indirectly have barely been touched. Awareness is limited only by our inability to see or imagine combined OCS patterns.

As stated, there is no way to illustrate all possible conditions, dynamics, and situations of OCS. There are, however, still a few common threads worth considering. These should be kept in mind by all others involved, and professionals. Doing so should enhance therapeutic progress, hopefully, at least to some degree.

Those with OCS and their families tend to be hypersensitive at times to everything. They can over-respond in the extreme. Many arguments, fights, and misunderstandings have this sensitivity as a basic cause. When hypersensitivity is at fault, tracing this back to its root can be a very helpful intervention. Eventually, becoming aware of the source can also work as a useful prevention tool.

People with OCS may struggle to listen or focus long enough for new information to be fully processed. As a result, the details that do get stored in the brain may not be complete. Such interference often comes from having an obsessive thought getting in the way that can't be let go of. Tracing this storage problem back to the source can be helpful for those who are not identified with OCS. It can soften these others' feelings of frustration and anger. Finally they can see that the person is not just irresponsible. It's not just that those with OCS don't care.

Others start to realize that the person is not intentionally tuning things out. These others' concerns are not just being repeatedly blown off. Remembering things at times can be difficult, if not impossible, for the OCS-affected. This can be especially true for certain kinds of details. Once the memory issues and processing problems are understood, progress can be made. This knowledge can lead to creative and successful approaches to better manage this type of problem.

For example, I am acquainted with a professional who takes a briefcase to work every day. To help manage his OCS-influenced memory issues, he tapes a stick-it note to the outside. The briefcase only opens from one side. So each time he goes to open it, whatever he doesn't want to forget is stuck to it right there in front of his face. He also writes things down without delay so they don't get lost in other thoughts later on.

There was another man who couldn't stand having anything in his right pants pocket. It would annoy him so much that he became an exclusive left pocket man. When *he* wanted to remember something important, he wrote it down on paper. He would then crumple it up into a ball and shove it in that right pants pocket. It bugged him so much that there was no way he was going to forget that it was there. If he did happen to forget what was written on it, which rarely ever happened, he'd just reach in and pull out the bothersome lump. After smoothing it out a bit he'd see what was written and "TAH DAH" the memory was back. This worked for him.

OCS-driven people get doing something and either appear not to want to or don't seem able to quit (compulsive). This problem can be at the heart of not getting around to completing chores. It can be the underlying cause of missed meetings and unfinished homework. It may prompt arguments and result in temper tantrums and threats. It can be the source of extreme anger and physically violent actions. Aggressive-like actions may also originate in this same way. This inability to stop when you are supposed to can be the cause of any of the concerns listed above, and even more. It is critical to realize that the causal link between this need to continue OCS reactions and related outcomes can be either direct or indirect.

An example of direct causation would be when a parent simply turns off a video game while a child is playing. The explosive outburst that follows is directly related to the interruption of the OCS need to play or finish the game. This is the cause. The aftereffects of such a disruption are a direct response to the interference of a symptom.

Indirect OCS-related outcomes may have just a few or a great many links and connected layers. They can be incredibly complex and the source may be hard to figure out. A simple indirect OCS-related outcome would be the homework that didn't get done or the meeting that was missed. This is a one step indirect result. A more complex indirect result is the argument with a parent the next morning when she finds out the homework isn't done. Yet another indirect consequence relative to the same source is the failing grade the child gets at school. Even more undesirable outcomes can be linked to this same OCS root cause. Remember, the underlying cause was the inability to disengage from an activity in a timely manner.

When those with OCS want something in an obsessive way, they want it *bad*. They will ask and ask and then ask again if they can have it. They will cajole, wheedle, whine, and demand. They may even make threats that they do not really intend to carry out. Such threats can be terrifying, nonetheless. These can include threats of physical injury and murder or the destruction of objects. There may be suicidal threats. Some of those driven by OCS may threaten to run away if they don't get what they want. When you are faced with OCS, responses such as these stand your ground. Don't take what is said or done while under the influence of OCS personally. Remind yourself and the driven one that these reactions are symptoms of OCS and nothing else. Don't let these symptoms push you around.

If one parent tells the OCS-driven child "no," anticipate that this child will go straight to the other. Parents need to do whatever it takes to make sure they talk to one another about their OCS child. They need to check-in regularly with each other. This is especially true for any questionable activities in relation to their children.

There can be extreme heightened responses to others' reactions. When they react it may appear to others to be way more intense than called for, but to the OCS responder it seems appropriate. For example, if the OCS child says or does something and senses that mom or dad is unhappy, it can crush them. Thoughts about how that parent must surely hate them can surface. Once such a thought occurs, they may not be able to shake it or be absolutely certain that it's not actually true. Circular thinking further muddies the water. "Why would such a thought come and refuse to go away if it wasn't true?" "I hate myself for having done what I did. So it only makes sense that they must surely hate me too."

The tension and anxiety brought on by powerful fear hyper-responses can begin to run a person's life. Because the tension and fear is so overpowering, adults and children alike will lie to avoid having to face up to it. Either that or they will hold back on telling the whole truth. This is a lie of omission. On both sides of the coin, it can be very distressing and difficult to deal with. That's because the actual misinformation the OCS person relates may also cause parents and others to be disappointed. When the disappointment expressed is founded on an untruth, though, it is easier for the OCS to handle. The OCS often can't stand to have anyone thinking bad things about them or being upset with them.

Sometimes it can be quite a bit easier for those with OCS to handle another's reactions towards them when they tell a lie. For example, if the one with OCS says she was at a nearby mall when she was really at a park across town, her parents may yell at her. They may say bad things about her and her poor choices and so on. The girl can handle this easily because everything the parent said about her was based on her lie and so doesn't count. She won't feel bad about being called stupid ad irresponsible for going to the mall without permission, because she didn't go to the mall. Her parents are berating her for something she didn't do.

Oh, how sweet it is! She just has to remind herself that her parent's responses to the fib don't really apply to her since it wasn't true anyway. The horrible things that a parent is saying or *thinking* about her may not bother her at all in this situation. If, however, a parent had been reacting to the actual truth by yelling at her it would be real. If her parents were screaming at her about how stupid she was for going to that park at night that's clear across town then that would have been different. If they'd been yelling about what she'd really done, then all their words and actions directed at her would have been true.

That simply cannot be allowed to happen. "Surely I would die," she might think. "Either that or *they're* gonna kill me." The distorted and exaggerated fear those with OCS feel in relation to how they think others will react to them, is often totally unjustified. Nevertheless, to the OCS, what they fear might happen they believe really could happen. Even though there is no evidence to support such fear, it remains in their mind and they often cannot shake it off. Once there it's there.

Now, what if the parents were to catch this child in a lie? Well, that would be even worse, of course. As a result, if the OCS lie is found out the person may expend incredible energy and time denying that the lie is a lie. Often, even when it is blatantly obvious that the person is telling a lie, this fact will be stubbornly denied. This makes no sense to others. Parents and teachers can become infuriated. Their frustration can build to a point that they have to walk away rather than take a chance on losing control and acting out some pretty horrible impulses. Walking away is not only okay, but sometimes it is the best possible response available.

The OCS-driven can often come up with a creative outlook through which their lie could actually be considered the truth. They can also take a stand and hotly deny that the lie is a lie. This disturbs parents and others greatly. They don't understand how such a pattern can be repeated over and over again. Doesn't this child or adult ever learn that the fear that drives them to lie doesn't even make sense? Don't they ever figure out that all the pain and misery they get from having lied is not worth the price of the lie?

No they don't, not really. Since each new incident may happen at a different intensity level (state of consciousness) than before, all else during that time period can be forgotten. Eventually, when emotions have been calmed and some time has passed, many are able to come clean about the lie. While in the throes of this chemically driven moment, however, the majority cannot admit that they have lied. This further baffles and angers parents and others.

OCS family members sometimes need their space. During an episode in which OCS actions and reactions are charged, nothing else can get through. Verbal debate is useless. Yelling or screaming makes everything worse. Touching or efforts to restrain usually do the same. At times like these, often everybody involved needs to be left alone. They need to calm down. Nothing good can come from continuing such a confrontation.

Creative use of the time-out or time-away method is needed. This is probably the healthiest way to respond in these situations. Professionals can help with this. They can work to create a family time-out system. Typically, this should include a backup plan in case someone gets too out of control. Things can get so intense that time-out and time-away may also be quite useless. Usually this is because one or more of those involved are either unable or refusing to honor the plan.

A family cue system can be helpful. This cue, signal, or reminder can be verbal, visual, or involve the use of touch. Each family member agrees to use the chosen signal the moment a problem situation begins. The success of a strategy such as this is dependent on family agreement. All must be willing to give it a try. Second, all must agree on what cue or signals will be used. If agreement is not unanimous, this approach should not be tried.

One family decided to cue each other by playfully saying, "Are you obsessing again?" This actually worked quite well for them. With some practice and a little time they were able to prevent most of the household fights. These episodes used to occur on a daily basis. Sometimes a person will have a symptom that makes it impossible to use a cue and signal strategy. One symptom that this happens with a lot involves extreme embarrassment at being signaled. Another common symptom you don't want to use cues with is extreme frustration and anger about being cued. This can be especially difficult if the cues are many and frequent.

Changes in routines or plans can be very difficult for those with OCS to handle well. Often this problem can be the reason that family members may not do much or go many places together. Vacations are way too often complete disasters. There are some methods that can help to make changes, transitions, and vacations go more smoothly. One of the best and most effective is, don't go! This is meant to be a bit in jest here, but sadly it happens far too often. Vacations and sudden changes in plans can lead to much misery and pain in an OCS family. As a result they simply give up. To avoid suffering the family stops going on vacations. This strategy isn't really a healthy one. It may be slightly healthier than continuing the yearly disasters with the hope that things will get better. Aren't things supposed to get better if you just keep on trying? Isn't that what persistence is all about? Continuing to confront a challenging situation makes it better right? Well, not necessarily. Never give up, never surrender! Yeah, right.

Of course treatment in the form of education, knowledge, and medication can all be very helpful. Another method that is probably one of the best for easing transitions and going new places is *preparation*. A family should begin talking about a planned trip or vacation months in advance. The closer to the date of departure, the more often and detailed these discussions ought to be. How often and how detailed depends on the age of children and how strong the family OCS symptoms are. It can also depend on whether or not other treatment methods are currently in use.

In doing this, each family member is getting mentally prepared. Having done this, they can better anticipate what will happen. They will respond better emotionally than they would have if they knew nothing. Fewer surprises on such a trip will translate into fewer behavioral and emotional issues. Possible sudden changes can be taken into account and processed. This can ease mental anguish, anxiety, and worry related to the fear of the unknown. When better prepared for changes and transitions, the emotional status of each family member is more resilient. The family is then much less likely to have another "disaster." Normally, with the use of the preparation method, things *will* go more smoothly.

All family members need to practice, practice, and continue to practice their PATIENCE. Patience is needed in relation to each other, as well as themselves. One of my favorite and most helpful mantras that I use is *"practice your patience."* It doesn't matter whether this is in reference to myself or to others. We could all benefit from practicing our patience. It truly *is* a powerful virtue.

OCS and the Individual

What is it like inside the mind of a person struggling with OCS? How do they think? What do they think about? How do they view other people? How do they see the world around them? What do they think about themselves?

"I want to die," one six-year-old told his mother. He was distressed by another *"sad sticker"* his teacher had put on his work paper that he took home. It was the seventh in a row that he'd gotten. It was only the middle of the second week of school. His mother brought him to my office, very concerned.

"I should just kill myself," said a fourteen-year-old to her friend at school. The friend reported this to the teacher. The teacher told the principal. The principal sent her to the school psychologist. She shared the same suicidal thought with him. The psychologist called her caseworker. The girl was in a foster home placement at the time. The caseworker had heard it before. He listened to the psychologist, but seemed unimpressed. The young lady had told the psychologist that her foster parents weren't all that great. This was probably true, the caseworker had admitted. This particular caseworker appeared to simply blow it off. The school psychologist began to see her two to three times a week. He tried to be there to support her as best as he could.

Every single week for the next month, this same psychologist phoned the caseworker at least one time. He shared that the girl was still feeling like she wanted to end her life. It appeared that the caseworker just couldn't seem take what the young lady was saying seriously. There were no changes made in her foster home situation.

Early one morning during the fifth week since this had all started, the girl knocked on the office door of the school psychologist. It was about ten minutes before school was to begin. He opened the door and motioned for her to come in and sit down.

As she entered the office, she looked at him. She appeared a little disheveled. Knowing fully well that the psychologist would have to report it, she calmly declared, "I did it."

She told him she had taken forty asthma tablets. Her heart was pounding. The psychologist immediately took her to the nurse. Paramedics were called. The psychologist was allowed to stay with her. Both of them went by ambulance to the hospital. He was at her bedside when they pumped her stomach.

The young lady was removed from the foster home placement before she left the hospital. The state put her in a *therapeutic* foster home. The school psychologist was able keep in touch a few times for the next couple of years. She thrived in her new environment.

Suicide is on the mind of many with OCS. It doesn't really matter if they are children or adults. When things never seem to go right or go the way that a person wants them to, the mind and heart can get stuck. It can think of no other way to get free from these constant feelings of misery. The OCS-tormented often can see no other options available to ease the pain.

"She doesn't love me. She probably *never* did. She hates me. I can't say that I blame her. I hate myself," he thinks. "I don't deserve to be loved by anyone. How could I possibly hope that she'd be any different? I'll bet if I just stepped right off this world no one would even notice. No one really cares. Not even me. Why should they?"

Thoughts such as those above come and go. When OCS-driven, they happen a lot. Mostly they come when things aren't going well. When a girlfriend dumps you they come. When a spouse declares that he or she wants a divorce they come. They occur when you don't get that promotion you expected and wanted so badly. They come when you can't stop thinking that everybody hates you. They happen a lot.

The main problem with OCS is that when these thoughts enter the mind they tend to stick around. Not only that, but feelings are greatly magnified by the OCS hypersensitivity. The intensity of thoughts and emotions are prone to be much stronger for those with OCS. Once these thoughts and emotions occur, they then seem to want to set up shop and refuse to leave. An entire day can be ruined by one little thing that goes wrong in the morning.

Other people who don't have a strong OCS influence are the *lucky* ones. They don't *feel* as deeply. They don't beat themselves up all the time over *stupid* things. *They* can actually be happy. *They* can let things go. *They* can forgive. The OCS-afflicted tends to have trouble doing all these things.

There is a great turbulence going on inside the OCS mind. It is almost *never* peaceful or calm. There's *always* something that isn't right or that needs to be done. There is *never* enough time. The OCS mind thinks in extremes. "All-or-nothing, black or white," these are its only working point of view. "If I can't do it well I'd rather not do it at all." "If I'm not going to win I don't want to play." "If I'm playing and start to lose I'll do whatever it takes to make sure that I win. If I *still* can't win no matter what I do I have to find a reason for the loss. I'll take a fall. I'll blame the referee for bad calls. I'll quit and walk away saying I didn't want to play this *stupid* game anyway. I'll bump the board by accident so that all the pieces fall off and we can't finish. I *cannot* accept defeat. I *cannot* lose. I *will not* lose."

People with OCS overreact to what are often considered the stupidest things. They become melodramatic and emotional over silly little things. To them, however, these things don't seem stupid or silly at all. Let's visit the mind of one OCS person during a moment when this was happening:

I was sitting in my car idling. My little girl was going to go with me to the store. She'd had to go to the bathroom at the last minute. While I waited I adjusted the rear view mirror. It only needed to be moved a tiny tad to the left. It had to be just right so I could see out the back window. I couldn't stand it when it was even the least bit crooked. If it was off center just the tiniest little smidgen it drove me crazy. It would take a long time and many adjustments to finally get that stupid little mirror in the proper place too. I glanced at it once again and felt it was *perfect*.

My daughter bounded out of the back door and raced to the car. She came to the driver's side and I opened the door to let her in. She immediately crawled over my lap to get to the other front seat. As she did this her head bumped into that rear view mirror. She knocked it way off center.

"Oh, no," I screamed. "You *bumped* my mirror!"

I quickly got her situated in the seat belt. Then my attention went instantly back to the hopelessly lopsided mirror.

"Now I'm *never* going to get it back to the right position." My voice was loud and full of intense anger. At that moment it felt like it was the most important thing in the world that had just been messed up. I ranted and raved. I shifted into reverse and rolled out onto the street. All the while I was heatedly shouting about how I'd *never* (those with OCS use that word *never* a lot) get it in the right place again. I grumbled and adjusted the stupid mirror all the way down our street. I was still complaining loudly and trying to get that mirror back into its *perfect* position when we stopped to turn at the end of the street.

I looked left. I looked right. It was then that I noticed my little daughter. She was crying. Her tiny hands were frantically wiping tears from her eyes.

"I'm sorry, daddy," she whimpered over and over again. "I'm sorry . . . ."

It was a rear view mirror, a *stupid* rear view mirror. They make those things so that they rotate. How else can they be adjusted for a different driver? They're supposed to move.

I thought to myself, "*What* am I doing?"

I looked down at my daughter who was still wiping away her tears. I wanted to die.

This man truly *did* want to die at that moment. He felt horrible about what he'd done. He did not want to be acting like this and especially not with his children. *His* parents had done that same kind of thing to *him*. How could *he* be doing this too? He knew that he would rather be *dead* than continue to cause such pain, fear, and sorrow in his own children. He vowed right then and there to *never* (there's that word again) do such a thing again. But then, he did. In fact he did it again and again and again over the silliest little things. He literally hated himself for a long, long time before finally getting the help he so desperately needed.

No one seems to get more excited about things than someone with OCS. They already feel emotions at an amplified level. It can only intensify from there. To understand this next example, it may help to rephrase something that the well-known Mr. Albert Einstein once said.

"Every recollection is colored by today's being what it is and therefore by a deceptive point of view."

According to him all memory is a least a bit slanted. What is actually happening at the moment and how we feel at any given time is culprit. We don't set out to distort reality. It just happens. As a result, probably no memory is as true as we might think it is.

It is usually difficult for the OCS-driven to work in groups. This tends to be generally true throughout their lifetime. If they feel a project *needs* to be done in a certain way, they are going to fight for that need against all odds.

There is a common belief that goes round and round in the OCS mind. It is that no one else is going to do things as good or proficiently as they will. This person *needs* things to be done well. The sad part about this is that much of the time it may actually be true. Unless also OCS-driven, the others in a group are probably not going to want to spend as much time and effort (be obsessive or compulsive) on a project.

Imagine for a moment there is a work group that has more than one OCS-driven person. What if each person with OCS thinks differently about the direction a project should go? Chaos may reign in the group at least for a while. Tension and stress would definitely be a factor. This only makes sense. Perhaps you can now envision the numerous issues and problems that a group with one or two OCS-driven people might face. Now what if such a working group has two or even three or four OCS types? Let the sparks fly.

"Money is made so that it can be spent." This was a comment made in a session by an OCS-driven male. That statement illustrates one of the common mind-sets for those with OCS relative to finances. "Why else do we make money?" such a person thinks. However, in the all-or-nothing style of the OCS-driven there *is* another side to this coin.

"A penny saved is a penny earned," is a famous quote by Mr. Benjamin Franklin.

"I make money so that I'll have it," is another similar statement that shows just a touch of the *miser* side of the coin where money is concerned. Ebenezer Scrooge is a good example of what happens to people on this side. He was a skin-flint, penny pincher, excessively stingy, tightfisted sort. These are characteristics of those who have trouble spending any money at all.

On the one hand, you've got someone who spends money as soon as they get it in their hands. And sometimes these can spend it before they get their hands on it. This kind of person has great difficulty managing money. This type wants to buy, buy, buy and doesn't seem to understand the cost of such behavior. In a marriage this can become a nightmare for the other partner. It is very common for the OCS spender to embellish the truth. They avoid sharing details about their spending. They may even outright lie about what they are doing when it comes to money. Eventually he or she *is* found out. Sometimes a married couple may get buried in debt before these issues are discovered.

One woman kept her secret right up until her deathbed. Her husband only found out about her gambling debt because of circumstances. During the last month or so of her battle against cancer, she was bedridden. She was then unable to handle her affairs. She could no longer secretly pay her monthly fee. There was a credit card she'd gotten behind her husband's back. The fact that she had it could no longer be concealed. When he did finally find out about this he was furious. How could she have done that? Arizona is by law a community property state. Because of this if *you* owe money, your partner has to pay it if you do not. When she passed away, there was still ten thousand dollars left on that credit card. Her hapless husband had known nothing about it up until the very end.

Another man owned his own business. He had worked very hard for his entire life and had been quite successful. You might not guess this by looking at his house or by the clothes he wore. Every penny he ever spent was cataloged and accounted for. He would spend only as much as he *had* to. This man was also very good at finding or making the *best* deals on *everything* he bought. He kept his wife on a very meager and tight budget. Most of the time, she had barely enough money for the household bills. There was nothing left whatsoever for her to use to purchase anything extra. As a result, his wife had to get a part-time job. She had to do this if she wanted money for the things she might want for her daughter or herself.

The secrecy behind which he handled their finances was also way over the top. His wife was not involved in any of the actual bill paying or financial planning, other than what was needed to run the house. She literally had no idea how much money he had amassed over the years or where it went.

In time this man passed away. It was a bit sooner than might be expected for most in this day and age. After his death the family discovered that he was actually a millionaire. *No one* knew. It was a huge surprise to them all. He had money in more banks than his wife even knew existed in Arizona. Of course he'd done this to be certain that the whole of it was FDIC insured.

Although this man gave generous gifts to his family over the years, it seemed that he never really got a chance to enjoy his wealth. It was very hard for him to let go of money. Not long after his passing, the family found file after file of business receipts in storage at the man's office. These were dated as far back as the 1930s. His surviving wife was completely overwhelmed by her sudden and unexpected wealth. She ended up needing a lot of help from her children to manage all her financial affairs. She had never learned how to handle such things. She didn't even have a clue how to proceed.

The OCS mind is constantly plagued by fear and *what ifs*. *What if* I'm not really who I think I am? *What if* I am not what others think I am? *What if* I am? *What if they* think I'm *bad* or *foolish*? *What if* others think I'm stupid or dull? *What if* I am stupid? *What if* I'm really ugly? *I* think I'm ugly, so surely others must think so too. *What if* they say I'm beautiful just to make me feel good? *What if* I *know* they are lying? *What if* no one *ever* tells the truth about things like that? Sometimes *I* don't tell the truth. *What if* I *lose*? *What if* no one likes me? *What if* I go bald or have to wear glasses? *What if* I get fat? *What if* people think I'm crazy? *What if* I really am? *What if* no one *ever* wants to marry me? *What if* the only reason she did marry me was because she felt sorry for me? *What if* she doesn't *really* love me? I don't really love myself so how could anyone else? *What if* nothing in this world is real and it's all just a dream? *What if* life is just an accident and there is no God? *What if* there is?

That's probably *enough* of that. A person could go nuts just from thinking like that. A great many of those with OCS are secretly afraid they might be crazy. With all the weird things that they think and do, who wouldn't wonder about it?

In the mind of the OCS, life is as uncertain as a tightrope walker on the high wire. A sudden wind could come up and knock her from that wire at any moment. Should this happen without a safety net, it would be all over *just like that*. Fortunately, most high-wire acts do make use of a safety net. There may be a lot of time and energy spent by the OCS person trying to make sure that they don't get knocked off of the wires of life. This can be extremely tiring. It can keep the person from being able to do much more than focus on themselves throughout their entire lives.

What would you be like if you felt as if you *were* walking on a tightrope for *your* entire life? What if *you* had to face every day the fear of losing your balance and falling? Don't you think it might be just a bit difficult to focus on anything but yourself? Do you think you could really pay any kind of decent attention to what others might be doing or saying? This is but one of the many long-term dilemmas suffered by those with OCS. It is very hard to focus on anything else when you feel a constant sense of danger to yourself. It doesn't matter that the danger may be unrealistic or irrational. The OCS mind thinks it's real. That or the mind simply can't shake the possibility that it *might* be real.

This is the same kind of phenomenon that takes place when a major disaster occurs. Take for example "nine-eleven" as it has become known by most that live in the United States. On September 11, 2001, terrorists flew two planes into the twin towers in New York, killing everyone on board and many other people. There are a lot of people who will never get on a plane again because of this. The very idea that such a thing could happen *even one time* is enough. These are the OCS people. That event acted as a trigger for the newly adopted decision to *never* fly again. Who can argue with their logic? It *could* happen again. It probably won't, but it could. I refer to an incident such as this as a "trigger event." There are many such trigger events that occur throughout the life span of an OCS-driven person.

Another woman described her specific OCS problem in detail. With her permission, I am sharing her story.

It's not so much that she was afraid to say something in public. It's just that she was afraid she wouldn't be able say what it was that she *really* wanted to say. When put on the spot she felt she wasn't able to think fast enough or clearly enough to be able to get out what she truly meant. Later, when she'd had some time to go over what *was* actually spoken, she would think of many alternative ways to have said it *better* or *more clearly*. She *should* have said *this!* She *should have* said *that!* If *only* she'd said this. That's what she couldn't get her mind to stop thinking about. She couldn't stop thinking about all those awful *should-haves*.

For her, this was like a form of mental torture. She would reflect on it for days and sometimes for weeks. She might beat herself up and be in mental agony for as long as a month. This was especially true if she'd said something that she was *sure* had hurt another person's feelings. That was the absolute *worst!* If she thought that she had hurt someone else by what she'd said she would get to feeling so bad she wouldn't want them to see her. In fact, she sometimes wouldn't want *anyone* at all to see her for a while. The mental suffering she would go through was so strong and deep-rooted that it would get very depressing.

Sometimes she would find herself wondering if she was just making up excuses for wanting to be alone. Should she *fight* it? Was this even something that she *could* fight and win? Did it make her a bad person because she couldn't share her ideas and beliefs with others openly?

Sometimes she would think and feel that maybe she *was* bad. She would hate going over and over in her mind the things she'd said in public. She hated it so much that she usually avoided sharing her thoughts and ideas in any public setting. The chance that she might not say things *right* kept her from saying much at all in public most of the time. She couldn't bear the unrelenting guilt she felt afterwards.

This woman was struggling with the letting go of a triggered thought. It would continue to torment and haunt her long after it had occurred. She didn't seem able to let go of those distressing thoughts most of the time. Her solution was to completely avoid doing those things that caused her to feel such pain. This makes sense. It was restricting her life.

The following is another very similar example, also used by permission. These words were written by the OCS-affected woman herself:

"I've always considered myself to be what I call a slow processor. It is hard for me to express my ideas vocally to others in a quick and understandable way. If the idea is simple or something that I am very familiar with, it isn't quite so hard for me. If I am asked to comment on something that is complex or unfamiliar to me, I have a very hard time organizing my thoughts and expressing myself.

It's kind of like baking a cake. If you take the cake out of the oven early, the edges might be cooked enough to eat a little, but the middle will be soggy and gushy and very unappetizing. If the cake is left in the oven for a longer time, it will come out golden brown and cooked through and through. It's like my thoughts are swirling around in my head like a soggy cake batter and I need the time to sort through them all and figure out what I want to say.

In life, time stops for no one and when I finally have figured out what I want to say, the moment has passed and I am left with my unexpressed ideas. This is a most frustrating experience and it happens over and over again and I wish more than anything that I could have said what I wanted to say when the moment for it was right. My ideas seem to swirl around the most when I am in a group situation, and people around me think that I am shy or quiet because I don't say much, but that is really not the case. I want to comment, but in my past experiences when I have tried to, it comes out half-baked and not what I really mean to say; so I usually keep quiet.

Of course, I keep thinking about it as I can't let go of the fact that I didn't say anything like I wanted to, and then over and over the thought goes on about what I wished that I had said. This tortures me and I get down on myself about what a stupid woman I am and shameful feelings always come with the thoughts. Over time the strength of the feelings lessen until I can eventually think about the incident with only a sting of pain instead of a blade. This usually takes about two months, depending on how intense the initial experience was. Then something else will happen that will start the cycle all over again."

Was she truly a slow-processor as she thought herself to be? Or was this an example of an anxiety-ridden OCS-driven person? When put in a position that forced her to respond verbally in public, she felt incredible anxiety. This was caused by what she anticipated was going to happen. After all, it *always* did. The very unease she underwent would then interfere with her ability to think clearly. Not thinking clearly would keep her from responding in a way that was consistent with her true opinion. Afterwards her anguish was magnified by thinking about all the things that she *should have* said. These would include all the things that she could easily think of when she wasn't worrying so much about what she might say, and so on and so on. The circle would simply continue and feed upon itself.

Two examples have been given from the perspective of women. I don't want anyone to get the false impression that the same thing can't happen to men. It can, and does happen to men. It just might not happen as often. Experience seems to suggest that it is a much more frequent trend with women. Men, however, *have* presented with such a tendency as well. There seem to be no absolutes in relation to the OCS mind.

Then there are the distractions. When most people think *obsessive* or *compulsive*, the idea of having trouble with attention probably doesn't come to mind much at all. This is a mistake. Take for example the following story told by an OCS-driven man:

I will never forget something that happened to me when I was about eleven years old. My dad was chewing me out and he was really mad. He was right up in my face yelling and carrying on about something or other he thought I'd done.

At first I was upset because I truly had not done what he was accusing me of. He wouldn't listen to me, though. The more I tried to tell him about it, the louder and angrier he got. He might have been a little tipsy at the time too. He usually was. Anyway, I finally decided to just wait out his anger. I figured it would eventually die down.

Well, it just kept going on and on. It went on so long that I began thinking of something else that had happened during the day with one of my friends. It had been kind of funny. As I remembered the funny thing with my friend, a smile must have appeared on my face. All of a sudden my father was bellowing louder than ever.

"Oh, so you think it's *FUNNY*, do you?"

"Uh, no," I said. "No I don't, not at all." But it was too late. I was in deep trouble. I got punished for whatever it was he'd been mad about, but I also got punished even worse for thinking it was funny. Trust me; I hadn't thought it was funny. Why does my mind do that to me?

When the OCS mind gets bored or is not interested in what is happening, it goes to another place. When such a mind is wrapped up in a thought or an idea, it can stay fixated on that idea. A mind in this state does not take in new information or follow instructions very well because it's already busy. At any moment the OCS mind may get caught up in a brand new idea or be unable to let go of the idea that's already there. While this is going on the mind may or may not be available for other tasks, thoughts, or instructions. Usually it is not. In this way the OCS-driven mind can seem just as distractible as the mind that is driven by an Attention Deficit Hyperactive Disorder (ADHD).

A young boy is overjoyed. "You mean all I have to do is clean my room and then I can go?" He quips to his mother.

"Yes," she replies, "but it has to be clean by my standards."

"No problem," her son assures her. "I'm going to go clean my room," he sings, "I'm going to go clean my room." He hurriedly leaves the backyard garden.

His mother returns to pulling weeds. "Come and tell me when you're done, so I can inspect it," she calls out after him.

"I'm going to go clean my room," the boy sings skipping up to the back door leading into the kitchen. "I'm going to clean my room," he dances on through the kitchen. "I'm going to clean my room," he chants under his breath as he enters the living room.

His big brother is watching TV. The boy doesn't want his brother to hear him singing, and especially not about something so stupid. If he was to be caught singing about cleaning a room, how uncool would *that* be?

"Hey, Jimmy," his brother suddenly calls out, "you ever see this commercial?"

Jimmy stops, but continues barely moving his lips, "I'm going to clean my room. I'm going to clean my room. "Huh uh, Josh," he mumbles as he turns to look. "I'm going to clean . . ." then all on a sudden it *had* him. The music was very up-tempo.

Josh was singing along and acting out moves like a rock star. It was really funny. He was mimicking exactly what the guy on the TV was doing; only, Josh was funnier.

Jimmy started to laugh. He sat down on the footstool between the chair and the couch. The next commercial was almost just as funny. The one after that was totally scary. It was about some new movie that Jimmy was sure *he* didn't want to see. Then the show his brother had been watching came back on.

It was Deal or no Deal. The lady was about to win either a million dollars or just one dollar. Jimmy moved from the stool to the chair. He couldn't stop laughing at the antics of Howie Mandell, the host of the show.

Two hours later Jimmy's mother stuck her head into the living room. "Okay guys, go wash up for dinner,' she told them. "Decided not to go over to Troy's after all, huh?" she nods at Jimmy.

"Wha-what," he stammers. "No, I uh . . . no, I really *do* want to go."

"Too late now, buddy," she smiles. "Dinner's on the table in three."

Jimmy was instantly enraged. He *had* promised Troy he'd be over. They had plans to ride their bikes together down *suicide hill*. Now he couldn't go. He wondered if Troy went down the hill without him. He hammered his fists against both sides of his head as he went to wash up for dinner. Why am I so stupid? Why? Why? Why?

Why indeed? The OCS mind can get yanked into a thought so quickly, with a focus so intense, that it takes the person by surprise. The two hours that Jimmy was riveted to the TV went by in a flash. At the moment that his mother called him to dinner it had seemed to him that he'd only just sat down. When the OCS mind is in the act of being *driven*, time seems to stand still.

The reality that *time* can often seem to stand still is something that can sometimes be used to the person's advantage. It is often very difficult for the OCS mind to wait patiently. Waiting in line or waiting for the fish to fry or waiting at a doctor's office or waiting for the TV commercial to get over feels like a *colossal* waste of time. The OCS mind *hates* to waste time. It *can't* be tolerated.

George had both ADHD and OCS. So not only did he hate wasting time, but he constantly bounced his legs and fidgeted. It was also very difficult for him to sit for long or stay in one spot. He couldn't stand waiting. If he went to eat at a fast food restaurant for lunch and there was a line of three or more people, he would turn around and go back to work. He'd rather not eat than have to spend time waiting in a line. Sometimes at a bank or in a doctor's office he had no choice but to wait. The longer he waited, the angrier and more restless he would get. After a long delay the anger that built up might linger for hours. Often it actually ruined the rest of his day.

One of the things George loved to do, however, was to draw. In fact it was a bit of an obsession. When in the act of sketching he would relax, stop fidgeting, and time would seem to rush on by. One day George needed to make a stop at the bank. He tried to prepare ahead of time mentally for the usual lengthy and irritating wait in line. It was late afternoon, and on top of that, a Friday. By chance he just happened to have a clipboard with him. On it was a new drawing he'd been working on. The line at the bank turned out to be very long. It looked to him like it might take "*forever*" to get up to the teller. He was not a happy camper.

After taking his place at the end of the line, George decided to work on his current drawing while standing there. Why not? He propped the bottom of the clipboard up against his chest. It was easy to support with his left arm underneath. Unclipping the mechanical pencil from the metal clamp at the top he began to draw. In his own words he explains what happened:

"All on a sudden a teller was calling and motioning for me to come forward. It was *my* turn. I glanced around thinking that maybe the others that had been waiting before me had gotten tired and gone home. As I took care of my business with the teller I asked him the time. I hate wearing a watch, you know. I was shocked to learn that forty minutes had passed since I'd first gotten in that bank line. *Forty* minutes! To me it had been like the blink of an eye. I couldn't believe it. On the drive home I realized what I now had to do from that point on, whenever standing in any line."

George had found the answer to his lifelong struggle with having to wait places. He started taking that drawing board (clipboard) everywhere he went. He could draw for hours and hours and enjoy every minute of it. He learned that as long as he was drawing he could easily wait anywhere for hours and hours too. No more frustration, anger, anxiety, or distress while waiting. This hobby (obsession) eliminated the problem. For him, it was truly like a dream come true.

His wife also felt hopeful about George's newfound ability to be more patient. It reduced George's nonstop grumbling when they were out together. He could even go shopping with her for clothes. George was now able to patiently wait as long as it might take and not get antsy or upset. As long as he had his drawing board with him, he could wait *forever*.

Others with OCS may find comfort in reading. Whenever one is in a situation that requires a long wait, the act of reading a book may cause time to fly. These are the OCS-driven readers. Time slips by so swiftly while immersed in a book that before they know it their wait is over. Still others might be able to *channel* an OCS-driven need to perhaps write poems, songs, letters, or stories, to pass the time. Negative thoughts can't influence the mind during an incompatible OCS-driven activity. Thoughts are the foundation from which anxiety, frustration, and anger are born. With no such thoughts relentlessly gnawing at the mind, accepting bothersome delays is a lot easier.

Finding a way to redirect OCS tendencies for practical use is healthy. Such an approach can reduce the guilt, frustration, and anger related to the feeling of wasting time. A person drawing, writing, reading, or keeping busy while waiting is *not* wasting time. Of course you need to be cautious, because even this, if taken to the extreme, can get out of hand. A strategy such as this should be managed wisely. Adjustments can be made as they are needed. And it *is* a good bet that sooner or later fine-tuning or modifications of this OCS channeling *will* be needed.

Those with OCS can benefit immensely from education. This involves learning the ins and outs about many of the more common characteristics. It is often very helpful to understand the personal issues associated with OCS. A few of those that are fairly common are as follows:

There is a tendency for the person with OCS to be viewed by others as extremely self-centered. The problem is that it *does* look that way. OCS individuals do appear to be very self-absorbed. Clinical experience suggests that this self-focus is based on the interfering symptoms. In the OCS mind, much of what they do is thought to be entirely for the benefit of others. The real dilemma lies in how their supposed selfless acts are put into practice. Given the popular notion of selfishness, this is a difficult concept to understand. It tends also to be hard to believe.

A simplified example may help. Let's say a child comes to visit his grandfather. In the backyard of the house they happen to have two big and healthy navel orange trees growing. The child loves oranges. So upon arriving, he asks his grandfather if they can go out back and pick one. He wants to eat it.

The grandfather is thrilled at his grandson's request. After all he'd hand-planted them both for this very reason more than twenty-five years before. They go out to the backyard together. The grandfather's entire purpose for planting those trees was for this grand moment. He begins telling the story of those special trees to his grandson.

The boy *wants* an orange. But the story must be told first. Grandfather insists. The boy must hear it in its entirety. The grandfather starts to tell the tale of exactly why it was the navel orange that he chose to plant.

The boy stretches his hand out towards the nearest tree.

"Not yet," his grandfather redirects his hand. "We're getting to the good part. I went to thirty-two different nurseries before I found these two very special kinds . . ." the grandfather drones on.

Need this go on? Can you begin to get a sense of what is going to happen here? The *writing is on the wall.*

Obviously this grandfather appears to be forcing his story on the boy to fulfill his own needs. This is exactly how it looks. To the grandfather, however, it has a whole different meaning. He is caught up in the obsessive need for this moment to be just right. Every single word along with twenty-five *plus* years of care has been totally for and on behalf of his grandson. But the boy only wanted an orange.

There is yet another way to interpret this story. If the grandfather has OCS, then his grandson may too. For the sake of this alternative explanation, let's assume that he does.

The boy wants an orange. I mean he really wants one. He must have one, now. His own OCS demands it. He reaches out towards the nearest tree.

Grandpa gently pushes the boy's hand aside. "Not yet, son," he tells him.

The boy can hardly stand it. He needs an orange. He must get one right away. Again he puts forth a hand.

"No, no, not yet," it is pushed away.

Orange, orange, orange . . . the word beats inside the grandson's mind. ORANGE!

Perhaps this is enough to share in the alternate view to get the picture. This time it is the grandson who might be seen as selfish. He appears completely focused on his own needs and oblivious to those of his grandfather. The OCS drive can all too easily be labeled as selfish behavior. When this happens, serious emotional baggage can be added over time.

Knowledge and awareness (and sometimes medication) are needed to make progress on this problem. Also needed are patience and commitment. The OCS person must be open-minded. There can be no signs of denial. Finally, the person must not be too defensive. They must learn to "catch" themselves in the act, so to speak. Most of the time, especially in the beginning, they will need to rely on others. They need someone to help them realize when it seems like they are being self-centered.

Remember, to the OCS-driven the action is not self-centered at all. This is why the person must be open and non-defensive. It's usually the only way they will be able to accept such cues. The moment the cue is given, the OCS should stop whatever they are doing. It can help to shift attention to another activity. With time and effort this obsessive pattern can be successfully managed. As this pattern improves, it leads to better relationships with others. This in turn makes it less likely that these OCS behaviors will be mislabeled and misunderstood.

The tendency to be very sensitive, and for this reason to overreact, can also become less of a problem. This, however, takes determined effort over time. Often medication can soften the intensity of such a response. It also gives them a chance to become a believer in the biological nature of OCS. As awareness grows through treatment, a person is better able to choose his or her actions. After being treated for a time and learning about OCS, the likelihood that the person will better handle triggers when they occur is strengthened. The person may then select another response rather than simply overreacting, as usually happened in the past.

Since the OCS mind is always busy, those with OCS tend to feel that there is *never* enough time. They seem to be continually in a rush. There is no way they will be able to do all that needs to get done. It is not unusual for the OCS individual to try to gain more time by getting others to do some of their work. This is true even though the work may be their responsibility. The OCS will also do this with tasks they don't like or don't want to do themselves. Often the person is quite unaware that they are doing this. They have no idea what kind of an emotional strain such behavior has on others. These others sooner or later become frustrated and angry. They may also feel intense resentment. Educate those with OCS about this need to get others to do things they aren't interested in doing. Make them more aware. Help them to understand and keep from creating and fostering such emotionally damaging antics. Resentment of the OCS can develop in family members, friends, and those at the workplace.

Personal obsessive standards of perfection can be a big issue. This trend is usually a no-win situation for all those involved. Those with OCS are often frustrated, as person after person fails to meet their standards. These OCS-driven standards are generally out of reach of most if not all others. All who come up against OCS-established objectives can in time become discouraged. Frustration and anger may develop as well. These others may get to a point where they no longer want to try. Why keep on trying if what you do is *never* good enough? This person cannot be pleased, and so others eventually quit even trying to please them.

Resentment towards the OCS person is a common outcome. Awareness can help those with OCS to refrain from imposing their own rigid standards on others. Expectations can still be high. They just need to make sure these expectations are not obsessively high and out of reach.

Be prepared for distortions and misperceptions. These are a prominent and frequent feature. Such distorted views can easily cause problems for those who do not know they have OCS. As treatment progresses and understanding and awareness grow, perception becomes clearer. Distortions and misperceptions become fewer in number. In time, the OCS person is better equipped to recognize and handle that they may have possible twists of view. With work, the rate and severity of misread cues diminish greatly.

OCS and Social Life

Depending on one's point of view this may not be considered a problem. That's because there often isn't much of a social life. Social issues are very common throughout the life span for those with OCS. Any combination of the already shared OCS symptoms can impact social life. This impact, though, can be either negative or positive.

On the negative side, there seem to be a lot of OCS people who can be categorized into one of two groups. To the uninformed, the two may look like polar opposites.

Group One

Those in the first group have developed strong fears and anxieties. These fears become intensified in social situations, where they are triggered. So these people tend to avoid social gatherings. Whenever they can get away with it, they simply don't go to social activities or events. A few of the symptoms underlying this group's social issues include the following:

- A heightened fear of what others may be thinking about them.
- The strong OCS fear that something might be said or done that wasn't right.
- Distress over being so physically close to other people.
- Feelings of a claustrophobic nature.
- Extreme generalized anxiety for which no clear cause has been established.

In my experience I have come to believe that there *are* specific factors at the heart of this anxiety. These factors can be hidden by other behaviors. These reactions can be so intertwined as to make it difficult for even the most savvy to disentangle. However, I believe that they *are* present. One must sometimes work hard to find them.

- There can be problems accepting personal blame.

The responsibility for all things tends to be shunned. This actually seems to be a hallmark trait associated with OCS. This trait also has a polar opposite symptom (accepting blame for everything). To accept responsibility or blame, one must admit that a personal mistake was made. This can be incredibly difficult for many with OCS. To those with OCS, to do so would be akin to committing emotional suicide. For them things are either "black or white" or "all-or-nothing" with no in-between. For the OCS to accept blame for an error or mistake is to acknowledge one's worthlessness as a human being. They can't do that. The need to keep others from seeing them as worthless or horrible triggers an instant rejection of even the slightest blame. Those with OCS can have a need to deny responsibility for any and all mistakes. It doesn't really matter how trivial the mistake may have been. The opposite of taking too much blame can also be true.

OCS-driven people can also have a need to accept the blame for everything. They also may do this in an intensely magnified manner. These may try to take responsibility for every problem or mistake made anywhere near their sphere of existence. This can be incredibly annoying for family members. It can be just as irritating to all others who must deal with them as well. Medication, awareness, cognitive restructuring, patience, practice, and time, all need to be combined to treat this form. It may be the only way to manage, and in time alter, this mind-set of self-blame.

Finally, there are those who, at times, play both sides of the coin. Neither the *self-blame* (always-to-blame) nor *other-blame* (never-to-blame) versions of this seems to be mutually exclusive.

Group Two

The second group of the OCS relative to social life appears to be the opposite of the one discussed above. The key word here is "appears" but we'll get back to that in a minute. The people in this group seem to *love* attending various social gatherings. They appear to enjoy social events, parties and the like. This, it seems, is their chance to shine. They can be the "life of the party." The social behaviors of those in this group tend to be enormously varied, but lean in the same direction. They are loud. They are often viewed by others as obnoxious. They can be intrusive and also hilarious. As a result they may be either the "life" or the "scourge" of the party or social gathering. They might be admired and loved for their frequently offbeat comments and antics. Either that or they may barely be tolerated as annoying buffoons.

Many others see this OCS group as desperate attention seekers that would sell their souls for a laugh. The dynamics that lead people down this particular path are not yet clear. It does seem fairly obvious, however, that no single event is the cause. Rather, it is a complex series of events. These events merge with the person's unique biological makeup.

The OCS underlying factors that seem to be driving this group include the following:

- There may be a need to regulate, control, or be in charge of social events or situations.
- The more the OCS person feels in "the driver's seat" the more it seems that anxiety, worry, and fear is less of a problem. Thus the OCS-driven "acting out" in social settings may be at least in part due to the need to be the one directing all that happens to them. This may work to reduce what might otherwise be a vast amount of free-floating anxiety.
- There may be an incompatible response occurring.

There is a behavior modification technique that's been called the Incompatible Response Method. This strategy can be used to slow down and stop unwanted behaviors and thoughts. It consists of a purposeful change in behavior or thinking. The unwanted behavior is replaced by another that is neutral. This neutral action keeps the person from being able to perform the unwanted behavior. If I want to stop sucking my thumb, I might sit on my hands every time I got the urge to stick my thumb in my mouth. The two actions are incompatible. When you do one, you cannot do the other. This is a simplistic example, but basically it is the way the method works. By engaging in one behavior or thought, the other cannot be performed.

A right-handed person who is busy writing on a piece of paper cannot at the same time chew or bite the fingernails of that hand. The act of writing and that of biting the nails is an incompatible response. OCD research has consistently pointed out that those who keep "busy" experience a reduction in symptoms. The OCS-driven may be highly active in social situations in order to manage their symptoms. Loud and obnoxious behavior may be needed for them to survive socially. At least some in this group may not be all that different from their apparent polar opposites in their feelings. The difference may lie more in the method that these OCS responders adopt to reduce their symptoms.

Extreme high energy levels are sometimes present.

Although debatable, it appears that this high energy subgroup may very well be made up of those who have both ADHD and OCS. The

ADHD component appears to be of the hyperactive type in this case. The frenetic and boundless energy of this hyperactive ingredient may help drive those in this group. Also, both ADHD and OCS symptoms often get worse in the presence of overwhelming external stimuli—in other words, when there are lots of things happening around them. Social events and gatherings are often full of abundant and frequently shifting people and happenings. Such constant stimulation can sometimes tax the sanity of the best of us. When stressed, the strength of the ADHD symptoms increase. This means you may get a temporary state of super-hyperactivity. Such a state can appear to be manic. A Bipolar diagnosis may be mistakenly made as a result.

An OCS-driven need to perform may be present.

On the more positive side, these OCS-driven people can be very good comedians and actors. The outlook of these people can be amazingly refreshing and inventive. The intensity they can bring to the characters and the roles they play could make anyone believe. Again, knowledge of OCS and knowledge of related issues are the keys to manage this effectively. The social behavior of those with OCS can be markedly improved. It does seem to take a fair amount of time, though. Also, there must be persistent effort to both achieve and sustain lasting social success.

We need to remember this:

There is no key to life: It has a combination lock.

Similarly one might also say:

There is no key to OCS: It has a combination lock similar to that of life.

17

Educational Implications

In my experience, OCS in the school setting is one of *the* most misunderstood problems that a student can have. A simple lack of awareness seems to be at the heart of this dilemma. The lack referred to, though, is not just found in the schools. It is present to some degree in the health care field as well. It has been very difficult to decide the best way to present the subject of OCS in the schools. We will begin with general issues that are fairly widespread and common. Then we'll move towards the more specific symptoms that may or may not be present when working with individuals.

Anxiety:

In one form or another, worry and excessive anxiety are common problems for those with OCS. The anxiety may be elusive and in any area of life. It can also be *very* specific. Transitions from one activity to another can be difficult. The same can be true when going from one environment to another. Change can trigger anxiety, frustration, and anger. This is especially so if the change is unexpected.

"I don't *want* to, mama," Jimmy wailed.

"Here we go again," bellowed his frustrated father. "Will you *please* tell me Jean, why . . . no matter where we are going, this *son of yours* never wants to go?"

Jean smiled just a bit before saying, "That's not true Tim, and you know it."

"Yeah, okay, but the only places he doesn't throw a fit about are the ones he's already been."

"There, you see," she said. "Doesn't that *tell* you something?"

"Yeah, it tells me something all right. I've got a spoiled child. That's what it tells me. And he's making *my* life miserable."

"No Tim," Jean gently corrected. "It tells you that he's worried. He's never been to that place before. He's afraid of what he isn't familiar with. Now who else are we aware of that is afraid of the unknown?"

Tim grimaced. "I don't know," he replied a little too quickly.

"Sure, you do," Jean grinned. "Your mother comes to mind and then let's see . . . who else? Hmmm . . . Could it be *you?*"

He was staring down at the floor. "Not me," he whispered halfheartedly.

"Oh, no, of course not you, heck no . . . not *you!* Who won't go anywhere without spending half the day studying every little detail on a map? *You!* Who won't go at all if even the slightest thing changes? And I mean the slightest!"

"Okay, okay!" He batted at the air with both hands. "Stop already."

There seems to be no hard rule regarding how, when, and where anxiety may come flying out. At least not that can be applied generally. There are some who are anxious about everything. There are others who are worried about only some things. One very important point to keep in mind is the actual *level of anxiety* that may be present. For it to be an OCS issue, the difficulty it causes needs to go beyond the norm. This is determined by its intensity as well as how long the anxiety lasts. It is also measured by how extreme or severe related issues seem to be.

The cause of the anxiety may seem very clear, or it may make no sense at all. There is an excessive quality to its expression. As a result teachers and other school personnel may soon become annoyed by this student. Irritation and frustration tend to build over time. Tolerance levels may be pushed to the limit. In time, patience may be all but gone.

Crystal approaches the teacher's desk slowly. She has in her hand an assignment she's been working on. She really needs to ask a question before she can go on to the next problem.

"What is it *now,* Crystal?"

She holds the paper up so the teacher can see. "Miss Green?" she whispers, "is . . . is this right?"

"You know, Crystal, if every student came up to my desk after every single problem they did, I'd *never* get my lesson plans done or papers graded."

"Yes, ma'am, but is it right?"

"Of course, it's right. It's always right. Surely you *must* know that by now."

"But Miss Green," Crystal persists, "you didn't check it."

"Oh, for goodness sakes," she grabs the paper from Crystal's outstretched hand. She hurriedly glances at it and then thrusts it forward for Crystal to take.

Crystal remains standing passively by the teacher's desk.

"What now!" Miss Green sighs.

"Is it okay? Did I do it right?"

"*YES!* Now don't come back up here until you've finished each one of those problems." Miss Green clenches her teeth in a forced smile and adds as gently as she can, "Do you understand?"

Crystal nods and returns to her desk. After finishing the very next problem she stands and approaches Miss Green at her desk once again. There is a question she *has to* ask before she can go on to the next problem.

In the example given above Crystal's anxiety is centered on whether or not a problem is correct. She *needs* to know this before she can move on to the next one. It doesn't matter that she usually does them all correctly. She *needs* to know. In her mind she is never quite sure that she knows what she knows. So she has to check it out.

Teachers and parents often confuse this behavior with a *need for attention*. There is yet another common mistaken explanation often made, as well. It is the belief that such a student is constantly seeking praise or approval. When OCS is the cause, neither of these explanations is accurate. The real reason is almost invariably an inner *need* to be absolutely certain that a mistake has not been made. Those with OCS don't want approval here. They want to know it's right.

In order to be sure, the ultimate authority figure *must* be consulted. This authority is the teacher. Common examples of how worry and anxiety may show up in the schools specific to the OCS student will now be addressed.

Work Resistance or Refusal:

There are many reasons why students may resist or refuse to do assignments. In fact, even when OCS is found to be the cause, teachers often continue to blame this behavior on other motives. This is one of the key reasons that attempted interventions may not work.

Resistance or refusal can come from an excessive fear of making a mistake or of failing. If the student can successfully resist and refuse to complete an assignment, his goal is obtained. By doing this, he can avoid even the possibility of doing it wrong. No mistakes today, thank you very much. The student may not be able to openly admit that such a fear exists. He may not even be aware of the fear at all. Usually when confronted by an adult as to why this is happening, the student will reply with "I don't know." This may or may not be the truth. Yet, true or not, it is nearly always considered an unacceptable response. The teacher, as a rule, will not generally accept such a response. Instead, they will *demand* that a reason be given for the behavior.

The OCS student will often work very hard to find a good motive for their behavior. Typically it's a reason they believe that the teacher will accept. A commonly attempted response is the statement, "I can't do it." Also similar explanations such as, "It's too hard or I don't know how," are often used. Teachers regularly take such remarks as proof of a student's "laziness." They may tell colleagues, counselors, or the school psychologist things such as, "She just doesn't want to do the work," or "She doesn't care."

When OCS is behind a behavior, such a mind-set is not only unfair, but may also be harmful. Damage can take place in the areas of both emotional and/or educational growth. Misjudgments like this impede the student/teacher working relationship. In time, flawed beliefs can have a very negative outcome. They can adversely affect the student's learning.

Students are also subject to what has been called the *self fulfilling prophecy*. In brief this suggests that students will become what teachers and other responsible adults believe them to be. For the OCS student, the self-fulfilling prophecy is even more likely to be a problem. This is because those who don't know why they do the things they do, tend to accept the most obvious reason available. When this is the case it makes the diagnosis of OCS even more difficult. That's because the OCS person really can come to believe that the reason they've adopted is true.

As time goes on, these errors develop twists and turns that further magnify the complex dynamics involved. Sometimes complete misunderstandings of the student's motivations are made. It then becomes even more difficult for school personnel to unravel the resulting mess. The real truth gets harder and harder to find. When the actual source of the problems *is* due to OCS, the account may seem absurd to the teacher. It may seem ridiculous to the student and her parents as well. To teachers it may sound more like a fanciful make-believe story than reality. If not shared with caution and care, some teachers will flatly reject the real cause as nonsense. This, of course, further complicates matters.

Work resistance and refusal may also occur from worrying about time and having a strong *need* to finish a task. This comes about when the OCS student gets an assignment with a time limit. There is often a specific amount of time allotted during class to complete the task.

"Mark," the teacher calls out from his desk, "see if you can stop daydreaming and start working. You've got fifteen minutes to get as much done on this assignment as you can." Mr. Donaldson then addresses the entire class. "Most of you should be able to finish the entire assignment in about ten minutes if you work hard. Remember, whatever you do not finish in class will go home with you tonight."

Several groans emerge from the disgruntled students.

"Enough of that . . . now get to work!" Mr. Donaldson sits back down at his desk.

Mark looks at the clock on the wall. There is no way he'll ever be able to get this stupid assignment done in ten minutes. He *knows* that. Maybe he could do it in thirty or forty minutes, but no way in ten. Why start the stupid thing at all if he's just going to have to take it home anyway? So he begins to look around the room instead.

He imagines himself inventing something. It would have to be simple, but useful. So useful in fact that everyone in the entire world would want one. After eventually catching up with all the back orders he'd be *rich* beyond his wildest dreams. Of course half of the money he'd give away to the needy and to his church. The headlines would read "Eleven-year-old billionaire makes good on his promise!" He'd be famous. Jay Leno would shake his hand and congratulate him on national TV.

There may or may not be time enough for students to finish an assignment in class. Typical instructions would be for those not finished to take the work home and turn it in the following day. For many OCS students, such conditions can create a real dilemma. The need to finish a given task without interruption once it has been started can be very strong. Giving this student a time limit can instantly trigger the engine of anxiety.

If the OCS student is a slow worker, there may be no decision to make about starting. This is because the student knows there is no way the assignment will get done. The slow-working OCS student's reactions to being assigned such a task vary. They may include sighing, wailing, or negative language said out loud or just under the breath.

Another common occurrence is to begin an alternate task. This may be something such as playing with bits of paper or micro-machines smuggled into school. It could be touching the hair of the girl sitting close by. There might be drawing, daydreaming, or even sleeping. Not uncommonly angry outbursts can occur if the teacher demands that the student work. This student soon learns to pretend that he's working, in an effort to keep the teacher from continued harassment.

If the OCS student in the above setting was not a slow worker, reactions may be different. The student may simply rush through the material as quickly as possible. There may be little regard for accuracy or penmanship. Keep in mind that in order to start, this OCS student must believe the entire task can be completed within the time limit given. The student described in this last part may finish well before the allotted time frame. This is because the speed is governed by the absolute need to get done. There is no pacing for such a student.

Sometimes those with the milder OCS are not aware of their inner need for completion. When this is the case, the OCS student may innocently begin working on the assignment. If time runs out on this student and the teacher tries to transition the class to the next subject, sparks may fly. When this happens it's because it has been a *trigger event* for the student. A host of reactions may arise including, but again not limited to, the following:

- The student may ignore the teacher and continue working on the assignment. If the teacher does not notice this or chooses not to interrupt or redirect, it may work in favor of the student.
- She may resist for a period of time while mumbling under her breath and then finally give in. Either that or she'll finish the assignment and then try to catch up on the new one.
- She might calmly resist, get angry, or blow up emotionally. She could display verbal disrespect or burst into tears. She may brood, glower, or gripe. She might even obstinately announce that if she can't finish what she is doing then nothing else will be done either, and so on.

Excessive self-doubt:

The tendency to doubt one's self seems to invade the lives of all those affected by OCS. In fact the French call OCD the Doubting Disease. These students are apt to be chronically unsure of everything. They hardly ever offer personal opinions if at all. If they do share their point of view, it is often done with great caution. They tend to retract what's been said at the first hint of another's dissent or even slight inquiry. This student cannot let go of the possibility that what they think, do, or say might be wrong.

In the classroom these OCS students may never raise a hand to answer teacher-directed questions. If the teacher calls on them the most common response is, "I don't know." Even when the OCS student does know the answer, they doubt the truth of this knowledge.

Such a student may have trouble completing assignments as well. This is because they doubt all aspects of what they do or at times what needs to be done. Such a student may constantly badger the teacher. They want to check the accuracy of every problem on every assignment. They are trying to relieve their uncertainty. Teachers often interpret the outward signs of this symptom as "attention-seeking behavior." However, in a case like this, it simply isn't true.

The excessive doubt can cause problems in decision-making. These students typically defer to others when a decision must be made. Their lack of confidence also makes them more hesitant to try new things or go places where they haven't been before. This can also have a negative impact on their ability to handle several tasks at once. There is a strong tendency to be easily overwhelmed when given more than one task at a time.

This also seems to affect the OCS student's capacity to prioritize. They have trouble figuring out which task or which part of a multiple-step assignment should be done first, which second, and so on. As a result, they can be to a large extent disorganized.

Hypersensitivity:

This OCS student tends to react to pain, whether physical or emotional, in an intense manner that is often well outside of the norm. Feelings get hurt much too easily. Their extreme sensitivity may convince them that others don't like them. They may also feel that other students are picking on them, even when they're not. This sensitivity can make them easy targets to actually be picked on by others. Some may also adopt a victim role.

This student may apologize in excess over minor things that others hardly notice. At times this can be annoying to a teacher because the student is always looking for reassurance. Not being able to make a decision and super-sensitivity seem to go hand in hand. The OCS-driven anxiety can be set in motion and maintained by the smallest infractions.

This student may relentlessly question if what they've said or done has hurt or bothered another. If he does not apologize, he experiences an inner turmoil or dread. There are even times that some can feel so badly about their words or actions that they may decide to administer their own punishment. It may occur in one of several possible forms. It could be the student who repeatedly pounds the palm of one or both hands against their own head. It can be the one who seems to have a desire or need to inflict pain and self mutilates. There have been some who will refuse to eat for two or three days in an effort to show their bodies just who is in control of what. Sometimes words may be spoken aloud in frustration. More often than not there are plenty of silent chastisements. Each may be repeated over and over again in the student's mind. Such thinking cannot help but influence the overall emotional and social well being of the student.

A few examples of common reprimands made might help to understand. Comments might be things like "What an idiot I am!" "I'm so stupid." "Boy; am I a jerk!" "I can't do nothin' right!" "What the heck am I doing?" "Well, what do you expect from such a worthless fool like me?" "Why do I even try anyway?" Sadly more often than you might think, self-statements also occur such as "I should just kill myself!" This last comment seems more an indicator of how deeply and badly those with OCS feel, rather than a true wish to commit suicide. Whenever any student makes such a comment, it is a good idea to consider the possibility of underlying OCS. It is also critical to always follow up on this student's intentions and get help.

Too much sensitivity leads to overreactions. It's almost as if the OCS student is "set up" daily to overreact. This student may work very hard to control the tendency to be hypersensitive. Some do this much better than others. In moments when control is lost, the sensitive student's actions may seem impulsive. Their overreactions often come as a complete surprise to others. The trend is for such events to flare up burn for a time and then die as quickly and mysteriously as they began.

While the flare is lit teachers and others can unintentionally make it stronger and prolong this OCS reaction. Some of the other common types of statements and reactions from these sensitive students are worth considering. You may hear, "Teacher, she's looking at me!" "Nobody likes me," "Shut up! (and quit talking about me);" "He did that on purpose!" In relation to assignments you might hear, "Do what?" "I can't do that!" "It's too hard," "Do we have to do *all* that!" "We'll *never* get done." The student may suddenly yell, push, or hit another. The sensitive OCS student may also be easily frustrated and is likely to shed tears at any given moment of the school day.

For teachers and other students, the hypersensitive OCS student can be a huge distraction. They can also be quite irritating. Over time it can be a challenge for others to treat this type of OCS student kindly. In fact, that is what can drive this particular student to take on the role of a victim. The situation in this way feeds on itself. The OCS student "victim" may feel that the teacher and other students are "out to get him," and in time this may actually come to be the truth. Hypersensitive students are good candidates to think about for possible OCS. When OCS is present, if not seen and treated for what it is, all other interventions are like using a Band-Aid to treat a three inch gash. The Band-Aid may help a little, but is ultimately ineffective.

Obsessive Thoughts/Compulsive Behaviors:

This refers to those students who obsess or can't stop thinking about ideas, needs, fears, or wants. A relentless need to do something or carry out some kind of an action repeatedly is the *compulsive* part. A simple example may help to make clear the relationship between the obsession (thought) and the compulsion (action).

The student is in the middle of a test. She feels a need to make her slightly dull pencil sharper, even though it still writes. In her mind pencils must be exactly sharp enough or she has a hard time using them. The class has been warned not to leave their desks for any reason during the test. This student will not experience relief from this need until she is able to sharpen the pencil. If she asks permission and the teacher refuses the need will intensify. If this urge is not *too* strong, the student may make it to the end of the test without too much interference. She will sharpen the pencil later. Although this troubling thought might have gotten in the way just a bit during the test, she won't be in trouble for disregarding authority.

When an OCS-driven need is *too* strong, a variety of reactions are possible. These tend to be more intense than in the situation just described. A typical response might be an argument with the teacher. The student could also respond by just getting up and going to sharpen the pencil anyway. Such a student may similarly announce in a huff something like "That's just fine by me; then I won't have to finish this stupid test." The student may then cross his arms and sit defiantly, doing nothing.

The behaviors reported above are real life choices that happened. They were taken from several case histories. This inability to let go of ideas, thoughts, and needs can be a big problem. It often interferes with the OCS student's ability to work well with classmates or in groups. This can be especially hard to deal with in a classroom setting.

When the OCS student begins to take on a group assignment, obsessive locks may occur. These usually involve the way things should or should not be done or who should do them. When this happens the student's drives can cause havoc within the normal group process. The affected student may seem obnoxious. They may appear to have a need to be in control of everything. This need, though, is not truly one for *control*; it is usually more of a need to do things right. The person *must* follow the inner demands dictated by this insidious OCS drive.

In time, the OCS student may avoid working in groups. It may appear to teachers and others that the student prefers working alone. They can appear to have no interest whatsoever in the class work of others. They may often seem unwilling to accept any suggestions from others. This is especially so if the suggestions are regarding changes in their own work.

Teachers may hear comments such as, "They won't do it right!" "They don't even care how good it is. They don't care if it's right or wrong!" "But we've just got to do it like this!" and so on.

Competition is another thing that tends to be influenced greatly. The inability to let go of ideas and their behavioral urges wreaks havoc in this area. The OCS student may often have a need to be first or the best at everything. For example the first in line, first to start, first to be done, first in a race (and anything can be made into a race), and so on. In all these instances of needing to be first, they may push, shove, hit, scream, cry, or throw tantrums in an attempt to get this need met.

When in a small group and one child receives praise from the teacher, the OCS child in the group may consider this a threat. This child may feel slighted as if the praise of another somehow lessens his own status with the teacher. As a result he may act out right away to get a similar degree of attention. This *is* attention-seeking behavior, but not for the sake of getting the attention. It's more like an actual need for the OCS student to "stay ahead" on the scoreboard. Either that, or at least an attempt to try and keep everything as evenly balanced as possible.

In the area of competition with sports or games, OCS students usually lean toward one or the other of two poles. They either tend to not want to play or they play and undergo a very powerful urge to dominate and win, often at all costs. In this emotionally charged setting the OCS-driven may come down hard on any player of his own team that makes even the smallest of mistakes. They may come down just as hard on those that they believe are not trying.

If an OCS student's team begins to fall behind, one of several common reactions may occur. Almost certainly this student would start to complain, gripe, and whine. The moaning would be about things such as the teams not being fair. Calls by the refs they might bellyache are not going their way. The other team keeps fouling. They may complain that the other team's players were playing dirty.

The OCS student may also start criticizing the weaker players on his own team. He or she will yell at them over incidents that don't really matter. This driven student may cheat, even if he or she would normally never stoop to such actions. Fights may break out. When playing board games, the fighting typically consists of yelling and the throwing of game pieces.

In either of these situations, interesting things can happen if the one with OCS thinks he might lose. If he truly believes a loss is imminent, he may leave the game. There could be many reasons given for this. It could be that he suddenly becomes injured. The injury has to be bad enough to be unable to continue. Of course, this one doesn't usually work for a board game.

She may accuse the other players of cheating and stomp off in protest. She might announce (as the bell rings) loudly that her team wasn't really trying. They were just "playing around" as it were. Statements like this are usually followed by comments further meant to "save face." Things are said such as, "If we had been trying, your team would have been vaporized," and "We felt sorry for you and let you win."

The OCS student also often strains under the anxiety of constant pressure. There is a strong need to "prove" himself over and over again. As a result prior accomplishments and successes mean nothing in the heat of the moment. This can be why a young child who just had three hours of parental attention can seem like a bottomless pit.

What has already happened simply doesn't matter. Getting this attention does not stop the apparent need for more attention. This is because it is not attention that the child is really seeking. It is a biochemically driven obsession or compulsion that looks just like crying out for attention. All the parental attention in the world will not change the intensity of the next *driven* urge.

Sometimes parents can fall into the trap of believing that they are satisfying an urge by giving more attention to the child. This is not true. In fact, by doing this the parent has helped the child to strengthen his obsessive and compulsively driven desires. That's why they come right back. The child may return as quickly as the next moment after satisfaction seems sure.

The hypersensitive nature of the OCS student makes them a shoe-in for not being able to let go of lots of fears. This touchiness also tends to extend to all the five senses common to human beings. An extreme *startle response* is not unusual. Such a response can be triggered by an unexpected touch, sharp or loud sound, or a nasty smell. Overreactions can also arise from an unpleasant, bitter, sour, sickly sweet or surprising taste. They can come from a visual element, which often consists of something moving quickly in front of the eyes. The over-response to a touch is most often a quick or frantic jerking away. There can be a tightening of body muscles in a rigid display. This can leave the one who touches with rather suspicious thoughts. Such thoughts usually center on concerns of possible physical abuse. These reactions to touch really nay be impossible to tell apart from the actual reactions that those who have been abused can have.

If OCS is the driving force, a clinical interview along with specific screening instruments, can be done. If OCS is at the heart of this reaction the assessment will reveal many other signs and characteristics as well. Many other OCS tendencies would show up that are not typical to patterns of abuse. A case of abuse alone would not have evidence of significant OCS signs and symptoms.

This is not to suggest that an OCS student could not have been abused. It is offered as a possible option, other than that of directly assuming that there has been abuse. Abuse may not always be a factor.

Yet another intense reaction related to touch is common. This has to do with texture in relation to food and its perceived consistency in the mouth. How the food feels in the mouth of the OCS-driven will determine whether or not it can be swallowed. It very well may result in a gag reflex or even throwing up.

There is yet another related variation of this that is worth noting. Some of the OCS-affected will be nearly unable to swallow even the tiniest pill. This can be especially true for children. Usually, it stems from having had an experience of attempting it once and choking. That choking experience gets locked into the brain. It can be very intense. They cannot free themselves from the memory. Interestingly, most of the time, the ability to swallow a pill improves when the person has been treated medically for a time. Fortunately, most of the SSRIs come in a liquid form. Within a few days to weeks after starting a fluid medication, the person can often be taught to swallow a pill. By this time it is also fairly easy to do. This is because the old OCS-driven choking fear no longer has a stranglehold on the mind.

There is also the tendency for some to over-respond to taste. When this happens, it is not unusual for them to immediately spit out what was put in their mouth. It doesn't matter what it is or where the person happens to be. This can easily offend others. Often it's because of the sheer intensity of the response. They may include words like "YUCH!" or "HOW GROSS!" Spittle may fly from the mouth area and land everywhere. This is particularly likely when tasting food that has been prepared by someone else. In fact, some of those with OCS will refuse to eat food prepared by anyone outside of their family circle.

The overreaction to sound is similar to that of touch. There tends to be an immediate startle reaction. It's a lot like the reaction seen with infants when an unexpected loud or sharp noise occurs. Usually the OCS student will "jump" and turn towards or shy away from the sound's source. There is another key point to remember about the OCS student. It is that the sound setting off the startle response may hardly even be noticed by classmates nearby. Students sitting near someone who has such a reaction may regard them as if there is something really wrong with them.

When the OCS student has such overreactions in school, teasing can often follow. This is one of the many ways in which the OCS student becomes a target. It is also how they can pick up the reputation for being a little strange, weird, silly or "out to lunch." Unfortunately these are the types of things that provoke others to pick on them. Others quickly realize that this student is an "easy target." They also can get a kick out of making such a student overreact. To make another student jump or yell can provide them with a sense of power. This can be quite intoxicating for the student who feels inferior or feels he has no say or power over his own life.

In relation to the sense of smell the OCS driven can have extreme difficulties. Problems may be encountered in many ways. If a smell is perceived there can be trouble focusing and completing work. This can come from sitting near another student who is wearing strong perfume or cologne. It could also arise if another student has less than adequate hygiene.

The problem of focusing can occur if the OCS student is hungry and the smells of lunch are wafting though the air around her. This smell over-reactivity can often create big problems with food. To others the reaction may seem quite silly, and yet these are very real issues for the person involved. If food does not have a pleasing smell to the OCS getting them to eat or to even taste it may be nearly impossible.

Attempting to force this issue can cause a commotion that may not be worth the fight. This often has a lasting negative affect on the eating habits of those with OCS. In time, this type of an issue can even interfere with the person's nutritional health. This person may also overreact to a sudden disgusting odor. This might happen if sitting next to a student who is suffering the effects of flatulence (a digestive gas problem), and so on.

An OCS-driven student may overreact to the movements of other students near him. This is even more likely if those movements are sudden. It can include any perceived threatening action on the part of another. These might be movements such as unexpected quick actions like the raising of an arm or leaning forward or turning around. These may result in a flinch, a startle, or a sharp fearful-like response. As said before this can easily lead another into thinking there may have been physical abuse, even though that may not be true. Caution is urged before making the decision in your mind that a case of physical abuse is probably occurring.

The OCS student is also likely to over-respond to any visual presentation. It can be worse if the materials are graphic or explicit. This may be true whether in the form of drawings, photographs, or films. Students will make comments such as, "Yuck, eeeuw!" and "Do they have to show that?" They may start to feel ill or feel like they are going to faint. There are even times when actual throwing up can occur in reaction to visual images that those with OCS experience as intense.

Most of the reactions related above, that those with OCS are likely to display, will occur apart from one another. There is a time when many do come together in one activity; that is worth some attention and a few words of caution. Movies, videos, and TV shows can all have a very powerful effect on people. These can have a much more powerful effect on anybody with OCS at any age. Movies have a limited amount of time in which to present their stories. Because of this, they tend to do so by manipulating time. They also exaggerate both visual and auditory channels often in the extreme. The OCS already feels things at an amplified level. As a result, the intensity applied to make a movie work can be overwhelming. It can leave the OCS essentially in a state of literal shock. If the movie is intensely exciting, the aftereffects of that thrill can last for hours, days, or even weeks. For a while it may be difficult to calm down enough to get to sleep at night. The various actions of movie characters may be played out in both the imagination and real life. This can go on as well for days, weeks, and months at a time. There may also be a desire or a very strong need to see the movie over and over again.

If the movie is frightening, an entire army of new fears may be born in the OCS mind. These fears can affect their lives in many ways and be harbored there in the mind for some time. This same handling of time and passion is common in horror movies as well. Just as they can in an action-adventure type of movie, a horror film's effects may persist as well. The aftereffects can last for a very long time.

In my work I have recorded notes for many OCS clients that point to specific movies as the root cause of their fears and anxieties. The influence and effects of these movies has at times been sustained for many years and some for an entire lifetime. An example is the ten-year-old boy who saw the movie *Twister*, which was a thriller about tornadoes, and very believable. After this he would not go out of the house during any type of inclement weather. This included simple windy days.

It seems that anything picked up by one of the five senses can get locked into place and be a trigger. Once triggered, the imagination can then take over and go wild. Over the years I have worked with many OCS-affected children, adults, and families. One of the most important and recurring problems involves the response to levels of intensity. It is also clear that as for ADHD, stress of any kind, fatigue, and emotionally charged incidents tend to make OCS much worse. Movies, TV shows, and even commercials work hard to achieve just such a reaction. Commercials about antibacterial soap come to mind. The more intensely experienced a thing is, the more likely it is that it will become an interfering factor in the OCS mind.

Adapting to the Difference

Some OCS students will begin to openly embrace their weirdness. They have no explanation why they can't seem to get control of these tendencies to over-respond and over focus. No one else seems to be quite so picky about food, clothes, and how things need to be done. Why does everything seem to matter so much? These weird little issues get in the way. They embarrass him. Others make fun of him. They call him names.

A lot of effort is often needed to survive amid so much confusion, stress, and the build up of emotional pain. The OCS student may literally start to take pride in her own strange behaviors. In this scenario, the OCS student begins to accept credit for all the weird behaviors. This includes the things others have noticed or teased them about. The typical response goes something like this:

"I wanted to do it. I like being that way because it's fun. I *want* to be different. I don't want to be just like everyone else," and so on.

At some point while still working to survive, the OCS student can begin to behave strangely on purpose. This strangeness is often not at all OCS-driven. This is the classic cover-up. It works as a very effective smokescreen. The purpose is to make it easier for others to believe that when they see the actual symptoms these too are deliberate.

One adult developed what I thought at the time was a unique and creative cover-up approach. Whenever introducing himself to others he would say "Hi! I'm Dave Crenshaw," after which he would pause raise the corner of his mouth in a sly smile and add, "I'm weird." By exploring his past he figured out where this odd introduction probably started. It was his unconscious method of protecting a battered self-esteem and a quite fragile ego. He came to realize that after such an introduction if someone later saw his OCS strangeness and said something like, "Mr. Crenshaw, you're weird," he could then protect himself. His ego would be spared.

He would respond, "I told you so," and brush his hand across his chest. This would be accompanied by a smile. It would prevent the comment from hurting as much as it otherwise might. "Yeah, I'm weird," he could tell them," and that's exactly how I want to be." He might say this, even though it wasn't really true.

In the school setting it is a whole lot easier for a teacher to believe the common explanations for a student's behavior. Teachers can more easily accept that a student's words and behaviors are intentional rather than driven. Otherwise, how can they possibly be held accountable for their actions?

When lies are easier to believe than the truth . . . the truth is not welcome.

Born Liars

"Why did you do that?" the teacher asks.

Often the OCS student's only way to answer this question is to lie. The genuine honest answer to this question is almost always, "I don't know." Teachers rarely accept this answer. As a result, many of those with OCS learn to replace "I don't know," with a more acceptable answer.

The OCS driven may also end up actually believing what their teacher thinks is the cause for their behavior. Most of the time, a teacher's perceptions as to why certain actions occur may be quite accurate. The major problem with this is that when the behavior in question is OCS-driven, they are often wrong.

Then the lying begins. When pinned down, these students will try to save face or avoid punishment altogether. This may be accomplished through grand as well as little white lies. Sometimes the student rationalizes that it's not really much of a lie. This is because they so often don't know why they do the things they do anyway. Therefore the student gives a reason that he thinks the teacher or adult is likely to believe. This can get the OCS-driven student into big trouble, but usually only if they are found out.

Depression and Depressive Characteristics

OCS-affected students often have a sense of sadness about them that teachers rarely fail to notice. This often will be described in tentative and questioning-like tones. Teachers may say things like, "Well she's not like this all the time, but she just doesn't seem happy."

The OCS student, at any given moment of the day, may be functioning in a state of overload. On top of that, so much of what they try to do doesn't seem to go the way they want it to, or simply isn't quite *right*. It's just not the way they feel that it should have been.

These students can be regularly misunderstood and shunned by nearly everyone. Is it really any surprise that this OCS student appears unhappy and sad, at times, or even depressed? They may be angry with themselves for their lack of success. So they beat themselves up inside.

They may also be angry with almost everyone else who is successful. There can be areas in which the student remains fairly intact and seems to function well. Within these areas they may continue to work adequately or even at levels of excellence. They may perform superbly on some tasks. These successful parts may be surrounded by, "pockets of depression." This is why so many of the OCS students can show that sort of apparent vague, yet visible, sadness.

Distractibility

This can be a primary factor that interferes with the learning process of the OCS student. Ponder for a moment the following setting.

The hyper-vigilant, unbelievably sensitive, and over responsive OCS student is there. He is sitting at a desk surrounded by other students, also seated. A movement is perceived out of the corner of his left eye. He furtively glances in that direction, but sees nothing. Was there a movement? He's not sure. If there was, it was probably that Bobby Fenton who sits just to his left. Bobby is always looking at him. Yeah, that must've been it. Bobby looked at him again.

The OCS student begins to focus on catching his tormentor in the act. He narrows his eyes, squeezing them down into very thin slits. Then he slyly moves his gaze across the back of Nancy's green sweater. Slowly, but surely, he moves them to the left. His eyes leave Nancy's back and move on.

There's the teacher Mrs. Westgate. She is gesturing animatedly at the front of the class. His eyes shift a tiny bit more. Mrs. Westgate's mouth is opening and closing like the clown's mouth on hole fourteen at Horton's Miniature Golf and Games. He wonders briefly what Mrs. Westgate might be saying: "Students, I want you to take notice . . ."

The OCS student does take notice. He notices everything. He noticed Bobby. Goofy-golf, yeah, that was it. Old man Horton should change the name of the place. Goofy-golf sounded so much more fun than . . . hey, maybe Disneyland would loan Goofy to old Mr. Horton.

He saw Bobby was still looking toward the front of the class. Class rhymes with glass. Another movement brought his eyes back. Bobby still hadn't looked at him. He must be looking whenever he glanced away. Suddenly a flurry of action occurs. The OCS student's eyes dart back to where his nemesis is sitting. The movements continue.

What the heck is Bobby doing? Is this some kind of a ruse meant to lure him into glancing away? Well, it isn't going to work! Bobby's just fiddling with that book to make everyone else think he's working and not looking this way. But Bobby hasn't been working. He's sure of it. He isn't going to work now. He's waiting for my eyes to wander away so he can look this way without getting caught.

At about this point, we might expect this OCS student's teacher to intervene by calling on him. The teacher might inquire why he is not following instructions. Why isn't he getting out his social studies book? She may have to call his name several times before he'll respond. She may be annoyed at his complete lack of awareness regarding her painstakingly given clear directions. Will the teacher be willing to repeat the instructions again? It's hard to say, but probably not.

The OCS student is distracted principally by the inner workings of his own mind. Any event or circumstance that occurs around him, though, can start a given train of thought. It is the mind, however, that takes that incident and carries it on "to where no *mind* has gone before."

The OCS mind seems perpetually in motion. Other than the times it is obsessively locked onto an idea, it tends to roam the entire universe and beyond. If a student's most common response to an unexpected direct question happens to be "Huh?" then perhaps OCS is the reason why. The comment given above is meant only to be an example, and is not necessarily considered to be an actual characteristic. Hopefully, though, a valuable point has been made.

A constant battle is being fought within the OCS mind. It is in regard to the purposeful direction of thought. For example, reading can be a very difficult and painstakingly slow process. The moment a word with powerful emotional connections is read, the OCS mind may react. It may embrace the emotion and follow it into oblivion, while the eyes alone read on. This OCS-related dynamic wreaks havoc on the comprehension aspect of what is read. It may seem that this student has a disability in reading comprehension. A sentence, paragraph, or page may need to be read several times before the gist of what is said is understood or remembered. As a result of the great effort required by OCS students in order to comprehend, they may avoid books and reading whenever possible.

There is also an OCS pattern that is completely opposite to that which was described above. This is manifested when the OCS drive is the need to devour the written word. Interestingly, there may only be very specific types of books involved. These, though, are obsessively sought after and compulsively read. This is the person who starts a book and often cannot stop until finished.

For example there are those with OCS who will only voraciously read science fiction or romance novels. They may only read westerns or how-to books. It may be only nonfiction biographies. When reading books of a specific sort or genre that is OCS-driven, there may be no comprehension problems at all. The moment the OCS-driven student is forced to read something they don't want to read, watch out. If a school-related assignment or book is not the genre they like, comprehension problems can surface big time. This same student who devours science fiction books at the rate of one to two in a single day may take weeks to plod through a mystery novel. The OCS-driven student also may not be able to get through such a book at all.

As already stated, there can be what seems like an intense stubbornness in the types of books that will or will not be read. What can happen is demonstrated by an incident that one high school OCS student had as the result of an English assignment.

This student was obsessed and read compulsively only science fiction novels and stories. His English teacher assigned a book report. She gave specific guidelines that it must be non fiction and not fantasy or science fiction. This young man became very angry. He ranted and raved to anyone who would listen to him. He went on and on about this horrible teacher who was trying to dictate what he could or could not read. How dare she! He wasn't about to read anything that he didn't want to. She couldn't make him. No one could force him to read something he didn't want to read. They never had, and never would.

Of course this OCS teenager was clearly over-responding just a bit. The intensity of his OCS thoughts kept him from seeing his behavior as over-reactive at the time. He carried on with his grumbling diatribes for about a week. He verbally blasted this teacher everywhere he went. Finally, he settled down to simply wallowing in his own thoughts. He would think things like, "She can't make me. No one can and no one will."

The teacher had a lever, though, which was his grade. For this young man it was a nasty dilemma. It was a matter of principle. If he gave in, he felt he'd never be able to look into a mirror at his own face again. He would be a traitor to himself. He simply couldn't give in and read a book that he did not want to.

The teacher really had no clue what this student was going through. She was not aware of his inner turmoil. To her he was just a stubborn teenager whom she felt needed to expand his horizons and *grow up*. She had already put up with his shenanigans far too long. The teacher had taken it upon herself to enlarge this young man's very narrow field of vision. She was hoping he'd develop additional interests. These would then enhance his life. She was not going to budge either.

The OCS teen sensed that his teacher had put her foot down. Her feet were in a hole that had been filled with quick drying cement. He was just as determined that he would not be forced to do something or act in a way that would be untrue to him. He also was not going to budge.

It is situations like this one that can sometimes get such a student to take a stab at doing something different. If this student had not actually been quite fond of his English teacher, they both might have ended up losers. As it was, because of this fondness, the young man was really in a predicament. You see he also had an obsessive need not to let anyone down who was important to him. It was a Catch 22.

If he let her down he would be devastated. If he let himself down, his "whole life would be like a useless piece of garbage." These were his very words. What could he do? He began to focus on this dilemma. He did so with the kind of intensity that apparently only those with OCS possess.

After thinking about it constantly for days, it finally came to him. He knew exactly what he had to do to satisfy both of these obsessive needs. It was a lucky thing for the teacher that this young man cared about her. He couldn't have cared less about a grade. She also cared about him. What he finally decided to do was done mostly so that he would not disappoint her. There was no other real motivator. Necessity *is* after all the mother of invention.

This OCS teen did the only thing he could think of. He knew of students who had based their reports on the vague descriptions of a book provided on the inside cover flaps. He wasn't stupid, though. He was aware that at least sometimes these students had gotten nailed. He knew that if he did that and got caught, it would be even worse. That would let his teacher down just as much if not more than not doing the report at all. He wasn't that thick. So he lied.

He thought up an interesting title and came up with what he thought was a decent sounding author's name. He then wrote a very credible book report on a realistic type of fiction novel that did not exist. This probably could not have been done, had it not happened 35 years ago. It was before the Internet.

If she had tried to check up on him and confront him with the fact that there was no such book in the school library, he was ready. He would casually inform her that he'd gotten the book at the main library in downtown Phoenix. He didn't think she'd go all the way into Phoenix just to check up on one stupid book. She also had no reason to believe that he might do something like this either. It was a good thing for him that she did not feel the need to check up on him. He was not aware at the time of the reference volume carrying the title "Books in Print." Even the school library may have had that volume.

The teacher had been thrilled. She thought that she had surely broadened the young man's world, even if only a tiny bit. He was just as ecstatic because he had remained true to himself (or his OCS). He hadn't read something he did not want to read; nor had he let his teacher down. At least, not as far as she could tell, he didn't.

She gave him an A. He couldn't have cared less. On the very same day she handed it back to him, he threw it away. The real reward had been received the moment she'd handed him that book report back. It told him she'd believed that he had done what she'd asked. He hadn't let her down. He hadn't let himself down either.

This is an example of just how far the OCS-driven may go. The energy and effort it takes is tremendous. What might it be like if that energy was to be able to be channeled in the right direction? Well, maybe it was.

Black or White; All-or-Nothing Responding

This paradox is seen so often in every aspect of OCS that it calls for a brief review of its own. Over-responding to many things is very common. Both an over-response and no response are examples of this. When symptoms are active, that's pretty much what you get. Hyper-responses can basically lean in one or two directions. On one of the paths the reaction can appear to be focused entirely on the negative side of things.

The OCS student is often difficult to be around. Generally this is because she can seem to be continually complaining about anything and everything. The most uneventful situations can be harshly condemned. It can get to be so bad that even the most patient, kindhearted and caring among us can become exhausted and frustrated. The OCS student manifesting this tends to view things as either good or bad. There is no in between. Neutral does not exist. For those with OCS as a concept neutral cannot be conceived. To them there is no such thing as a *middle* ground.

You either win or you lose. There is no second place. Things are either exactly right or they are *not* right. If they're not *right* they're wrong. Many of the OCS-affected who display this kind of focus tend to do so in a negative vein.

The other path taken is a constant focus on the positive. Experience suggests that those in this OCS group are far fewer in number than its counterpart. Even so it is possible this assumption has been based on an under-represented sample. These people are less likely to seek therapeutic assistance. Why would they? They don't have a problem. Heck, they're considered to be *optimistic*. Very few of the OCS-affected on the optimistic side of the coin can view what they have as a "problem" in any sense of the word. These people, though, can also irritate others at times. Generally, this is due to their often outrageous positive outlook. Still, they are more easily tolerated by others than those who are focused mainly on the negative.

In the optimistic group *everything* is viewed as good. The OCS-affected with this chronic positive symptom can always find something they can comment on that is good. This is true even in the most awful of situations. It's almost as if they have an inability to allow themselves to see the bad. Perhaps this is the real truth. The anxiety they experience may spring from any negative thought they might have. So they are positive to a fault. This makes sense.

Others tend to value and praise this eternal optimism as virtuous. Realistically, though, it is often *way* beyond virtuous. It's also way past the euphemistic notion of "finding the silver lining" or the "making of lemonade when given lemons." The all-or-nothing factor can leave this group incapable of even considering a negative thought of any kind. Those I have come in contact with, professionally and socially, sometimes appear to be what might be called "the secretly depressed." The look this need predisposes them to show the world is just too positive. They cannot truly accept or admit to weakness in any form. They cannot so much as consider the existence within themselves of something like depression. They often suffer silently, hiding reality from even themselves. These OCS optimists rarely seek out therapeutic assistance. They truly can sometimes be the saddest OCS-driven people of all. They don't often get help. No one would believe they need it. Not even them.

OCS in the Schools: What to Do about it

Make it known. Education is without a doubt the most powerful and vital component. It is the most important of all the possible interventions for OCS. Knowledge opens the doorway to understanding. Whether or not someone walks through the door or slams it shut and runs the other way remains out of our control. No one can force understanding, any more than a horse can be forced to drink. It is the physically experienced crisis of thirst that motivates the horse to drink.

Without sufficient knowledge and insight, a healthy adjustment cannot be made. When a competent teacher is made aware of a condition such as OCS, insight is gained. This acts to eliminate faulty beliefs. Education also frees the teacher from common chronic errors and beliefs. The kinds of errors referred to are those that can cause disruptive classroom confrontations. A new level of predictability will also come with this new knowledge. Teachers are better able to anticipate many of the OCS reactions. This skill can then be used to better manage incidents when they occur. The knowledge applied by the teacher can also further reduce problems. The student's inappropriate behaviors can be managed more effectively. This can be true regarding the intensity as well as the frequency.

It is important to remember at all times that *OCS is an explanation, not an excuse*. Do not let sympathy get in the way of appropriate disciplinary measures. Flexibility with such students is required, not sympathy. In order to establish a good learning relationship structure with flexibility is needed. Rigidity or inflexible routines in teaching the OCS student is like a setup for confrontation and war.

Think about the example of the young man in high school. His teacher was actually quite flexible, which is why he did so well in her class. It is also why he developed an emotional connection with her. That is what really mattered. When she put her foot down, a battle ensued, although she didn't really know how intense it was. If that young man had been a little less intellectually endowed it might have been different. If he had not been as creative or had a learning disability in writing, it might have turned out differently. Or, if he had not had an emotional tie to this teacher the same outcome would not have occurred. If any of these things had not been what they were, the end result would have undoubtedly been quite different.

Teachers in a war with an OCS student are fighting a "no-win" situation. The teacher with the OCS teen and the book report issue lost the war. She just didn't know it. Does this mean I am suggesting that teachers should never assign an OCS student a task that they seem driven to resist? Of course not! It just means that in those circumstances when a teacher feels the need for strict control, he or she had better be prepared for war.

By being prepared, the teacher is able to be more effective. He or she will not get too emotionally involved in the struggle. A teacher in this situation really needs to take a step back, and not view the OCS behavior personally. The student may verbally rail against the assignment in front of the class. If so, surely there are class or school discipline procedures for such occasions. The teacher needs to calmly follow through with them.

Finally, teachers should be much more able to withstand the student's overreactions if they understand OCS. They should also be less likely to take the student's behavior as a personal attack. They will not feel their authority as a teacher is being questioned. The teacher will not routinely consider the behavior a sign of disrespect. It *is not* disrespect. There is no real lack of respect without true intent. Teachers should keep in mind that they are dealing with a student who at times is internally driven. Because of this, sometimes these students only have partial control over their actions and reactions. This student has an honest-to-goodness problem that they cannot always control. It is real and when identified can be treated successfully.

The OCS student in such a situation is not vying for attention, in spite of how it may seem to the teacher. This student is not being manipulative out of laziness. He may manipulate but when OCS is present, the manipulation is not for the reasons most people think. In fact, such manipulations can be for very strange reasons that no one understands, or would believe. To the OCS student, this experience is like a life-and-death situation—his own. The great anxiety the OCS student feels may be exaggerated tremendously, but not by choice. These larger-than-life feelings are not established on purpose or with some sinister goal in mind. Teachers need to know this. Both teachers and parents need to follow through with discipline calmly. Emotions should not be allowed to get in the way.

Some OCS students will shutdown either right away or later after their blow up. Don't take it personally. Understand. Fail them when they do this in relation to a specific assignment. Teachers should not allow their emotional reactions to dictate the OCS student's grades. On assignments for which no symptom struggles were present, grade them just like everybody else.

Emotions also must not be allowed to cloud the judgment of a teacher. This is especially important in relation to the performance of the OCS student as a whole. During obstinate shutdown periods, as long as the student is not disrupting others, don't make a scene. Let her be.

Sometimes the strength of an OCS problem will fade with time. This may be the way it goes, especially if there is no early confrontation. Teachers have had success following these suggestions. They have reported that in many instances they have observed such students eventually begin an assignment. The teachers find that this seems to often work when they themselves don't overreact at the start. This is the same assignment for which the student had originally experienced a shutdown. An OCS-driven war is neither worth the effort nor the potential casualties. It's usually a no-win situation for the one that is not OCS-driven.

Sadly, a conflict with an OCS student is often not quite as simple as that described above. That's why flexibility is such an important concept to understand. If the OCS student balks on a particular aspect of an assignment, ask yourself the following question. Is staying firm in the best interests of the student? If it is, remain firm and be prepared. Think.

Remember, a true OCS student is not trying to usurp your authority as a teacher. Ponder.

There are many possible ways to travel to a neighborhood grocery store. Most might agree that a few of these paths are probably "better" than others. This is often true for school assignments, as well. You as a teacher may have assigned the path that you know by way of experience as the best one to take. What if the agreed upon "best" path to the neighborhood store happens to go over curbs inaccessible to those in a wheelchair? What if the path includes a stretch with no sidewalk where the street's shoulder is made up of tiny rocks two inches thick? What if on the other side of the rocks there is an irrigation ditch? Isn't it possible that the best route for the disabled wheelchair-bound student may be quite different from what is thought 'best' for most others? It may take a little longer, but is much less dangerous. It also may actually be easier. If you've ever tried to navigate a wheelchair over a distance covered by two inches of tiny pebbles, you know what I mean. If the goal is to arrive safely or to make it easier for the specific person involved, then it doesn't really matter what route is taken. The one that works best for the person is the one that is best to achieve that goal.

OCS is a condition that is managed and not cured. There are natural fluctuations of symptoms and intensity throughout the course of a day, a week, or a year. Symptoms come and go. They change over time. Stress and fatigue make them worse. There can be periods of time during which no observable interference is apparent. Teachers must insure that they don't take these periods of remission as evidence that the student really is in complete control. If not, it is too easy to believe that the symptoms must be intentional when they reoccur.

If teachers begin to get a sense that a student's behaviors have this "OCS flavor," the ideas discussed so far may help. It can be much like a Band-Aid can help a small cut or sore to heal. The actual healing process itself doesn't have much to do with the Band-Aid, and yet the Band-Aid remains useful to the process. Discussing the student and situation with an OCS-aware school counselor or psychologist can help. This professional may then interview the student and parents to get more information. This can be a very positive and appropriate action.

Depending on the frequency and intensity levels of the OCS, the school psychologist may want to refer the student to a medical professional. Sometimes it is necessary to educate the physician in regard to OCS (see sample generic letter in appendix). This is okay. It's why the letter was written in the first place. There are times when these physicians may not feel comfortable prescribing certain medications such as Anafranil or one of the SSRIs. It helps sometimes if they understand exactly what the target symptoms are. It is also helpful if there is a general description of the likely responses to treatment.

A psychologist or counselor can assist physicians. This is done by interviewing teachers and parents after a medication is started to determine a child's response. At times the professional involved can re-administer behavior inventories to parents and teachers. They can also interview the student involved in order to get firsthand personal insights. It has been my experience that the most appropriate way in which to complete follow-up interviews is to start with the general and then move towards the specific.

There are two main reasons for starting a personal interview with general types of questions. One is to figure out how much of a change the person may be aware of, without questioning. It is not unusual in the first follow-up session about a week or so after the start of a medication, to report no difference. Either that, or only slight improvements may be reported. Typical things that do improve a little include problem behaviors, which may be less frequent. They also become less intense and when issues do occur, recovery may be quicker. The student may report feeling calmer. They may not get into as many fights with siblings, parents, teachers, or other students. Improvements often reported by teachers and parents tend to be similar. They may include being easier to get along with. The OCS student may be less intense about everything. When they do get upset it may not last as long. They may not seem as irritating as before. They also may be a bit more on task than previously.

There is another good reason for starting a personal interview with general questions. It has to do with personal insight and education in relation to the problem of OCS. There are specific symptoms that tend to improve with medical treatment. These then result in the general types of progress noted in the previous paragraph.

Experience indicates that the OCS student's difficulty in noticing what may have gotten better after starting medication is understandable. When a symptom is better, it is no longer on the student's mind as it was prior to a medication trial. A good response results in fewer episodes of these persistent thoughts. Fewer thoughts mean fewer compulsively driven actions or urges. This very fact makes it unlikely that a given symptom, even though improved, will be noticed by the student. This is simply because it is no longer interfering in their daily functioning. If it's no longer an issue, why would one notice whether or not it was better? Why would one think about it at all? The idea to consider it as an improved symptom doesn't cross their mind.

The Leyton inventory is given again. The student is then faced with reassessing each and every symptom that was first identified. If parents or teachers see a positive response, it is important to redo the Leyton. It doesn't matter if the student thinks there's been little or no response. After the Leyton is redone the student often realizes that many of the symptoms are now better. The symptoms have become less frequent, less intense, better, or are no longer present. The response is usually good enough that the student can definitely state that many symptoms are "better." This means that they are better than they had been prior to the onset of medication. The term "better" typically refers to one or more of the following descriptors, depending upon the question:

1.   The symptom is less intense when it does occur.
2.   Problems are less frequent than they had been previously.
3.   The symptom's presence does not persist as long as it once did.

Once the symptom occurs, it is easier to calm down than it was. Also, another person may be able to intervene as a calming influence. This calming effect can occur rather than making things worse or more intense, as used to happen.

Typical comments made by OCS students when reminded by the symptom checklist can include the following: "Oh yeah . . . you know, I haven't done that in a while." "Now that I think about it . . . you're right! That's not the same anymore." "I haven't even thought of that one . . ." and so on.

It is also not unusual for the OCS student to be fairly cautious when answering. They may respond with something like, "Well, yeah, that's a little better . . . maybe." This seems due to the self-doubt and tendency to be unsure of most opinion and decision type questions. They will also often report a group of symptoms as being about the "same." These are usually the strongest of all the symptoms. The strength of these may be related to long-term habits. They are also related to social acceptability. Many are also related indirectly to the root source. As a result, such symptoms do not simply fade away as others do when serotonin levels are addressed in the brain. Strategies for working with and managing these stronger or more persistent problems will be considered in more detail later.

It is important to do follow up interviews with the Leyton or something like it after the start of medication. The importance cannot be stressed enough. It is from this that those with OCS gain their insight. Parents, and even teachers, can also benefit in a big way from this information. It helps them to realize what specific symptoms are improving as a result of the medication. The results tend to make them believers in the biologically driven OCS.

As the skeptic of a chemical cause begins to see the connections between the improving symptoms, there is often a change of heart. As others see a change in behavior it becomes hard to keep a skeptical attitude. Parents, teachers, family members, and the OCS person, now begin to really learn about the primary cause. Their previous behavior problems are seen in a whole new light.

This awareness and knowledge can be helpful to all involved. They are now ready to use a well-known cognitive behavior therapy technique. This method has been proven by longstanding research to be effective in the treatment of OCD. It is known as "exposure and response prevention."

Knowledge enables those with OCS and others to identify symptoms. These symptoms are finally recognized for what they are as the medication may begin to level off. When this occurs it suggests a dosage change may be warranted.

What if medication for some reason or another cannot be tolerated? What if it's not effective? What if you or your parents are unwilling or unable to follow through with such treatment? What if everyone involved is putting forth good and honest effort in attempts to treat the problem? What if the correct diagnosis still does not seem to be forthcoming? What if the problem is not quite severe enough to be easily recognized? What if it still interferes with a student's quality of life and education? What if the difficulty seeing OCS keeps others from being able to consider that an actual real problem exists?

The answer to each of these questions centers on one shared factor. This factor is intensity. Levels of intensity dictate what typically is or is not effective when faced with trying to educate or treat an OCS student. The mild-moderate OCS student, whose symptoms are fairly intense, may need special education services. When they do need such services they are often viewed as those with an emotional disability.

These OCS students can fall under one or several categories used to make an educational diagnosis. Often OCS symptoms lead to serious depression. This is one of the categories under which a student can be considered emotionally disabled (ED). OCS students at moderate levels also tend to have difficulty making or keeping friends. They often struggle as well in getting along with teachers. As a result they may also be eligible as an ED due to an inability to build and maintain relationships with peers and teachers. There is yet another descriptor relating to possible eligibility under the ED category. OCS students may show inappropriate types of behavior or feelings under "normal" circumstances.

As already discussed, many observed OCS symptoms do not seem to make much sense. This is especially true when compared to other students in the same environment. There is one final picture relating to ED eligibility that can also be considered for the OCS student. This is the tendency to pick up physical symptoms linked to personal or school problems. The hypersensitivity of the OCS student can become overly focused on their physical health. When this happens, the OCS student will tend to have a high number of visits to the school nurse's office when compared to the average for other students. They may also have a significant number of absences from school.

Another category that an OCS student may qualify for special education services is known as Other Health Impaired. If ADHD co-exists with OCS, this may be the best category for the student.

This book is not intended as a treatise on special educational requirements and the law. Still, there are a few more important points relating to special education services that should be known to all. A student may clearly have one or any combination of the ED types. Even though this is true, they may not be entitled to special education services as defined by the law. If the symptom does not adversely affect a student's educational performance, they are not eligible. The adverse effects have to be deemed not able to be fixed without special education.

These adverse effects are usually determined by a comprehensive psycho-educational team evaluation. This helps to rule out other possible reasons for school related problems. There must be a major discrepancy between measured potential and actual achievement. Usually potential is indicated by an IQ test. Achievement is normally determined by scores on standardized achievement tests. A major discrepancy is necessary for eligibility in many of the special education categories.

One other element is usually needed. Also required for eligibility is a concept that can be summed up in one simple word. That word is *failure*. The evaluating team is in charge of determining academic failure. Still, a ballpark figure for general use would be consistent grades of low Ds or below. This is added to the evidence that the student is capable of much better performance.

There is a component to also rule out that involves what is called "social maladjustment." This means that the poor grades must not result from a determined lack of effort. If social maladjustment is considered to be blamed for poor grades, the student is not eligible for special education services.

So where does that leave the teachers who must educate, put up with and somehow survive the OCS student? Right back to the beginning of this section of the chapter entitled, "What to do."

I am convinced understanding is the key. In spite of any treatment given, the teacher or parent who understands can have a positive effect on this student. Those who accept limitations and truly work to enable this student to succeed will have success. This will require a firm, yet compassionate, reality-based approach. However, doing so will be what's best for the student. In doing what is best for the student, teachers also do what is best for themselves as teachers. It is not an easy task to live with, teach or even be a friend to the true OCS student. Remember, just like the presence of a wheelchair implies a disability, OCS can be a sign of a disability too. It is also important to remember that just like the wheelchair-bound paraplegic, OCS is an explanation, not an excuse. Teachers and all others need to work hard not to let it be an excuse. Knowledge sets us free from the chains of uncertainty.

No article or book can substitute for actual real life experience with its tons of genuine complications and subtleties. It is my sincere hope that this information enables the reader to get a solid glimpse of what the OCS-affected may be experiencing. I hope that knowledge and insight are achieved. Perhaps this insight and knowledge gained will be sufficient. If it just enables a better and more positive working relationship that may be enough. All those who are or may yet be diagnosed as having OCS will benefit, if this can be done.

They couldn't see into the Heart

I used to think if they could just see the one I know that's really me
then they . . . would surely understand
somehow I knew . . . something was wrong
though I didn't know what . . . it was so strong
I was like an ostrich . . . with its head in the sand

but all they believed of me . . . just wasn't true
they couldn't see into the heart
so many things I'd do . . . were so often misunderstood
and then they'd turn away . . . whispering . . . that boy's no good

but I believe we can be what we want to be
if we'll put in the kind of time and effort it takes
all we have to do is try . . . and never give up . . .
though we may ache
to stop . . . to quit . . . to run . . . in fear our dreams will break

somehow I sensed . . . that I could stand
all by myself . . . as we all can
when we believe . . . it's something we can do
and though I may fall . . . a thousand more times
I'll get back up . . . 'cause that's a part of life
I know I'll make it . . . if I just keep on . . . I've learned this is true

'cause all they believed of me was from their own point of view
they couldn't see into my heart
so many things I'd do . . . were so often misunderstood
and then they'd turn away . . . whispering . . . that boy's no good

but I believe we can be what we want to be
if we'll put in the kind of time and effort it takes all we have to do is try . . .
and never give up . . . though we may ache
to stop . . . to quit . . . to run . . . in fear our dreams will break

Words and Music by Ron D. Kingsley
May 20, 1993

18

You're in Good Company

The Positive Side of OCS

I feel absolutely confident in conveying what I am going to suggest. Nearly every great inventor, artist, musician, writer, and actor seems to have either ADHD and/or what I refer to as OCS. As you read about the people in this chapter, I hope that you will realize that you are not alone. Many have had it and have been able to accomplish truly remarkable feats.

A middle aged Albert Einstein once wrote, "Every reminiscence is colored by today's being what it is and therefore by a deceptive point of view." I begin my discourse with Mr. Einstein and his life with this statement. This is because what I am about to say is surely colored by today's being what it is. It is also colored by what Albert Einstein perceived himself to be in his own writings. It is even further colored by how others who knew him saw him. And finally, it is sometimes colored by what others may have suggested, based on their opinion of his writings.

After exploring the life of Albert Einstein I have come to several conclusions. I am convinced that throughout his lifetime he showed evidence of what is known today as an Attention Deficit Hyperactivity Disorder (ADHD). He also had obsessive and compulsive symptoms (OCS) in the mild-moderate range. In describing my case for Mr. Einstein, I hope to share enough evidence to make a special case. Many, if not all, genius level innovators are in my opinion the products of their biological "wiring." It was this that "drove" them to the heights they often reached. By understanding the lives of these "driven" great men and women, perhaps we can better know our generation. Maybe it can help us better understand

ADHD/OCS-affected children. Hopefully we can then better accept their progress and current life status. That which we understand . . . we no longer fear. As fear diminishes, real change is able to occur.

There are many subtle hints made about the parents of Albert Einstein. These hints point to evidence of OCS tendencies. They show the genetic link. Ronald Clark asserts that "Einstein was nourished on a family tradition which had broken with authority; which disagreed, sought independence, and had deliberately trodden out of line."

Regarding Mr. Einstein's memory Dr. James Plesch wrote the following. "It has always struck me as singular that the marvelous memory of Einstein for scientific matters does not extend to other fields. I don't believe that Einstein could forget anything that interested him scientifically, but matters relating to his childhood, his scientific beginnings, and his development are in a different category, and he rarely talks about them—not because they don't interest him, but simply because he doesn't remember them well enough."

In reply to this statement Einstein himself commented as follows. "You're quite right about my bad memory for personal things. It's really quite astounding. Something for psychoanalysts—if there really are such people."

Those with ADHD and OCS are often considered by parents and teachers to have "selective memories." Many of these children and adults can remember some specific events or details. This is especially true in areas of strong interest or study. This tends to be a common OCS-related characteristic. The things for which one has an obsession are generally remembered with ease. Often the OCS person couldn't forget even if they wanted to. In relation to memory parents, teachers, and others can get incredibly frustrated. This frustration comes from the OCS inability to remember common sense rules of behavior. They forget the times tables. They can even forget what time dinner is served, although the supper time may be at exactly the same time day-after-day.

Einstein represents the essence of what has become known as the "absentminded professor." Mr. Ronald Clark quickly points out that Einstein was "absentminded only about things that didn't matter . . . or Einstein was absentminded when he knew there was someone to remember for him." From the OCS point of view I will not argue that it seemed to others that when Einstein had someone there to remember for him, he was forgetful. I would argue though that over time someone came to be there because he *was* absentminded. If they had not been there appointments would have been missed and everyday things would not have gotten done.

It has been noted that there was nothing in Einstein's early history to suggest the presence of latent genius. In fact some writers have suggested that the exact opposite seemed more likely to be the case. These would cite the "lateness with which he learned to speak" as supportive evidence. It has been recorded that "even at the age of nine Einstein was not a fluent speaker." Einstein's personal memories of his youth were of speech hesitancies. That and the fact that he would reply to questions "only after consideration and reflection." His parents reportedly feared he might be mentally slow. From an OCS perspective there is another explanation that cannot be proven, but makes a lot of sense. When OCS is a factor, there is a characteristic that might make sense out of Einstein's apparent speech and language problems. In the past twenty-five years I have worked with quite a few children who had been diagnosed with Elective Mutism. These also tended to demonstrate a wide variety of OCS characteristics. After treatment for the OCS, the "Elective Mutism" greatly improved.

Common symptoms of OCS that can relate to these children's unwillingness to speak include the following:

1.) An irrational yet undeniable fear of not saying the right thing.
2.) An irresistible need to find *just the right* words before one answers.
3.) The compelling fear that others will reject or accept them based on what is said.

What if Einstein's delayed speaking and hesitation were actually caused by something else? What if his tendency to answer only after careful thought could be explained differently? What if both question and answer was the product of OCS characteristics? I believe they were.

In my experience it has not been that common for OCS persons to be rendered mute. To have symptom intensities at a level strong enough to do that seems somewhat rare. I have, however, seen a few wherein this clearly has been the case. Thus I consider it quite possible that Einstein's reported childhood language troubles might not have been language "problems" at all. They could have been secondary and tertiary reactions to the unidentified symptoms of OCS. If this is true, then his inherent genius was always present. It could have been well camouflaged, though, amid a host of behaviors and reactions that tended to suggest otherwise.

This too is common for those with OCS in the public schools. They are too often viewed as underachievers. They are also often considered by teachers to be less intelligent than they in fact are. On the other hand they can also be thought of as brilliant and wonderful students. This can depend on whether or not they are overwhelmed in school. It can also depend on whether the teacher can see through the smokescreen of symptoms into the heart of who the student really is.

Another secondary symptom common to the OCS, shown by Einstein, has been reported by his son Hans Albert. He has said that his father was withdrawn from the rest of the world. This was true even as a boy. He was also a student for whom teachers held out only poor prospects. Einstein's father had asked one of his teachers regarding what profession his son should pursue. He was told point blank: "It doesn't matter; he'll never make a success of anything."

Authors agree that Einstein grew to loathe educational discipline. He also hated the Luitpold Gymnasium where he'd spent six of his boyhood years in school. Reportedly Einstein did not seem able to express his dislike in regard to his school experience until his midlife years. Even then he was said to be unable to actually say he "hated it." Often those with OCS have difficulty expressing some types of feelings and thoughts. This can be especially true when aimed at respected institutions or persons of authority. Sometimes this is the result of an unfounded fear of condemnation or other dubious fears. Interestingly the exact opposite can also be true.

Einstein left the Luitpold School before graduating. History reports that Einstein had been trying to leave the school to join his parents in Italy. He wanted to leave by means of a "medical" release. This was to be owing to a "nervous breakdown." However, Einstein had not yet received the medical certificate when he was expelled from the school. He was let go on the grounds that "your presence in the class is disruptive and affects the other students." This is such a common feature of OCS and ADHD that it again points towards other reasons for many of Mr. Einstein's life events.

A description of Einstein as he appeared to others during this period in his life is also revealing. He was described as a "precocious, half-cocksure, almost insolent youth and young man." Some of the most difficult and disruptive students in the public schools of today could be described in this same way. Many of these students of today might also be portrayed as having ADHD and OCS.

Einstein had an intense dislike of every kind of authority. He wanted nothing to do with authority figures and was also suspicious of the same. A large number of those with OCS have major problems with authority figures early-on. It usually starts with parents, teachers, coaches, rule-oriented institutions and so on. If the OCS person has not finished an assignment and has a compulsion to complete the task, it can be a problem. If the teacher directs the class to move on to the next subject the student may have a problem with authority. The intensity of the student's *need* to finish defines the extent to which a problem will occur. It can become a problem if the compulsion is strong and the teacher pushes the student to stop what he is doing and transition as directed. The student will appear to be defying authority on purpose. It doesn't matter that he is simply reacting to an unknown drive for task completion. What it looks like is usually what it is believed to be. Remember the thought shared earlier. When lies are easier to believe than the truth, the truth is not welcome. This could also be quoted in another way. When alternative explanations are easier to believe than the truth, the truth is not welcome.

An idea or thought that cannot be let go of can lead to defiant behavior. This is especially true if the idea is not in line with the content of the teacher's lesson. Directions coming from a teacher, principal, parent, can feel like intrusions into the way the OCS feel things must be. Such intrusions need to be rejected. The same reaction can occur in relation to established rules. This is particularly so when these rules are rigidly held. If the "rule" interferes with needs or compulsions, the OCS student may appear to be flagrantly breaking those "rules." In reality they are only following through with a chemically driven impulse. They are only breaking the "rule" because it just happens to be there and in the way.

If the presence of OCS/ADHD was a significant factor in Einstein's life many things about his life would make sense. It is easy to imagine how he might develop strong negative attitudes towards authority figures. Also, it might explain his extreme stubbornness. In addition, it might explain his unwillingness to let go of an idea, and so on. Note that some of these things are not necessarily always bad or undesirable. It all depends on the circumstances and eventual outcome.

Einstein is said to have been "always sensitive to beauty and abnormally sensitive to music." An abnormal sensitivity to things is common for OCS. Over-responding to many things is also common. In fact, this tendency to overreact seems to be almost essential in diagnosing OCS. This includes under-responding too. After all, what is under-responding but an over-response in the opposite direction?

Colleagues spoke of Einstein's "single-minded determination with which he followed his star without regard for others." Also, he is said to have had a "desperate need to find order in a chaotic world." Such accounts fit easily into the OCS patterns of behavior.

OCS-affected people are often charged with being very selfish and self-centered. The obsessive need to do certain things gets in the way. So does the inability to let go of certain thoughts. Both of these can interfere with the ability to notice anything else that may be going on. Obsessions and compulsions create a form of tunnel vision.

It has been my experience that the OCS-affected usually do hold a deep and meaningful regard for others. When accused of being otherwise, they vehemently will not accept this assumption or believe it. During times that are OCS-driven, though, nothing else seems to matter. There is almost no consciousness of anything beyond the current focus. The undeniable thought or need of the moment is the only thought or need that exists. There is nothing else.

Einstein conveys yet another interesting idea in his own words. He wrote, " . . . but you must recognize it at least as a modest attempt to overcome the laziness in writing which I have inherited from both of my dear parents." This is of interest because it is common for those with OCS to have great difficulties in the area of writing. Others often label this as laziness. In fact the OCS themselves typically come to accept what others think as well. So they commonly come to feel that they must indeed be "lazy." The OCS can also be great and prolific writers when this is the direction that their OCS drives them.

A fellow student's account of Einstein as a young man suggests some ADHD-like behavior. It also hints at what seems to be evidence of OCS. This fellow considered Einstein "impudent" and then went onto say that he was "sure of himself, his gray felt hat pushed back on his thick, black hair. He strode energetically up and down in a rapid, I might almost say crazy, tempo of a restless spirit which carries a whole world in itself." He felt Einstein showed an "intellectual disinclination to give a damn for anybody." He further said Einstein had a "prickly arrogance" and was "a young man of the world." He was "well filled with his own opinions" and "careless of expressing them without reserve regarding the passing scene." Furthermore he would do so "with a sometimes slightly contemptuous smile." He was at times "moodily aloof" from his peers and companions. Again, all these characteristics are common for those dealing with OCS and/or ADHD.

Einstein was "casual of dress" and "unconventional of habit." He went around "with the happy-go-lucky absentmindedness of a man concentrating on other things." He was to retain this "all his life." "That young man," a friend's parent once said, "will never amount to anything because he can't remember anything." Einstein would frequently forget his key and have to awaken his landlady late at night. He would call out: "It's Einstein—I've forgotten my key again."

Emotional hypersensitivity relating to his music (playing of the violin) was often shown. During "musical evenings" to which he'd been invited by friends, certain problems would arise. If attention to his performance was not deemed adequate, he would simply stop playing. Sometimes he would add a remark that would verge on impetuousness. He considered it an affront when a group of elderly ladies went right on with their knitting as he played.

A great deal of Einstein's "genius" has been credited to "an imagination which gave him courage to challenge accepted beliefs." From an OCS perspective this could be restated. His challenge of accepted beliefs may have been more of an inability to see it any other way. It may have been tunnel vision rather than a true challenge to the status quo. The inability to let go of new ideas could be viewed as a challenge to the ideas of old. Indeed, that's what it is, but not necessarily because of courage. Although I suspect Einstein himself would prefer that account. Who wouldn't prefer courage over a suggested biological drive? If accepted beliefs got in the way of what was "driven" well then they may just have to be rethought. They might be rethought or changed completely.

After failing the initial entrance exam to a college level school known as the ETH, Einstein waited. He was going to try and take the exam again. Eventually he was allowed to register. This was reported to be due to the principal of the ETH having been "impressed by his mathematical ability." It appears to have been more likely that it was because this principal was impressed with Einstein's "character."

The principal set Einstein up in a nearby school. In that school it was expected that a year of specific study would enable him to pass the ETH entrance exam. Minkowski who was one of Einstein's teachers at the ETH has said that Einstein was "the lazy dog who never bothered about mathematics at all." To the professors at the ETH Einstein became one of the floundering scholars who might or might not graduate. Nevertheless he was a great deal of trouble. A certain professor Weber, after admitting to Einstein's cleverness, then told him, "but you have one fault; one can't tell you anything." This type of comment is very common for parents and teachers when dealing with the OCS-affected. Their obsessive and compulsive symptoms lock in on the way they think things should be. Often this keeps them from being able to accept another's direction or advice.

Einstein's over-reactive and sensitive nature is once again found in a comment made in later life about the four years he spent at the ETH. "The coercion," he wrote speaking of the required exams "had such a deterring effect upon me that after I had passed the final examination I found the consideration of my scientific problems distasteful to me for an entire year!" He then tried to get a job at the ETH. The refusal of this institution to hire him was a blow to both his prospects and his pride. It seems that he had been enough trouble as a student that no one wanted to have to deal with him as a colleague. It was said of him at this time "Einstein was the graduate who denied rather than defied authority." Einstein was also said to be "the perverse young man whom 'you must' was the father of 'I won't." He was "The keen seeker out of heresies to support; a young man who was written off as virtually unemployable by many self-respecting citizens."

Somewhere around a year after trying to get on at the ETH Einstein was offered a position at a technical school called Winterthur. About this offer he wrote "I have no idea who recommended me because as far as I know not one of my teachers has a good word to say for me." In another part of this same letter he adds, "I am fully aware that I am a curious bird . . . ." After just one year Einstein was dismissed from the post at Winterthur. It is believed this was because his ideas about minimum routine and minimum discipline were quite different from those of his employer Jakob Neusch. "One thing that remains clear is that neither Zurich nor any other Swiss University would have refused to hire Einstein or sent him looking elsewhere for a position had they seen in him at the time anything more than an awkward, somewhat lazy, and certainly obstinate young man who thought he knew more than his elders and betters." The impression that Einstein was a "know-it-all" is a basic error that often occurs when OCS is present. Symptom dynamics make it appear to be this way, when it is not.

Einstein's first marriage failed. This is also not that unusual for those with OCS/ADHD. These people tend to be very difficult to live with. A student visiting him a few years after he'd married described what he saw. "He was sitting in his study in front of a heap of papers covered with mathematical formulas writing with his right hand and holding his younger son in his left. He kept replying to questions from his elder son Albert who was playing with his bricks with the words, 'Wait a minute, I've nearly finished.' He gave me the children to look after for a few moments and went on working. The irresponsible cad! Did he care so little for his children that it didn't matter to him who looked after them?"

Seeing what that young man saw one could easily come to an assumption such as this. The more accurate account might be that Einstein was in the throes of an obsessive thought process, with a compulsion too. With this filling his conscious mind it would keep him from being able to think about any other activity. At that particular moment in time *caring* was not the real issue. It is obvious that another might argue that it was. If he truly cared one might say he would not have done this. Never under any circumstances would a caring parent give their children to a practical stranger. This line of thinking does not take into account or even begin to grasp what it means to be biologically driven. The OCS truly are driven thus and I believe that Einstein was, as well. It only makes sense. This is not meant to excuse unsafe or thoughtless behavior. Rather, it is meant to be used as a basis for understanding OCS behavior. Knowledge is after all the first thing that is critical to most successful forms of management or treatment.

A confession made in Einstein's own words is of interest. It hints further at the inner workings of what for the OCS-affected is a common event in their minds. He wrote "I must confess that at the very beginning when the Special Theory of Relativity began to germinate in me I was visited by all sorts of nervous conflicts. When young I used to go away for weeks in a state of confusion." Confused thoughts along with noteworthy anxiety are common for many people with OCS. In fact these tend to be the main reasons linked with difficulties in writing. Also, the comprehension problems connected with reading may be due to these characteristics.

Einstein was always ready to declare that imagination and intuition were critical in his work. He called it "the very stuff of which artists rather than scientists are usually thought to be made." He said "When I examine myself and my methods of thought I come to the conclusion that the gift of fantasy has meant more to me than my talent for absorbing positive knowledge."

The OCS-driven tend to be obvious dreamers and are often described by others as "out to lunch" or "lost in their own world." This *is* one of the positive and sometimes negative features of the OCS-affected. Only those "lost in their own world" can envision "other" worlds as musicians, artists, and writers often do. Only they can imagine what could or might be because their thoughts are not locked into the common sense realities of society. At the same time this tendency sets them apart from most others and causes them to be labeled strange, weird, or down right "crazy." This weirdness can have a fairly negative impact on their social status. It can also impact the willingness of others to include them as members of their community.

Those who have OCS tend to isolate themselves and withdraw from most, if not all, social groups. They may belong to various social groups but are inclined to feel as if they are members, but don't really "fit in." When asked, they regularly describe themselves as "different." They even feel different from the majority of group members that they regard as their own. Seeing themselves as peculiar when compared to others seems to have a disturbing quality. This sense of turmoil sticks with them throughout their lives. The feeling is always there. It is in the background. It reminds them that they will never truly fit in with any group. It often makes them dismal and lonely.

Among his colleagues, Einstein "moved with a calm assurance and a quizzical smile; and both came, for all his innate humbleness, from an inner certainty of being right." He has been described as kind, but in a slightly casual fashion. He was also thought of as friendly "as long as others allowed him to get on with his work." The unspoken message, of course, was that if people interfered with his work he could be quite nasty, surly, and mean. This is a good description of what is often seen from the OCS-affected when a compulsion or obsession is interfered with. The same description applies if attempts are made to block its completion. The OCS-afflicted tend to over-respond or give up and completely abandon all efforts towards completion. Einstein was one who seemed more apt to react with passion and hostility relative to the interference of other people.

Winston Churchill is someone to whom Einstein's generation has made comparisons. He too appears to have had OCS. C. P. Snow said: "Of Churchill it has been written that almost obsessional concentration was one of the keys to his character. It was not always obvious but he never really thought of anything but the job at hand. He was not a fast worker, especially when dealing with papers, but he was essentially a non-stop worker." In my opinion, this "almost obsessional" state that Churchill and Einstein would attain was indeed just that. It was truly an obsessional state of mind at the moderate level on the continuum. Nevertheless, it was obsessive. Einstein displayed a "ferocious concentration on the task to be done." He also showed a "determination that nothing should be allowed to divert him from it." The comparison with Churchill rings true.

In 1908, Einstein wrote: "I am ceaselessly occupied with the question of the constitution of radiation." These incessant preoccupations seemed to change with the wind. It was like this throughout his entire life. Einstein evidently had a great variety of such obsessions, many of which were triggered by whatever currently occupied his mind.

Obsessions and compulsions are known to change with time, situations, and circumstances. Exactly why this occurs is not well understood. Experience suggests that the milder the symptoms are, the more likely they are to shift and change, as well as vary over time. As one moves up the continuum towards the severe, it seems that fewer symptoms are detected. These few are less likely to dramatically change over time due to their severity.

In the early 1900s Einstein was known as the man who could not seem to fit in. He was also thought of as disrespectful to professors. He was called the "dispenser of conversational bricks." He was "the bumbling Jewish customer." He was also "the man who at almost the age of thirty nevertheless, continued to prefer the company of students." To prefer the company of students was strange behavior indeed. This could have been due to an OCS-related hypersensitivity to criticism. Einstein, it seems, had heaped upon him by others more than his share of criticism. This came mostly from the professors and educated elders of his time. For Einstein to associate socially with them might have been equal to a form of emotional suicide. Students would be far less likely to criticize and would because of this be the obviously preferred company.

OCS children and adolescents do tend to hang around others that are younger. The reason appears to be similar to that which was just suggested for Einstein. They also tend to be considered socially immature. They can be two to three years behind their same-aged peers, socially. Their interests are prone to be more like those who are younger, as a result.

Another enlightening description is offered by one of Clark's statements. "Einstein," he has said, "was as he himself has admitted the kind of man who did not work well in a team." This same difficulty is very common for the OCS person. In fact, it is so common that it nearly seems a universal symptom. The primary problem when working with others on a team effort is inflexibility. This occurs when the OCS person feels a need to do things in a certain way. Either that or their direction of focus is contrary to the direction that others in the group want to take. The OCS-driven do not usually back down, bend, or compromise even a little. Of course, it is obvious what kinds of problems can occur, given the dynamics of such a situation.

Those with OCS may also feel that no one else will do specific tasks at a level equal to their own. They often feel resentment and fear that their project grade could be the result of another's inferior efforts. So the OCS student has trouble allowing another to complete his or her part of the project alone. Like a mother hen, they hover over the other team members' work. They direct suggest, argue, and sometimes demand that it be done exactly the way they feel it should. Such behavior does not win friends; nor does it foster smooth running group dynamics.

Another element of Einstein's character which is also common to the OCS-driven is suggested in more of Clark's statements. He has said that Einstein was always "dissatisfied with earlier work." He would "worry round it until he unearthed the chance of providing experimental evidence." The typical OCS child or adult is never really satisfied with anything that they do. The effort involved doesn't matter; the outcome is never quite good enough. As a consequence, two common results seem to occur. One is like that of Einstein who obsessively considers and reconsiders. He then writes and re-writes things, striving for perfection. The need to reach perfection overrides everything else. All thoughts and frustrations relating to never actually getting there are subsumed and beaten back. In spite of the personally perceived failures, this OCS type does not give up.

The other type can actually be a mixture or an apparent direct polar opposite. They show a similar need to reach perfection. They seem more focused on the idea and awareness that nothing they do will *ever* be good enough. These share a tendency to resist work. They often don't want to try. These seem to already be sure that they won't be able to complete the task satisfactorily. Each new failure is yet another painful reminder of their personal incompetence. These OCS-driven seem to be saying too: "So why even try?" Depression seems more common in this group, though it is certainly not unheard of in the other. Whatever the factors may be that cause or influence a person with OCS to go down this particular path, it is certain that they must be quite complex.

It should be obvious that there is no "simple" course to enable professionals to help those with OCS. There is no cook book manual from which to treat them. There is no easy guide to direct them towards a more evenly lived healthier lifestyle. This, however, appears to be a goal worthy of research.

The strength and levels of Einstein's over-focus are hinted at in a verbal summary offered by Dr. James Plesch. He said "As his mind knows no limits, so his body follows no set rules. He sleeps until he is wakened; he stays awake until he is told to go to bed; he will go hungry until he is given something to eat; and then he eats until he is stopped."

This statement was made at a time in Einstein's life when he had become so severely ill that there was some concern that he might actually die. Apparently, Dr. Plesch felt that the illness was a result of how poorly Einstein cared for the physical parts of his being. During the illness of 1917, his cousin Elsa took care of him and a bond grew between them. This bond eventually led to their marriage. It appears that Elsa's character was that of a "mothering" type. She was exactly what Einstein needed. She took care of him and for all the reasons already mentioned. Einstein had a great need to be taken care of. She watched over him as one might watch over a child.

It has been implied that "It was part of his genius that he could isolate himself from his surroundings." This "isolation" tendency may not be so much an element of genius but rather an OCS tendency. This is not to suggest genius was not present, for it surely was. The isolation inclination probably enabled the genius to flourish. There was a time when one of Einstein's colleagues was expressing his joy regarding the results of an experiment. The experiment was viewed as proof of Einstein's previously longtime unproven theory. Einstein himself, though, had been reportedly unmoved and said: "But I know that the theory is correct." The colleague then suddenly asked him, "But what if there had been no confirmation of the theory?" Einstein is said to have replied: "Then I would have been sorry for the dear Lord—the theory is correct!" Was this true *arrogance* or obsession? You know by now my thoughts on the matter.

Yet another thing shared about Einstein by his son Hans Albert is also quite common in the OCS population. He pointed out that his father was always willing to exaggerate, in his attempts to explain. There were also times, according to Hans, when Einstein would "delight in making up a story to please the audience." Common to those with OCS is the tendency to often exaggerate. They also distort accounts of events and experiences. They tell stories. This may have something to do with the OCS emotional oversensitivity to much of what they go through in life.

Sufficient data appears to exist on Mr. Einstein to make a posthumous diagnosis of OCS/ADHD. In examining Einstein's life, it is my hope that the reader will perhaps see parts of themselves. It is hoped that you will be able to draw parallels to your own lives or those of others who have OCS. By doing so, you can ultimately recognize it for what it truly is. Those who are OCS-driven are not alone. It can interfere with your life. It can be the very thing that makes you great in the eyes of others. It can make you the best of the best. Even so it can alienate you from others in ways that no one would believe unless they understood OCS. It is not always negative. It is not always positive. It is wonderful and it is horrible. No one can feel lonelier than the one who is OCS-driven. No one can feel as much joy over even the simplest of things.

Although not yet well recognized, there is and has always been a large community of those with OCS. Some of the greatest and most productive men and women ever to live owe their success, at least in part, to OCS/ADHD. The undeniable drive and seemingly boundless energy linked to the OCS/ADHD condition has led them to greatness. You who have OCS are in good company.

Those with OCS/ADHD tend to have unlimited energy. Thomas Alva Edison seems a good example of this. History records that he needed very little sleep. OCS appears to do several things for these people as well. First it drives the person to focus on a given problem with such intensity that nothing is likely to get in the way. Nothing could keep them from obtaining whatever happens to be the sought-after aim. Secondly, OCS has made them hypersensitive well beyond the norm. In fact they can be so sensitive that they tend to over-respond to just about everything. Many circumstances and "facts of life" that others seem perfectly capable of ignoring, these individuals cannot.

Regarding Beethoven, history records that when he was a child: "Soon his mother noticed that Ludwig wasn't quite like other little boys. He heard things that most children never noticed." It is true that many people can become annoyed with tasks that they have reason to believe are difficult. This irritation, though, usually isn't enough to push them into thoughts or actions of change. Most people will not spend extra time and energy in search of a better way. They won't necessarily try and make something easier. It doesn't really matter to them. The old or established way of things works just fine. The idea that it could be done differently and more easily, probably doesn't even enter their minds. This is not so for those with OCS. These folks tend to be bothered to an intolerable level by things that most others can simply "shrug off." This is why they tend to create things. It is why they invent and do things that have never been done before or thought of before by others.

It is also not unusual for those with OCS to spend a lot of time and energy trying to get out of doing something. They can spend more time avoiding tasks than would have been needed to complete the task in the first place. This often prompts teachers and parents to shake their heads in dismay and disbelief. Comments frequently include things such as: "I just don't understand what the problem is." "I wish she'd put as much effort into accomplishing things as she does in avoiding them." "He's making a mountain out of a molehill." "What's the big deal!" and so on. The exact "problem" can be hard to determine. It can be just as difficult to accept as credible. The identified "problem" can be such a small part of a given task that others simply don't get it. Remember, what to most others may be unbelievably trivial, can feel like a life-and-death situation to those with OCS. Is it really a life-and-death matter? Well no, it's not. Not really. Do they believe that it is, though? Yes.

Question: Why do inventors invent?
Answer: Because things *"bug"* them.

There was a young man who was being irritated by something on a daily basis. It hadn't always been so. It had all started after he and his wife got their first house. They moved from a rental. After the move the young man's commute to work doubled to about twenty miles one way. The young couple accepted this burden as positively as they could. After all, what was a bit longer of a commute compared to owning a house?

For this young man the irritation began to build as the days and weeks went by but it wasn't the travel that so irritated him. It was the sun. You see, in his small car there was a window shade that was inadequate to the task at times. This hadn't really bothered him before because his travel time in the car was not very long. Now, though, it was extended to five times what it used to be. Not only was that a problem but the direction of his commute to work had also changed. In the morning the sun was just coming up and would drench the full left side of his car in its brilliance. On the way home it was going down and was once again brightly shining on the left side of his car. The visor on the inside of the front windshield could be adjusted to swing over his left shoulder and provide shade from a blaring left side sun. This was one of its main purposes. It was supposed to be able to do this. The problem was that it just wasn't long enough. The young man would pull it down and slide this eye shade past his head. He'd have to duck just a bit to do this. Then he would position that visor for shade. Ah . . . shade, wonderful shade. His eyes were very sensitive to light. The sunlight coming in from the left could make his eyes water. It was also so bright it made it hard to see ahead sometimes. It bothered him. What else could he say?

Once the visor was positioned over the left window there would be about four to six inches of space between it and the door frame. That space wasn't shaded. The sun shot right through this space and into his eyes. If it had been only for a few minutes it probably wouldn't have mattered so much. The drive he now had twice each day could go from forty-five minutes to as long as two hours. He had the sun in his eyes now for one-and-a-half to as long as four hours every single day. It was maddening.

He complained often and loudly to his wife. After about three weeks it was annoying him so much he began having difficulty getting to sleep at night. One late evening he decided he was going to do something about it.

In frustration at his constant complaining his wife had snapped at him. She'd said: "Fine then, let's just sell our house and go back to the rental if that's what you want!" She'd walked away mumbling to herself about the big bad sun and how stupid could someone be and the like.

The young man was determined that he would somehow solve the problem. He turned his focus on this and nothing else. For the next three days he thought about it day and night. Then it came to him.

It was a Saturday afternoon. He grabbed his car keys and excitedly got behind the wheel of the car. The grocery store was only a few minutes away. Once there he went to the school supply isle. He found a cheap plastic three ring binder. The covers were thin and flexible. That was important. He had wanted to get red because that was the color of his car. He settled on blue because they were out of red. He was too excited and driven to want to waste time going to another store just because of a stupid color.

At home he nearly ran over his wife in his rush to gather the tools he would need. First he pulled out the strip of metal with the three round clasps meant to hold paper from the binder. He then took the folder out to his car. There he marked off a spot a couple of inches down from where the visor already hung. He reasoned that there might be a time he would want the shade a little lower than it now was. Plus he would need a little space past the mounted shade to anchor it in place. He wasn't certain how he would anchor it just yet. He'd thought about maybe Velcro. That probably would be best. The problem would be that the Arizona heat would surely melt any self-sticking Velcro tabs and keep them from holding it together. He could sew them on. No, he didn't really *know how to do that. Besides, the plastic was pretty thick and he was sure it would be hard to get a needle through it.*

He took the gutted folder into the kitchen. He sat down at the table where he'd left his tools. The young man picked up some scissors and cut along the spot marked off on the folder. He rounded the edges so that no one would get poked by a sharp corner. He sat for a while staring off into space. He was trying to figure out how to get his new "shade extender" attached to the visor in the car and ready for use when it was needed.

All of a sudden, he knew exactly what he had to do. He rummaged through the kitchen junk drawer until he found an old stapler. He then placed a staple every inch or so along the edge of the newly cut folder. He did not staple either of the ends but left both open. He rushed back out to the car.

The young man slid the cut and stapled folder right over the top of the permanent visor. It went on easily. He then adjusted the visor down and swung it out over the seat past his bent head and stooped shoulders. The gap between the fixed visor and the frame of the door remained. It was like the gaping maw of a laughing monstrosity only seen in dreams. Smiling broadly the young man reached up and pinched the edge of the folder between his thumb and forefinger. He tugged and it slid easily over the visor. At six inches or so he stopped. The gap was closed. He breathed a sigh of relief. The extend-a-shade was born. He went for a drive. It worked. A few weeks later, while on a trip with his wife and kids, he bought another plastic folder for the visor on the passenger side of the car. This time he cut it quite a bit wider. His kids were young and for it to be useful to them the extension had to cover more of the window space. Again, it worked like a charm.

The young man in question above invented his shades in the early 1980s. He didn't do it for money. He did it out of necessity. That sunlight coming through really bothered him. This was long before automakers finally began to figure it out. Even so, they still didn't get it right at first. The young man thought what they tried to do in the beginning was hilarious. Someone somewhere got the idea to put an extender right into the visor. When unhooked it would slide out of the visor itself and cover the sun gap. The funny thing was they only made the extender about two inches wide. After it was slid into place there was still a space about an inch wide at the top and a couple of inches at the bottom where the sunlight could sneak through. More recently, these extenders made by auto companies and put in the visors have been getting wider. The young man still occasionally shakes his head and smiles at those initial lame efforts the big auto companies made on a problem he had solved quite successfully more than fifteen years earlier.

Another more widely known inventor Thomas Edison was without doubt a brilliant man of many talents. He also displayed all the signs of significant ADHD and also OCS. It is doubtful that many professionals knowledgeable about ADHD and familiar with Mr. Edison's life history would disagree with this post hoc diagnosis of ADHD. However, the idea of OCS may be new to many. It clearly makes sense.

Mr. Edison has been portrayed as a "lively child" by historians. He was one who "was always taking things apart and putting them together again, or, trying to put them back together." He started a little fire in the corner of the family barn once to see what would happen. He ended up paying for the burnt down barn with a sound whipping by his father in front of the townspeople in the village square. He was thought to be "a creative little fellow" by a neighbor. He'd found Thomas in the midst of his barn sitting on a nest. Thomas was trying to "hatch" some goslings from eggs he'd found there. His mother is quoted as having said, "It's always interesting. I only wish he didn't get into so much trouble."

Thomas' first and only experience in an organized school setting was in Port Huron, Michigan. It was after a family move out of financial necessity. Thomas was placed on a school bench for about six hours a day. It was a hardly bearable experience and not really conducive to young Thomas' learning style. He bounced. He fidgeted. Mostly he is reported to have been lost in his own thoughts and daydreams. This was probably the only way he could survive being cooped up in a small classroom for as long as was expected. Students of today who show this same inclination are often labeled by teachers and classmates alike. It is said that they are "out to lunch," "a space cadet," "off the wall," and "weird." These, of course, are names of just a few of the most common labels.

Thomas Edison would get so caught up in thought that he literally would not acknowledge the lessons of his teacher. Even when directly called upon, he might not respond. Reportedly, after about three months of this Thomas' teacher arranged a meeting with his mother. This teacher informed Mrs. Edison that her son was unteachable because he was "addlepated," which implies that he was "retarded." Thomas Edison's mother, as you might imagine, was furious at this assertion. In response she kept him home and taught him herself. He was home schooled thereafter. Thomas never returned to public education. Obviously he was not *retarded*. Those with OCS, though, are sometimes singled out by teachers who believe they may be intellectually deficient.

Thomas set up his own "laboratory" in the basement of his parent's house. Although they allowed him to do this, they were also worried, and perhaps understandably so. Their son did nearly blow up the basement once while trying to make a cannon work. Also, in the interest of studying "static electricity" he once tied the tails of two tomcats together. One can only imagine the aftermath of that experiment.

As a young man, Thomas Edison never kept a job for long. By the time he reached his twenty-first birthday he was, by his family and those who knew him, considered to be a total failure. He was also regarded as "stubborn, independent, and hardworking." While he was courting the woman he was to eventually marry, there was a lot of teasing and laughter from her co-workers. The teasing was directed at her because of Thomas Edison. To this she was not immune. It has been reported that she was quite flustered and embarrassed. Nevertheless, she did marry him.

Historians report that Thomas Edison was a man who simply could not grasp mathematics. This, is in spite of the fact that he is said to have put forth great effort to do so. Regardless of this he has some 1,093 patents to his name. These include the phonograph, the electric light, and the motion picture projector. There are dozens of other electronic devices he invented that most of us in this day and age take for granted.

Mr. Edison was once addressed by a well-meaning individual. This person said "Remember many famous scientists, people who knew all about how light and electricity work, have tried to make such a lamp—and *none* of them could do it. Maybe you should read what they have written about this very difficult problem before you spend a lot of time and money on experiments that might not work." Thomas' reported reply to this man is fascinating. He told him: "That could just get in my way. When I start on an invention I don't read books. I don't want to know what has already been done. I start from scratch."

This is probably exactly what Mr. Edison did. It is also possible that the entire truth of the matter might just be a bit more complicated than it seems. Many with OCS find reading an extremely tedious chore. They avoid it as much as they can. This isn't usually due to an inability to read or a learning disability, although it could be. It is most often the result of an active and obsessive mind-set that has trouble staying with the written word while reading. This is especially true when the reading is forced or of no interest to the person. To comprehend what is read, the OCS-affected may have to read and re-read a given page several times before they "get it."

Reading for them becomes a chore similar to mowing the lawn or doing the dishes.

This next idea is pure conjecture and is used only to show the condition and not to suggest this was true for Mr. Edison. If his reading was interfered with by OCS it might have been a real chore for Thomas Edison. He might not want others to know this. He might not even realize it was happening himself. He would have been frustrated often when he did attempt it. He just might have reasoned it out as explained in his words earlier. Mr. Edison could have convinced himself that he didn't want to read what others had tried.

If driven by OCS, reading could have been very tedious and difficult. Obviously, he didn't actually *need* to read the things others wrote. Not doing so did not keep him from being able to invent things. He might have convinced himself that what he thought the reason was that he didn't read was true in order to make sense out of what others were saying. He might have said it was that way to justify his non-reading behavior. In this fashion the OCS person may find a way to hide or explain weaknesses in such a way that they might not be considered weaknesses.

Perhaps if he had read what others had done in relation to the light bulb, it wouldn't have taken him some 2,000 experiments to get it right. Then again, reading about others' failures could have locked Mr. Edison into a way of thinking that may have kept him from succeeding. We will never really know because he didn't do that reading. It doesn't really matter, but OCS reading difficulties do clearly exist. The reasons for the reading trouble can be as varied as a person is imaginative. The OCS person needs to find a reason for the troubles they have other than that they are stupid or dumb.

A motivational speaker once said that Mr. Edison had been asked by an interviewer how it felt to have failed 2,000 times. He was referring of course to how many experiments it took before the invention of the light bulb. According to this speaker Mr. Edison had responded by first looking the individual square in the eyes. He then said "Fail, what do you mean fail? I never failed, sir! It was a 2,000 step process." The speaker then used this to support the idea that we should try to be as optimistic as Mr. Edison.

There is another possible reason for Mr. Edison having said what he did. Those with OCS tend to be extremely sensitive to the slightest forms of criticism. They can refuse to accept anything viewed as critical, even in the face of all odds. Incensed at the thought that anyone would even hint that he had failed, Mr. Edison's reported response could have been a simple cover-up. It was a brilliant quip meant to cut-to-the-quick of the insensitive jerk that had asked such a question. Let historians interpret what they will. Of course, such interpretations are no more than an educated guess, as well.

It has been said that Mr. Edison would not give up even when he failed. It would make perfect sense if he were to have seen every project he worked on as "in process" until he eventually succeeded. If he thought this way, then he could literally say at any time "I never failed." The only failure would be to stop trying. As long as projects were being worked on, there could be no failure. Instead, he might say "the project you are referring to is not yet done."

Mr. Edison is reported to have never stopped forging ahead. He might have given up if he hadn't been obsessive and compulsive about everything he did. How many people do you think would keep on trying after 100 failed experiments, let alone 2,000? It would seem that Mr. Edison's accomplishments represent what is often a very positive part of OCS as well as ADHD. Depending on how strong the symptoms may be, an individual might just never give up. Once locked into a given task or project, they continue until a solution is reached. Success in a chosen endeavor is often just a matter of time and effort. Sometimes obsessive and compulsive actions may be vital to success.

Mr. Edison needed very little sleep and had an enormous amount of energy that drove him both day and night. He is said to have attributed this energy to his ten minute "catnaps." He would take these off and on day or night wherever he happened to be when the urge for rest came. Mr. Edison's astonishing energy may have really been due to ADHD and perhaps a bit of OCS as well. This was not diagnosed during his lifetime. How would he know how to explain his tremendous energy to others?

It is also likely that Mr. Edison's output as an inventor was from one of the often positive features of ADHD. This might be the abundant and unyielding endurance, drive, and energy of ADHD. Mr. Edison was considered "a strange man who gradually became deaf but never needed much sleep. After working all day he would sit up till four in the morning studying electrical science. His first invention was one for killing cockroaches by electricity within the Boston telegraph office. At one time he was working on 45 different inventions simultaneously."

*　　*　　*

Let us briefly consider Mr. Alexander Graham Bell. Everyone knows that Alexander Graham Bell was the inventor of the telephone. What many do not know is that "it was simply not in Bell's nature to fixate for long on any one specific area. All his life he retained a childlike joy in the world's diversity." But before he became world-famous, Bell's love of variety caused serious doubts in some who knew him. His future father-in-law scolded him for his tendencies. These tendencies were "to undertake every new thing that interests you and accomplish nothing of any value to anyone." That reprimand occurred less than five months before the telephone was patented. What saved Mr. Bell from mere aimless floundering was his talent for total absorption in the concern of the moment. This is yet another trait that might be called childlike.

"My mind," he once wrote "concentrates itself on the subject that happens to occupy it and then all things else in the universe including Father, Mother, wife, children, and life itself, become for the time being of secondary importance." Does this or does this not sound a lot like OCS and perhaps a little ADHD too? Even though very brief, this biographical sketch has elements that clearly imply the presence of ADHD and OCS. These conditions appear to have surely enabled Mr. Bell to accomplish much of what he is known for having done. These tendencies also perhaps may have disabled him at times as well.

*   *   *

The following is reported of Marie Curie. "With a passion to learn everything she possibly could, Marie worked far into the night and for weeks would live on nothing but bread and butter, fruit and tea." By now this has got to seem very familiar.

*   *   *

During a short vacation from his university studies Albert Schweitzer, it has been reported, made a life-changing decision. He decided that he would spend his time up until the age of thirty absorbing the things of the mind that he loved. Thereafter he would devote his life to serving mankind. History records that he never wavered from this decision.

It was his humanitarian efforts in Africa that earned him fame. It won for him the Nobel Peace prize. He was not just a doctor. He was also a philosopher, a theologian, and a musicologist.

*   *   *

Eleanor Roosevelt's entire life was devoted to the service of others. She remained steadfast in her accomplishments, even in the face of quite serious setbacks. As a young girl she was very shy and withdrawn. This was thought to be due to what appeared to be constant internal feelings of inadequacy. As first lady, she was said to have been "an energetic and outspoken representative of the needs of the people suffering from the Great Depression." She traveled broadly, held news conferences, and corresponded with hundreds of men and women. This she did in both her private and public life. Eleanor displayed an absolute concern for others. She taught at a school she had set up for poor children. She ran a factory for jobless men and was a supporter of equal rights, when it was not a popular thing to do. She is said to have had a lifelong yearning to be needed and loved.

*   *   *

Confucius held that the reason for life was for people to "obtain perfection within themselves." As his fame grew as a teacher, more and more people wanted to study with him. Once he taught poetry, history, ceremonies, and music to about 3,000 students. His standards though were so high that he felt only seventy-two of these pupils were able to master the subjects he taught.

*   *   *

Hans Christian Anderson's father was a shoemaker who dreamed of a better career for himself. His mother was uneducated and known to be quite "superstitious." Hans' school-age years were reportedly "not happy." In his teens he traveled to Copenhagen, determined to win fame as a singer, dancer, or an actor. According to reports, Hans was "a complete failure at all of these professions." He was in due course relegated to almost begging. Throughout his life Mr. Anderson was considered "difficult" with a "complex character." He has been depicted as "vain, sensitive to criticism, and bedeviled by his own moods." Those with OCS tend to be very moody too. Mood changes can be rapid and intense. Often others describe relationships with an OCS person as like being on an emotional roller-coaster.

*   *   *

The inventor of the modern day sewing machine, Elias Howe, became more than a millionaire. In spite of his riches and success, history records that right up until the end of his life Mr. Howe continually built "small machines." Some of these machines were very strange. There were many that nobody could figure out. As far as others could tell, they had no purpose or use at all.

*   *   *

The most prolific and greatest inventors clearly appear to be or have been OCS-driven. The most productive and widely known authors also seem to have been or be OCS candidates. The most diverse, impressive, talented and believable actors seem to have OCS. Olympians of all varieties are surely driven to do what they do by their OCS. The majority of gifted professional athletes almost certainly have it. The most dedicated, ambitious and well-known artists have OCS. Artists don't have to be well-known, though, to be driven so in this way. The best musicians are energized and driven by OCS. The most persuasive and successful salespersons are also OCS-driven and so on.

Perhaps you can now clearly sense an emerging pattern. Those who make up the OCS population are not alone. These people are also most definitely in very good company. The very best of the best in nearly every vocation and avocation got there more than likely because of a helpful dose of OCS. The best of the best *are* OCS-driven. So it's not all bad news when you find out that OCS is present. There is some very good news as well.

Many OCS people will never give up even in the face of insurmountable odds. It may be labeled bravery. It may be considered certain suicide. No one can force others to see it differently. Education is the most likely tool that might successfully help someone see it differently. The OCS-driven artist draws, paints, sculpts, and sketches at every possible opportunity and location. As a result of this unrelenting work, the artist becomes very good at what he or she does.

Michelangelo, Vincent Van Gogh, and Leonardo Da Vinci are historical figures that immediately come to mind. Surely these were all examples of what OCS can drive one to accomplish over time. Van Gogh went so far as to cut his own ear off. If that's not an overreaction, then what is? Rather than *crazy*, perhaps this deed was really one driven by his obsessive and compulsive needs. That would seem to make more sense. He literally felt that he *had* to do it.

Similarly musicians such as Beethoven, Bach, and Mozart, to name a few, also seem to have had the OCS factor. This is not to suggest that they weren't also gifted musically. The OCS may account for their tremendous productivity. It might make sense out of their frequently reported odd and strange behaviors, as well.

There are many authors or writers that seem to exhibit the OCS drive. The OCS appears to have pushed quite a few to prolific heights of historical significance. A few worthy of mention might include Shakespeare, H.G. Wells, Edgar Allen Poe, and Charles Dickens. These, of course, are only a few among the many.

These artists, musicians, and authors, if OCS-affected, should have many things in common. One such thing would be a relentless drive to produce, to perform, and to persevere. Even when not published or recognized, they would turn out work after work after work. Endless production alone over time brings about ever greater skill. For these individuals, the OCS drive would press them to be prolific well beyond the norm. OCS gives them a ferocious undeviating drive. Without this, they would undoubtedly not do the many things that they do.

Actors and salespersons that are OCS-affected also seem to have a lot in common. There is a powerful dynamics that begins early in life for these people. The OCS drive surely shapes some of these people towards their destinies. Early on, when OCS begins to show up, these individuals must face a variety of problems. Their behavior is often persistent and frustrating to parents and teachers. They usually have no idea why they behave as they do again and again. Especially, they may wonder after being told not to do something, and then they go ahead and do it again. They really don't know why this happens.

Some things those with OCS do are downright strange. It makes no sense to them why they continue to act in such ways. As a result they begin to learn how to come up with explanations for their behaviors. It can actually become a honed skill. They soon learn that the excuse must be reasonable in order to make it believable. To cover up for their weird actions, they learn to be *very good liars* and storytellers. In order to survive, they spend a good deal of their lives working out lies to get others to accept their reasoning. They strive to convince others as well as themselves that things are not as they may have seemed. They also are not who they seem. In short, they experience a lifetime of practice in the art of lying.

When OCS driven no one would believe the *real* reasons for most of their actions. "I don't know" or "I just *had* to do it" doesn't cut it for very long. Others have a very hard time accepting as truth that a person doesn't know why they do some of the things they do. By the way, what are actors anyway if not very good liars? They are people working hard to get us to believe that they *are* actually someone different from who they truly are. The very best actors in the world are by default the very best liars. If they weren't, they wouldn't be any good.

A good salesperson can sell people things they wouldn't normally think of buying otherwise. Both actors and salespeople are amazingly persuasive. This has to be at least in part due to their years of practice. Also in part because they too, like all those with OCS, tend to be so intense about everything they do. They will go to almost any lengths to make a sale or to make the part they are playing more believable.

There was once an actor playing the part of a person chased through the streets and alleys of a big city for three days and nights without sleep. In order to prepare for the scene the actor actually spent three days and nights out in the streets without sleeping. He sauntered and ran from place to place pretending that someone was after him. He trudged through bar after beaten-down bar and crawled through alley after alley. All this he did in order to make the character become more realistic. The word on the street was that when this particular performer finally got to the place where they were shooting his scene, an interesting event took place. Another actor getting ready for the very same scene took a hard look at him and quipped: "Ever consider having a go at *acting?*"

No one can be more believable playing the role of another than someone who is obsessed with getting it right and compulsive about doing so. When ADHD is a component as it often is, there may be an added bonus. This actor or salesperson will have an abundance of energy as well. He or she will be able to work long, grueling schedules that can sometimes seem almost superhuman. In thinking about many of the best actors and salespeople of today it would be surprising if several names didn't come to mind that seem to fit the OCS, ADHD, or OCS/ADHD pattern.

Professional and Olympic athletes starting at a very young age tend to get hyper-focused on becoming the best. To become the best requires practice. There needs to be lots and lots of practice. The best of the best eat, drink, and breathe their sport. They put in unbelievably long hours day after day and year after year to attain their goal. OCS supplies them with the relentless drive needed to stay motivated. The drive necessary to continue perfecting skills relative to their sport long after they have already become better than most, is hardwired into them. The highly touted "will to win" in this case is more of an "obsessive need" than an actual *will*.

Let's consider this question. Does it *really* matter what the motivating force is behind *genius*? The answer is a resounding *NO*! It does not absolutely make a difference exactly what is at the heart of brilliance. What *does* matter is whether or not that basic force interferes with the living of one's life. Such interference can occur in one or more of several areas. It might disrupt social or emotional well being. Mental welfare may be disturbed. Physical health can be undermined. Finally, professional life can be damaged or destroyed. The very thing that caused one to become the best of the best can later do the exact opposite. This occurs if the OCS interference is ignored or allowed to run wild.

Keep in mind that having OCS can be a tremendous asset, depending on your point of view. It also may depend on the situation or circumstances in which it occurs. It can depend as well on how much influence it may or may not be having in a given person's life. To have OCS can also be a huge inescapable burden. It can be burdensome, even though its presence may result in an eventual positive outcome.

Whether to treat or not medically will depend on the strength and frequency of the symptoms. It is also subject to the observed interference. If a person does not see the OCS influence in their life then for that person it does not exist. Unhealthy behavior cannot be changed if it is not recognized as an issue worthy of change.

The adult with OCS has been living with its influence for a lifetime. The effects are so tangled up in their personality it doesn't feel like influence or interference to them at all. It just feels like who they are. Helping the OCS-driven to become self aware can be a very difficult task. When it is a factor, helping the person to see and understand their OCS, is critical to therapeutic progress. Knowledge about this convoluted condition that impacts so many people's lives is enormously valuable.

Whether or not formal treatment is begun, knowledge alone can equip the OCS-driven to better manage their symptoms. It can also profoundly help others who have to spend a lot of time with an OCS person. Education is always important. It is *always* important. Almost without exception, it *is* the *most* important step in the appropriate treatment of anything. Truly knowing what is going on enables anyone to better manage their reactions and responses. Keep in mind that OCS, just like so many other physical conditions, is managed and not cured.

Remember: Disorders, Disabilities, and Handicaps
Should be Regarded as Explanations
Never Excuses

So you have OCS. Okay. Now what are you going to do about it? That is the question.

So All Alone

I've never felt so all alone . . . as I do today
been searching for the answers . . . yet still can't find a way
to take this yearning that I feel and that I can't deny
and turn it into something that will keep my hope alive

we're told just how we're supposed to feel
and all we're supposed to need
but I'm not sure just what is real or what I should believe
there's no room left to wonder about life and the things we do
it's all preshrunk and pre-thunk to fit us
so that we'll end up like we're expected to

> but the world I see is not the same as the one others must see
> those who look with their eyes but don't include the heart
> and it's not that I want to try and see it differently
> it's just the way it's been right from the start

no one knows what I'm thinking . . . there's no way that you can
and you can't feel what I'm feeling . . . and you don't know who I am
though it seems you listen to me at least until you think I'm through
yet you don't hear what I'm saying it might change your point of view

—repeat—
—chorus—
I've never felt so all alone . . . as i do today . . .

Words and music by Ron D. Kingsley
June 24, 1997

19

Additional Insights into OCS

Debbie was a thirteen-year-old teenager who physically resembled an adolescent of at least sixteen or seventeen. She and the other members of her family did not get along most of the time. She was described by her mother as having problems lying, stealing, being lazy, being extremely stubborn, being disrespectful, not keeping house rules, being irresponsible, and fighting constantly with her siblings. Debbie also seemed to be riding an emotional roller-coaster every single day. No one knew at any given moment whether she'd be emotionally up or down or somewhere in between.

About three weeks before the incident to be described Debbie had had another one of her frequent emotional flare-ups. It had been just before her mother was about to leave the house on an errand. As her mom attempted to depart, Debbie got right up in her face. She demanded that she be allowed to go and hang out with her friends, in spite of the fact that it was a school night. To her mother's credit, she ignored the theatrical antics of her Drama Queen daughter. Debbie's mother reported having made the following simple statement.

"You know the rules, honey. I'll be back around seven. Dad will be late tonight, so don't hold up dinner for us. You can order pizza if you want. Make sure your brother puts his dirty football uniform in the hamper."

Debbie's mother had been working on setting boundaries in family co-therapy. She was working on following through, with realistic consequences if these were violated. As practiced, Mrs. Caruso had calmly restated to her daughter the house rule about not going out on school nights. She also stated that this particular issue was not negotiable.

As her mother turned to go, Debbie began to rant and rave.

"It's not *fair*," she screamed! "You never let me do anything!" This angry young lady even started jumping up and down like a two-year-old and wailing at the top of her lungs. "I hate YOU! Do you hear me? I HATE YOU! You never do anything for me."

Mrs. Caruso *had* heard what her daughter screamed, but wisely chose not to respond. Instead of responding to those hurtful words, she bit her lower lip and continued on to the car. The last image seen as she drove away from the house was that of her daughter. She had her hands flattened against the living room picture window with her mouth wide open as if howling. Mrs. Caruso also couldn't help but notice her daughter's expensive straightened bright white teeth. She also smiled as she saw a lolling tongue, thinking momentarily how ungrateful and selfish she was. Again, rather than allow *that* thought to roll around in her mind and cause havoc like she used to, Mrs. Caruso smiled and waved enthusiastically. She broadened her smile at her daughter's tantrum as she backed the car out of the driveway. It looked to her as if Debbie was repeatedly shouting something. Her mouth kept rapidly opening and closing in the same way. She had the fleeting thought that her daughter might even be screaming obscenities. She couldn't be certain, though, as she was no longer able to hear the sound of her voice. She smiled again triumphantly this time and *this time* it was also a smile of pure joy.

Meanwhile, back at the house Debbie was much more than mad. She was fuming. She was livid! How could her mother do this to her! She couldn't believe it. Debbie swore. She began looking for something to destroy. No luck in the living room. She picked up a couch pillow and threw it at her mother's lazy good-for-nothing cat. The cat was stretched out across the arm and cushion at the other end of the sofa. It connected and the cat went mewing to the carpet. Upon hitting the carpet it took off as if its tail had been set on fire. Debbie smiled in satisfaction. Her aim was usually not that good when she was angry. This time it must have been fate. She felt vindicated just a bit but still desperately wanted to find something to tear apart, preferably something of her mother's.

When all else fails go to the source, her mother was always telling her. That would be her bedroom, thought Debbie. She wasn't supposed to be in there when her mother wasn't home. It was a house rule. Too bad there wasn't another soul around to notice. Too bad for mom, that is. She made her way to the end of the hall where she found the master bedroom door closed and locked. She knew it probably would be. It had never stopped her before, though. Not when she was this angry anyway. She could no longer simply bend a hangar and use the metal tip to open the cheesy lock in the middle of the doorknob. Her mother had gotten wise and bought a real lock. She knew that most likely there was a place where an extra key would be hidden. Once her mother had lost her key and had to crawl through a window to get into her own bedroom. Debbie found herself smiling at that thought. It served her mother right. Now, where would it be? She began to search.

It was way too easy. The key was in the second place she looked. It was duct-taped to the back of the toilet in the hall bathroom. How unoriginal, Debbie thought. When was mother *ever* going to make stuff like this a true challenge for her? It was almost like asking someone to break into her room. Getting into the bedroom had been so simple that she half expected a booby trap to go off when she pushed the door open, but nothing happened. Face it; she had a dull, less-than-creative mother.

Debbie trotted right over to the dresser drawers. She leaned over and pulled open the biggest one that was lowest center. If she remembered right that was where her mother put all her stupid little keepsake things. Debbie smiled thinly as the contents came into her view. Yep, this was the drawer. She began roughly rummaging through the objects inside. She wasn't sure exactly what she was looking for, but figured she'd know it when she saw it. She was right.

Debbie slammed the drawer shut and stood victoriously holding a silly birthday card. It was one that she'd given her mother when she was only nine years old. Mother had been so proud of her because she had made it all by herself. There was a picture glued on the front, of mother and her. Their faces were contorted in a mixture of laughter, joy, and fear. They were zipping down the last steep drop of Disney's Matterhorn ride. The photo was a little crooked, but so were the words "HAPPY BIRTHDAY MOM" scribbled in red crayon on the front cover. Red was Debbie's favorite color. She opened the card and grimaced at what she'd written inside.

A sound like a muffled door slam interrupted her thoughts. She quickly stuffed the card into the back pocket of her jeans and rushed towards the open bedroom door. The key was still inserted in its hole just below the doorknob. Debbie hurriedly turned the handle to keep the latch from making too much noise as it shut. She stepped out of the room and pulled the door tight behind her. Turning the key slowly to the left, she soon heard the slight click that told her it was locked once again. Now all she had to do was return the key to its place at the back of the toilet. No one would be the wiser. She doubted that her mother would even notice the theft. It wasn't like her mom went through that stuff in her drawer and examined it every day. With any luck she wouldn't notice at all until Debbie *wanted her to notice*. She had plans for that ratty old card. Her mother was going to pay for keeping her from her friends.

Debbie sat on the sofa trying to look and act as innocent as possible. The cat had returned and was once again sprawled across the other end of the couch. Debbie just ignored it as a part of her plan. She waited five minutes. After that she figured since no one had shown themselves, the noise she'd heard must not have been the door. She got up from the couch barking loudly. The cat awoke with a start. Its body got so contorted that as it scrambled for purchase it lost balance and fell, all on its own. Debbie was doubled over laughing as the cat tore out of the room.

She went straight away towards her bedroom. Debbie took the card from out of her pocket on the way. She stopped at the end of her bed. She was trying to remember where she had last seen the scissors.

A door slammed and she jumped. Someone was definitely in the house now. It sounded like it came from the back. It must be her brother. She quickly stashed the card under her bed on top of a pile of old photos. She had been meaning to put them into some kind of a scrapbook, but hadn't yet gotten around to it.

"Hey, ugly," she heard a loud voice proclaim, "I'm home. What's for dinner?" It *was* her brother.

The incident described above provides the background necessary to understand what happened three weeks later. After ditching the card, Debbie had hastily left her room. She wanted to ward off her brother and make sure he didn't get suspicious. In doing so she had had to change her mind's focus. It had to go from anger and revenge to one of indifference and isolation, which was her normal attitude around her brother. The plan was quite successful and her brother never suspected a thing. It was *so* successful, however, that she totally forgot all about her earlier anger. She also forgot about that old birthday card and what she was going to do with it, as well.

About three weeks later, in a therapeutic session with her mother, the rest of the story unfolded. Mrs. Caruso was very upset that Debbie had somehow gotten into her bedroom. She was more than upset that Debbie had taken something of very special meaning to her. She was convinced that she was going to cut it to pieces or burn it. If not that, she might find some other way to destroy it. She shouldn't have been in the bedroom in the first place. Debbie knew that. To her mother the idea of actually having taken something of hers that was irreplaceable was beyond belief. But to top it *all* off, Mrs. Caruso was absolutely enraged at what had happened when she'd caught her with the goods. She couldn't believe it when Debbie had looked her right in the eye and had the audacity to tell a *bold face lie* about it. As told by Mrs. Caruso this is what happened on the night in question.

"I got home from work a little later than expected. I had been a bit worried that there might not have been enough money left in the cookie jar to cover the cost of the pizza I'd told them they could order. That thought kept turning over in my mind and I felt it churning in my gut.

I came in through the kitchen and was relieved to find an opened pizza box left on the dinning room table. I called out that I was home and went to my bedroom to change clothes and relax. Since no one had answered my call when I came in, I got curious and went to Debbie's room. She was sitting on the bed. It looked like she had scrapbook things spread out all around her. Scissors were in her hand and she was trimming a picture. As I got closer to the bed, something familiar caught my eye. At first I dismissed the possibility that it could be what it looked like. I knew *that* card was safe in the third drawer of my personal chest of drawers. The closer I got to it, though, the more worried I became. Soon I knew beyond a shadow of a doubt that it was indeed *that* very card. Debbie had made it for my birthday when she was only ten years old. It was one of my most precious keepsakes.

'What are *you* doing?" I found myself screaming. I can't believe that you would do such a thing!'

Debbie looked up at me innocently. She had sort of a confused look on her face and said, 'What are you talking about, mom?'

'You know damn well what I'm talking about,' I yelled. I actually used curses much worse and stronger than that. But since this is going to be read by others, I thought it should be toned down some. You can imagine for yourself what I might have said.

Debbie's blank stare unnerved me just a bit. I wanted to smack her, but I didn't. Instead I reached past her and grabbed the card. 'Where did you get this?' I yelled sort of unkindly.

Without even blinking an eye she stared right back into mine and said, 'Oh that, from under my bed.'

'What?' I almost choked on the word, I hollered it so loudly. 'YOU MOST CERTAINLY DID NOT!' I shrieked. 'You had better come clean. Just tell me where you got this from or I'm through with you, done, finished. I'll ask the doctor to recommend a residential treatment center where I can send you to rot.' I was so very angry that I think I may have said several things like that during my ranting and raving. It's kind of hard to remember.

Debbie was in her element. She is such a good liar. After I slowed down a little and paused for a breath I asked once again, 'Now where did you get this?' I held the card right in front of her nose.

She pushed my hand away saying, 'I told you. I got it from under my bed.'

'Liar,' I roared. 'You little liar! I can't believe you can just sit there and lie like that right to my face. I *know* where this was and it was *not* under *your* bed.'

'Yes, it was.'

'What? Are you going to just keep right on with that same weak and stupid lie even though I've caught you in the act?'

'You didn't catch me doing anything.'

'You had this! And that's enough to prosecute, convict, and sentence you.'

Then Debbie came out of her seeming calm shell like a hungry shark on the attack. 'Look at you,' she screamed. 'You're always harping on me to *tell you the truth*,' her words dripped with sarcasm. 'And then when *I do*, you don't believe me anyway.'

'That wasn't the truth," I came down on her hard, "and *you* know it!'

I had to leave her room right then or I would have done something I would have regretted. As I got to the doorway, I turned. I reminded her rather forcefully and undoubtedly with colorful words, '*Stay out of my Room!* And don't look for the key to the lock. You won't find it this time.' I didn't know that she had gone out and made an extra key so that when she promised me, 'I won't,' it would be the truth. Frankly, I didn't believe her for a second, even though it turned out to be the truth. She didn't have to look for a key anymore. She had a key of her own."

Mrs. Caruso was sitting on a small couch in my office with Debbie right next to her as she finished telling this story. The last part about the key wasn't a part of the story at the time. This was because Debbie's mother did not become aware of the extra key until much later. I wanted that part explained early on, though, to further illustrate the point of this story.

"Debbie," Mrs. Caruso began, "now you tell the doctor exactly where you got that card."

It appeared that Debbie's mother thought that perhaps the presence of a psychologist would make a difference. She must have thought that she would finally hear the truth from her deceitful daughter's mouth, once and for all.

Debbie smiled and said, "I got it from under my bed."

Perhaps you can imagine what happened next. The fireworks started all over again with an intensity that would have melted lead. The exact words and phrases spoken by either do not warrant repetition. Let's just say that had I not intervened, things may have gotten physical. The only reason it had not up until this point was that Debbie's mother had decided not to speak about the incident at all until their next counseling session. She'd made it, barely. But here they were again and Mrs. Caruso's anger was incredibly magnified. It was amplified by the many times in the past that her daughter *had* been dishonest with her. It was all those times her mother had believed what Debbie had said, only to find out later that it had been a lie. This time Mrs. Caruso had thought that she had her daughter dead to rights, and *still* she lied.

It was clear that the two would have to be separated in order to unravel the mystery of what was going on. Mrs. Caruso was directed to the lobby. She left the session, still shaken and visibly fuming.

I closed the door and sat in a chair directly in front of Debbie. She was still on the couch chewing gum and looking smug.

"So," I started calmly, "you got that card she was talking about from under your bed?"

"Uh-huh mmm . . . yeah," she said resolutely.

It seemed clear that she was expecting the same kind of a fight to start up with me that she'd been having with her mother. There was no doubt in my mind that she was ready. What she wasn't ready for was what I actually did say. Knowing the patterns and dynamics of the OCS mind in situations like this enabled me to take what she said at face value. Somehow she was telling the truth—of that I was pretty sure. "You were telling the truth, weren't you?" I asked.

"Yep," she announced smugly.

"I believe you," I told her.

"You do?" She seemed quite surprised. Suddenly her eyes narrowed. "Yeah?" She questioned, "How come?"

I shared with her the fact that this kind of a thing happened a lot. Especially between people who are driven by their symptoms. As I spoke she relaxed and during a lull in our conversation I asked her casually, "So where was that card anyways BEFORE it was under your bed?"

Debbie appeared stunned much like a deer caught in the headlights. Her eyes drifted downward then up and around in a lazy roll. "Uhmmm," she muttered.

We then had a serious and honest chat about the entire incident. It became clear why Debbie had become so unwavering about the issue of her having lied. She didn't lie. The card actually *was* under her bed exactly as she'd said. She wasn't going to offer a more detailed account, because she didn't want to get in even more trouble. But the main issue that had provoked her own explosive retaliation was being called a liar. She hated being called a liar when in fact she was telling the truth.

If Mrs. Caruso had been aware enough of the OCS driving force and asked the right question, it might have ended quite differently for them. Asking the OCS-driven the right question can make all the difference in the world. There is no guarantee that they won't still lie, but it makes it a lot harder when a question leading to the truth is asked. Then when you accuse the person of lying it may be an accurate accusation. If the question had been worded correctly it would have been harder for her because Debbie knew exactly where the card had been originally and that her mother had caught her. She would have either had to lie or come clean.

In a perfect world where communication is clear the right question is asked it might just lead to an open discussion. During this discussion Debbie might have admitted that she had been very angry with her mother. All she could think about was getting back at her mother and making her pay for the pain and discomfort she'd caused. She couldn't get it out of her mind and the adrenalin was flowing freely. Once energized, there was no stopping her until the quest was complete. By the time Debbie had found something to exact her revenge upon, her adrenalin had begun to falter. As a result, her energy level and ruminations decreased. When finally interrupted by her brother, she was able to stash the card under her bed. The intention was to inflict her vengeance at a later time. She could do this because the intensity level was no longer the same. The interruption had given her something else to do at that moment. Keeping busy, it is known, does indeed keep other symptoms at bay. Education is our most powerful tool in the resolution and/or management of any problem. This truth will never change.

*   *   *

Mild-moderate obsessive and compulsive symptoms (OCS) are not readily seen or easily identified. There is no digital sign over a person's head announcing that they have exactly *this* much OCS in their system. There is no code telling you just how disruptive to a person's life these symptoms may be at any given moment. OCS tends to be misunderstood frequently and often missed entirely. This happens to such an extent that these symptoms in my opinion qualify as one of the many *invisible* enemies that people must deal with throughout their lifespan. It's much like *pain*. Pain is another one of those invisible enemies that is often difficult to understand. There is no scale over everyone's head that clearly registers the amount of pain being felt. If there was such a scale, people would be much more understanding and appreciative of another's pain and situation in life.

*   *   *

The guilt endured by those with OCS can be very distressing. The regret and sorrow can reach enormous proportions if not recognized and treated for what it is. It's obsessively driven guilt. There are many other words that have basically the same meaning as the word guilt. These include: shame, blame, fault, remorse, condemnation, responsibility, and self-flagellation. A lot of mental energy can be used trying to avoid people, places, and events where guilt might be expected. Over-remorse can also drive a person to say, do, or act in ways that they would really rather not have acted. Afterwards they can even feel guilty about having felt guilty in the first place.

The over-responsive, OCS-driven person will experience everything at a heightened level. Hence guilt and shame can drive them into either fits of rage and/or complete states of withdrawal and serious depression. Is it any wonder that especially in their early years, those with OCS are often thought to display Asperger's (a milder form of Autism)? They will not look you in the eye. They are too ashamed about whatever it is they *think* they did or were accused of doing. They look away. They tend to believe that others can see the guiltiness in their eyes. They do not want to discuss it. If you insist on talking about it, they may shut down completely and refuse. They may not speak a word. The guilt and shame they feel can be much more powerful than anything you might want them to do at the moment.

* * *

"If you don't do your homework you won't be doing anything else, young man," growls a father to his son.

"I don't care!" the son shouts back. He hollers because he's trying very hard not to care, very hard indeed. It's the only way to endure it because no matter what he has done, it doesn't matter. His homework takes *so* long and is *so* boring he just can't seem to get it done. If he cares too much about going somewhere it will *kill* him emotionally. The only way to get by is to convince himself and everybody else that he just doesn't care. First it was the homework. As long as he still cared about not being able to get it done, it hurt and he felt stupid. It made him miserable. Once he had decided not to care it got easier. Then it was the punishments or *"consequences"* as his parents liked to call them. These he also had to try and not care about. Then it was his friends. Soon he didn't have any. But who cared anyway? Depression ensued.

* * *

Jessica was worried, "but if I don't get my homework done, everyone will think I'm stupid."

"Not only that," her mother added, "if you don't get it done there will be no TV or privileges of any kind either."

Tears began to roll down Jessica's face. Soon she was blubbering, "I can't do it," she whined. "I just can't."

Her mother tried to comfort and motivate her. "Sure you can," she said. "You've done it before. Besides I know you like watching TV and playing with your friends."

"I don't have any friends," she wailed suddenly. This was followed with, "and I don't care what you do to me." She crossed her arms and sat down to pout. "If I don't do any homework everybody's going to think I'm stupid." She was afraid. She was crying. She wasn't going to go to school anymore. That was the only way. Eventually Jessica made the decision that it just didn't matter anymore. It was the only way to survive. To her it was worth not caring in order to avoid the anxiety and panic that she felt when she did care. That was the bottom line. Stupid was better than being freakin' anxious all the time.

* * *

"Do you think I CARE?" shouted Jeremy at the top of his lungs. "Cause if you do, *I don't!*" He threw one of his tennis shoes at the half open door of his room. It slammed into the door so hard that it nearly closed all the way. The shoe also put a heel-sized hole right smack in the middle of the hollow panel where it hit. "Serves 'em right," reasoned Jeremy. "I bet they'll think again before telling *me* what I can or cannot do!" He smashed a fist into the wall to emphasize his point.

*   *   *

"I should have been punished," thought Leslie. She was grounded to her room and lying on top of her bed, pondering what had happened. Leslie knew that her parents didn't understand. If they had, they would have given her a much harsher consequence. They didn't know that she lied to them most of the time. They thought it was only this one time, but she knew it wasn't. If they knew how often and in how many ways she had stretched the truth they'd ground her for a year. That, of course, would be in addition to getting a whipping and whatever else they might think of. But they didn't get it.

"You'll be grounded for this evening, honey," her mother had told her in that sickly sweet and syrupy voice she used at times like this. "Just do the stuff you know you need to do tonight while you're in your room. Tomorrow things will be back to normal."

What a joke. Normal is one of those words her mother always mentioned. Leslie was so far from normal that she didn't think she'd ever get back. That is if she ever really was *normal* in the first place. She was going to have to punish herself. It needed to be done *right* or justice would not be served. A punishment should fit the crime. Let's see, there were straight razor blades in her parent's bathroom. If she was going to go on in this way Leslie knew she needed to pay the price. She needed to pay the *right* price. She would just have to take care of it herself. She figured her parents probably wouldn't have the guts to follow through with the punishment. At least not the level that was right for justice to be served. After all, an eye for an eye was even in the Bible.

Sometimes not caring about things seems to be the only way to survive. Like so many other things in life, caring is greatly magnified by OCS. The OCS-driven cares so much about some things and sometimes about *every* single thing, that they can hardly stand it. Most people would be frustrated when things go wrong. Most would be upset over the loss of something that they valued. Those with OCS can be totally devastated. To them it can feel like it's the end of the world. This is usually an end it is felt that must be avoided at all costs.

*   *   *

"I can't believe I'm so stupid!" Marie cried.

Her mother was holding the test in her hand. She held it out at arms length to get a better look. She didn't have her magnifying glasses on. "What do you mean, honey?" she questioned. "You got a ninety-eight. You only missed two."

"I know," Marie went on, "but I shouldn't have missed any!"

"Isn't that still an A?"

"Yes mother! That is an A. But it's a spoiled one!"

"But . . ."

"Dumb, dumb, dumb," Marie interrupted. "How can I show my face at school again?"

Nothing Marie's mother said could comfort or console her. This young lady remained angry at herself for not getting 100% on a test that most students would be happy to simply pass. Marie also had a very difficult time when anyone criticized her in any way, shape, or form. In her mind such criticism was just more proof of how stupid she really was. As a result, it would devastate her.

*   *   *

It was twenty minutes before noon when she pulled into the driveway. She felt a huge feeling of relief wash over her. She had promised Shawn she'd be there to take him to his practice at noon. She glanced at her watch as she walked in the front door. There were nineteen minutes to spare. As she closed the door behind her, she called up the stairwell "Shawn, c'mon, if we go now we'll be sure to get there on time."

"What!" Shawn's reply sounded from an upstairs bedroom. "You've got to be kidding mom. We'll get there too early. Besides, I'm right in the middle of something that I really want to finish. I'll be down in a few minutes."

Shawn's mother shrugged her shoulders. She started looking around for something to occupy her time for those next few minutes. She was not one to waste time simply waiting. Finding nothing that needed doing in the living room she headed out to the kitchen. Once there, she saw some dishes left in the sink and opened the dishwasher. "Oh, drat!" she said aloud, "when are those kids going to learn how to put these dishes in here the way they're supposed to go?" She began to systematically take each dish out. She had gotten all but a few back in and arranged correctly, when Shawn appeared.

"Okay, mom, let's go," said Shawn heading for the back door on the other side of the kitchen.

At the same moment a crash was heard, followed by a loud wail.

"Shawn, will you put the rest of these in place? I'd better go and make sure your little sister isn't dying." His sister was howling at the top of her lungs.

Shawn stopped mid stride. "It's twelve o'clock, mom!" he exclaimed.

"I know, honey," she said, "but this will only take a minute." Suddenly Shawn screamed, "You promised! You promised and now we're going to be late just like all the other times! You never do anything you say! I hate you!"

*   *   *

They were on a cross-country vacation trip. The side windows of the old Chevy had fogged up on the outer surface from the mist in the air. One of the older children complained that they could no longer see the passing countryside. Their father was driving.

"Open the window just enough to get your arm through. Try wiping the outside glass with this," he said. He held up a handkerchief he'd snatched from his breast pocket.

Nine-year-old Jimmy took it and did as he was told. "It worked," he cried in delight. He reached out to give the handkerchief back to his father.

"I want to see too," said six-year-old David from the other side of the car. "Can I do my window too? Can I, please?"

Jimmy pulled the handkerchief towards his chest. "I don't know, dad," he said, "he might not be able to hold on to it."

"Aw c'mon," David pleaded. "I can do it. I can! Please dad, can I? I want to see too."

"The wind is pretty strong out there," warned Jimmy.

"Go ahead and let him try it," their father finally told the older boy.

"Okay, dad, but I still think he might let it go."

"I won't, I won't!" whined David. "You'll see." He grabbed the handkerchief from his brother's outstretched hand.

"Careful," said Jimmy.

David was too excited to be careful. Dad was letting him use his 'snot-rag' as he sometimes called it, although there didn't seem to be any snot on it at the moment. He was being trusted with something special of his father's. David quickly cranked the window down.

"That's too far," Jimmy cried suddenly as the air came rushing into the back seat.

Theresa, their ten-year-old-sister, moaned. Her hair went flying in all directions with the sudden gust of air let in. "Roll it back up a notch, dummy!"

"Hey," cut in their father's gruff voice, "there's no need for name calling."

David spun the handle around once.

"That's good," coached Jimmy. "Now, do it now. And remember to hold on to dad's hankie."

David reached up but couldn't get his arm far enough out of the window. He got to his knees on the car seat and tried again. He was so thrilled he could hardly stand it. He reached his arm out and bent his elbow to dab at the glass. He felt the full force of the wind snatch at his arm and slam it up against the window. He tightened his grip on the handkerchief. The muscles of his arm quivered. David hadn't noticed that his hand was so tightly gripping most of the rag that there was no cloth left with which to wipe. He knew it then, though. He would have to loosen his hold on his father's handkerchief just a bit if he was going to wipe anything with it. The moment he loosened his grip the handkerchief was whipped by the wind and stolen from his grasp. He watched helplessly as his father's handkerchief rocketed away from the speeding car. David burst into tears.

"I told you so," shouted Jimmy over his brother's wails.

David cried and cried and cried. He kept apologizing and pleading with his father to go back. He had to go back so he could look for it.

The rest of the family was now wide awake from David's hysterics. Nothing any of them could say or do would calm him down. His father and mother both reassured David over and over again that it was just a 'snot rag.' He had *thirty* more. It was no big deal.

David whimpered and blubbered for three-quarters of an hour. He finally cried himself to sleep.

For days thereafter, David seemed sad and in a funk. He was miserable. He'd lost his father's handkerchief and now he would never be trusted again.

The distress lasted so long that David's father began to worry. He wondered if it might have been better for them all if they'd just got off the freeway and gone back to search for the stupid little snot rag.

David never forgot this incident. It plagued him for years. Even as an adult, when he shared this story, there were still times when he would be moved to tears.

*   *   *

Blake absolutely hated reading. Don't get me wrong, he was a good reader. That wasn't the problem. He had even passed out of reading at a twelfth-grade-plus level when he was still in grade school. So it wasn't that he couldn't read. It was just that for him, it had become almost painful to try and read.

Whenever Blake attempted to read these days, the same thing would happen. He would open a book and start to read the words on the page. As he did so, he would think the words in his head at the same time.

"This is a story about a little blond-haired girl and three bears that lived in their own little house and could talk . . ." a story might start. If so, he would already be thinking how stupid the story must be, because he certainly *wasn't* stupid and *knew* that bears not only couldn't talk but also did not live in houses, but rather in caves. He might go on from those thoughts to ideas about the kind of person who might write such a story and what he or she might be trying to do by bringing animals to life in children's stories. Perhaps the writer wanted children to feel sorry for the plight of bears in the wild. Perhaps the underlying motivation was just the opposite.

Suddenly Blake would realize it was time to turn the page. Although he had continued reading the words for the entire length of time he'd been thinking he would realize that he had no clue what those words had said. He might then breathe out a sigh and go back to the beginning to start over again.

"This is a story about a little blond girl and three bears that lived in their own little house and could speak human language. They had learned the language of humans from a fairy who just happened to live nearby in a huge oak tree. The fairy had thought . . ." Fairies . . . Blake might start to think. I have to read about fairies! If I have to read about stupid things that aren't real, why can't I at least read about scientific stuff? Why not things like time travel or a journey through space? Fairy tales are so boring. Boring . . . *Boring* . . . Boring . . . .

Once again, Blake would become aware that a page was due to be turned. Once again, he had not grasped what the page had been about. His thoughts had taken him on a ride somewhere else while his eyes had still been reading the words.

After giving it a third and *sometimes* maybe even a fourth try with about the same results, Blake would slam the book shut in frustration. Once he had angrily thrown a book to the ground. That turned out to be a bad idea. The binding tore along with some of the pages. It was a library book. His parents had been forced to pay for a new one, so the library could replace the one he'd ruined. He got to keep the book he'd damaged, but that wasn't really much comfort. He didn't even like the stupid thing.

*   *   *

"Leslie," Miss Greene asked, "is that a book you're reading?"

Looking up suddenly Leslie stammered, "Uh book . . . what . . . where?"

Miss Greene tapped her pencil on the desk from where she sat glaring at Leslie. "On your lap, dear," she replied. "I believe it's under your desk."

"Oh that. Yeah well . . . it *is* a book," Leslie confessed.

"Are you supposed to be reading during class?"

"I don't think so," whispered Leslie.

"Don't make me come over and take that book away from you. Are you finished with today's assignment?"

"Uh, not yet," she admitted. Leslie took one last forlorn look at the treasured book as she lifted it from her lap. Slowly she slid it into the storage space of her desk. She left it open to the page she'd been reading.

Miss Greene was watching her intently. "Are you sure you want to risk the temptation," she asked?

"What do you mean, Miss Greene?" Leslie inquired innocently.

Miss Greene smiled. "Your grades are reflected by unfinished assignments, as you are aware. Do you really think that you can resist the call of an open book only a few inches from your grasp for very long?"

Her fingers were already lightly touching the pages of the book inside her desk. Leslie gulped, "Uh, no . . . I guess not."

"Well then," Miss Greene went on, "you might just want to close it or better yet give it to me to hold for you until the end of this period."

"Yes, Miss Greene." Leslie blushed as she quickly placed a bookmark between the pages. She longingly brought it out and closed the latest escape hatch she'd found from life.

"And just how many reading hours do you have so far this week (it was only Tuesday)?" asked Miss Greene as Leslie handed over the beloved prize. Each week reading hours were counted up from Saturday to Friday.

Leslie blushed yet a brighter shade of red. She was extremely embarrassed at being asked by her teacher to share this information out loud. The entire classroom of other students sat breathlessly listening. "Twenneetahwoooooooo," she mumbled.

"What was that?"

"Twenty-two," she repeated, in a barely audible whisper.

"Twenty-two?" Leslie heard a boy from the class proclaim loudly. "Man I haven't read twenty-two hours all year."

Leslie silently congratulated herself for not having told the truth. It had actually been more like forty-two hours. She had really gotten into that last book she was reading. It had resulted in her staying up all through the night on Saturday and well into Sunday morning and that same evening. If the other students were freaking out over a mere twenty-two hours, how she wondered, would they have reacted if she'd told the truth? She was glad she wouldn't have to find out.

"Why haven't you recorded those hours," questioned Miss Greene. "You only get credit, you know, if the hours are recorded."

"I know," said Leslie, looking down at the tile floor.

"Is this a school library book," Miss Greene asked? She held up the one she'd just taken from Leslie.

"Yes."

"How many does that make that you've borrowed this year?"

"I'm not sure," Leslie twisted her hands in a gesture of awkwardness. "Uh . . . two hundred and thirty . . . I think," she said softly.

"You must have some lengthy library card," Miss Greene smiled.

"Actually," Leslie confided, "I have three stapled on top of each other. There's not enough room on one to list all the books I've checked out."

"It's rather nice," Miss Greene said dreamily. "To have a student who truly likes to read for a change. However, let's try not to let it interfere with class time. You *do* love to read, don't you?"

"Oh, yes," smiled Leslie, "I'd rather read than eat." In her excitement, she'd spoken rather boldly and much louder than planned.

"That's why she's so skinny," a voice from the back of the class called out. The other students cracked-up.

"That's enough of that," Miss Greene said sternly over the murmuring students. Silence ensued at once.

Leslie went red in the face again.

"I'll tell you what," said Miss Greene. "If you complete all your assignments each day and let me check them, I'll let you read for the rest of whatever time is left, if you like."

From that day on Leslie finished every single assignment in Miss Greene's class early. Her grade went from a C—due to incomplete and missing assignments, to a solid A. She came to love Miss Greene's sixth grade class. In later years she remembered her fondly as one of the best teachers she ever had.

* * *

A young man of about twenty had come in for an initial visit. He was dressed casually and a bit sloppily. It wasn't too different from most that were about his same age, though. He did seem quite nervous and a little out of sorts. To insure confidentiality, we'll call him Joe. He stood about six feet five and towered over me, though it didn't seem like he was that tall. This was because when he sat or walked, he sort of hunched over, with his eyes cast downward towards the ground.

As Joe stood to come in from the lobby to the office, I noticed that the fingers of his right hand were in a constant state of movement. His thumb would touch each finger one after the other in an apparent purposeful and rhythmic pattern. Joe came in and sat down on a small sofa and began to explain his reasons for wanting to see a psychologist.

I asked questions or made comments for clarification purposes, mainly. I also observed and took notes. About ten minutes into the interview, I offered him an interpretation in the form of a question.

"How often," I asked, "do you find yourself counting like that?" I gave a nod in the direction of his constantly shifting fingers. They had not stopped moving in that same pattern since I had first set eyes on him out in the waiting room.

Joe quickly pulled the hand back behind his thigh to where I could no longer see it. At the same time he quickly sat forward and fixed his eyes on mine. *"All the time,"* he said with a sudden intensity. This response also brought his shoulders up from their slouched position. The look on his face seemed a bit alarmed, and yet perhaps hopeful, at the same time.

No professional had ever said anything like that to him before. None had said much about his moving fingers. Some had assumed that it was simply another sign of his obvious anxiety. These had *informed* him of this. None had asked him if their declaration was correct. No one had known that he was counting. Joe had been interested right away in the comment made, because it had been accurate. The next thirty minutes were replete with first time insights and understanding. He left that initial meeting with hope in his heart. He also left with awareness about what might be going on, that he had not had up until that time. He was a compulsive counter. Progress could now be made.

* * *

No one likes being locked up or kept from doing certain things. This is one of the reasons we have prisons. Prisons serve two main goals. One is to inspire people to stop breaking the law and doing bad things. If they do, they will be locked up and lose their freedom. The other reason is to keep people who have broken the law from going right back out and doing more of the same. The risk of losing your freedom is usually a strong enough motivation for people to obey the law. These prisons are made from walls made of concrete and steel. There are many other kinds of prisons, though. Some of them don't have walls or bars at all.

There are some prisons that we make ourselves and others that grow around us, without any recognition on our part. A prison can be anything that keeps us from being able to do what we want or from becoming all that we could be. Thus there are "external prisons" which are all those that are outside of us. There are also "internal-prisons" or those that are physical, biological, or in our minds. Mild-moderate OCS are of the "internal" variety. A person plagued by such tendencies can feel like a prisoner as the OCS determines what he or she can or cannot do.

The child in a classroom setting, who knows that if she starts an assignment she will have to finish it or she will go ballistic, is not free. She may choose not to start at all. When the teacher confronts her about why she isn't working on the task she may say, "I can't do it," or "I don't understand it." This can cause a problem if the teacher already knows the student *is* able to do the work. In that case the student may instead say, "I don't feel well." She'll say that or whatever she feels might keep her from having to start something that she is sure she won't have time to finish. Such a student may then come home with loads of homework. Often when this is the case she won't be able to finish at home either. On the other hand, if the need is strong enough, she may work the entire afternoon, evening, and late into the night to get it done. The next day she may be tired and cranky. Yet, the very same thing may happen all over again. This child is in a prison from which she cannot escape.

* * *

"*Fly* . . . on a plane?" she asks fretfully. "Uh . . . I don't think so."

"Hey, it's no big deal," he reassures her. "If we fly, we can get to Anaheim in a little over an hour instead of driving for eleven or twelve."

"You'll get there without me then!" she assures him emphatically.

This couple is in a prison that could be called "partial" or "limited." They can still go to Disneyland, just not on a plane.

* * *

"I can't believe that after they invited us over, *you* only ate bread!" she shouted in frustration.

"What *is* your problem?" he returned. "I don't eat food that's all mixed up together. You know that. Besides I don't think it really mattered to them."

"Are you crazy? Of course they made it *look* like it didn't matter! They were acting!" Her voice raised in pitch. "I have never been so embarrassed in my entire life. I just can't believe you'd do such a thing. It's mind-boggling."

He tried to shrug it off, "I still don't see what the big deal is."

"Oh, you're impossible! I'm never accepting another invitation to someone else's house to eat again." She stormed upstairs and slammed the bedroom door.

The bars of the prison for this couple are just developing.

True freedom from the prisons that can be created by OCS symptoms begins with education and treatment. What prisons have developed around you? What symptoms may be keeping you bound? What would you like to do, that you just can't bring yourself to do? These are questions worth answering.

*   *   *

Priorities can be a big problem for someone who has trouble letting go of an idea or stopping a task they are doing. It also tends to be a real problem for those who feel they must make the *best* deals. It may pop up and get in the way when looking for a house, car, spouse, or food in a supermarket. It can arise when looking for the best gas price to fill a car or even when faced with something as simple as which candy bar to choose.

There was a student who signed up for a speed-reading course while at a university. A vocabulary test had to be passed at a certain level before a student was allowed to take the six-week course. This was done as an attempt to weed out those who would be less likely to finish. Over time it had been found that those scoring below a certain level usually dropped out before completing the class. This student easily passed the test and was consequently allowed to begin the lessons. He dropped out anyway after only two-and-a-half weeks into the course. Why? His vocabulary level was adequate. That wasn't the issue. What could have been the problem?

Not long after starting the speed-reading course, this student began to have issues. He did have OCS, and one of the symptoms he had long been plagued with was the compulsion to read. As a result he became a very good reader, albeit a bit slow perhaps. He became a good writer for the same reason as well. He loved words. Whenever he would find a word that he didn't know, he would look it up in a dictionary. He wanted to know what it meant. In this way his vocabulary was always growing. His favorite books included a dictionary and a thesaurus. He used them every day.

Those who are aware of the methods taught in speed-reading courses may have an idea about what this student's problem with the program might have been. It was the words. This student had been passionate about the written word since childhood. The idea of skimming through a page, looking for key words while leaving out whole sentences, was absolutely unthinkable. To this student *every* single word was important. Time and time again as he tried to practice the method, he would be totally stumped. He couldn't seem to figure out which words should be attended to and which ones should be ignored. It didn't feel right to be leaving words out. Words to him were like art. They flow together to help those who read them experience exactly what the writer had planned. To skip words and ideas would be to take a chance on missing what the writer was really trying to say.

He was obsessively focused on the idea that every word was of equal importance. To him, it felt like he'd missed something when he didn't read each word. He couldn't do it anymore. He quit the course.

A similar situation can occur with the friend who calls on the phone. This friend always feels she must tell her story from beginning to end. She can talk for hours. Every little detail must be shared. Many people can have trouble remembering details in their proper sequence. She is no different. As a result there may be a lot of backtracking and getting off the subject. When this type of OCS symptom is present, no one who has a caller ID may want to pick up the phone when they see who is calling. Probably a lot of the time no one does. Nobody wants to get stuck on the phone for thirty or forty minutes at a time. There are too many other things to do.

How can one set priorities when everything is of equal value? Sometimes they can't. For those with OCS, everything can seem to be of equal value and equal importance. How can priorities be set when this is the case? Quite honestly, the answer is that they can't. These people need help in prioritizing. This skill can be taught. It just takes time.

* * *

From the life of an adult survivor of OCS we read the following:

What you are about to read is a personal experience. It is a true story. These words are written in the hope that others may find pieces of themselves. In so doing, maybe they will come to the realization that they are not alone.

I was fortunate to have gotten the opportunity to visit my father a little less than a year before his death. This was a very important time period for me. At one point during this visit, my father and I stepped onto the porch, preparing to reenter his house.

He had just opened the screen door and was reaching for the doorknob when I blurted out, "Dad, what was I like when I was a kid? I don't really remember very much about my childhood years."

His hand paused on that doorknob. He then glanced back over his shoulder. His neck quivered and through tightly clenched teeth he spoke just one word. There was an intense passion in his voice as he looked at me and said, "ROTTEN!" He then turned the knob and pushed open the door and walked into his house.

As I paused momentarily to collect myself, I remember thinking, "No, I wasn't." But frankly, back when I was a child, that's what everyone else thought too.

*   *   *

When I got out of bed this morning I tripped on a shoe and twisted my ankle. I maybe even broke my arm. I cut my chin while shaving. Then I found out that my walking cane had been sawed-up by my little boy. He was going to use it for an airplane he was making. The cane was now in four pieces instead of the one that it was supposed to be. There wasn't enough time for breakfast. I couldn't get my car to start. So I quickly limped in the direction of the bus stop, but saw it leave before I could get there. I then sat down on a nearby bench to wait for the next bus. That's when I noticed the *wet paint* sign. While I was sitting there a bird flew overhead and I felt something wet land in my hair. I'm already twenty minutes late for work and am now absolutely certain that this day, just like every other one before it, is going to be a horrible, no good, very bad day.

No one, it seems, can be more negative than the OCS-driven. Nobody can complain and grumble more about anything and everything. And they go on and on and on and on.

*   *   *

He wanted oatmeal for breakfast and it was all gone. He had cold cereal with milk instead. The whole time while he sat at the table eating that cold cereal, all he could do was grumble and complain. He also complained about the spoon he had to use. The one he really liked best hadn't been washed the night before. On top of that, he didn't get to take a shower as long as he liked. Thirty seconds after he had begun, someone else had started their shower in one of the other bathrooms. He couldn't stand it when the water pressure wasn't what it was supposed to be. At that moment he wondered if he shouldn't just get out of the shower and go back to bed. So that's what he did. What else could he do? After all, the whole day had already been ruined.

*   *   *

A fourth grade boy came to my office with his father for the first time. It was clear that they had a very good warm and caring relationship. This was the reason they had come in for help. The boy—let's call him Adam Strong—was struggling with some baffling issues and both father and son were very concerned. After interviewing Mr. Strong, he was sent out to the lobby with a behavioral inventory to fill out, while Adam was interviewed alone.

During one of the scales the question was asked, "Do you ever count things?" He obviously knew what was meant by this because his head drooped suddenly as did his shoulders. He seemed rather stunned.

"Well yeah . . ." he whispered, "sort of."

He was gently coaxed. "Can you tell me what you mean by *sort of?*"

Adam appeared very uncomfortable. He seemed anxious and afraid. "I don't know," he sighed.

Again in a very soft voice I whispered, "Try if you can."

His eyes were still glued to the floor and he was wringing his hands just a bit. "Well," Adam began, "when I . . . I come home from school each day I kind of write the numbers from one to a hundred five times before doing anything else." His voice faded as he spoke. "Is that the kind of counting you mean?"

"Maybe," I said to him. "Can I ask you a few questions about that?"

"Sure."

"Do you write numbers like that every day because you want to or do you feel like it's something that you just *have* to do?"

"I kind of feel like I h . . . have to do it," he stammered.

"If it was possible," I asked him, "to figure out a way to stop yourself from doing that, would you like to try it?"

Adam lifted his gaze from the floor to my face. "Yes," he replied.

Later in the session, Mr. Strong returned. He sat beside Adam on the small leather couch. It was explained to him what the evidence seemed to suggest might be underlying his son's behavioral and emotional issues. He was informed about some of the mild-moderate obsessive-compulsive characteristics that Adam had reported were present. As the *number writing* need was shared, Mr. Strong interrupted suddenly.

With apparent pride and excitement he spoke. "Oh, yeah," he beamed, "Adam *loves* writing numbers." He patted his son on the back as he said this and displayed a huge smile. "He writes them every single day."

There was no real need to confront Mr. Strong about this blatant misconception. Instead, my gaze turned towards Adam. "Adam," I began and as he glanced my way I went on, "Is that true? Do you really *LOVE* writing those numbers every single day?"

Adam once again lowered his head. There was a rather long pause. An audible sigh escaped his lips.

Mr. Strong nudged his son encouragingly. "Go ahead son and tell the doctor how much you like writing numbers."

Very softly I questioned him yet again, "Do you, Adam? Do you *really* like writing those numbers?"

As his father smiled broadly down at him as only a proud parent can, Adam slowly shook his head from side to side.

There was a moment of shock and disbelief visible on his father's face. It told the rest of the story.

Fortunately Adam and his father truly did have a good relationship. As a result, all it took was a little education. The problem was explained to him from Adam's perspective. Adam felt a very, very strong *need* to write those numbers every day. It had to be done as soon as he got home from school. He was afraid to tell his parents that he had this feeling. If he didn't do this every day he was afraid something bad would happen.

He had tried to tell them before but all he got out of that was a lecture. He would be reminded of the many reasons why he should not feel the way he did. So he did the only thing he could think of. He made it seem like writing those numbers was something that he simply *loved* doing. He made his parents think that he actually looked forward to writing them each and every day. Obviously he sold this idea to his parents. He couldn't, however, sell it to himself. It didn't matter how hard he tried. Finally being able to unload that burden was a very important and healing event for Adam. It turned out quite differently than he had feared. Mr. Strong felt very bad that his son was forced to play out such a ruse over time and apologized sincerely. It was a good beginning for them both.

*   *   *

There was this sixth grade boy. We'll call him Rick. His after school sports team was playing for the championship in softball. The umpire made a call that Rick knew was a bad call. He was in a better position to see what had happened than the umpire in the field. Because of this he saw that the kid on the other team who was at second base had not tagged-up after a fly ball was caught. The kid had made a motion to the bag but his shoe never touched it. In fact it had still been a good foot away from the bag when he took off.

When the ball was then thrown to Rick and he stepped on the base, the kid on the other team should have been called out. The umpire, however, had said he was safe. Rick started screaming that the other kid had not tagged up. The umpire would not change the call. Rick just couldn't let it go.

It wasn't fair. He knew that the other kid had not touched the base. The umpire signaled for the game to begin again. Rick just kept screaming that it wasn't fair and finally the umpire threw him out of the game.

The loss of that championship game was never directly linked to Rick. He was one of their best players. Rick knew it wasn't his fault they lost. It wasn't even his fault that he got thrown out of the game. He was livid about it.

In Rick's mind the umpire had cost his team the game. If only he'd made the right call. If only Rick had been able to play the remaining five innings, the outcome would have been different. He was devastated. He was livid. He was sure the rest of the team blamed him for the loss.

It was only years later when working on this with a professional, that Rick was to realize that it was his fault he had not been able to play the rest of that game. It wasn't the umpire. If only he could have let go of that bad call. If only he could have stopped ranting and raving. If he had simply continued to play he would have been able to help his team, both offensively and defensively, for the rest of the game. He was also able to realize that had he stayed in the game, the outcome might or might not have been different.

With help, he was able to quit blaming himself for the loss. He was also able to let go of his anger towards that umpire and quit blaming him for the loss as well.

*   *   *

It was Christmas. Rob and Jill Moore had six children. They talked together about gifts they thought they might be able to get for each of their children. For the little ones it was little things, and fairly inexpensive. For the older three, however, the things they had wanted were quite expensive. Jill had a strong need for everything to be even or fair. They decided to spend the same amount of money on each child. Jill was still struggling with the reality that while the younger kids would be opening many gifts, the older ones would have only one to open.

"It still doesn't seem fair," Jill would say. "I know it *is* fair as far as how much we spent but Sarah is going to be opening fifteen presents while Robert junior will have only one. He's only thirteen years old. I just can't get past the fact that even though it cost the same, it's still only one."

The closer it got to Christmas the more distressed Jill became. About one week before the twenty-fifth, Rob discovered other presents under the tree for the older children. There were many more than he and Jill had originally agreed upon.

He questioned his wife about the *extra* gifts. She told him they were nothing special and not very expensive. Jill was just trying to *even* things up a bit. From Rob's point of view the presents had already been *"even"* because the cost had been the same. She was spending more money that frankly they didn't have. Also it wasn't really fair to the younger children either. This became an argument just like it had the year before and the year before that. It was going to be the same as in years past. By the time Christmas came they would likely be very upset with each other. It was going to be a horrible day again rather than the day of joy it was supposed to be.

*   *   *

I remember reading an article back when I was still a graduate student. It was about a study where they gave college students speed (a stimulant) the night before a test to see if it would help them learn better. The next day when they took the actual test the researchers got some interesting results. They found that if the students did not have about the same level of stimulant in their system as they'd had the night before, they could not remember what they had learned. The researchers called this State Dependent Learning. The theory was that the stimulant had somehow created a different state of consciousness in their brains. Anything they learned while in this different *state* was dependent on the brain being in that exact state again for retrieval. Like a file locked by a key, it could only be unlocked if the right key was used.

I was fascinated by that study and have thought about it over the years since I graduated. I have come to believe that this State Dependent Learning may explain a lot about the fairly common OCS-related problems with memory. It would seem that there are probably many levels of what might be called *States of Consciousness* that we all must deal with at some time or another.

"I get so panicked just before a test. It's like I had buried a bone in the backyard, but now I can't find it. I know it's there . . . but where?"

This comment came from a college student with interfering OCS. She would start to obsess hours before a test was given over the fear that she wouldn't be able to remember the things she'd studied. During the time that she had studied the material she wasn't anxious or particularly worried.

She had focused hard on studying what it was she needed to learn. She did learn it too. She would feel worry and mounting anxiety, the closer it got to the test time. It appears to have put her mind into a *different state of consciousness*. When she finally sat down to take the test, she could not retrieve the information she had worked so hard to learn. Perhaps this was because it had been filed at a different level of consciousness. She could only open that file by somehow getting her mind to reach the same level of consciousness it had been at when it was learned.

After about thirty minutes had passed, she would suddenly start to remember bits and pieces of the material. Not long after that it would all come flooding back and she would complete the test. Sometimes, though, she was unable to remember anything until after she had left the testing center. Usually an hour or so after leaving the test site, her memory would unexpectedly return. Then all that she had studied would come back into her mind once again.

*   *   *

"It's like there's an enemy you're fighting that you don't even know you're fighting."

*   *   *

"The medication has quieted the committee in my head."

*   *   *

"I feel mortal." This was said in response to the fact that he would now occasionally *forget* some things, although not really important things. He had been discussing the fact that he never used to forget anything. The trade off, though, was considered well worth it.

*   *   *

"I definitely notice that I don't have that knot in my stomach anymore."

*   *   *

"It's easier to be me."

*   *   *

"It doesn't feel like I'm trying to escape from the inside out anymore."

*   *   *

"There was a bomb in the boys' bathroom," the third grader declared. "Kids had to be evacuated. We stood out in the sun and it got real hot while they were searching for the bomb."
"Did anybody get hurt?"
"Yeah, a couple of people did."
"What happened to them?"
"They got sunburned."

*   *   *

"When my mother—the kid's grandmother—would come over for a visit, I'd have them mess up all the stuff in the cabinets the day before she came. That way she would spend the two days organizing and putting all the things away. She would put them back in the order that she thought they ought to be in. My mom would be so preoccupied doing this during the time she was with us that everything would go well. It took all the pressure off of me."

*   *   *

Working with an OCS client and making a list of right and left brain functions, the word "right" was printed on the paper. Under this was written a list of the major areas this part of the brain controlled. On the other side of the paper was written the word "left." Under this word was listed the major functions of the left hemisphere. The paper was then handed to him.

He glanced at it then hesitated awkwardly before saying, "Did you notice that you put the right brain functions on the left side of the paper?" That had not been noticed or even thought about. It didn't matter. However, to this client it mattered. It mattered a lot. The paper was retrieved and the things written down were cut out with scissors. Each list was then taped in place on another sheet of paper. Left was on the left and right was on the right. This greatly relieved the client.

*   *   *

Simon continued to argue with his father. He was furious inside. "YOU THINK YOU KNOW EVERYTHING!" he shouted. "I don't want to hear no more!" Simon was yelling in his father's face.

Mr. Shuler was about to lose it with this twelve-year-old ill-mannered son. "Back off!" he said, sternly.

Simon moved a little closer. He tried to move ahead and get past his father. It was a tight squeeze in the hall.

Mr. Shuler pushed his son back a few feet. "Back off, Simon!" he warned.

"*Back off yourself*," Simon fired and tried once more to get around him.

"Don't come at me like that, son," said his father.

Simon ignored his father's words and suddenly lunged to the right. He caught the old man off guard. He got half of his body past where his father had been. Then the old guy regained his balance. His dad reacted by grabbing him under the armpits. With an enormous burst of adrenaline-charged strength, he lifted Simon right off the floor. He then turned, and got ready to shove him back down the hall. This would send him away from the shelter of his bedroom.

"You're not getting by me. You can't just run and hide in your room whenever you don't like what's going on," he announced. "You're not leaving until you've calmed down a bit and we've talked this through."

Simon resisted.

Mr. Shuler had had quite enough. He gave his son a firm shove.

Simon's legs became tangled and he tripped over his own feet. As he was falling his arms flailed out before him. Simon's left arm rammed into the wall next to the family room. His hard elbow made a hole the size of a large grapefruit in the sheet rock. It was about two feet from the floor.

"Son, are you okay?" Mr. Shuler immediately bent down. He tried to help Simon up.

"I'm fine." He snapped. He got to his knees. Simon glared up at the man. Then he yanked his arm away from his father's hands.

The scene described above is from a real life experience. The names of the father and son were changed to protect their privacy. The event was explained as clearly as possible. Readers need to understand the details. This is because the final outcome was truly an accident. The boy, however, did not remember it that way. He would bring it up whenever he and his father got into a heated argument. What had actually happened would be magnified. It would be twisted to fit the anger of the moment.

He would yell out something like, "So what are you going to do, throw me through the wall again, dad?"

At first this account greatly troubled his father. His own reply was to straight away deny that he had ever thrown the boy through a wall. That would amount to big time child abuse had he done this, he knew. Next he would try to assist his son in remembering the incident correctly. He would go over in great detail exactly what had actually happened.

To the boy, however, the simple truth of the matter was that he had been thrown through a wall by his father. It had never happened before that incident, and it never did again. The shock and surprise, though, left an unforgettable OCS larger-than-life mark in the boy's mind. The experience itself was intense. The retelling of it was also subject to sensationalism and overstatement. Changes were even more likely when the story was retold during a fit of anger.

With OCS there is a tendency for some experiences to become locked into place in the memory banks of the mind. This is especially true for incidents that are traumatic. It is also true for those occasions when emotions are at a high level. These sharp and sensitive memories can be had at a moment's notice. They can flood the mind and heart of the person involved. When a frozen memory is triggered, that person feels the emotions exactly the same as when they first happened. These feelings from the past then magnify whatever is currently going on. Also, whenever such a *frozen memory* is called to mind by choice, the same thing can happen. As the one with OCS recounts a memory, the emotion gathers strength. If not careful, the person can work himself or herself up into a frenzy.

*   *   *

Jeremy recalled, "When I was in second grade we were having a family get together and sort of a party. After dinner, all the adults were sitting around in the living room sipping drinks, smoking, and talking. My stepmother had made a cake for desert. After a while she went out to the kitchen. She got the cake and put it on the table. She was a little tipsy. She began by asking everyone whether or not they wanted some of the cake. Her words were a bit slurred and kind of hard to follow. She went from one person to another asking if they wanted a *big piece* or a *little piece*."

At about this point in the story Jeremy's hands began to clench into fists. His vocal tones rose. Color came into his cheeks.

"Everybody that she asked before me had told her that they only wanted a little piece. I know today that they were just being polite. With so many people at the party and only one cake they were trying to make sure that everyone got a piece. Back then, though, I didn't know about that! I was only eight years old. What in the heck did she expect?"

Jeremy's hands slammed down on the arms of the chair and then against his thighs. His movements became jerky and seemed restrained.

"I was always hungry when I was a little kid. My stepmother finally got to where I'd been waiting. She asked if I wanted a *BIG* piece or a *little* piece. *She* asked! *She's* the one who asked!"

If Jeremy had been able to somehow go back in time, I could imagine him taking a swing at his stepmother with a fist. He seemed infuriated.

"I told her what any eight-year-old probably would. I said that I wanted a big piece of course. She looked at me like I'd just broken every one of the Ten Commandments. '*Big piece?*' she questioned me. 'BIG PIECE! I'LL GIVE YOU A BIG PIECE!' Then she grabbed me by the arm and dragged me over to the table where the cake was. 'Here you go, she told me. Here's your BIG PIECE! You wanted a BIG PIECE. Here it is! Now you better EAT IT!'"

The veins in Jeremy's neck started sticking out. His entire face flushed. He looked ready to kill. If anyone had crossed him at that moment, he looked like he would have ripped them to shreds.

"She *made* me sit there and eat the *whole* thing! Nobody else stopped her either. Not one person came to my rescue. Maybe they were too drunk to notice? *No*, that couldn't be right. Maybe they were afraid of her too? Here I was, this little terrified boy. I was sitting there with this big mean ogre of a woman hovering over me. She was forcing me to eat a whole cake. It was kind of like that big fat kid in the movie Matilda. When I saw that movie I was cheering out loud right along with those kids in the auditorium of his school. I wanted Brucie to do it! I wanted him to get the last laugh. I wanted him to beat his ogre because I didn't get to beat mine. About three fourths of the way through my stepmother's cake, I had to run to the bathroom and throw up. I guess it's a good thing I don't have bulimia today. At least she didn't make me eat any more after that. I suppose my throwing up was reward enough for her. I still can't believe nobody stopped her, not *even* my own father. He was there too, you know. I guess he didn't really care about me enough to want to stop her. I don't know."

Jeremy would end up brooding like this for hours or even days. The mixture of anger and sadness would every now and then become overwhelming. It would get hard for him to focus on just about anything. Jeremy would withdraw from others. He would beat himself up over not being able to just *let go* of the incredible anger he still felt. He *hated* his stepmother. He told himself that his dad *must* have *hated* him. He would *vow* that he would *never* do such a thing to his own children. He would also fear that he might not be able to keep his vow. He hated himself. The amount of time Jeremy spent thinking about this was enormous. It interfered with his concentration. It sapped his energy. It made it very hard to get to sleep at night. Later, weariness drained his energy even further.

In time, Jeremy would start to think less and less about those past events. He'd be able to focus again. Things would begin to get done again. As stuff got done he'd start to feel better about himself. Thoughts of his past distress faded away. Life got better. It might stay better for quite a while. Then something would happen to remind him of that old cake incident again. Either that or it was some other hurtful event from the past. The same pattern would return and start up all over again.

*   *   *

What if OCS is a major underlying feature of Post Traumatic Stress Disorder (PTSD)? People with Post Traumatic Stress respond well to treatment with the SSRI group of medications. In pondering this it seems quite possible. This may explain why there has been a recent upswing in the diagnosis. It also may be why it is being recognized more and more in relation to events and incidents that never were considered potential causes of PTSD before. Perhaps this is why some people can get PTSD related to incidents that many others might not. Could this be due to the OCS tendency to overreact? It sure seems plausible.

*   *   *

Over the past fifteen or twenty years, clinical experience has suggested to me that PMS or Pre-Menstrual Syndrome may actually be due at least in part to OCS. What if these obsessive compulsive symptoms are magnified by the stress and fatigue put on a woman's body during that cycle? It makes a lot of sense. It's certainly worth exploring.

Early in the history of Prozac's introduction to the world, it became clear that Prozac appeared to improve other identified mental health issues as well besides depression. Like many other medications physicians could write prescriptions for what is known as "off label" use. This simply means that in clinical practice, evidence suggests a medication might be effective for another condition. This means other than the one it was originally intended for and FDA approved for. In the Physician's Desk Reference (PDR) published each calendar year, each medication has listed the conditions for which it has been approved. There is also a list of those that are still considered *investigational* or "off label".

The use of Prozac for PMS was discovered in this way. Apparently women who were taking Prozac during the clinical trials in the mid 1980s reported some interesting results to the researchers. They were apparently telling them things like "not only has my depression gotten better, but my PMS is better too." The researchers listed the treatment of PMS with Prozac as an off-label possible benefit.

During the 1990s some physician colleagues shared with me that the Prozac sales people were encouraging them to try it for women with PMS. Women would come in and tell the doctor "Gee, Doc, I've got PMS really bad. Isn't there anything you've got that might help?"

When the doctor suggested Prozac, the women would tend to sort of freak out. "Hey, I'm not depressed. I've got PMS. I don't need Prozac. No thanks . . . no happy pill for me . . . thank you very much."

It seems that the bad things they'd heard, along with the general disdain held by most others relative to someone who was taking Prozac at the time, made it hard for most women to even consider it. The general public, it seemed, didn't want to have much to do with Prozac for much of anything for a while.

Prozac eventually went to generic status. I assume that the company was no longer making as much money as they had before it went generic. It doesn't seem much of a stretch to think that perhaps someone got the bright idea to do a study on PMS. Why not? They had experience based evidence that it seemed to help. The approval would be sought for the use of Fluoxetine (Prozac) in the treatment of PMS.

Fluoxetine was approved by the FDA on July 6, 2000, for the treatment of PMS. The company marketed it under the brand name Sarafem. That was brilliant marketing. Now, when a woman went in to see a doctor asking for relief from her PMS, the doctor could say, "Why don't we try a little . . . Sarafem, shall we?" Say each syllable slowly Sara . . . fem. It sounds so nice and smooth and feminine. The name alone is calm and soothing. Do you think a woman hearing that word would freak out? I wouldn't think so. Not too many people in the general population would know what the word underneath the name Sarafem would signify. It of course is Fluoxetine or Prozac. It would appear that the company selling it named it carefully so that women would be more inclined to take it. Not only that, but Sarafem for PMS is a name brand and the company was able to charge more money for it as a result. This is not the only company to have done something like this. There are several others who've done the same.

In spite of all these politics, the point being made here is that perhaps Prozac works for PMS because it really is OCS. What if this postulation is true? This is an interesting hypothesis that is so far off the beaten path that to get someone to do the research might just be close to impossible. It might be very interesting to do such research, though.

Trapped

trapped . . . but only I can see the walls around me . . . they say relax . . .
it's something I can't do until I know the truth . . . but what is truth . . .

is it what we think or believe . . .
or could it be . . . everything we feel . . . it always seems so real . . .

sometimes I think I know the answer . . . and then I don't . . .
as it slips away . . . into another day . . . in the story of my life . . .
I can't remember . . . I don't remember . . .

    I just want to live my life and not be misunderstood . . .
    I want to uncover (discover) all the truth . . .
    I want somehow to find myself . . . anyway I know I should . . .
    but sometimes I just don't know what to do . . .
    (there are times when I just don't know what to do)

stripped . . . of everything I need to be sure of who I am . . .
they slip . . . into my mind these lies . . . and I don't understand . . .
perhaps in time I can . . .

in this world of make believe the masks are up . . .
everywhere we go . . . didn't you know . . .

I'm not sure what you may think . . . but in the mirror . . .
I don't want to see . . . a different me . . .
in the story of my life . . .
I can't remember . . . I don't remember . . .

—chorus—

trapped . . . but only I can see the walls around me . . .

Words and Music by Ron D. Kingsley
January 12, 2000

PART V

For the Professional

20

Becoming a Believer:
Treatment Issues for OCS/OCD

Believing may be the biggest problem that gets in the way of treatment for obsessive and compulsive issues. In order to put into action the strategies that work, a person must accept as true that this is what she is dealing with. Not only that, but she must also have a desire to change. He must want to get better. She must believe that change *can* occur. She also needs to be certain that *better is* what she's going to get. Otherwise, why put in all the effort and work required? It wouldn't be worth it. He simply must believe that it will be profitable for him to even want to try. Can you see the red flags related to treatment success popping up all over the place if this is really true?

In the last twenty-three years or so clinical experience with this has taught me a lot. There are some things you don't want to do when evaluating, working with, and/or trying to set up a treatment plan for those suffering from OCS/OCD. Most of the articles and books out there about OCD seem to come from the same kind of a setting. They tend to be authored by those working in university settings or special treatment centers with programs specifically for OCD. Not that there's anything wrong with that. It's just that the people who come to such centers tend to do so because they have somehow become aware. They are believers. They know or highly suspect that OCD is, or might be, their problem. Many of these first sought treatment with various others who had not been able to figure out what was really going on. Most therapeutic gains in such instances were small or nil or did not last. By the time such a person hears of or finds out about an OCD center, he is hungry for answers. Many are practically self-diagnosed before they arrive. They are already believers. He is ready for the diagnosis. She knows it is OCD. It just *has* to be.

On the other hand most OCS/OCD sufferers out in the real world don't know that this is their underlying issue. They are brought by another or seek out a professional themselves for some other reason. He is struggling. She is depressed. He is miserable. She must be Bipolar. He doesn't really know why things aren't going well. She's always so cranky. He says and does weird things. She does *strange* stuff. Neither understands why. He may have some ideas, though. Like they told you he's depressed! He's afraid. So he comes in for help.

She was sad and depressed. It's been this way for most of her life. Why? She has no idea. Neither does her parents. They finally decide to take her to see a mental health specialist. It was a very difficult decision to make. There appear to be no outward signs of obsessive and compulsive symptoms at all. She looks, sounds, and even says that she's depressed. Assessment goes no further. The mild-moderate OCS at the heart of her lifelong melancholy is left undiscovered. I believe this type of scenario happens in the real world way too often.

He has OCD but cannot admit this to himself or to anyone else. When counselors had first worked with him years ago, none recognized the OCD. Instead they focused on "control issues," "anger management," "assertiveness training," and "anxiety management." One even focused entirely on the client's unhealthy relationship with his mother. Finally, one of the professionals he went to realized that OCD was present. Unfortunately her manner and approach in sharing this information with him was less than therapeutic. He ran out of her office and never returned.

Most people have at least heard something about OCD. It scares them. Sometimes out of fear they may laugh at it. They know such a person "washes her hands all the time, right?" "Aren't they the ones freaking out over germs everywhere they go?" "They can't even open a doorknob without using a Kleenex or something, right?" There are other things people might think or know about OCD as well, but they generally do not truly understand it. OCD frightens us. The symptoms don't make sense. "I mean, isn't having OCD like, uh, being two steps *past* the doorway into crazy?" Insane is just not a place people want to visit. Nobody wants to have OCD, and so even those that suffer from such symptoms often feel tremendous pressure to deny it.

When a person's symptoms are in the mild-moderate range (OCS) trying to read the literature on OCD can be more harmful than helpful.

Often if given such information to consider, the client will return to the next session convinced that this can't be *his* problem. Remember that first of all *he* doesn't want it to be true. Secondly, in such writings, he would be faced with reading OCD cases that are much more severe than his own. Thirdly, many of those books actually say that mild-moderate symptoms are *not* OCD. And of course they aren't. Did you say they *aren't*? I thought you were saying that they are. No, they aren't. Now, don't get this wrong. They *are* OCS; defined as mild-moderate obsessive and compulsive symptoms. As a result of such statements, though, it's all too easy to come to the conclusion with absolute certainty that "*that's not* me." Then, since they obviously don't have OCD, it follows that they must not be obsessive and compulsive. The diagnosis must be incorrect. During the first few years of my clinical practice this kind of a thing was happening too much of the time.

This is not to suggest that there is not good information for those with OCS within the articles and books about OCD. There truly is. OCS under stress and over time can become OCD. OCS and OCD are born of the same genetic and biological cause. Treat one and you're treating the other. In my experience, the difference is that the same medications work sooner and at lower doses for OCS than for OCD. This only makes sense. Both can respond equally well to behavioral therapy. Sometimes, however, it can be very difficult to get sufferers in either group to comply with CBT. Also, some people are more open to the use of medication or it may even be preferred. Others may be very much against it in general or because of its possible side-effects. Judith Rapoport, M.D., in *The Boy who Couldn't Stop Washing* (1989) wrote: "for patients willing and able to use its precepts, behavioral treatment should be the first approach." She also went on to say "through using . . . Anafranil, I became convinced that getting rid of these symptoms as quickly as possible is the only rational treatment for my patients." It also seems the more humane thing to do. Clinical experience over the years has taught me that Dr. Rapoport's strategy makes sense. I believe it remains true even today.

On the one hand, those with OCS may have trouble viewing their tendencies as symptoms or sometimes as problems at all. Their symptom picture is often not quite as clear as full blown OCD. Compulsions and rituals may be weak and few in number or not there at all. These symptoms are also more likely to be effectively hidden or camouflaged. The obsessions in OCS are also not as strong. Mental rituals, if present, may not be frequent.

It can be very hard to convince a person that behavioral treatment will help. He may reason that he has *control* issues and *not* OCS. A couple may state "it's *not* obsessive-compulsive that's *our* problem, it's *communication.*" She may laugh after her OCS is explained. "Doesn't everybody have some of that?" she asks. Notice that this very statement could actually be a mental and/or verbal ritual. If so, she would be using it in an effort to get reassurance to reduce her anxiety or distress about the matter. When she hears the truth that *indeed* most of us *do* have at least a little OCS, it *will* lower her anxiety for the moment. "Of course we do," she repeats to herself in a whisper. This can also work as a reason why actually trying to treat mild-moderate obsessive and compulsive symptoms may not be regarded as necessary.

After having read the first few severe cases in a book on OCD the clients with *OCS* may "freak out" and put it down. They're not going to read another word from *that* book. Remember the concept of literal thinking which many of these individuals have? If the examples described don't fit his or her own experience exactly, then the view often taken is that it doesn't fit at all. When reading accounts about OCD, the details would generally have to be precisely the same as what the person with OCS is going through, or no connection is made. He or she will not feel such an explanation or example relates to their lives. This can sometimes create a problem because whether it's OCS or OCD, it tends to be expressed a little differently in all who have it.

Perhaps the most important distinction between OCS and OCD is in the levels of severity. Because of this contrast it can be tough for those with OCS to view their issues as obsessive or compulsive in nature. OCS issues often tend to only faintly resemble those of full-blown OCD. Also, the time lost throughout the day due to symptom interference is not as easy to see or establish. The lost time in an OCS affected life is more understated and insidious. It tends to be only a few minutes here, a few minutes there, and so on. By the end of the day, several hours may have been used up in actions and thoughts that were OCS-driven. However, since each thought or act was only for a short duration, the OCS sufferer may not feel that much time was actually wasted or misused. For OCS, it is not so much an obvious block of time that is lost during each obsessive-compulsive incident. It is the accumulation of many short periods of time that it steals over the course an entire day, week, or even year.

It is fascinating how this seems to happen. Often by the afternoon or evening the OCS person begins feeling a *time crunch,* but doesn't know why. He feels like he *never* has enough time for himself. Also, he may be frustrated and angry. If just *one* more person asks him to do something he's going to "*lose it.*" He has no idea how this happened. He started the day feeling like he was going to have plenty of time to finish all that was planned. That, however, was early in the morning when he was reviewing his planner. He may frequently scratch his head and wonder "Where did all the time go?" Whoever thought up that old saying "time flies" sure had it right.

With actual OCD, there can be a problem of applying CBT that is opposite that of OCS. When OCD is severe, a person may be so caught up in the symptoms that she cannot extricate herself. Telling her she has to confront each symptom on her own is a lot like saying: "Things will get better if you just stop breathing!" Medications might or might not make up the difference. Often the right medication will take the edge off. When it does, the chances are much better that she'll be able to successfully apply behavior therapy principles. Over time and with hard work she'll learn to manage many of even the most severe of her symptoms.

Dr. Lee Baer points out an important issue in his book *Getting Control* (2000). He says that should a person with OCD select goals to work on that are too easy to change, it may cause a problem. Such symptoms are not likely to bother her enough to motivate her to change. If she does not soon see sufficient improvement in her life functioning, she may not keep on with the behavior therapy practice. She will likely become frustrated by a lack of perceived progress and give up.

The same problem stated above is one of the main reasons it is often difficult to use CBT when working with those who have OCS. Usually the person is looking to get help for a problem other than OCS. It can be for depression, anxiety, anger control, explosiveness, panic, relationship issues, extreme shyness, oppositional behavior, educational struggles, control issues, chronic illness, stomach aches, headaches, and so on. All the above and many more can be either directly or indirectly related to underlying OCS. The effects on the mind and the body of the many milder symptoms together over time are subtle. They are difficult to recognize. These effects do, however, appear to accumulate. Eventually these connected outcomes can become overwhelming. They are not only hard to recognize but also hard to change. It's much like when one considers the strength of toothpicks. One toothpick is easily snapped between the two fingers of one hand. However, don't lash 150 of them together and try that. You won't be able to do it even using both hands.

Generally any single symptom of OCS is *no big deal* all by itself. It is easy to see why those with OCS might question the use of a behavior therapy plan. Why should they spend time trying to change something that's not even related to the reason they came in for help? Remember, *he* came to see you for his depression. *She* was seeking assistance for her anger control issues. *They* are seeking couples therapy for their communication problems. When the underlying issue at the heart of such problems *is* OCS, it should be treated first. In my experience, doing so has resulted in a more positive outcome and lasting improvement. If the OCS is left untreated, whatever gains made in therapy will have a tendency to fade. The original problems will tend to return as gains fade.

Therefore, following Dr. Baer's lead it makes sense that a person with OCS might not do well with the typical behavior therapy approach, at least not at first. Trying to force the use of CBT might even cause the person to doubt the treatment provider's capacity to help him. This is not to suggest that behavior therapy would not be effective for those with OCS. It is! It will work. It does work. One major problem is the number of symptoms involved (many). Also, none are sufficiently strong for a diagnosis of OCD. As a result, they come and go and wax and wane quite frequently.

Inconsistency is a hallmark of OCS. Furthermore, the effort it would take to change enough of the symptoms to begin to see a positive difference is enormous. A clear life change for the better does not occur until after quite a few of the symptoms are under the person's control. This takes time. Often it takes too much time to remain motivated and retain hope during the process. If there is no clear and fairly quick favorable result, hope and motivation weaken fast. People give up or won't even try.

It is important to remember that by the time a person comes to see you he has probably tried many times to fix the problems himself. He has also failed just as many times. With a history of failure already behind you, it can be hard to keep on trying. This is especially true if she has significant doubt about the diagnosis or the suggested treatment methods. And when it's OCS/OCD, you can bet a strong doubt at least in the client's mind is going to be present. Hey, the French called this "the Doubting Disease," remember? So this is a major dynamic that must be worked through.

Most researchers and practitioners in the field agree that sometimes medication is needed. Without it some people are not likely to get better. Dr. Jeffrey Schwartz likens the use of medication to a child using "water wings" to learn how to swim. As the child learns and gets better, the air is let out of those water wings until eventually she is swimming on her own. Medication takes the edge off of the overwhelming fear, anxiety, and distress that those with OCD feel. It lowers the intensity or strength of the person's symptoms. As this occurs she is more likely to be able to carry on with the principles of behavior therapy. Over time, as behavior therapy is applied, the symptoms weaken even further. During this process medication can be slowly withdrawn. In due course, most are able to stop medication completely. They are then able to manage their OCD much better than ever before.

In my clinical experience, those with OCS (or sub-clinical OCD as some researchers dubbed it) also respond to the SSRI group of medications. This is not surprising, if indeed OCS is an extension of OCD. Most researchers agree that when OCD is treated with only medication a certain problem can be expected. Too often, within a short time after discontinuing, OCD symptoms return and the person relapses. Without the help of CBT tools to manage their symptoms it doesn't take long before they are at the mercy of their OCD once again. Evidence suggests that the relapse rate is less of a problem for those treated with only behavior therapy. A large part of this may be due to their level of understanding regarding OCD symptoms. An acute awareness is needed to succeed with the method. The gains made using CBT tend to last longer and the person generally manages better during a relapse. A relapse prevention plan is usually an important part of CBT.

A recent study by Martin Franklin, PhD Reported in *The Thought That Counts* (2008) examined the effectiveness of CBT, SSRI medication, or a combination of both for the treatment of OCD. The focus was on children and teenagers. The study was a randomized controlled trial. There were 112 subjects from three separate university treatment centers. Overall results showed that the subjects did better on a combination of CBT and an SSRI than on either treatment alone.

In a study of people without OCD, Rachman and de Silva (1978) found that 80% indicated that they had experienced obsessions at some time in their lives. Furthermore, trained clinicians had trouble discerning these obsessions by content from those described by persons with an OCD diagnosis. The study suggested that those without OCD had obsessions that were less frequent. The non-OCD obsessions, although the same, were also easier to dismiss, were less upsetting, and more acceptable to have had. Those with OCD, in addition, seemed to have a stronger urge to counteract their obsessions. Such reports may have been because those without OCD were reporting obsessions they'd had in the past.

The great physicist Albert Einstein once said "every reminiscence is colored by today's being what it is and therefore by a deceptive point of view."

We all know that usually distress recalled from the past is not nearly as intense or troublesome as when it is experienced in the present. It may be that when the obsessions occurred for the non-OCD group they might have been a little more difficult to deal with than what they remembered and reported in the present.

Joseph Ciarrocchi concludes in his book *The Doubting Disease* (1995) that "obsessions, therefore, are part of normal experience." He goes on to suggest that in the normal population the obsessions do seem to be less frequent. They are also less upsetting and easier for the person to let go of than it is for those with OCD. There is yet another study of interest in this area, though. Edwards and Dickerson (1987) found that indeed it took persons who did not have OCD longer to dismiss what were considered intrusive rather than neutral thoughts. This was because invasive thoughts were considered harder to ignore than those that were neutral.

When identifying a child with OCS parents often have a very hard time accepting such a diagnosis. They don't understand. Parents see it as willful resistance and a complete lack of respect for them as authority figures. Teachers tend to do the same. When OCS is found to be at the heart of a child's issues there is no better way to make believers out of the adults in her life than to treat it. Once positive behavioral changes begin everything else starts to make sense.

There are three main treatments of choice when treating OCS/OCD. I believe the absolute most important treatment is education. The better a person understands what he is facing, the better he will be able to manage it and get it under control. There are usually years of misunderstandings, blaming, hurt feelings, frustrations, anger, masking and hiding of symptoms, lies, secretiveness, pain, and sorrow that must eventually be untangled. There are often huge guilt feelings on the part of parents and sometimes siblings. "If only I had known!" is a common verbalized regret. Longstanding family patterns and unhealthy reactions must be challenged and worked through. By itself, education is sometimes enough to inspire people to make changes. Parents begin to treat a child with understanding and kindness. Such a change can often improve the child's behavior and symptoms too. This is due to the fact that life becomes less stressful as family dynamics improve. Often these changes don't last very long if one and/or both of the other treatment methods of choice aren't also brought into play.

These are CBT (already discussed) and medication. Both these methods have been shown to play a part in changing brain functions that result in OCD symptom improvements for most that are able and willing to implement them. Both methods should be introduced as viable treatments for OCS/OCD. Experts in the field agree that CBT should be the initial method and approach used when treating OCD. Medication along with CBT is the preferred next best approach recommended. Some people cannot tolerate the medications. Some cannot tolerate CBT. It is important to remember that in the real world often creative combinations of these three methods are needed when treating individuals.

Clinical experience over the last two decades with the group that I refer to as OCS and the one known as OCD has led me to a conclusion. I believe that a continuum does indeed exist relative to OCD. At the one end we have practically no obsessive and or compulsive behavior. Sometimes I joke that a person at this end of the continuum would surely be like the "Ultimate Couch Potato." She would not be motivated to go anywhere or do anything. She would have virtually no drive to achieve.

At the other end of this continuum would be absolute OCD. A person at this end would be freaking out about every little thing. His drive to accomplish and need to do things would be so strong it would tend to overwhelm him. He would be caught up in such strong obsessions and compulsions that he would have no other life. There don't seem to be too many at these absolute extreme ends of this hypothesized continuum. Perhaps the old *normal curve* statistic is applicable here. Why couldn't it be? Brain chemicals and brain functioning do essentially the same thing for all of us.

OCS is not OCD. This is very clear. The DSM-IV depiction restricts us from considering alternative definitions as obsessive and compulsive "*disorders*." This is as it should be, since to add OCS into the mix would require a radical change in the diagnostic category of OCD. Better to call it OCS (mild-moderate obsessive and compulsive symptoms) and keep it separate from the OCD diagnosis. Clinical experience has suggested that many who have OCS can go on to develop OCD or OCP (Obsessive-Compulsive Personality Disorder). This seems to be particularly true if not identified and/or the OCS is left untreated. Stressors and *trigger events* play a role in the worsening of OCS, as well.

OCS responds to the same methods as those that work for OCD, as might be expected, with only a slight difference. Starting first with CBT seems normally unwise when OCS is targeted for treatment. Education is still *the* most important early intervention based on my experience. This seems true whether it's OCD, OCS, ADHD, Bipolar or whatever. We need to know what it is we are dealing with.

Medication appears to be the next best option to consider when treating OCS. We want noticeable results as quickly as possible. Also the SSRI dose range for OCS is generally a lot lower than that typically needed for OCD. On top of that some OCS characteristics often respond in a positive direction within just a few days. It can take up to ten weeks for OCD symptoms to begin to respond positively to an SSRI.

There are other benefits of starting the treatment of OCS in such a manner. These include emotional and intellectual awareness. Once a person experiences a tempering of their OCS in a positive direction it is harder to assert that OCS isn't real. They suddenly become believers.

Mild-moderate obsessive and compulsive symptoms really *can* interfere with one's life. This interference can also be at a level that warrants active treatment. Clinical experience has taught me that OCS wreaks havoc with our lives long before OCD may or may not enter the picture. I have not yet found anyone with OCD who didn't have elements of OCS before being diagnosed and treated. In the same vein, after successful treatment for OCD, at least some OCS lingers on.

Over the years there have been quite a few times when a person began treatment medically for OCS whose positive response seemed miraculous. Within a few weeks after starting a medication all symptoms would appear to have vanished. It is hard to believe how many times a parent has called or told me in a session not long after the onset of a medication, "Thank you for giving me my child back." These are perhaps the ones whose symptoms haven't been around long enough to create strong secondary or tertiary intertwined responses. Maybe these are those whose symptoms were milder than most and not quite as tenacious because of this. Perhaps they were exceptionally good responders to the medication that was used. It doesn't really matter what the reason might have been for their phenomenal responses. The bottom line is that the targeted OCS symptoms improved to an incredible degree. As a result, many of them no longer needed *therapy* for their presenting issues. As OCS improved and symptoms steadily faded so did many of the major concerns and reasons for seeking help in the first place.

There are several interesting dilemmas that often surface and that need to be addressed in the treatment of OCS/OCD. These are particularly relevant in relation to OCS, but should be kept in mind even when treating OCD. There are reports in the research of similar amazing responses to medication when treating actual OCD patients as well. Such a complete remission of all or nearly all active symptoms with only medication is not the norm when treating OCD. However, sometimes it does happen. Therefore the concerns that we will now explore can be of import for the entire OCS/OCD continuum.

Perhaps the dilemma of greatest concern is the lack of interest in taking the time and effort to learn CBT tools. This is a very common reaction when such a positive and complete response to medication occurs. Why should they learn skills to treat something that is no longer a problem? Those with OCS/OCD often have a hard time doing *busy work* or anything that they consider a waste of time. The symptoms are gone, they reason. Thank you very much but what else is there to do? I'm cured, doc. These individuals far too often simply see no need to continue with counseling sessions. They commonly simply stop coming. Knowing that this might happen can help the professional anticipate such a reaction and prepare for it.

Quite frankly, expecting a person who suddenly finds himself symptom-free to want to learn CBT makes no sense at least not from his point of view. If you think about it for a minute it doesn't make much sense from a professional perspective either. Would *you* expect someone to put in their time, energy, and money to learn about something they don't think they will ever need? This is one of the reasons an important part of the therapeutic process needs to be spent helping the client become a believer. He *needs* to believe in the diagnosis. She *must* understand and believe that her symptoms *are* symptoms.

There is recent evidence suggesting that after treating OCD with a medication alone when discontinued the dose should be tapered slowly. When it *is* decreased gradually the tendency to soon relapse seems to be less of a problem. This makes sense. It may be that as the dosage is lessened some symptoms do begin to reappear but are less strong or intense. As a result, the person quite naturally resists these weakened tendencies more easily. In doing so she is actually carrying out *in-vivo* exposure and response prevention. She may not even realize it. It would be better if she did so that this CBT tool could be used again in the future as needed. Each symptom she refuses to give in to creates a track record of her success. Every victory builds on itself making it more likely that she'll be able to continue to do more of the same.

When dealing with OCS, relapses after a medication is stopped seems less of a problem than it does for OCD. In clinical practice it has appeared to be related to mainly three things. First; learning about the symptoms puts her in a better position to do something about them. Second, when medication is effective the symptoms will not interfere at all or at least not as much in her life. This experience will strengthen her belief that OCS is real. Third, during the time that the symptoms are more out of the way she has the chance to put into practice and learn skills that were usually interrupted by those symptoms before. As this new way of reacting to the world is repeated again and again without OCS getting in the way her confidence grows. These new reactions then get a chance to set in and replace old habits or responses. Once new ways have been consistent for three months to about two years the OCS-driven reactions tend to be experienced as no longer needed.

It seems that becoming aware of the symptoms is critical to the successful treatment of OCS. Without awareness, once a medication is stopped old connections and habits can, and too often do, return. Family dynamics and stressors may revert to previous times. If a person doesn't recognize a symptom he cannot resist what it makes him feel like he must do. Old patterns return and the same issues reappear. With mild-moderate OCS it sometimes takes a while for this to happen. However, if he is already aware of the symptom when it tries to reassert itself, he recognizes what it is. It's a symptom. He can now deal with it. He may say to him self something like:

"Hey, I don't think so. I know what you are. You're a symptom and I'm not going *there* again. Thank you very much!"

From this point on resistance is no longer seen as futile.

the night

where do I go from here . . . nowhere I fear
sometimes I want to find a way to disappear

I used to be able to see . . . oh . . . and take care of my needs
now I can't seem to remember what I believe

> it's been dark so long I can hardly imagine the light
> 'til the pain is gone . . . I'll pray for the night
> for the night . . . oh . . . the night . . . yeah the night
> it's so cool and dark there I can safely hide
> in the night . . . oh . . . the night . . . yeah the night
> even though I'm afraid . . . I know I'll survive

in some things I've found release . . . ahh . . . but no lasting peace
as the chains of habit grow tighter each day . . . I am less free

I know what you want me to say . . . but I've got to find my own way
if I'm ever really gonna make it
I've got to strive for my own light each day

—chorus—

I'm not made of steel . . . no . . . I . . . I think and feel
I want to learn to run from the fake and go for what's real
and if I believe I can be whatever I want to be
then I'll begin to do all I need . . . to get free

—chorus—

Words and music by Ron D. Kingsley
November 23, 1992
For Sharp RM 3

APPENDIX

Sample Letter to a Physician: The OCS/ADHD Connection

It can be a fairly easy task for most professionals to talk someone with mild-moderate OCS (or the parent of an affected child) out of the desire and/or need for treatment. Usually these people have already experienced long-term self-doubt about their own sanity and have spent a great deal of energy rationalizing, hiding, or camouflaging symptoms. Often, they have also created or accepted a host of rational sounding reasons for their uninvited thoughts, and sometimes rather odd-seeming behaviors.

When those with OCS or parents with children who have OCS initially present with this seemingly vague and inconsistent symptom picture misdiagnoses are quite common. The more typical assumption upon hearing the suggestion that such an obsessive-compulsive pattern exists is far too often that, if such symptomology is not "all consuming" as suggested in the DSM-IV description of OCD (Obsessive-Compulsive Disorder), it is not a viable diagnosis. As a result aggressive intervention is sometimes not considered warranted. Such an attitude, however, has not proven helpful to those individuals manifesting this symptom picture. Misdiagnoses and/or a determination that "nothing is really wrong" are all too common. Depression (for significant others and the symptomatic individual) along with frustration, severe stress, anxiety, and blaming are typical outcomes over the long term.

As you may know when obsessive and compulsive symptoms are present such a biochemically driven problem often significantly affects mood, emotional control, and self-esteem. Secondary and tertiary symptoms frequently include relationship difficulties, anxiety, panic states, sleep difficulties, depression, a labile mood, anger control issues, attention problems, and a variety of possible physical and/or psychological ailments.

The individual with mild to moderate Obsessive Compulsive Symptoms (designated hereafter as OCS) can sometimes "hold things together" at work or school for specific periods of brief duration (inhibit many symptoms). Upon returning home for the day or having *held things together* for a while, however, accumulated fatigue and stress can cause loss of control which may result in discharges of pent up anxiety, explosive episodes, emotional shutdown, and significant withdrawal behaviors as well as symptom exacerbation in all related areas.

Obsessive and compulsive symptoms are often very effectively treated with the Specific Serotonin Reuptake Inhibitors (SSRIs) along with education and cognitive-behavioral therapies (CBT). With the use of an SSRI, these symptoms often decrease swiftly and dramatically and as the OCS decreases, focusing issues, related depression, anger control, withdrawal tendencies, and anxiety problems improve as well. Relationships also tend to improve, as do sleep patterns and self-esteem. Emotional lability declines and at times disappears altogether. Irritation and moodiness when present follow the same path of improvement, as do attentiveness and a sometimes-surprising new level of apparent awareness and more appropriate responsiveness to others' needs is achieved. Thus, relationships tend (with time) to become much better. The behavior modification technique known as "Exposure and Response Prevention" can also significantly ameliorate OCS/OCD, but tends to be an extremely difficult intervention in regard to compliance especially for children and mild-moderate sufferers. Nevertheless this and other related CBT techniques are viable and worthy of exploration, attention, and active practice and are therefore always a part of the psychological treatment in addition to and sometimes in place of psychopharmacological interventions.

The most essential treatment factor—whether it is for the individual, parent, or treating professional—is without question, accurate knowledge. This can be obtained through pertinent articles, books on the subject, and an up-to-date knowledgeable counselor, psychologist, psychiatrist, or physician. In fact, counseling is typically only beneficial to the extent that it focuses on coping skills with an understanding of the dynamics associated with OCS/OCD and ADHD. Many families and individuals have lived for years with these specific undiagnosed problems and enabling them to untangle the chronic misinterpretations, cognitive distortions, and long standing emotional distress can be invaluable.

Whenever ADHD is determined to be a co-morbid factor that is also interfering with daily life functioning, the addition of a stimulant such as Concerta or Adderall in conjunction with an SSRI is a common viable treatment with quite positive outcomes and vice versa. Neither the SSRIs nor the stimulants can effectively treat both conditions alone when both are a hindrance to an individual's day-to-day functioning. Research points to the brain chemical serotonin in relation to OCS and Dopamine/Norepinephrine is most often implicated in cases of true ADHD. Treating the apparent more prominent one first should enable us to determine if ADHD and OCS are active co-morbid conditions, or if those suggestive symptoms were primarily related to one or the other, since both conditions share a large number of similar symptoms.

The medications commonly used that can alleviate and/or ameliorate obsessive and compulsive symptoms include the following:

Fluoxetine (Prozac)   Sertraline (Zoloft)
Fluvoxamine (Luvox)   Paroxetine (Paxil)
Clomipramine (Anafranil)   Escitalopram (Lexapro)
Citalopram (Celexa)

All medications have potential side effects. Sometimes there can be a side effect bothersome enough to merit the discontinuance of a medication. There is evidence that if one SSRI causes uncomfortable side effects it doesn't necessarily mean that another will do the same. Thus, if unwanted side effects do occur with one SSRI it is often worthwhile to attempt another.

Although depression itself typically responds therapeutically in 4 to 6 weeks to the SSRIs actual obsessive-compulsive symptoms in the mild-moderate range and resultant anxiety and emotional difficulties frequently begin to improve within just a few days. This makes sense if the manifest depression that responds to these medications truly is a secondary symptom resulting from the insidious underlying OCS.

Brief Intervention Guide for OCS/OCD

Mild-Moderate Obsessive-Compulsive Symptoms (OCS) and Obsessive-Compulsive Disorder (OCD)

- **Education:** Beyond a shadow of a doubt the most worthwhile and helpful intervention tool is knowledge. There is no better approach available than learning as much as you are able to learn about these symptoms and the disorder itself. The goal is to begin to understand the links and interconnections between symptoms and behavior. You need to find out what having OCS/OCD means. What impact can it have on a person within the school, work, social, and home setting? Such details are vital in relation to how best to cope when you, someone you care about, or someone you work with has this problem.

- **Medication:** Generally these are in the SSRI (Specific Serotonin Reuptake Inhibitor) category. They include the following: Fluoxetine (Prozac), Sertraline (Zoloft), Fluvoxamine (Luvox), Paroxetine (Paxil), Citalopram (Celexa), Escitalopram (Lexapro), and even though not truly an SSRI Clomipramine (Anafranil), which is a Tricyclic (also very effective when treating OCS/OCD). Without medical treatment the symptoms are sometimes not seen for what they really are and true change is not possible. This may be especially true in the mild-moderate range.

  A person may believe that their OCS driven behavior is not driven at all. They may see it as choices that are logical and that accurately reflect what they think and who they are. If so, there may not be a desire to change anything. Where there is no desire there can be no change. Often, early-on, medication can take the edge off symptoms. When it does certain undesired behaviors that are no longer as driven tend to improve. With this improvement comes a realization that OCS symptoms are genuine. It helps those with OCS to become believers. All those who believe can use the other methods of treatment for OCS/OCD much more effectively.

- **Cognitive Behavior Therapy (CBT):** What a person thinks and what a person does are used to change what a person feels. These methods help to manage and reduce the symptoms and related problems.

- **Incompatible Response Method:** Have those with OCS make a list of symptoms and related behaviors. They can then practice replacing them with an incompatible response. An incompatible response is an action or thought that, when busy doing, gets in the way of acting out or thinking of the symptom. For example, there may be a need to pick at scabs or sores or even clothes. If a person sits on both hands it is impossible to pick at the clothes or the skin during that time. Singing a song or reciting a poem can be an incompatible response to certain thoughts such as worrying obsessively that something bad is going to happen and so on.

- **Exposure and Response Prevention:** The CBT technique of Exposure and Response Prevention is employed more than any other for OCS/OCD. It has been shown in research to be the most successful of such methods available. It does have a few dilemmas that can sometimes get in the way and keep it from working for certain individuals. Children and those whose symptoms are either in the mild-moderate range or very severe range may not be able to use this method, at least not at first. Later, that can change.

- In brief this strategy consists of exposing yourself (confronting) a situation that causes you to feel distress, anxiety, or fear. Because of these feelings you are compelled to respond in a certain way. Instead, you consciously do not respond in the way that you feel you must. You do this over and over again as often as possible. In time this exposure will lessen the strength of the symptom and make it more manageable.

- **Work Resistance and Work Refusal:** There are a host of possible and viable reasons why children may resist and refuse assignments at school, chores at home, and why adults may respond similarly at work or in the home setting. In fact even when OCS or OCD has been found to be the underlying cause teachers and others still have trouble believing. They often seem to wrongly assign the response to some other very different and yet believable unrelated cause. This is one of the reasons that attempts to correct and change OCS behavior can be notoriously ineffective. Those with OCS truly may not know why the resistance/refusal occurs. Or similar to teachers and others, those with OCS may also assume an inaccurate cause. One begins to sense why confusion has run rampant in relation to OCS/OCD.

- **Issues with Time:** If this person is having issues that appear due to time limitations the lengthening of such time limits may be helpful. Those with OCS/OCD can take an extremely long amount of time to complete work or what is asked of them for a variety of reasons. These don't really need stressing here. Depending on other factors, extra time may or may not help. It is certainly worth trying, although it may only work in specific instances.

- **When Overwhelmed by Workload:** Shortening certain tasks or breaking things up into smaller segments can be helpful if the OCS person will allow it. Many with OCS/OCD absolutely do not want to be viewed as different from their classmates or co-workers. When this concern about being seen as different is a current issue, then cutting down or breaking up tasks or the work load may not help.

- **The need to Finish:** If the OCS adamantly insist that there is just no way to complete a task in the time allotted, he or she may not start working. If it is possible to do so, suggest that the work be taken home if unfinished. Don't be surprised if the entire project is taken home.

- **Avoid power struggles:** Those with OCS/OCD will hardly, if ever, give in—no matter what the cost. To them the situation is of "do or die" intensity, not unlike the well-known fight or flight pattern of many mammals. If left alone to ponder the situation, the person will often eventually come around. If confronted, a battle may ensue that is not worth the time and effort, let alone the emotional drain on all those involved.

- **Participation Issues:** Do not try to force those with OCS/OCD to become involved, answer a question, or respond. When their body language and words are telling you that they absolutely do not want to participate, forcing the issue will only create problems. This is the time when it will appear that the OCS-driven has no respect for authority. This is not usually true. Still, when cornered, they may lash out at teachers, principals, parents, and spouses or even bosses.

- **Craving Attention or Praise:** This is a common pseudo-symptom relative to the unrelenting OCS/OCD need to always know that they are right in what they are doing. This can be very frustrating to a teacher or boss as it looks as if such a person is craving attention. They are not. They just need to make sure what they're doing or thinking is right. Patience is of supreme importance when working with this population.

- **Consultations:** Consult the school psychologist for ideas on how best to work with this type of a student. The psychologist can speak with parents of a child about a possible more thorough evaluation outside of the current setting. Adults may be referred to employee assistance teams, physicians, or human resource specialists when such a need is determined.

- **Prioritizing and Organization Issues:** Help these OCS/OCD students and adults to structure their day and prioritize tasks. These are notoriously problematic areas for the OCS/OCD-affected. They often cannot decide what the most important tasks are when several need to be completed. Helping them to do so can lower stress and enable them to complete tasks in a timelier manner.

- **Issues with Change:** Prepare them in advance for any changes that may occur that are apart from the normal routine. Change of any kind is a well-known difficulty that can be very distressing for many OCS/OCD students and adults. Knowing ahead of time can reduce distress and related problems.

- **Overreactions:** If the OCS over-responds emotionally or physically, do not get directly in their face unless they are a danger to themselves or others. Give them space and use time-out and time-away procedures to enable them to calm down. Let this person walk away or sit alone for a time, until he or she is calm. Then re-engage them in conversation or task completion.

- **Working in Groups:** Those with OCS/OCD tend to have great difficulties working in groups unless they are in charge. Even when in charge, however, problems can still arise due to excessive rigidity and unrealistic expectations. Consider allowing this person to work alone, if it is possible.

- **Hypersensitivity Issues:** Be careful about touching such a student or adult. The tendency to overreact extends to all areas and it can be very hard for them to be touched. This is especially true if they are not expecting to be touched. However, the exact opposite can be true, as well. They can be overly touchy-feely, to the dismay of all those around them. Be aware and be understanding.

- **Depression Issues:** Report excessive sadness and evidence of possible depression to the school nurse, school psychologist, human resource team, or other appropriate professional. Depression is a very common secondary condition brought about by OCS/OCD symptoms. It tends to come and go a lot in this population. Still, it can be a serious problem that needs to be addressed.

- **Always keep in mind the following:** OCS/OCD is an explanation, not an excuse. Once you know it is there, all involved should ask the question: "Okay, what are we going to do about it?" Also remember that this condition is *managed and not cured.*

BIBLIOGRAPHY

Baer, L. 2000. *Getting Control: Overcoming Your Obsessions and Compulsions.* Little: Brown & Company.

Baer, L. 2001. *The Imp of the Mind.*

Barkley, R.A.1995. *Taking Charge of ADHD: The Complete Authoritative Guide for Parents.* New York London: The Guilford Press.

Braun, A. 1993-94. *Neurobiological Relationship of Tourette's Syndrome, Obsessive Compulsive Disorder, and Attention Deficit Hyperactivity Disorder.* Tourette's Syndrome Association: No. 3.

Bruce, R.V. 1988. Alexander Graham Bell. *National Geographic,* September.

Bruun, B., and R. Bruun. 1994. *A Mind of Its Own: Tourette's Syndrome: A Story and A Guide.* Oxford University Press.

Carter, Rita. 1998. *Mapping the Mind.*

Chansky, T. E. 2000. *Freeing Your Child from Obsessive-Compulsive Disorder.*

Ciarrocchi, J.W. 1995. *The Doubting Disease: Help for Scrupulosity and Religious Compulsions.*

Foa, E. B., and R. Wilson. 2001. *STOP OBSESSING!*

Huebner, D. 2007. *What to Do When your Brain Gets Stuck.*

Hyman, B.M., and Pedrick. C., R.N., 1999. *The OCD Workbook: Your Guide to Breaking Free from Obsessive-Compulsive Disorder.* New Harbinger Publications Inc.

Johnson, A.D. 1981. *The Value of Creativity-The Story of Thomas Edison.* La Jolla, CA: Value Communications.

Johnson, A.D. 1984. *The Value of Self-discipline: The Story of Alexander Graham Bell.* La Jolla, CA: Value Communications.

Johnson, S. 1979. *The Value of Dedication: The Story of Albert Schweitzer.* La Jolla, CA: Value Communications.

Johnson, S. 1979. The *Value of Fantasy: The Story of Hans Christian Andersen*. La Jolla, CA: Value Communications.

Johnson, S. 1979. *The Value of Honesty: The Story of Confucius*. La Jolla, CA: Value Communications.

Kant, J.D., M. Franklin, and L. W. Andrews. 2008. *The Thought That Counts*.

Kelley, K. and P. Ramundo. 1993. *You Mean I'm Not Lazy, Stupid or Crazy?!: A Self—Help Book for Adults with Attention Deficit Disorder*. Tyrell & Jerem Press.

Kingsley, R.D. 2002. *Making Sense of the Senseless: Mild-Moderate Obsessive-Compulsive Symptoms (OCS) Unveiled*.

Leman, K. (1985, 1998), *The New Birth Order Book*. Fleming R. Revell.

Leman, K. 1989. *Growing up First Born*. Delacorte Press Bantam Doubleday Publishing Group.

Leonard, H. L., J. S. Rapoport, and S. E. Swedo. 1992. Childhood Obsessive Compulsive Disorder. *Journal of Clinical Psychiatry* 53:4 (Suppl-, April).

Levert, S., and K. R. Murphy. 1995. *Out of the Fog: Treatment Options and Coping Strategies for Adult Attention Deficit Disorder*. Skylight Press.

Levinson, H. D. 1990., *Total Concentration: How to Understand Attention Deficit Disorders*. M. Evans & Company.

Lund, J. L., ed. 2004. *Without Offense: The Art of Giving and Receiving Criticism*. American Fork, UT.

Covenant Communications, Inc.

March, J. S. and K. Mulle. 1998. *OCD in Children and Adolescents: A Cognitive-Behavioral Treatment Manual*.

March, J. S. 2007. *Talking Back to OCD*.

McLean, P. D., and S. R. Woody. 2001. *Anxiety Disorders in Adults: An Evidence-Based Approach to Psychological Treatment*. Oxford University Press.

Nadeau, K. G., ed. 1995. *A Comprehensive Guide to Attention Deficit Disorder in Adults: Research-Diagnosis-treatment*. Brunner/Mazel.

O'Neal, J., R. Pharm, J. Preston, and M. Talago. 1994. *Handbook of Clinical Psycho-pharmacology for Therapists*. New Habinger Publications.

Penzel, Fred. 2000. *Obsessive Compulsive Disorders: A Complete Guide to Getting Well and Staying Well*. Oxford University Press.

Peterson, C., S. Maier, and M. Seligman. 1993. *Learned Helplessness: A Theory for the Age of Personal Control*. Oxford University Press.

Phillipson, S. 2008. The Center for Cognitive-Behavioral Psychotherapy (7/29/2008), *The Right Stuff: Obsessive Compulsive Personality Disorder: A Defect of Philosophy*

Pratt, F. 1955. *All about Famous Inventors and Their Inventions*. New York: Random House.

Rapoport, J. L. 1989. *The Boy Who Couldn't Stop Washing*. New York: E.P. Dutton.

Rapoport, J. L. 1991. *Recent Advances in Obsessive Compulsive Disorder*. Neuropsychopharmacology, 5(1): 1-10.

Rapoport, J. L., S. E. Swedo, and H. L. Leonard. 1992. *Journal of Clinical Psychiatry 53:4*. Rapoport, J. L. 2008. *The Boy Who Finally Stopped Washing*. Cooper Union Press.

Ratey, J. J., and E. Hagerman. 2008. *Spark: The Revolutionary New Science of Exercise and the Brain*.

Rompella, N. 2009. *Obsessive-Compulsive Disorder—The Ultimate Teen Guide*. The Scarecrow Press, Inc.

Rosenberg, D., J. Holttum, and S. Gershon. 1994. *Textbook of Pharmacotherapy for Child and Adolescent Psychiatric Disorders*. University of Pittsburgh Medical Center: Brunner/Mazel Publishers New York.

Schwartz. J. M., and B. Beyette. 1996. *Brain Lock: Free Yourself from Obsessive Compulsive Behavior*. Harper Collins Publishers.

Shimberg, E. F. 1995. *Living with Tourette Syndrome*. Simon and Schuster.

Singer, H. S. 1993. Tic Disorders. *Pediatric Annals*. 22:1 22-29.

Steketee, G. 1993. *Treatment of Obsessive Compulsive Disorder*. Guilford Press.

Steketee, G., and T. Pigott. 1999. *Obsessive Compulsive Disorder: The Latest Assessment and Treatment Strategies*. Dean Psych Press Corp, Compact Clinicals.

Steketee, G., and K. White. 2001. *When Once is Not Enough: Help for Obsessive Compulsives*. New Harbinger Publications, Inc.

Swearingen, G., with illustrations by Niner, H.L. (for children). 2004. *Mr. Worry: A Story about OCD*.

Talley, L. 2006. *A Thought is Just a Thought*.

Vasey, M. W., and M. R. Dadds, eds. 2001. *The Developmental Psychopathology of Anxiety*. Oxford University Press.

Wagner, A. P. 2004. *Up and Down the Worry Hill*.

Wagner, A. P. 2006. *What to do When Your Child Has Obsessive-Compulsive Disorder*.

Witcher, A. E. 1989. The Grief Process: As Experienced by Parents of Handicapped Children. *Principal*: March 31-32.

INDEX

CPSIA information can be obtained
at www.ICGtesting.com
Printed in the USA
FSOW02n1839240915
11485FS

9 781441 556639